משניות

ArtScroll Mishnah Series®

A rabbinic commentary to the Six Orders of the Mishnah

Rabbis Nosson Scherman / Meir Zlotowitz

General Editors

the mishnah

ARTSCROLL MISHNAH SERIES / A NEW
TRANSLATION WITH A COMMENTARY **YAD
AVRAHAM** ANTHOLOGIZED FROM TALMUDIC
SOURCES AND CLASSIC COMMENTATORS.

Published by

Mesorah Publications, ltd

ששה סדרי מִשְׁנָה

FIRST EDITION
First Impression . . . April, 1992

Published and Distributed by
MESORAH PUBLICATIONS, Ltd.
Brooklyn, New York 11232

Distributed in Israel by
MESORAH MAFITZIM / J. GROSSMAN
Rechov Harav Uziel 117
Jerusalem, Israel

Distributed in Europe by
J. LEHMANN HEBREW BOOKSELLERS
20 Cambridge Terrace
Gateshead, Tyne and Wear
England NE8 1RP

Distributed in Australia & New Zealand by
GOLD'S BOOK & GIFT CO.
36 William Street
Balaclava 3183, Vic., Australia

Distributed in South Africa by
KOLLEL BOOKSHOP
22 Muller Street
Yeoville 2198
Johannesburg, South Africa

THE ARTSCROLL MISHNAH SERIES ®
SEDER ZERAIM Vol. III(a); *KILAYIM*
© Copyright 1992, by MESORAH PUBLICATIONS, Ltd.
4401 Second Avenue / Brooklyn, N.Y. 11232 / (718) 921-9000

ISBN
0-89906-322-2 (hard cover)
0-89906-330-0 (paperback)

Typography by Compuscribe at ArtScroll Studios, Ltd.
4401 Second Avenue / Brooklyn, NY 11232 / (718) 921-9000

Printed in the United States of America by Moriah Offset
Bound by Sefercraft Inc., Quality Bookbinders, Brooklyn, N.Y.

~§ Seder Zeraim Vol. III(a):
מסכת כלאים
Tractate Kilayim

The Publishers are grateful to

YAD AVRAHAM INSTITUTE

and the

MESORAH HERITAGE FOUNDATION

for their efforts in the publication of the

ARTSCROLL MISHNAH SERIES

This volume is dedicated to
the memory of

Jerome Schottenstein ז"ל

יעקב מאיר חיים בן אפרים אליעזר הכהן ז"ל
נפטר ה׳ אדר ב׳ תשנ"ב

He was a man whose ideals were untainted by success,
whose compassion was uncorrupted by power,
whose humility was undiminished by adulation,
whose benefactions to institutions were boundless,
and whose kindnesses to individuals were
too numerous and quiet ever to be known.

His untimely passing is a grievous loss
not only to his loving family
and the the many who were close to him,
but also to the countless people
of this and future generations
whose lives were and will be enriched by the good he did
and the Torah study he made possible.

May the study of the Torah in this volume
be a source of merit for a man
who supported Torah study throughout the world.

תנצב"ה

Dedicated by
Mr. and Mrs. Louis Glick

הסכמה

Rabbi Moshe Feinstein
455 F. D. R. Drive
New York, N. Y. 10002

משה פיינשטיין
ר"מ תפארת ירושלים

בע"ה

[חתימת יד — מכתב בכתב יד של הרב משה פיינשטיין]

אברהם פיינשטיין

בע"ה

הנני מברך בזה את ידידי הרב הנכבד מהר"ר מאיר בן ידידי הרב הגאון ר' אהרן שליט"א
זלאטאוויץ ואת ידידי הרב הנכבד מהר"ר נתן שערמאן שליט"א שעמדו בראש הנהלת **חברת ארטסקרול,**
אשר הוציאו כבר הרבה חבורים חשובים בשפת אנגלית לזכות את הרבים, וגם הוציאו על משניות כרך
אחד ועכשיו מוציאים לאור עוד כרך שני, ויש בו לקוטים מספרי רבותינו מפרשי משניות על כל משנה
ומשנה, מלוקטים בטוב טעם ע"י תלמידי חכמים חשובים ומומחים לרבים, והוא לתועלת גדול להרבה
אינשי ממדינה זו שלא התרגלו מילדותם במשניות, וגם יש הרבה שבעזוהשי"ת התקרבו לתורה ויראת
שמים כשכבר נתגדלו ורוצים ללמוד, שיוכלו ללמוד משניות בנקל בשפה המורגלת להם, שלכן הם ממזכי
הרבים שזכותם גדול ואני מברכם שיצליחם השי"ת בחבור זה ובעוד כרכים.

וגם אני מברך בזה את ידידי הרב הנכבד מאד עסקן ותומך גדול לתורה ולתעודה מוהר"ר אלעזר גליק
שליט"א אשר עזר הרבה להדפסת משניות אלו לזכר נשמת בנו המנוח החשוב מאד מר **אברהם יוסף** ז"ל
ונקרא הפירוש **יד אברהם** על שמו והוא זכות גדול לעילוי נשמתו בלמוד הרבים. יהי זכרו ברוך. וע"ז
באתי על החתום בער"ח אלול תש"מ.

משה פיינשטיין

מכתב ברכה

יעקב קמנצקי

RABBI J. KAMENECKI
38 SADDLE RIVER ROAD
MONSEY, NEW YORK 10952

בע"ה

יום ה' ערב חג השבועות תשל"ס, פה מאנסי.

כבוד הרבני איש החסד שוע ונדיב מוקיר רבנן מר אלעזר נ"י גליק
שלו' וברכת כל טוב.

מה מאד שמחתי בהודעי כי כבודו רכש לעצמו הזכות שייקרא ע"ש
בנו המנוח הפירוש מבואר על כל ששת סדרי משנה ע"י "ארטסקראל"
והנה חברה זו יצאה לה מוניטין בפירושה על תנ"ך, והבה נקוה שכשם
שהצליחה בתורה שבכתב כן תצליח בתורה שבע"פ. ובהיות שאותיות
"משנה" הן כאותיות "נשמה" לפיכך סוב עשה בכוונתו לעשות זאת לעילוי
נשמת בנו המנוח אברהם יוסף ע"ה, ומאד מתאים השם "יד אברהם" לזה
הפירוש, כדמצינו במקרא (ש"ב י"ח) כי אמר אין לי בן בעבור הזכיר
שמי וגו'. ואין לך דבר גדול מזה להפיץ ידיעת תורה שבע"פ בקרב
אחינו שאינם רגילים בלשון הקדש. וד' הסוב יהי' בעזרו ויוכל לברך
על המוגמר. וירוה רוב נחת מכל אשר אתו כנפש מברכו.

יעקב קמנצקי

מכתב ברכה

ישיבת טלז
YESHIVAT TELSHE
קרית טלז-סטון
Kiryat Telshe Stone
ירושלים
Jerusalem, Israel

בע"ה — ד' בהעלותך — לבני א"י, תשל"ט — פה קרית טלז, באה"ק

מע"כ ידידי האהובים הרב ר' מאיר והרב ר' נתן, נר"ו, שלום וברכה נצח!

אחדשה"ט באהבה ויקר,

לשמחה רבה היא לי להודע שהרחבתם גדול עבודתכם בקודש לתורה שבע"פ, בהוצאת המשנה בתרגום וביאור באנגלית, וראשית עבודתכם במס' מגילה.

אני תקוה שתשימו לב שיצאו הדברים מתוקנים מנקודת ההלכה, וחזקה עליכם שתוציאו דבר נאה ומתוקן.

בפנותכם לתורה שבע"פ יפתח אופק חדש בתורת ה' לאלה שקשה עליהם ללמוד הדברים במקורם, ואלה שכבר נתעשרו מעבודתכם במגילת אסתר יכנסו עתה לטרקלין חדש וישמשו להם הדברים דחף ללימוד המשנה, וגדול יהי' שכרכם.

יהא ה' בעזרכם בהוספת טבעת חדשה באותה שלשלת זהב של הפצת תורת ה' להמוני עם לקרב לב ישראל לאבינו שבשמים בתורה ואמונה טהורה.

אוהבכם מלונ"ח,
מרדכי

מכתב ברכה

RABBI SHNEUR KOTLER
BETH MEDRASH GOVOHA
LAKEWOOD, N. J.

בע"ה

שניאור קוטלר
בית מדרש גבוה:
לייקוואוד, נ. דז.

בשורת התרחבות עבודתם הגדולה של סגל חברות ,,ארטסקרול", המעתיקים ומפרשים, לתחומי התושבע"פ, לשים אלה המשפטים לפני הציבור כשלחן ערוך ומוכן לאכול לפני האדם [ל' רש"י], ולשימה בפיהם — לפתוח אוצרות בשנות בצורת ולהשמיעם בכל לשון שהם שומעים — מבשרת צבא רב לתורה ולימודה [ע' תהלים ס"ח י"ב בתרגום יונתן], והיא מאותות ההתעוררות ללימוד התורה, וזאת התעודה על התנוצצות קיום ההבטחה ,,כי לא תשכח מפי זרעו". אשרי הזוכים להיות בין שלוחי ההשגחה לקיומה וביצועה.

יה"ר כי תצליח מלאכת שמים בידם, ויזכו ללמוד וללמד ולשמור מסורת הקבלה כי בהרקת המים החיים מכלי אל כלי תשתמר חיותם, יעמוד טעמם בם וריחם לא נמר. [וע' משאחז"ל בכ"מ ושמרתם זו משנה — וע' חי' מרן רי"ז הלוי עה"ת בפ' ואתחנן] ותהי' משנתם שלמה וברורה, ישמחו בעבודתם חברים ותלמידים, ,,ישוטטו רבים ותרבה הדעת", עד יקויים ,,אז אהפוך אל העמים שפה ברורה וגו' " [צפני' ג' ט', עי' פי' אבן עזרא ומצודת דוד שם].

ונזכה כולנו לראות בהתכנסות הגליות בזכות המשניות כל' חז"ל עפ"י הכתוב ,,גם כי יתנו בגוים עתה אקבצם", בגאולה השלמה בב"א.

הכו"ח לכבוד התורה, יום ו' עש"ק לס' ,,ויוצא פרח ויצץ ציץ ויגמול שקדים", ד' תמוז התשל"ט

יוסף חיים שניאור קוטלר
בלאאמו"ר הגר"א זצוק"ל

מכתב ברכה

ב"ה
לכבוד ידידי וידיד ישיבתנו, מהראשונים לכל דבר שבקדושה
הרבני הנדיב המפורסם ר' אליעזר הכהן גליק נ"י
אחדש"ה באהבה,

בשורה טובה שמעתי שכב' מצא את המקום המתאים לעשות יד ושם להנציח זכרו של בנו **אברהם יוסף ע"ה שנקטף**
בנעוריו. "ונתתי להם בביתי ובחומתי יד ושם". אין לו להקב"ה אלא ד' אמות של הלכה בלבד. א"כ זהו בית ד' לימוד
תורה שבע"פ וזהו המקום לעשות יד ושם לנשמת בנו ע"ה.

נר ד' נשמת אדם אמר הקב"ה נרי בידך ונרך בידי. נר מצוה ותורה אור, תורה זהו נר של הקב"ה וכששומרים נר של
הקב"ה שעל ידי הפירוש **"יד אברהם"** בשפה הלעוזית יתרבה לימוד ושקיעת התורה בבתי ישראל. ד' ישמור
נשמת אדם.

בנו אברהם יוסף ע"ה נתברך בהמדה שבו נכללות כל המדות, לב טוב והיה אהוב לחבריו. בלמדו בישיבתנו היה לו
הרצון לעלות במעלות התורה וכשעלה לארצנו הקדושה היתה מבקשתו להמשיך בלמודיו. ביקוש זה ימצא מלואו על ידי
הרבים המבקשים דרך ד', שהפירוש **"יד אברהם"** יהא מפתח להם לים התלמוד.

התורה נקראת "אש דת" ונמשלה לאש יש לה זה הכח לפעוע מכל כוחות האדם, הניצוץ שהאיר בך רבנו הרב
שרגא פייוועל מנדלוויץ זצ"ל שמרת עליו, ועשה חיל. עכשיו אתה מסייע להאיר נצוצות בנשמות בני ישראל שיעשה חיל
ויהא לאור גדול.

תקוות עזה שכל התלמידי חכמים שנדבה רוחם להוציא לפועל מלאכה ענקית זו לפרש המשניות כולה, יצא עבודתם
ברוח פאר והדר ויכוונו לאמיתה של תורה ויתקדש שם שמים ויתרבה שם שמים על ידי מלאכה זו.

יתברך כב' וב"ב לראות ולרוות נחת רוח מצאצאיו.

הכו"ח לכבוד התורה ותומכיה עש"ק במדבר תשל"ט

אלי' שווי

מכתב ברכה

דוד קאהן

ביהמ"ד גבול יעבץ
ברוקלין, נוא יארק

בס"ד   כ"ה למטמונים תשל"ט

כבוד רחימא דנפשאי, עושה ומעשה
ר' אלעזר הכהן גליק נטריה רחמנא ופרקיה

שמוע שמעתי שכבר תקעת כפיך לתמוך במפעל האדיר של חברת ארטסקרול — הידוע בכל קצווי
תבל ע"י עבודתה הכבירה בהפצת תורה — לתרגם ולבאר ששה סדרי משנה באנגלית. כוונתך להנציח
זכר בנך הנחמד אברהם יוסף ז"ל שנקטף באבו בזמן שעלה לארץ הקודש בתקופת התרוממות הנפש
ושאיפה לקדושה, ולמטרה זו יכונה הפירוש בשם ,,יד אברהם"; וגם האיר ה' רוחך לגרום עילוי לנשמתו
הטהורה שע"י יתרבה לימוד התורה שניתנה בשבעים לשון, על ידי כלי מפואר זה.

מכיוון שהנני מכיר היטב שני הצדדים, אוכל לומר לדבק טוב, והנני תקוה שיצליח המפעל הלזה לתת
יד ושם וכות לנשמת אברהם יוסף ז"ל. חזקה על חברת ארטסקרול שתוציא דבר נאה מתוקן ומתקבל
מתחת ידה להגדיל תורה ולהאדירה.

והנני מברך אותך שתמצא נוחם לנפשך, שהאבא זוכה לברא, ותשבע נחת — אתה עם רעיתך תחיה —
מכל צאצאיכם היקרים אכי"ר

ידידך עז
דוד קאהן

[xiii]   *Approbation*/מכתב ברכה

Preface

אָמַר ר׳ יוֹחָנָן: לֹא כָּרַת הקב״ה בְּרִית עִם יִשְׂרָאֵל אֶלָּא עַל־תּוֹרָה שֶׁבְּעַל
פֶּה שֶׁנֶּאֱמַר: ,,כִּי עַל־פִּי הַדְּבָרִים הָאֵלֶּה כָּרַתִּי אִתְּךָ בְּרִית . . ."

*R' Yochanan said: The Holy One, Blessed is He, sealed a
covenant with Israel only because of the Oral Torah, as it is
said [Exodus 34:27]: For according to these words have I
sealed a covenant with you . . . (Gittin 60b).*

With gratitude to Hashem Yisborach we present the Jewish public with
tractate Kilayim, one of the most complex tractates in Seder Zeraim. The
majority of the tractates of the Mishnah is now complete, and work is
proceeding on the orders of Zeraim and Tohoros. All of this is thanks to the
vision and commitment of MR. AND MRS. LOUIS GLICK. In their quiet,
self-effacing way, they have been a major force for the propagation of Torah
knowledge and the enhancement of Jewish life for a generation. The
commentary to the Mishnayos bears the name YAD AVRAHAM, in memory of
their son AVRAHAM YOSEF GLICK ע״ה. An appreciation of the niftar will
appear in Tractate Berachos. May this dissemination of the Mishnah in his
memory be a source of merit for his soul. תנצב״ה.

By dedicating the ArtScroll Mishnah Series, the Glicks have added a new
dimension to their tradition of service. The many Mishnah study groups in
synagogues, schools, and offices throughout the English-speaking world are
the most eloquent testimony to the fact that thousands of people thirst for
Torah learning, presented in a challenging, comprehensive, and comprehensi-
ble manner.

We are proud and grateful that such venerable luminaries as MARAN
HAGAON HARAV YAAKOV KAMENETZKI זצ״ל and להבל״ח MARAN HAGAON
HARAV MORDECHAI GIFTER שליט״א have declared that this series should be
translated into Hebrew. Baruch Hashem, it has stimulated readers to echo the
words of King David: גַּל־עֵינַי וְאַבִּיטָה נִפְלָאוֹת מִתּוֹרָתֶךָ, Uncover my eyes that I
may see wonders of Your Torah (Psalms 119:18).

May we inject two words of caution:

First, although the Mishnah, by definition, is a compendium of laws, the final halachah does not necessarily follow the Mishnah. The development of halachah proceeds through the Gemara, commentators, codifiers, responsa, and the acknowledged poskim. Even when our commentary cites the Shulchan Aruch, the intention is to sharpen the reader's understanding of the Mishnah, but not to be a basis for actual practice. In short, this work is meant as a first step in the study of our recorded Oral Law — no more.

Second, as we have stressed in our other books, the ArtScroll commentary is not meant as a substitute for the study of the sources. While this commentary, like others in the various series, will be immensely useful even to accomplished scholars and will often bring to light ideas and sources they may have overlooked, we strongly urge those who can, to study the classic sefarim in the original. It has been said that every droplet of ink coming from Rashi's pen is worthy of seven days' contemplation. Despite the exceptional caliber of our authors, none of us pretends to replace the study of the greatest minds in Jewish history.

This volume is by RABBI MORDECAI RABINOVITCH, *who is familiar to ArtScroll readers from his masterful work on both Mishnah and Talmud.* RABBI YONOSSON ROSENBLUM, *a very welcome newcomer to our editorial staff, reviewed the entire manuscript and assisted greatly in the editing of this volume. We are proud to have him.* MRS. FAYGIE WEINBAUM *read the galleys meticulously as did* MRS. JUDI DICK, *whose efforts in coordinating the production of the final version of this book were invaluable;* MRS. ESTHER FEIERSTEIN *did the typing.*

We are also grateful to the staff of Mesorah Publications: REB SHEAH BRANDER, *the leader in bringing beauty of presentation to Torah literature, who is responsible for the layout; and his co-workers in the art department,* REB ELI KROEN *and* YITZCHOK SAFTLAS; RABBI YOSEF GESSER, AVROHOM BIDERMAN, YOSEF TIMINSKY, SAID KOHAN FOLAD, YEHUDA GORDON, LEA FREIER, SHEILA TENNENBAUM, MRS. ZISSI LANDAU, BASSIE GOLDSTEIN, NICHIE FENDRICH, ESTI KUSHNER, RAIZY BRANDER *and* MRS. DEVORAH MORGENSTERN.

Finally, our gratitude goes to RABBI DAVID FEINSTEIN שליט״א, RABBI DAVID COHEN שליט״א, *and* RABBI HILLEL DAVID, *whose concern, interest, and guidance throughout the history of the ArtScroll Series have been important to its success.*

Rabbi Nosson Scherman / Rabbi Meir Zlotowitz

ז׳ ניסן תשנ״ב / *April 10, 1992*
Brooklyn, New York

מסכת כלאים ⇜
⇜ **Tractate Kilayim**

Translation and anthologized commentary by
Rabbi Mordecai Rabinovitch

General Editor
Rabbi Yehezkel Danziger

אֶת־חֻקֹּתַי תִּשְׁמֹרוּ בְּהֶמְתְּךָ לֹא־תַרְבִּיעַ כִּלְאַיִם שָׂדְךָ לֹא־
תִזְרַע כִּלְאָיִם וּבֶגֶד כִּלְאַיִם שַׁעַטְנֵז לֹא יַעֲלֶה עָלֶיךָ

Leviticus 19:19

*You shall keep My statutes: You shall not mate your animal
with a diverse kind; you shall not sow your field with
diverse kinds of seed; and a garment [containing a] shaatnez
mixture shall not come upon you.*

דברים כ"ב:ט־י"א

לֹא־תִזְרַע כַּרְמְךָ כִּלְאָיִם פֶּן־תִּקְדַּשׁ הַמְלֵאָה הַזֶּרַע אֲשֶׁר תִּזְרָע
וּתְבוּאַת הַכָּרֶם. לֹא־תַחֲרֹשׁ בְּשׁוֹר־וּבַחֲמֹר יַחְדָּו. לֹא תִלְבַּשׁ
שַׁעַטְנֵז צֶמֶר וּפִשְׁתִּים יַחְדָּו.

Deuteronomy 22:9-11

*You shall not sow your vineyard with a mixture; lest the
fullness of the seed which you have sown be forfeited with
the product of the vineyard. You shall not plow with an ox
and a donkey together. You shall not wear shaatnez, wool
and flax together.*

General Introduction

The title of the present tractate is כִּלְאַיִם, *Kilayim*, a term whose precise meaning is somewhat obscure. *Targum Onkelos* (to *Leviticus* 19:19) renders it עֵירוּבִין, "mixture" or "confusion." *Ravad* (quoted by *R' Shlomo Sirilio* to *Kilayim* 3:5) makes a connection with the word כְּלָא, *prison*, as in *Isaiah* 42:22: וּבְבָתֵּי כְלָאִים הָחְבָּאוּ, "and they were hidden inside prisons." Evidently, the idea behind this term is that a species which is mixed up and confused with another is as if imprisoned.

The word כִּלְאַיִם, *kilayim*, occurs four times in the Torah. In *Leviticus* 19:19 we read: אֶת־חֻקֹּתַי תִּשְׁמֹרוּ בְּהֶמְתְּךָ לֹא־תַרְבִּיעַ כִּלְאַיִם שָׂדְךָ לֹא־תִזְרַע כִּלְאָיִם וּבֶגֶד כִּלְאַיִם שַׁעַטְנֵז לֹא יַעֲלֶה עָלֶיךָ, *You shall keep My statutes: You shall not mate your animal with a diverse kind; you shall not sow your field with diverse kinds of seed; a garment [containing a] shaatnez mixture shall not come upon you.* This verse contains three distinct prohibitions: a prohibition on crossbreeding animals of diverse kinds, a prohibition on sowing a mixture of seeds of diverse kinds, and a prohibition on wearing a garment containing a forbidden mixture of materials known as *shaatnez* (see also *Deuteronomy* 22:11). In *Deuteronomy* 22:9, the Torah states: לֹא־תִזְרַע כַּרְמְךָ כִּלְאָיִם פֶּן־תִּקְדַּשׁ הַמְלֵאָה הַזֶּרַע אֲשֶׁר תִּזְרָע וּתְבוּאַת הַכָּרֶם, *You shall not sow your vineyard with a mixture; lest the fullness of the seed which you have sown be forfeited with the product of the vineyard.* In this verse the Torah issues a specific prohibition on *kilayim* of the vineyard. In the following verse (*Deuteronomy* 22:10), the Torah prohibits working with a team of animals of diverse kinds. (The term *kilayim* does not occur in the Torah in connection with the latter prohibition.) These five prohibitions — two involving plants, two involving animals, and one involving clothes — form the subject matter of the present tractate.

ﹸﹶ כִּלְאֵי זְרָעִים, Kilayim of Seeds

The first three chapters of *Kilayim* deal with *kilayim of seeds* (*kilei zeraim*). This refers to the prohibition on sowing together seeds of diverse kinds of grains or greens,[1] and includes also a prohibition on grafting together plants of diverse kinds.[2] According to most authorities, there is no prohibition on planting a

---

1. According to most authorities, this is a Scriptural prohibition. However, *Rashi* in several places (*Shabbos* 84b, *Bechoros* 54a and others; cf. *Rashi Kiddushin* 39a) states that planting *kilayim* of plants is a Rabbinic prohibition (see *Eretz Chemdah* p. 215).

2. The grafting prohibition is derived by the Gemara (*Sanhedrin* 60a) from the juxtaposition of *you shall not mate your animal with a diverse kind* and *you shall not sow your field with diverse kinds of seed*. This indicates that there is a prohibited method of growing which

mixture of tree seeds, regardless of whether the mixture is only of diverse types of trees, or whether it includes seeds of grains or greens (see *Rambam, Hil. Kilayim* 1:6 and *Hasagos HaRavad* ad loc.). However, grafting is forbidden even with trees (mishnah 1:7).

It is not only forbidden for a person to plant a mixture of species together in his field, but even if it grew there on its own, the mixture must be eliminated (mishnah 2:5). Someone who preserves a mixture of species in his field, even if it arose on its own, is guilty of "maintaining *kilayim*" (see *Avodah Zarah* 64a).

In its treatment of the laws governing a mixture of diverse kinds of seeds, the mishnah seeks to clarify what exactly constitutes "a mixture," as well as how to define a diverse kind. For example, if a single seed of wheat is mixed with several tons of barley, is this a mixture which it is forbidden to plant (see mishnah 2:1)? And what about two adjacent rows, each planted with a different species? Is this also considered a mixture? If so, then what are the parameters which determine how closely together different species may be planted? These questions are treated extensively from mishnah 2:6 through mishnah 3:7. In some cases, gaps or separators must divide between two species (see mishnah 2:10); in others, distinctive planting formations enable two species to approach one another (see mishnah 3:1).

The mishnah teaches its system of classification of the species by way of numerous examples (mishnah 1:1-5). While it is certain that the halachic system does not correspond to the modern scientific system (see *Kilei Zeraim VeHarkavah*, p.20 ff.), it is not altogether clear what criteria are used by the mishnah. From *Yerushalmi* (1:5) it emerges that three factors are taken into account: the morphology of the leaves, the morphology of the fruit, and the taste of the fruit. *Rambam* (*Hil. Kilayim* 3:1-6 as understood by *Mikdash David* 61:4) lays down the following rules for classification: Where the leaves or the fruits of the two species seem "almost identical," the species are considered a single kind even if the tastes of their respective fruits are very different; where the leaves or fruits are similar in appearance (not "almost identical"), they are classified as one kind only if the taste of their fruits is also similar. In the latter case, if the taste of their fruits is markedly different, then they are considered diverse kinds (cf. *Tos. Yom Tov* to mishnah 1:5; see also *Eretz Chemdah* 1:3 pp. 181-188). [*Rash* and *Rosh* have a different approach (see commentary to mishnah 1:5).]

In addition to the difficulty posed by the obscurity of the criteria for classification, the identity of many of the plants listed by the mishnah is not known with certainty. We have attempted as best as possible to unravel the definitions used by *Rav*, with special attention to deciphering his many foreign-language definitions (most of which were taken from the major commentators or *Aruch*).

---

resembles the coupling of animals, viz., grafting. The grafting prohibition applies even outside of the Land of Israel under Biblical law (*Kiddushin* 39a; see Mishnah 1:7).

The product of a forbidden mixture of seeds, or a forbidden graft, is permitted for consumption (*Kiddushin* 39a).[3] Sowing a mixture is forbidden only in the Land of Israel; however, grafting diverse species together is forbidden even outside Israel (ibid.; *Rambam, Hil. Kilayim* 1:1 and 1:5).

כְּלָאֵי הַכֶּרֶם, Kilayim of the Vineyard

The mishnah devotes chapters 4 through 7 to the elucidation of the very complex laws governing this type of *kilayim*. The prohibition of *kilei hakerem* (*kilayim* of the vineyard) refers to the prohibition on planting grain or greens[4] in the vicinity of a single grapevine, or in the vicinity of a vineyard. Not only is it forbidden to plant *kilei hakerem*, but in contrast with *kilei zeraim*, the products of *kilei hakerem* are forbidden for use (mishnah 8:1; see also 5:5). However, the prohibition on use takes effect only when the components of the *kilayim* have grown a specified amount, or have reached a particular stage in their growth (see mishnah 7:7-8).

The area around a vineyard in which foreign planting is prohibited is much more extensive than the area forbidden around a single vine, and for this reason it is important to know what arrangement of vines and how many vines are needed to constitute a vineyard. This is clarified in mishnah 4:5-6. In addition, the extent of the condemnation from use of the vines or the foreign seed depends on the location of the foreign seed relative to the vines: If foreign seed is planted inside a vineyard, it condemns all the vines within a sixteen-cubit radius (mishnah 5:5); if planted outside a vineyard, within the area forbidden for such planting, it condemns only two rows of the vineyard (mishnah 4:5).

There are also special laws governing clearings within a vineyard (mishnah 4:1; see also mishnah 5:1), the area between a vineyard and its surrounding wall (mishnah 4:2-3), and the gaps between the rows of a vineyard (mishnah 4:8-9). A crawling vineyard is governed by a different set of rules than a hanging vineyard, and this is elaborated on by the mishnah in chapter 6.

One of the fascinating problems with the mishnah's treatment of *kilayim* of the vineyard is the seeming inconsistency between the mishnah's examples and the Talmudic definition of *kilei hakerem*. The *Gemara* (*Berachos* 22a; see also *Yerushalmi Kilayim* 8:1) defines *kilei hakerem* as a grain of wheat, a grain of barley, and a grape-seed, planted together simultaneously. That is, *kilei hakerem* involves *two* foreign species (e.g., wheat and grain), in addition to the grapevine. Yet, numerous *mishnayos* seem oblivious of this requirement (see

---

3. *Rashbam* (*Bava Basra* 94a s.v. כל סאה) speaks of *kilayim* of plants becoming forbidden for use once the seeds take root. This would seem to be in open contradiction to mishnah 8:1 as noted already by *Tosafos* (*Bava Basra* ibid. s.v. סאה). See also *Ri ben Malki Tzedek* to mishnah 2:11 and *R' Shlomo Sirilio* there.

4. Not all greens are included in this prohibition. The relevant criteria are discussed in the commentary to mishnah 5:8.

e.g., mishnah 7:5 and 7:8). A summary of the more prominent resolutions to this vexing problem may be found in the commentary to mishnah 8:1.

⊱ כִּלְאֵי בְּהֵמָה, Kilayim with Animals

Chapter 8 of the tractate is devoted to this type of *kilayim*. The Torah prohibits crossbreeding animals of diverse kinds (*Leviticus* 19:19), as well as working with a team consisting of animals of diverse kinds (*Deuteronomy* 22:11). Incidental to its illustrations of diverse species of plants, the mishnah already gives some examples of animals which are diverse kinds in mishnah 1:6. In chapter 8, the mishnah elaborates on the scope of the prohibition (kosher and non-kosher animals, wild and domestic animals), and on what exactly constitutes "work" which is forbidden with a mixed team. An interesting question discussed by early authorities is what constitutes a forbidden team: Must the animals be tied together? Must they work in unison? (See commentary to mishnah 8:4.)

⊱ שַׁעַטְנֵז, Kilayim of Clothes

The *kilayim* of clothes is known as *shaatnez*, and it is the form of *kilayim* is the most familiar to the average person. It refers to the prohibition to wear (*Deuteronomy* 22:11), or to have upon oneself (*Leviticus* 19:19),[5] a fabric containing a mixture of linen and wool. In mishnah 9:8, the Mishnah explains the Biblically forbidden *shaatnez*: This is a mixture that has undergone the three processes of *shua*, *tavui*, and *noz*, the initials of which spell *shaatnez*. There is a great controversy about the meaning of these terms, as well as whether they must all be performed on a mixture in order to constitute *shaatnez* on the Biblical level; and these issues are discussed at length in the commentary. Several *mishnayos* (see esp. 9:2 and 9:5) elucidate the type of wearing which is forbidden,[6] while others give examples of different sorts of garments that are forbidden Biblically or Rabbinically as *shaatnez* (see mishnah 9:9). It is perhaps interesting to note that the modern Shaatnez Laboratories were anticipated already in Mishnaic times, as is evident from mishnah 9:7, which speaks about examining certain garments for *shaatnez*.

---

5. See commentary to mishnah 9:5 for the difference between wearing and having upon oneself.

6. A common practical question is whether or not it is permitted to try on *shaatnez* for size. Although the principles deriving from these *mishnayos*, and expounded in the commentary, have direct bearing on this question, in view of the fact that this is not a practical guide to *halachah*, this question was purposely not addressed.

✒ Bibliography:

The major early Mishnah commentaries used were: *Ri ben Malki Tzedek*, *Rambam Comm.*, *Rash* and *Rosh*. As noted in the General Introductions to *Sheviis* and *Peah*, wherever possible, the most complete critical editions of these commentaries have been used. An unfortunate exception in the case of tractate *Kilayim* is the commentary of *Rash*, the Paris manuscript of which was recently published (in the Mutzal Me'esh edition of *Yerushalmi Kilayim*), but was not yet available at the time our commentary was written. A number of additions and corrections have been added based on this most important manuscript. However, it is to be regretted that a more thorough study of it could not be undertaken at present.

There follows a comprehensive listing of the more specialized sources used. Standard general works such as the Rom family edition of the mishnah (יכין־ובועז) are not included here:

ארץ חמדה, ר' שאול ישראלי, תל אביב – תשי"ז
אמונת יוסף, ר' חיים יוסף דינקלס [בתוך: מסכת כלאים עם פירוש ר' שלמה סיריליאו]
באור ההלכה ראה דרך אמונה
דרך אמונה [באור ההלכה – **ציון ההלכה**], ר' חיים קניבסקי, בני ברק – תשד"מ
החקלאות בארץ ישראל בתקופת המשנה והתלמוד, יהודה פליקס, תל אביב – תשכ"ג
הערות במשניות כלאים [בתוך: אוסף מאמרים מתוך חוברות הדרום],
ר' נ. א. ראבינאוויטש, ניו יורק, תשכ"ו
חדושי כלאים לתלמיד הרשב"א
חזון איש (זרעים), ר' אברהם ישעיה קרליץ, בני ברק – תשל"ג
כלאי זרעים והרכבה, י. פליקס, תל אביב – תשכ"ז
כפתור ופרח, ר' אישתורי הפרחי, מהד' עדעלמאן, ד"צ ירושלים – תש"מ
מנחת יצחק ראה עטרת יצחק
מסכת כלאים עם פירוש ר' שלמה סיריליאו, מהד' ר' חיים יוסף דינקלס
מסכת כלאים עם ביאורים, ר' חיים קניבסקי, בני ברק – תשמ"ו
מצוות הארץ, ר' קלמן כהנא, ירושלים – תשמ"ד
מקדש דוד, ר' דוד הכהן ראפאפארט, ירושלים – תשמ"ו
משנה זרעים עם פירוש ריבמ"ץ, מהד' ר' ניסן זק"ש, ירושלים – תשל"ה
משנה עם פירוש הרמב"ם, מהד' ר' יוסף קאפח, ירושלים – תשכ"ד
משנה עם שינויי נוסחאות, בעריכת ר' ניסן זק"ש, ירושלים – תשל"ב
משנת חכמים, ר' משולם פייבוש הלוי איש הורוויץ, ד"צ בני ברק
משנת נחמיה, ר' נחמיה רוז'נסקי, ירושלים – תשכ"ט[7]
משנת רבי נתן [בתוך: ספרי רבי נתן אדלר],
בעריכת ר' צבי בנימין אויערבך, ד"צ ירושלים – תשמ"ג

---

7. This little known work is unique in its penetrating study of *kilei hakerem*.

עטרת יצחק על תוספתא [מנחת יצחק – שירי מנחה],
ר' יצחק הכהן שבדרן, ירושלים – תשמ"א
ציון ההלכה ראה דרך אמונה
רש"ס ראה מסכת כלאים
שירי מנחה ראה עטרת יצחק
שלום ירושלים, ר' נחום טרייביטש, ירושלים – תש"מ
תורת הארץ (ב"ח), ר' משה קליערס, ירושלים – תשל"ב
תורת זרעים, ר' אריה פומרנצ'יק, תל אביב

A curiosity that ought to be mentioned here is the presence in *Shulchan Aruch Yoreh Deah* of two separate sections each of which is numbered 297. The first deals with the laws of *kilei zeraim*, while the second deals with *kilei beheimah*. The reader is advised to identify the section being referred to from the context. As a rule, references to *Yerushalmi*, *Tosefta*, or *Mishnah*, without specification of the tractate, are to tractate *Kilayim*. Likewise, unless otherwise specified, references to *Chazon Ish* are to *Hil. Kilayim* in the Bnei Brak, 5733 ed., of *Chazon Ish* to the Order *Zeraim*.

The botanical information in the commentary has been culled primarily from: *Plants of the Bible*, M. Zohary, Cambridge University Press, 1982; *Kilei Zeraim VeHarkavah*, Y. Feliks, Tel Aviv, 1969; and, *HaTzomeach VeHaChai BaMishnah*, Y. Feliks, Jerusalem, 1983.

※ ※ ※

Tractate *Kilayim* is among the most difficult of the entire Mishnah,[8] and at times the preparation of this commentary seemed almost an overwhelming challenge. If, as is hoped, the commentary succeeds in making *Kilayim* somewhat more accessible, credit is due to others aside from the author alone. In particular, Rabbi David Strauss of Jerusalem, with whom the author labored night after night in study of *Yerushalmi Kilayim*, deserves special mention. Special thanks are due also to the renowned Jerusalem sage, R' Shlomo Fisher, who was always available to discuss *kilayim*-related issues, and to share his vast knowledge of the writings of *Gra* and *Chazon Ish*, and to R' Chaim Kanievsky of Bnei Brak, whose encyclopedic work *Derech Emunah* is

---

8. Consider the following remarks of some of our greatest sages:

And I myself know that the laws of *kilayim* are so muddled because it has no *Gemara* (Talmud Bavli) and the *mishnayos* are not as clear to us as other tractates . . . we are like blind people in a chimney and feel around to pick up some of the laws here and there. Responsum that R' *Meshulem ben R' Yaakov* sent to R' *Avraham b'R' Yitzchok Av Bes Din*. Found in *Orchos Chaim* vol. 2, *Hil. Kilayim* pg. 221.)

The chambers of *kilayim* have been concealed from me [a play on the words of the *posuk* in Isaiah 42:22] and have been hidden from my eyes and its principle foundations have escaped me (*Rosh* comm. Chap. 3, Mishnah 5).

frequently quoted in this book and who graciously clarified many questions addressed to him in writing by the author. A debt of gratitude is owed to Mr. Allan Smith, formerly of the Max Cohen Memorial Library, who was of considerable assistance in locating source material.

Finally, mention must be made of my dear wife Chana whose infinite patience was tested to the limit many times during this project. Her constant encouragement and concern were vital to seeing this book to completion. May Hashem grant that this book lead to an increased knowledge and study of the special *mitzvos* peculiar to *Eretz Yisrael;* and may we all merit thereby to witness the completion of the redemption speedily in our days.

Mordecai Rabinovitch

Adar II, 5752
Jerusalem, Israel

[א] הַחִטִּים וְהַזּוּנִין אֵינָן כִּלְאַיִם זֶה בָזֶה. הַשְׂעוֹרִים וְשִׁבֹּלֶת שׁוּעָל, הַכֻּסְמִין וְהַשִּׁיפוֹן, הַפּוֹל וְהַסַּפִּיר, הַפֻּרְקְדָן וְהַטֹּפַח,

יד אברהם

Chapter 1

1.

The mishnah opens with a list of plants, grouped in pairs, such that the members of each pair are not *kilayim* with one another, but a member of one pair with a member of another are *kilayim* (*Rav, Rosh, Rash* from *Yerushalmi* 1:1). Our translation is based on *Rav's* definitions of the mishnah's nomenclature. Other opinions are presented in the commentary.

The mishnah here lists six pairs of plants. The first three are grain and cereal plants. The remaining three pairs are all leguminous (i.e. beans or peas). Thus, the familiar halachic groupings תְּבוּאָה, *grain*, and קִטְנִיּוֹת, *legumes* (see *Peah* 1:4), are the first to be treated by the mishnah (*Tos. Anshei Shem* to mishnah 2).

הַחִטִּים וְהַזּוּנִין אֵינָן כִּלְאַיִם זֶה בָזֶה. — *Wheat and darnel are not kilayim with one another.*

Darnel is a noxious weed that grows in grain fields. Its grains are similar in weight and form to grains of wheat, and are thus difficult to separate from wheat grains by sifting. The grains of the darnel are poisonous for man, but do not affect certain birds, such as doves, for which they are occasionally used as feed. In Arabic, darnel (*lolium temulentum*) is known as *ziwan*, the same term given by *Rav*.

Aruch (s.v. זונין) renders this plant as *zuwan* in Arabic and describes it as producing black grains. His reference is apparently to Syrian scabious (*cephalaria syriaca*), which grows among grain crops and has black grains that resemble certain varieties of wheat. Like darnel, the scabious is poisonous. In Arabic it is called *zuwan aswad*.

In the context of the laws of *kilayim*, darnel (or scabious) is considered a variety of wheat, and it is thus permissible to sow wheat even if there is darnel (or scabious) mixed with it. Indeed, *Yerushalmi* (1:1) describes זונין as arising when wheat grains planted in the ground degenerate. *Midrash Rabbah* (*Bereishis* 28:8) traces its origin to the generation of the Flood, when people degenerated morally, and

likewise the earth degenerated, so that crops planted as wheat came up as זונין (*Rav; Rosh; Rash; Rambam Comm.*; see Y. Feliks, *Kilei Zeraim VeHarkavah*, p. 22). Interestingly, this phenomenon is reflected in the Hebrew name זונין, which derives from the root זנה, *to go astray*, and thus describes wheat which has gone astray (*Rambam Comm.*).

As noted in the prefatory remarks, the varieties paired together by the mishnah are not *kilayim* with each other, but are *kilayim* with the other varieties listed by the mishnah. Thus, for example, it is forbidden to sow darnel together with barley (the next variety in the mishnah's list). Although darnel is not suitable for human consumption, it is nonetheless governed by the laws of *kilayim* since it is used as bird feed. However, something suitable for neither man nor beast is not subject to the laws of *kilayim* (*Rav, Rosh, Rash* from *Yerushalmi* 1:1). Strangely, *Rambam* (*Hil. Kilayim* 1:4) appears to regard only produce suitable for human consumption as subject to the laws of *kilayim*. This is in conflict with *Yerushalmi's* statement that darnel is *kilayim* with barley, since darnel is used as bird feed. For this reason, *Kesef Mishneh* (ad loc.; quoted here by *Tos. R' Akiva*) struggles to reinterpret *Rambam's* wording in a manner that conforms with *Yerushalmi's* contentions. See also *Mishnah Rishonah; Tif. Yis.* — *Batei Kilayim* 1:2; *Chazon Ish* 1:2; and *Derech Emunah* 1:4, *Beur HaHalachah* s.v. הראוי.

1. **W**heat and darnel are not *kilayim* with one another. Barley and oats, spelt and rye, broad bean and Nile cowpea, grasspea and red grasspea,

YAD AVRAHAM

הַשְּׂעוֹרִים וְשִׁבֹּלֶת שׁוּעָל, — *Barley and oats,*
Rav follows *Rashi* (*Pesachim* 35a and *Menachos* 70b) in rendering שִׁבֹּלֶת שׁוּעָל as *avena*, oats.

From *Rabbeinu Nosson Av HaYeshivah*, however, it is evident that שִׁבֹּלֶת שׁוּעָל is two-rowed barley, as distinct from שְׂעוֹרִים which is six-rowed barley (*Kilei Zeraim VeHarkavah*, p. 24).

Rambam Comm. describes שִׁבֹּלֶת שׁוּעָל as *wild* (desert) *barley*, and it is likely that he means Tabor barley, the wild progenitor of the two-rowed barley (*Kilei Zeraim VeHarkavah*, p. 25 n. 20).

Aruch (s.v. שבל) identifies שִׁבֹּלֶת שׁוּעָל as either rye or oats.

הַכֻּסְמִין וְהַשִּׁיפוֹן, — *spelt and rye,*
Rav follows *Rashi* in rendering כֻּסְמִין as spelt. However, *Aruch* (s.v. דשר) defines שִׁיפוֹן as spelt. [Modern scholars have identified כֻּסְמִין as rice-wheat, also known as emmer.]

As for שִׁיפוֹן, Rav (following *Rashi*) renders it as *seigle*, i.e. rye (*secale cereale*). *Rambam Comm.* describes שִׁיפוֹן as a variety of wild barley. Nevertheless, it does not constitute *kilayim* with כֻּסְמִין (which Rambam describes as a variety of wild wheat) since שִׁיפוֹן and כֻּסְמִין are similar in appearance (*Rav; Rambam Comm.*).

As already mentioned above, *Yerushalmi* asserts that sowing two varieties belonging to different pairs in the mishnah's list is forbidden. It follows therefore that כֻּסְמִין and חִטִּים, for example, constitute *kilayim* since they belong to different pairs. Similarly, שִׁיפוֹן would be *kilayim* with שְׂעוֹרִים. This would indicate that כֻּסְמִין and wheat, for example, are regarded as distinct kinds. While this is true with respect to the laws of *kilayim*, it is not universally so. Thus, in connection with the laws of *challah* (the portion of the dough which must be set aside and given to a *Kohen*), we find that כֻּסְמִין and חִטִּים are regarded as one kind, and so too שִׁיפוֹן with שְׂעוֹרִים (*Pesachim* 35a, *Menachos* 70a; see *Tos. R' Akiva*). Obviously, the classification criteria for the laws of *kilayim* differ from those of *challah*. What counts for the latter is the nature of the dough. Since כֻּסְמִין dough is very similar to חִטִּים dough, the two are considered one kind for the laws of *challah*. Accordingly, the *challah* portion due from a כֻּסְמִין dough may be taken from an equally liable חִטִּים dough (first explanation of *Rash* and *Rosh*; see *Rav* and *Tos. R' Akiva*). However, with *kilayim*, factors such as the morphology of the plant play a role (see below, mishnah 1:5 s.v. אף על פי), and these different considerations lead to a different system of classification. Accordingly, to sow כֻּסְמִין together with חִטִּים is forbidden as *kilayim* (*Rav; Rosh; Rash*).

הַפּוֹל וְהַסָּפִּיר, — *broad bean and Nile cowpea,*
The plant סָפִּיר is not encountered elsewhere. From *Yerushalmi* it appears that it corresponds to the garden pea (Y. Feliks, *Kilei Zeraim*, pp. 35-37). *Rambam Comm.*, along with *Rabbeinu Nosson Av HaYeshivah*, define it in Arabic as *maash*, or Nile cowpea (Y. Feliks, *HaTzome'ach*, p. 163). This is cited by *Rav* as an alternative interpretation.

Rav's first suggestion, based on *Aruch* (s.v. פול, quoted by *Ri ben Malki Tzedek*), is that סָפִּיר is the Latin *cicercula*, which Y. Feliks (*Kilei Zeraim*, p. 38 n. 48) identifies as the grasspea (ibid. p. 37 n. 45). [In our translation we have adopted *Rav's* alternative interpretation (based on *Rambam*) and have rendered סָפִּיר as *Nile cowpea*, rather than grasspea. This was done in order to avoid confusion with טֹפַח in the next pair mentioned in the Mishnah.]

הַפֻּרְקְדָן וְהַטֹּפַח, — *grasspea and red grasspea,*
Rav following *Rambam Comm.* gives *jelban* as the Arabic for פֻּרְקְדָן. This closely resembles the term גילבונה used by *Yerushalmi* to define פֻּרְקְדָן. In English this is the grasspea (*lathyrus sativus*).

וּפוֹל הַלָּבָן וְהַשְּׁעוּעִים אֵינָם כִּלְאַיִם זֶה בָזֶה.

[ב] הַקִּשׁוּת וְהַמְּלָפְפוֹן אֵינָם כִּלְאַיִם זֶה בָזֶה.
רַבִּי יְהוּדָה אוֹמֵר: כִּלְאַיִם. חֲזֶרֶת
וַחֲזֶרֶת גַּלִּים, עֻלְשִׁין וְעֻלְשֵׁי שָׂדֶה, כְּרֵישִׁים וּכְרֵישֵׁי
שָׂדֶה, כֻּסְבָּר וְכֻסְבַּר שָׂדֶה, חַרְדָּל וְחַרְדָּל מִצְרִי,
וּדְלַעַת הַמִּצְרִי וְהָרְמוּצָה, וּפוֹל הַמִּצְרִי וְהֶחָרוּב.

יד אברהם

However, *Rav* also reports a teaching to the effect that טֹפֵחַ is called *jelban*. [Indeed, this teaching is preserved in *Peirush Rav Hai Gaon* to *Tvul Yom* 1:2.]

As for טֹפֵחַ, *Rav* following *Rambam Comm.* describes this as a plant with hard white seeds which shares certain properties with barley grains. The reference is apparently to the red grasspea *lathyrus cicera* which like the grasspea is also a member of the genus *lathyrus* (Y. Feliks, *Kilei Zeraim* p. 36, n. 49; see ArtScroll *Peah* 5:3).

Ri ben Malki Tzedek gives *dolichos* (דוליקי) as a translation of טֹפֵחַ. This is the hyacinth bean [*dolichos lablab*] (Y. Feliks, *Kilei Zeraim*, p. 38 n. 49, and *HaTzome'ach*, p. 119).

וּפוֹל הַלָּבָן וְהַשְּׁעוּעִים — *hyacinth bean and cowpea*

Yerushalmi (as explained by *Shenos Eliyahu, Peirush HaAroch;* cf. *Tos. Yom Tov*) explains that these are two varieties

of the same bean: (a) the white bean (פוֹל הַלָּבָן) and (b) the laxative bean (פוֹל הַשְּׁעוּעִים). The root of שְׁעוּעִים is שׁוּע meaning to smooth out, and refers to the use of the פוֹל הַשְּׁעוּעִים, *laxative bean*, in cleaning out the digestive system.

אֵינָם כִּלְאַיִם זֶה בָזֶה. — *are not kilayim with one another.*

That is, the members of each pair listed above are not *kilayim* with one another; but a member of one pair with a member of another pair is *kilayim* (see preface).

The ruling here that the members of a pair *are not kilayim with one another* is the same as that given by the mishnah for its first example, the pair of *wheat and darnel.* In that case, the inclusion there of the ruling *wheat and darnel are not kilayim with one another* would seem superfluous! *Tos. Yom Tov* suggests that it was inserted in order to indicate that the mishnah's list should be read as a list of pairs, and not as if all twelve are permitted with each other (see also *Meleches Shlomo*).

2.

The coming mishnah consists of three parts. The first deals with a dispute concerning melons. Next, the mishnah deals with plants which come in both wild and cultivated varieties. And finally, the mishnah lists plants which come both in a local, as well as an Egyptian variety.

הַקִּשׁוּת וְהַמְּלָפְפוֹן אֵינָם כִּלְאַיִם זֶה בָזֶה. — *The chatemelon and muskmelon are not kilayim with one another.*

The translation of קִשׁוּת as *chatemelon* follows *Rambam Comm.* (see Kafich ed.) and *Targum Yonasan* to Numbers 11:5 (see Y. Feliks, *Kilei Zeraim* , p. 50). *Ri ben Malki Tzedek* defines it as cucumber.

[*Rav* records both definitions as if they are equivalent.]

The translation of מְלָפְפוֹן as *muskmelon* follows *Ri ben Malki Tzedek* (as explained by *R' Sh. Sirilio*), *Rabbeinu Nosson Av HaYeshivah,* and *Targum Yerushalmi* to Numbers 11:5 (see *Ri ben Malki Tzedek,* ed. Zaks, p. 76 n. 36; see

hyacinth bean and cowpea are not *kilayim* with one another.

2. The chatemelon and muskmelon are not *kilayim* with one another. R' Yehudah says: [They are] *kilayim*. Lettuce and wild lettuce, chicory and wild chicory, leek and field leek, coriander and wild coriander, mustard and Egyptian mustard, Egyptian gourd and ash gourd, Egyptian bean and carob bean

YAD AVRAHAM

also Y. Feliks, *Kilei Zeraim*, p. 49, n. 20). *Rambam Comm.* identifies it as a cucumber. The word מְלָפְפוֹן is of Greek origin and is a contraction of two Greek words: *melo* (apple) and *pepon* (melon). *Yerushalmi* explains that R' Yehudah believed the *melopepon* to be the product of a cross between an apple seed and a watermelon seed. The first *Tanna*, however, regarded the *melopepon* (muskmelon) as a derivative of the watermelon, which itself was believed to be a derivative of the chatemelon.

Thus, in the *Tanna Kamma's* opinion the *melopepon* (muskmelon) is just another form of chatemelon, and hence the two are not *kilayim*.[1] On the other hand, according to R' Yehudah the *melopepon* was an independent variety and thus was regarded as *kilayim* with chatemelon.

In *Terumos* 2:6 the same dispute recurs: The anonymous first *Tanna* regards chatemelon and muskmelon as one kind with respect to the laws of *terumah*, and R' Yehudah maintains that they are distinct kinds. In both instances (that is, concerning *kilayim* here and *terumah* there), the halachah rejects R' Yehudah's position (*Rav; Rambam Comm.*).

רַבִּי יְהוּדָה אוֹמֵר: כִּלְאָיִם. — *R' Yehudah says: [They are] kilayim.*

R' Yehudah does not subscribe to the theory that the chatemelon and the muskmelon are different forms of the same variety. According to R' Yehudah, they are independent varieties and dis-

tinct kinds of melon. Thus, they are *kilayim* with one another.

חֲזֶרֶת וַחֲזֶרֶת גַּלִּים, עֻלְשִׁין וְעָלְשֵׁי שָׂדֶה, כְּרֵישִׁים וּכְרֵישֵׁי שָׂדֶה, כֻּסְבָּר וְכֻסְבַּר שָׂדֶה, — *Lettuce and wild lettuce, chicory and wild chicory, leek and field leek, coriander and wild coriander,*

As with mishnah 1, members of the same pair are not *kilayim* with one another, but a member of one pair with a member of another are *kilayim* (*Rosh, Rash* from *Yerushalmi* and *Pesachim* 39a).

Although the "wild" member of each of these pairs presumably differed somewhat from the cultivated one, the mishnah does not regard the wild strain as *kilayim* with the domestic one. Indeed, both strains bear essentially the same name (see *Mishnah Rishonah*).

The names for the wild strains of most of the varieties listed here are characterized by the addition of שָׂדֶה (field) to the name. Wild lettuce however is called חֲזֶרֶת גַּלִּים. The term גַּלִּים (lit. heaps) apparently refers to high points in the field (*Rosh*), or to mountains (*Rav; Rambam Comm.*), where this variety of lettuce grew (cf. Y. Feliks, *Kilei Zeraim*, p. 54).

חַרְדָּל וְחַרְדָּל מִצְרִי, וּדְלַעַת הַמִּצְרִי וְהָרְמוּצָה, וּפוֹל הַמִּצְרִי וְהֶחָרוּב — *mustard and Egyptian mustard, Egyptian gourd and ash gourd, Egyptian bean and carob bean*

In each of these three pairs, one member is the Egyptian variety of the plant.

---

1. [*Yerushalmi* does not explain the etymology of *melopepon* according to the first Tanna. Presumably, the chatemelon was so called because its taste resembles that of a watermelon (*pepon*) while its color is similar to an apple (*melo*) (Y. Feliks, *Kelei Zeraim*, p. 49).]

אֵינָם כִּלְאַיִם זֶה בָזֶה.

[ג] **הַלֶּפֶת** וְהַנָּפוּץ, וְהַכְּרוּב וְהַתְּרוֹבְתוֹר, הַתְּרָדִים וְהַלְּעוּנִים אֵינָם כִּלְאַיִם זֶה בָזֶה.

הוֹסִיף רַבִּי עֲקִיבָא: הַשּׁוּם וְהַשּׁוּמָנִית, הַבָּצָל וְהַבִּצַלְצוּל, וְהַתֻּרְמוֹס וְהַפִּלָסְלוֹס אֵינָן כִּלְאַיִם זֶה בָזֶה.

Egyptian mustard is apparently what is today called white mustard (the standard mustard is black mustard).

The Egyptian gourd was a variety of calabash (or bottle) gourd. The ash gourd was a variety of bottle gourd which was made edible by heating in ashes (*Rav; Rambam Comm; Rosh to Nedarim* 51a).

Alternatively, רְמוּצָה is a place name, and here refers to a variety of gourd which grew in that place (*Rash; Rosh; Rashi to Nedarim* 51a; see *Tos. Yom Tov*).

The Egyptian bean was a variety of cowpea. The carob bean is apparently the yard-long bean (or asparagus bean), the fruit of which resembles the fruit of the carob tree and was known also as carob. Because the leaves of the Egyptian bean plant and the carob bean plant were similar (*Rash, Rosh from Yerushalmi*), the two were not considered *kilayim*. Rather, the carob bean was viewed as a variety of Egyptian bean (*Rav; Rambam Comm.*).

אֵינָם כִּלְאַיִם זֶה בָזֶה. — *are not kilayim with one another.*

[The members of each pair, which are viewed as varieties of the same plant, are not *kilayim* with one another, but a member of one pair would be *kilayim* with a member of another pair.]

3.

הַלֶּפֶת וְהַנָּפוּץ, — *The turnip and the radish,*

The translation of נָפוּץ as radish follows *Rav* and *Rambam Comm.* The reference is to the elongated radish (*raphanus sativus*), as distinct from the rounded radish known as צְנוֹן (*Peirush Rav Hai Gaon to Uktzin* 1:2). *Yerushalmi* (1:5) explains that לֶפֶת and נָפוּץ (var. נפוס) are not *kilayim* since their leaves are very similar (*Rav; Rosh; Rash*).

The identification of נָפוּץ with the elongated radish is problematic. This is because *Yerushalmi* (1:5) and *Rambam* (*Hil. Kilayim* 3:6) state that the taste of נָפוּץ is substantially different from the taste of the rounded radish or צְנוֹן. But in fact, there is little difference between the tastes of the rounded and elongated radishes. Additionally, it is stated that the נָפוּץ is very similar in appearance to the צְנוֹן, when in fact the rounded radish is easily distinguished from the elongated one. It has been suggested that perhaps נָפוּץ should be identified as rape (*brassica napus*), a plant which complies with the above criteria (see Y. Feliks, *Kilei Zeraim*, pp. 78-79).

וְהַכְּרוּב וְהַתְּרוֹבְתוֹר, — *the kohlrabi and the garden cabbage,*

Kohlrabi, a word contracted from the Italian *cavolo* (cabbage) and *rapa*

are not *kilayim* with one another.

3. **T**he turnip and the radish, the kohlrabi and the garden cabbage, spinach beets and shrubby oraches are not *kilayim* with one another.

R' Akiva added: Garlic and chives, onion and shallot, lupine and yellow lupine are not *kilayim* with one another.

(turnip), is the name for the race of cabbages having greatly enlarged, fleshy turnip-shaped stems. Specifically, it is likely that the term כְּרוּב refers to kale (*brassica oleracea var. Acephala*).

The תְּרוֹבְתוֹר is explained by *Yerushalmi* as a small variety of cabbage; that is, one with a negligible stem (*Rav, Rambam Comm.*). This would aptly describe the garden cabbage [although *Rambam* indicates that the cabbage in question is a wild variety].

הַתְּרָדִים וְהַלְעוּנִים — *spinach beet and shrubby oraches*

The translation follows *Rav* and *Rambam Comm.* as interpreted by Y. Feliks (*Kilei Zeraim*, pp. 82-84). Although much different in appearance, both plants belong to the beet family — *chenopodiaceae*.

Recent scholars have suggested that לְעוּנִים might be garden sorrel (*rumex acetosa*), which belongs to a different botanic family than the beet, but has strikingly similar leaves (see Y. Feliks, *Kilei Zeraim*, pp. 85-86).

אֵינָם כִּלְאַיִם זֶה בָּזֶה. — *are not kilayim with one another.*

[The members of each pair are not *kilayim* with one another, but a member of one pair would be *kilayim* with a member of another pair.]

הוֹסִיף רַבִּי עֲקִיבָא: — *R' Akiva added:*

According to R' Akiva, the following three pairs are also not *kilayim*. Since *Rambam Comm.* states that the halachah rejects R' Akiva's opinion, it is evident that the first *Tanna*, whose view is accepted, does consider these pairs to be *kilayim*. Thus, for example, R' Akiva permits planting שׁוּם and שׁוּמָנִית together, while the *Tanna Kamma* forbids this. The crux of their dispute is unclear (see *Mishnah Rishonah*).

הַשּׁוּם וְהַשּׁוּמָנִית, הַבָּצָל וְהַבְּצַלְצוּל, וְהַתֻּרְמוֹס וְהַפְּלָסְלוֹס אֵינָן כִּלְאַיִם זֶה בָּזֶה. — *Garlic and chives, onion and shallot, lupine and yellow lupine are not kilayim with one another.*

The translation of שׁוּמָנִית as chives follows the suggestion of Y. Feliks (*Kilei Zeraim*, p. 85). *Rav* does not name this plant, but follows *Rosh* in describing it as a wild variety of garlic, smaller than the garden variety of garlic (see *Hagahos R' Yechezkel Landau* to *Rash*; see also *Ri ben Malki Tzedek*).

Rav takes the term בְּצַלְצוּל to be a diminutive form of בָּצָל (onion) and to refer to a wild variety of onion which is smaller than the regular onion (see *Rambam Comm.*; cf., however, *Rashi* to *Lev.* 13:49; see *Gilyon HaShas* to *Yerushalmi* 1:3). We have translated this as shallot following the identification adopted by Y. Feliks (*Kilei Zeraim*, p. 88).

Our translation of R' Akiva's third pair, פְּלָסְלוֹס and תֻּרְמוֹס, follows Y. Feliks' interpretation of *Rambam Comm.* (*Kilei Zeraim*, p. 89).

Rav (following *Rash* and *Rosh*) notes that the *Gemara* (*Beitzah* 25b) describes תֻּרְמוֹס as so bitter that it could be eaten only after being cooked seven times.

[ד] **וּבָאִילָן:** הָאֲגָסִים וְהַקְרֻסְתּוּמֵלִין, וְהַפְּרִישִׁים וְהָעוֹזְרָדִים אֵינָם כִּלְאַיִם זֶה בָזֶה. הַתַּפּוּחַ וְהַחֲזַרְד, הַפַּרְסְקִים וְהַשְּׁקֵדִין, וְהַשִּׁיזָפִין וְהָרִימִין — אַף עַל פִּי שֶׁדוֹמִין זֶה לָזֶה, כִּלְאַיִם זֶה בָזֶה.

[ה] **הַצְּנוֹן** וְהַנָּפוּץ, הַחַרְדָּל וְהַלַּפְסָן, וּדְלַעַת יְוָנִית עִם הַמִּצְרִית, וְהָרְמוּצָה —

יד אברהם

4.

The *kilayim* prohibition for legumes and grains forbids sowing together the seeds of diverse kinds. With trees, there is no such prohibition. Thus, for example, to sow apple seeds with orange seeds would be allowed. The only form of mixing which is forbidden with respect to trees is grafting (הַרְכָּבָה) (*Rambam, Hil. Kilayim* 1:6, *Yoreh Deah* 295:3; cf. *Ravad, Hil. Kilayim* 1:6).

Our mishnah begins with examples of trees which may be grafted together, since they are regarded as one kind with respect to *kilayim*. It then gives examples of trees which are in fact regarded as diverse kinds, but might mistakenly have been thought to be one kind. These may not be grafted together.

וּבָאִילָן: הָאֲגָסִים וְהַקְרֻסְתּוּמֵלִין, וְהַפְּרִישִׁים וְהָעוֹזְרָדִים אֵינָם כִּלְאַיִם זֶה בָזֶה. — *With respect to trees: Pears and gall-nut pears, quinces and hawthorns are not kilayim with one another.*

The first pair of trees, הָאֲגָסִים וְהַקְרֻסְתּוּמֵלִין, are different varieties of pear. *Rav* (following *Ri ben Malki Tzedek's* second interpretation) explains קְרֻסְטוֹמֵלִין[1] as a variety of small pears which resemble gall-nuts. Alternatively, this might refer to the crustaminum pear, which is a superior variety (see *Ri ben Malki Tzedek's* first interpretation and Y. Feliks, *Kilei Zeraim*, p. 93). Despite having distinct names, these two trees do not constitute separate kinds, and they may be grafted together.

The next pair in the mishnah, הַפְּרִישִׁים וְהָעוֹזְרָדִים, is problematic. *Rav* follows *Ri ben Malki Tzedek* and *Rambam Comm.* in rendering פְּרִישִׁים as quinces (*cydonia*

oblonga). This is a large fruit which is edible only after cooking (*Yerushalmi*). Since the mishnah states that פְּרִישִׁים and עוֹזְרָדִים are not *kilayim* with one another, one would expect עוֹזְרָדִים to resemble פְּרִישִׁים (quinces). However, עוֹזְרָדִים is identified by *Rambam Comm.* (followed by *Rav*) as *zerur* which is hawthorn (*crataegus azarolu*) in Arabic, and by *Ri ben Malki Tzedek* as sorbus. Both of these produce tiny fruits, hardly resembling quinces. It is therefore entirely unclear why these should not be viewed as *kilayim* with quince (*Rash*; see *Kilei Zeraim*, p. 96).

הַתַּפּוּחַ וְהַחֲזַרְד, הַפַּרְסְקִים וְהַשְּׁקֵדִין, וְהַשִּׁיזָפִין וְהָרִימִין — אַף עַל פִּי שֶׁדוֹמִין זֶה לָזֶה, כִּלְאַיִם זֶה בָזֶה. — *Apples and wild-apples, peaches and almonds, jujube and wild jujube — even though they are similar to one another, they are kilayim with one another.*

In this list, the members of each pair

1. *Rav's* spelling of this word (with a ט) differs slightly from the spelling in the mishnah.

1
4-5

4. **W**ith respect to trees: Pears and gall-nut pears, quinces and hawthorns are not *kilayim* with one another. Apples and wild-apples, peaches and almonds, jujube and wild jujube — even though they are similar to one another, they are *kilayim* with one another.

5. **T**he rounded radish and the elongated radish, mustard and field mustard, Greek gourd with the Egyptian [gourd], or the ash [gourd] — even

YAD AVRAHAM

belong to different species. Although they bear some morphological similarity, they are *kilayim* one with the other (*Rambam, Hil. Kilayim* 3:4).

The term חֲזָרָד is related by *Ri ben Malki Tzedek* to חֲזִיר, meaning *pig*. This wild tree produced an apple-like fruit which was eaten by pigs. *Rav* (following *Aruch* s.v. חזרד) notes that Onkelos to Exodus 25:35 renders כַּפְתֹּר (knop) as חֲזוּר. [*Kilei Zeraim* (p. 100) suggests that חֲזָרָד might be identified with the Syrian pear.]

Almonds, when young, are covered by a fleshy pericarp which makes them look very much like peaches. For this reason, the mishnah stresses that these are distinct kinds and may not be grafted together.

The translation of שִׁיזָפִין and רִימִין follows *Kilei Zeraim*, p. 104.[1] *Yerushalmi* views the שִׁיזָף as a cross between olives and pomegranates (or according to a variant text, olives and wild jujube). The wild jujube is the source of the lotus fruit (see *Kilei Zeraim*, p. 105, n. 42).

5.

In mishnah 4, the listing of plant pairs which are not *kilayim* with one another was concluded. Examples from the grain and legume world were presented in mishnayos 1-3, and this section was ended in mishnah 4 with examples from trees. The mishnah then began a new listing of plants which are *kilayim* with one another, even though they are similar. Following on the first list which ended with trees, the new list of plants which are *kilayim* began with trees (mishnah 4). This list of plant pairs which resemble each other but are nevertheless *kilayim* is continued in the coming mishnah with examples of legumes (*Meleches Shlomo; see Mishnah Rishonah*).

הַצְּנוֹן וְהַנָּפוּץ, — *The rounded radish and the elongated radish,*

[See commentary to 1:3, s.v. הלפת והנפוץ.]

הַחַרְדָּל וְהַלַּפְסָן, וּדְלַעַת יְוָנִית עִם הַמִּצְרִית, וְהָרְמוּצָה — *mustard and field mustard, Greek gourd with the Egyptian*

[gourd], or the ash [gourd] —

The Greek gourd is *kilayim* with either the Egyptian gourd or the ash gourd (*Rambam Comm.*). [Egyptian and ash gourds themselves are *not kilayim* with each other, as stated above, mishnah 2.]

1. The full scientific name, *zizyphus jujube*, bears a strong resemblance to the Hebrew שִׁיזָף. [The Mishnaic שִׁיזָף should not be confused with the modern Hebrew שָׁזִיף, *plum*.]

אַף עַל פִּי שֶׁדּוֹמִין זֶה לָזֶה, כִּלְאַיִם זֶה בָזֶה.

[ו] **הַזְּאֵב** וְהַכֶּלֶב, כֶּלֶב הַכָּפְרִי וְהַשׁוּעָל, הָעִזִּים וְהַצְּבָאִים, הַיְּעֵלִים וְהָרְחֵלִים, הַסּוּס וְהַפֶּרֶד, הַפֶּרֶד וְהַחֲמוֹר, הַחֲמוֹר וְהָעָרוֹד —

יד אברהם

אַף עַל פִּי שֶׁדּוֹמִין זֶה לָזֶה, כִּלְאַיִם זֶה בָזֶה. — *even though they are similar to one another, they are kilayim with one another.*

Although the members of each pair are similar to each other as far as the appearance of their leaves and fruit, they are nonetheless *kilayim* with one another. *Yerushalmi* explains that because the tastes of their respective fruits are different, they were viewed as diverse kinds with respect to *kilayim* (*Rav; Rosh; Rash*). According to *Rambam* (*Hil. Kilayim* 1:6), two plants which have similar leaves and fruits will be *kilayim* only if the tastes of their respective fruits are markedly different (see *Mikdash David* 61:4, p. 460; *Eretz Chemdah* 2:3:1-5, p. 181 ff.).

From *Rash* and *Rosh* to our mishnah, it appears that for two plants to be considered a single kind with respect to *kilayim*, they must exhibit similarity in all of the following three domains: the appearance of their leaves, the appearance of their fruit, and the taste of their fruit. Divergence in just one of these areas causes them to be classified as diverse kinds. For example, two varieties with similar-looking leaves but dissimilar fruit will be regarded as distinct kinds and will constitute *kilayim* one with the other. However, above (mishnah 3) in the case of צְנוֹן and לֶפֶת, they indicate that

similarity of leaves by itself suffices to rule that the two are *not kilayim* with each other (*Tos. Yom Tov*).

It is possible that *Rash* and *Rosh* accept *Rambam's* principle that a markedly different taste of their fruits will cause two plants to be regarded as *kilayim* despite complete similarity in the appearance of their leaves and fruit. Similarly, two plants with markedly different leaves will be *kilayim* even if their fruits are similar in appearance and taste; and so also, if the taste of their fruits and the appearance of their leaves are the same, but the appearance of their fruits is markedly different. As long as one of the three criteria — appearance of leaves, appearance of fruit, taste of fruit — is *markedly* different between two plants, they are *kilayim* and similarity with respect to the other criteria will not suffice to permit them to be sown together. What *Rash* and *Rosh* mean here in our mishnah is that צְנוֹן and נָפוּץ differ markedly in the taste of their fruits. Therefore, despite the similarity in the appearance of their leaves and fruit, they are *kilayim*. In mishnah 3, however, their reference is to two plants that are not markedly dissimilar with respect to any of the three criteria, and on the other hand have very similar leaves. Accordingly, this common trait is relied on to rule that they are not *kilayim* one with the other (*Beis David* from *R' Moshe Zaccutto; Mishnas Rabbi Nosson* quoted by *Tos Anshei Shem; cf. Chazon Ish* 3:4).

6.

There are two prohibitions in the Torah concerning the mixing of animals. The first is: *Do not mate your animal with other species* (*Lev.* 19:19), which forbids mating one kind of animal with another. The second is: *You shall not plow with an ox and a donkey together* (*Deut.* 22:10), which teaches that two kinds of animals may not be driven or worked when harnessed together. According to *Rambam* (*Hil. Kilayim* 9:7-8), the latter prohibition is Biblical only when one animal in the harness is kosher and the other is non-kosher (see *Beur HaGra, Yoreh Deah* 297:21). The present mishnah lists seven pairs of animals in which the members of each pair bear some resemblance to each other but are nonetheless regarded as diverse kinds.

though they are similar to one another, they are *kilayim* with one another.

6. **T**he wolf and dog, village dog and fox, goats and gazelles, ibex and ewes, horse and mule, mule and donkey, donkey and wild ass — even

הַזְּאֵב וְהַכֶּלֶב, — *The wolf and dog,*

The *Tanna Kamma* of mishnah 8:6 below considers a dog to be a wild animal (חַיָּה), while R' Meir regards it as a domestic animal (בְּהֵמָה). Thus, according to the view of the *Tanna Kamma* there, both the wolf and the dog are wild animals. They are nonetheless *kilayim* with one another since they are diverse kinds (see 8:2 and see *Mishnah Rishonah*).

כֶּלֶב הַכֻּפְרִי וְהַשׁוּעָל, — *village dog and fox,*

According to *Rav* (*Rosh*; *Rash*), the village dog was a small dog raised by villagers. The adjective כֻּפְרִי thus derives from כְּפָר, meaning *village*.

Rashi (*Bava Kamma* 80a and *Yevamos* 59b) maintains that this was a large dog used by hunters. *Rambam Comm.* also identifies the village dog as a hunting dog originating in the villages. A Geonic tradition describes this dog as black (*Otzar HaGeonim, Bava Kamma,* p. 54).

Although the exact strain of dog referred to is uncertain, it is clear that this dog resembled a שׁוּעָל, which is normally assumed to be a fox.[1]

Yerushalmi states that a dog together with a village dog is *not kilayim*. It is possible that *Tosefta* (*Kilayim* 5:5) disagrees (*Tzofnas Pane'ach, Hil. Kilayim* 9:5).

הָעִזִּים וְהַצְּבָאִים, — *goats and gazelles,*

The meaning of צְבִי in Mishnaic Hebrew is disputed by *Rashi* and *Tosafos* (*Chullin* 59b). According to our texts of the *Gemara* (ibid.), the צְבִי does *not* have branched horns — a statement which

would seem to eliminate any identification of צְבִי as deer. (However, *Tosafos* emend the text of the *Gemara* and accept this definition.)

Rashi (to *Chullin* 59b) identifies the צְבִי as the stein buck (rock goat) — i.e. ibex or wild goat; but in his commentary to *Deut.* 14:5 and *Rosh Hashanah* 26b, *Rashi* translates יָעֵל as stein buck. In our translation we have followed *Kilei Zeraim* (p. 126-127) and explained צְבִי as gazelle. [This identification satisfies the traits attributed to the צְבִי both in Rabbinic literature as well as in the Bible — see especially Y. Feliks, *The Song of Songs, Epic and Allegory*, Jerusalem 5734, p. 14.]

The mishnah's grouping of goats together with צְבָאִים may also be marshaled as proof that צְבִי does not mean deer. This is because the mishnah clearly states that these two resemble each other — a valid statement for goats and gazelles (or wild goats), but not a valid statement for goats and deer (*Rashash; Tos. Anshei Shem*).

הַיְּעֵלִים וְהָרְחֵלִים, הַסּוּס וְהַפֶּרֶד, הַפֶּרֶד וְהַחֲמוֹר, הַחֲמוֹר וְהֶעָרוֹד — *ibex and ewes, horse and mule, mule and donkey, donkey and wild ass —*

Rav (following *Rosh, Rash*) explains יָעֵל as a type of wild animal, as is evident from *Job* 39:1. *Onkelos* renders אַקּוֹ (*Deut.* 14:5) as יַעֲלָא. *Rashi* and *Tosafos* (*Rosh Hashanah* 26b) identify the יָעֵל as the stein buck — i.e. a wild goat or ibex.

It is somewhat puzzling that the mishnah does not list *sheep and goats* (כְּבָשִׂים וְעִזִּים) as a pair which resemble each other but are nev-

---

1. Inasmuch as modern foxes are easily distinguishable from the known varieties of dogs, and because, moreover, the fox is not a member of the canine species, it has been suggested that שׁוּעָל may refer to the jackal (*canis aureus*) (Y. Feliks, *Kilei Zeraim*, p. 123).

אַף עַל פִּי שֶׁדּוֹמִין זֶה לָזֶה, כִּלְאַיִם זֶה בָּזֶה.

[ז] **אֵין** מְבִיאִין אִילָן בְּאִילָן, יָרָק בְּיָרָק, וְלֹא

יד אברהם

ertheless *kilayim*. The mishnah (*Bechoros* 9:1) seems to state that these are *kilayim*. See, however, *Chiddushei R' Eliyahu Guttmacher* ad loc.

A mule (פֶּרֶד) is a hybrid between a horse and a donkey and may not be mated or teamed together for work with either a horse or a donkey. Moreover, a male mule may only be mated with a female mule if both their mothers were mares or both their mothers were donkeys. A mule whose mother was a mare cannot be mated with a mule whose mother was a donkey (mishnah 8:5; *Rambam, Hil. Kilayim* 9:6).

The עָרוֹד is explained by *Rav* (*Rosh*;

Rash) as a wild ass. This might be an onager or a kiang. The wild ass roamed in the desert (*Rosh* from *Gem. Rosh Hashanah* 4a and *Jeremiah* 2:24; the term פֶּרֶה in *Jeremiah* ibid. is defined by *Targum Yerushalmi* to *Gen.* 16:12 as עָרוֹד).

— אַף עַל פִּי שֶׁדּוֹמִין זֶה לָזֶה, כִּלְאַיִם זֶה בָּזֶה. *even though they are similar to one other, they are kilayim with one another.*

Rambam (*Hil. Kilayim* 9:4) explains that even though they resemble each other and can generate offspring, they are distinct kinds and may not be mated together.

7.

The coming mishnah discusses the prohibition on grafting together different kinds of plants or trees.

אֵין מְבִיאִין אִילָן בְּאִילָן, — *One may not bring [together] a tree with a tree,*

I.e. one may not make a graft between two trees of different kinds. This is prohibited as long as at least one of the trees is fruit-bearing. If, however, both components of the graft are non-fruit-bearing, it is permitted. This is because all non-fruit-bearing trees are regarded as a single kind (*Rav, Rosh, Rash* from *Yerushalmi*).

According to a variant text of *Yerushalmi*, the prohibition on grafting applies even when both components are non-fruit-bearing (*Rosh; Rash*).

At the opposite extreme, *Rambam* (*Hil. Kilayim* 1:5) makes no mention at all of the law for grafts involving non-fruit-bearing trees, and his language suggests that only where *both* components of the graft are fruit-bearing is a graft forbidden (*Mishnah Rishonah; Derech Emunah* 1:5; *Beur HaHalachah* s.v. כגון).

In practice, *Shulchan Aruch* (*Yoreh Deah* 295:3) and *Rama* (*Yoreh Deah* 295:6) forbid a

graft even if one of the components is non-fruit-bearing, but permit one in which both components are non-fruit-bearing. However, *Pischei Teshuvah* (*Yoreh Deah* 295:3) quotes the *Chasam Sofer* as having advised that scrupulous people should avoid even this, since according to one version of *Yerushalmi* this too is forbidden.

In its formulation of the *kilayim* prohibitions (*Lev*. 19:19), the Torah does not speak explicitly about trees. However, the words, *You shall not sow your field kilayim* (*Lev*. 19:19), are understood to include a prohibition on grafting between different kinds. This is learned by comparison with the immediately preceding prohibition: *You shall not mate your animal kilayim*. The mating of animals of different kinds involves the physical joining together of two entities — the male of one kind with the female of another (*Bava Metzia* 91a). Likewise, *kilayim* in the field includes physically uniting two entities — i.e. grafting (*San-*

though they are similar to one another, they are *kilayim* with one another.

7. **O**ne may not bring [together] a tree with a tree, nor greens with greens, nor a tree with

YAD AVRAHAM

hedrin 60a). Thus, *kilayim* in the field entails two sorts of prohibitions: (a) a prohibition on sowing a field with a mixture of kinds; and (b) a prohibition on physically uniting diverse kinds by grafting them together.

It should be noted that it is not forbidden to sow a mixture of tree seeds. This is because the term sowing used in the prohibition (*Lev.* 19:19) does not refer to trees (*Yerushalmi Peah* 1:4). Thus, *kilayim* with respect to diverse kinds of trees comes only under the second prohibition — namely, the ban on grafting together diverse kinds (*Rambam, Hil. Kilayim* 1:6; *Shulchan Aruch Yoreh Deah* 295:3).

A second source for the prohibition on grafting is the story of Creation (*Genesis* Chapter 1). The verse concerning *kilayim* (*Lev.* 19:19) opens with the words: אֶת־ חֻקֹּתַי תִּשְׁמֹרוּ, *You shall guard My statutes.* This is understood by the Rabbis (*Toras Kohanim* ad loc.; *Yerushalmi* 1:7; *Chullin* 60a-b) as referring to the natural statutes embodied in the Creation — namely, the differentiation of flora and fauna into diverse kinds. Thus, for example the verse (*Gen.* 1:11): *Let the earth put forth . . . fruit — tree-bearing fruit of its kind,* is a statute indicating that each kind of fruit tree shall be distinct. The verse (*Lev.* 19:19) concerning *kilayim* which calls for the guarding of the statutes thus amounts to a prohibition on tampering with the existing kinds of trees by procedures such as grafting, which attempt to manufacture new kinds through combinations of existing diverse kinds (*Beur HaGra* to *Yerushalmi* 1:7).

יָרָק בְּיָרָק, — *[nor] greens with greens,*
I.e. one may not graft together greens of different kinds (*Rav*).

Diverse kinds of greens may be neither sown together, nor grafted. The source for

the prohibition on sowing mixtures of greens is clear-cut. It derives from the verse (*Lev.* 19:19): *Your field you shall not sow kilayim,* in which the term sow (תִזְרַע) is understood as referring to seeds (זְרָעִים) of grains and greens and the like, but not to tree seeds (*Yerushalmi Peah* 1:4). However, the source for the prohibition discussed here by the mishnah, namely, the grafting together of greens of diverse kinds, is not as clear. If grafting of greens is considered sowing, then the source for this prohibition would be the same as that for sowing a mixture of greens seeds — i.e. *Lev.* 19:19: *Your field you shall not sow kilayim.* Additionally, or alternatively, grafting between diverse kinds of greens might be outlawed under the same prohibition as that which forbids grafting between different kinds of trees. If this prohibition is modeled on the mating of diverse kinds of animals (see above), then just as grafting of trees is forbidden as a physical union between two entities, so too grafting of greens is forbidden. If however, the source of the prohibition is the Divine statute at Creation which defined the kinds of flora and fauna, then the matter is not straightforward. For in the case of greens and the like, the Torah (*Gen.* 1:11) does not record any Divine command for *distinct kinds* of greens to emerge. Although in their actual emergence the Torah (*Gen* 1:12) does speak of *herb yielding seed after its kind* (לְמִינֵהוּ), it is unclear whether this suffices for the diversification of the greens into distinct kinds to be considered a "statute which must be guarded." Indeed, *Bavli* (*Chullin* 60a-b) leaves this question undecided, whereas *Yerushalmi* (1:7) clearly indicates that the diversification of greens into distinct kinds is *not* considered a statute. Now, if the diversification of greens is regarded as a statute, then grafting between diverse kinds of greens would be forbidden under *You shall guard My statutes* (*Lev.* 19:19), as explained above concerning trees; if it is not a statute, then this prohibition would not apply.

The question of which verse serves as the

אִילָן בְּיָרָק, וְלֹא יָרָק בְּאִילָן. רַבִּי יְהוּדָה מַתִּיר יָרָק בְּאִילָן.

[ח] אֵין נוֹטְעִין יְרָקוֹת בְּתוֹךְ סַדָּן שֶׁל שִׁקְמָה, אֵין מַרְכִּיבִין פֵּיגָם עַל גַּבֵּי קִדָּה לְבָנָה, מִפְּנֵי שֶׁהוּא יָרָק בְּאִילָן. אֵין נוֹטְעִין יִחוּר שֶׁל תְּאֵנָה לְתוֹךְ הֶחָצוּב שֶׁיְּהֵא מְקָרוֹ, אֵין תּוֹחֲבִין זְמוֹרָה שֶׁל גֶּפֶן לְתוֹךְ

יד אברהם

source for the prohibition on grafting greens has practical consequences. This is because the grafting of diverse trees is forbidden even outside of Israel, whereas sowing diverse kinds is forbidden only in the Land of Israel (*Kiddushin* 39a). Thus, if grafting of greens is forbidden as a subset of the prohibition on sowing, then it should be permitted outside Israel. If however, it is forbidden like grafting of trees because grafting resembles mating, then it will be forbidden even outside Israel (*Tos. Chullin* 60a, s.v. הרכיב; see also *Kesef Mishneh, Hil. Kilayim* 1:5; *Beur HaGra, Yoreh Deah* 295:2; and see *Chazon Ish* 1:15).

וְלֹא אִילָן בְּיָרָק, וְלֹא יָרָק בְּאִילָן. רַבִּי יְהוּדָה מַתִּיר יָרָק בְּאִילָן. — *nor a tree with greens, nor greens with a tree. R' Yehudah permits greens with a tree.*

Tos. Yom Tov understands R' Yehudah to permit grafting greens to trees and vice versa. Unlike the *Tanna Kamma* who forbids grafting trees with greens as well as greens with trees, R' Yehudah permits both combinations. R' Yehudah's

rationale would seem to be that since in grafts between trees and greens, the components do not fuse together, this does not qualify as a real graft (see *Tos. Yom Tov* and *Kilei Zeraim* pp. 148-150).

Gra (*Shenos Eliyahu Peirush HaAroch*) understands R' Yehudah as permitting only the graft of greens onto a tree. But a graft of a tree onto greens would be forbidden even by R' Yehudah. It is not clear why R' Yehudah would differentiate between these two cases (see *Chazon Ish* 2:16).

It should be noted that according to most authorities, the issue under discussion here is grafting. However, to take seeds of a fruit tree (e.g. apple seeds) and sow these together with seeds of greens is not forbidden (*Rambam, Hil. Kilayim* 1:6). This is because the term sowing used by the Torah (*Lev.*19:19) in prohibiting the sowing of diverse kinds does not refer to tree seeds (*Yerushalmi Peah* 1:4). Nevertheless, *Ravad* (*Hil. Kilayim* 1:6), as understood by *Chazon Ish* (3:11), maintains that even this was Rabbinically forbidden.

8.

The mishnah gives examples of forbidden grafts of greens to trees, trees to greens, and greens to greens, discussed in the previous mishnah.

אֵין נוֹטְעִין יְרָקוֹת בְּתוֹךְ סַדָּן שֶׁל שִׁקְמָה, — *One may not plant greens inside the stump of a sycamore,*

The sycamore tree was regularly chopped for its wood in such a way that a stump of between three and ten hand-breadths' height was left to regenerate new wood (*Rav; Rosh; Rashi;* see

ArtScroll *Sheviis* 4:6). Although the sycamore is regarded as a non-fruit-bearing tree (*Tos. Yom Tov* to mishnah 6:4, s.v. והשאר), combining greens with it is forbidden (*Mishnah Rishonah*). Additionally, the mishnah teaches that although this was a rather tenuous graft, the first *Tanna Kamma* of the preceding

greens, nor greens with a tree. R' Yehudah permits greens with a tree.

8. **O**ne may not plant greens inside the stump of a sycamore, nor may one graft rue to cassia, as this is "greens with a tree."

One may not plant a scion of fig inside *chatzuv* so that it will cool it, nor may one insert a branch of grapevine

YAD AVRAHAM

mishnah (mishnah 7) still forbade it (*Chazon Ish* 2:18).

The mishnah (*Sheviis* 4:6) indicates that it was common to cover the top of the sycamore stump with earth in order to preserve its moisture and enable regeneration. *Kilei Zeraim* (p. 153) suggests that the procedure discussed here was the planting of greens in the earth covering the stump. This was forbidden lest the greens draw nourishment from the sycamore.

אֵין מַרְכִּיבִין פֵּיגָם עַל גַּבֵּי קִדָּה לְבָנָה, מִפְּנֵי שֶׁהוּא יָרָק בְּאִילָן. — *nor may one graft rue to cassia, as this is "greens with a tree."*

[I.e. as these two cases are illegal combinations of greens with trees.]

Although rue, a strong-scented perennial herb, was normally not cultivated (see *Sheviis* 9:1), the mishnah teaches that it is nonetheless governed by the prohibition on grafting (*Mishnah Rishonah*; see *Meiri* and *Ramban* to *Chullin* 60a). Additionally, the mishnah selects this example in order to teach that קִדָּה לְבָנָה, cassia, is a tree (*Chazon Ish* 2:18).

Cassia is mentioned in *Exodus* 30:24 as an ingredient of the anointing oil. From *Onkelos* (ibid.) it is evident that this is the cassia (*Rav; Rambam Comm.*), a tree the oil of which was used as a perfume (see *Kereisos* 6a). The *Gemara* (*Eruvin* 34b) distinguishes between קִדָּה לְבָנָה which, as is evident from our mishnah, is a tree, and plain קִדָּה which is a type of green (*Rosh; Rash;* see *Chazon Ish* 2:18).

Some other proposed identifications of קִדָּה לְבָנָה are: (a) citrus trifolita and (b) pegnanum harmala. Both of these are systemically close to the rue, which makes a graft between them

somewhat more feasible (*Kilei Zeraim,* pp. 159-161).

אֵין נוֹטְעִין יְחוּר שֶׁל תְּאֵנָה לְתוֹךְ הַחַצּוּב שֶׁיְּהֵא מְקֵרוֹ, — *One may not plant a scion of fig inside chatzuv so that it will cool it,*

Rav (following *Rosh* and *Rash*) explains that the fig branch cools down the *chatzuv*, which is very hot. (Presumably, this refers to moderating the pungent taste of *chatzuv*.) Alternatively, מְקֵרוֹ may be derived from קוֹרָה meaning beam or ceiling, and the idea here is that the beams of the fig branch give shade to the *chatzuv* by forming a canopy over it.

However, *R' Yehosef Ashkenazi* (quoted by *Meleches Shlomo*) points out that both of *Rav's* interpretations are inconsistent with the sentence structure of the rest of this mishnah. In the other examples of the mishnah in which the purpose of the graft is given, the species mentioned second is combined with the species mentioned first in order to assist the one mentioned first (see below). Accordingly, in our case as well, one would expect the mishnah to mean that the *chatzuv* cools the fig branch. In agricultural terms, what this means is that the tip of the fig branch embedded in the *chatzuv* receives a constant supply of moisture and nourishment from the latter, and is thus enabled to develop roots (see also *Kilei Zeraim,* p. 162).

The *chatzuv* (or *chatzav*) is described by the *Gemara* (*Beitzah* 26b) as a plant with roots which penetrated vertically deep into the ground without branching. It was used by Yehoshua to mark the borders of each tribe's province in Eretz

כלאים
א/ט

הָאֲבַטִּיחַ שֶׁתְּהֵא זוֹרֶקֶת מֵימֶיהָ לְתוֹכוֹ, מִפְּנֵי שֶׁהוּא אִילָן בְּיָרָק.
אֵין נוֹתְנִין זֶרַע דְּלַעַת לְתוֹךְ הַחַלָמִית שֶׁתְּהֵא מְשַׁמַּרְתּוֹ, מִפְּנֵי שֶׁהוּא יָרָק בְּיָרָק.

[ט] הַטּוֹמֵן לֶפֶת וּצְנוֹנוֹת תַּחַת הַגֶּפֶן — אִם הָיוּ מִקְצָת עָלָיו מְגֻלִּין,

יד אברהם

Yisrael (Bava Basra 56a). The name is apparently related to the root חצב, meaning to hew or chisel, and refers to the deep penetration of the roots. Kilei Zeraim (p. 162) identifies the chatzuv as the squill, a bulbous herb.

The mishnah selects this example to teach that although the purpose of the graft is not in order to generate a new variety, but merely to provide one plant with assistance from another, the combination is forbidden (Mishnah Rishonah; Chazon Ish 2:18).

אֵין תּוֹחֲבִין זְמוֹרָה שֶׁל גֶּפֶן לְתוֹךְ הָאֲבַטִּיחַ שֶׁתְּהֵא זוֹרֶקֶת מֵימֶיהָ לְתוֹכוֹ, מִפְּנֵי שֶׁהוּא אִילָן בְּיָרָק. — nor may one insert a branch of grapevine into a watermelon so that it will spill its waters into it, as this is "a tree with greens."

[I.e. as these two cases are illegal combinations of trees with greens.]

The exact case here is not entirely clear. Rash (based on Yerushalmi) explains that the branch of a grapevine was inserted into the root of a watermelon plant in order that the grapevine could benefit from the abundant juices of the melon plant. Even if this is done in a manner consistent with the special laws governing grapevines,[1] the mishnah teaches that this is forbidden, as it

violates the general law forbidding the grafting of trees to greens (Tos. Yom Tov).

According to Rash the combination outlawed here involves two growing plants — one a vine, the other a melon plant. From the language of the mishnah alone, the case might easily have been explained as referring to a grape branch which has been severed from its vine, and is introduced into a watermelon fruit (i.e. the fruit — not the plant) in order to stimulate regeneration (see above concerning a scion of fig). Although this would certainly be forbidden as "a tree with greens," it is evident from Yerushalmi that this was not the case under discussion (Chazon Ish 2:1 s.v. ולפי; see Kilei Zeraim, pp. 162 ff.).

אֵין נוֹתְנִין זֶרַע דְּלַעַת לְתוֹךְ הַחַלָמִית שֶׁתְּהֵא מְשַׁמַּרְתּוֹ, מִפְּנֵי שֶׁהוּא יָרָק בְּיָרָק. — One may not put a gourd seed inside a mallow so that it will protect it, as this is "greens with greens."

The gourd was normally planted in the spring and harvested in the summer. Gourd seeds cannot be planted before the ground is sufficiently warm, as germination of these seeds requires a minimum temperature. In order to enable early planting of gourd seeds, it was common to insert the seeds into the stem or root of some winter plant (in the mishnah's example: mallow), and the heat released

1. In order to accommodate the special laws governing grapevines, it must be assumed that above ground the melon plant was at least three (or, according to another view, at least six) handbreadths away from the vine. Moreover, the insertion into the watermelon root must be at a depth of at least three handbreadths below ground (Rash; see below, 6:1). Under such circumstances, the combination does not violate the special laws regarding grapevines.

into a watermelon so that it will spill its waters into it, as this is "a tree with greens."

One may not put a gourd seed inside a mallow so that it will protect it, as this is "greens with greens."

9. [I]f] someone stores turnips or radishes under a grapevine — if some of their leaves are exposed,

---

YAD AVRAHAM

by the growing plant enabled the gourd seed to germinate (*Kilei Zeraim*, pp. 166-167; see *Tos. Yom Tov*). The mishnah teaches that this procedure is forbidden, even though the objective was merely to prevent the seeds from dying, and not in order to develop some new variety (*Mishnah Rishonah*).

9.

הַטּוֹמֵן לֶפֶת וּצְנוֹנוֹת תַּחַת הַגֶּפֶן — *[If] someone stores turnips or radishes under a grapevine —*

It was normal to store these vegetables underground in order to preserve them. *Yerushalmi* explains that the case here concerns a bundle of turnips or a bundle of radishes which is stored under a grapevine. Now, if a person wanted to plant turnips, he would hardly bury a bunch of them bundled together. Clearly, by burying the turnips in bundles, the person shows that he does not want these turnips to take root, and his intention in burying them is merely to protect them from drying out (*Rav; Rosh; Rash*). Because the mode of underground storage here is such as cannot be confused with planting, and because the person's intentions are for storage and not for planting, the mishnah goes on to assert that indeed these buried turnips or radishes are not considered to be planted (see *Tosafos, Shabbos* 50b, s.v. הטומן).

Rav appears to maintain that in the mishnah's case a bundle of turnips was buried *together with* a bundle of radishes. This does not seem indicated by the *Gemara* (*Bavli* and *Yerushalmi*), nor is it assumed by any of the commentators (*Meleches Shlomo*). [*Tos. Yom Tov* and *Mishneh LaMelech* (*Hil. Kilayim* 3:6) infer from *Rashi* to *Eruvin* 77b that the case here involves turnips and radishes together under a grapevine. However, their reading of

Rashi is refuted convincingly by *Merkeves HaMishneh* (*Hil. Kilayim* 3:6) and *Derech Emunah* (3:6, *Beur HaHalachah*, s.v. הלפת).]

אִם הָיוּ מִקְצָת עָלָיו מְגֻלִּין — *if some of their leaves are exposed,*

[The printed text has *its* leaves. Some versions have the more consistent מִקְצָת עָלִין — some of the leaves (*Shinuyei Nuschaos*; cf. *Tos. Anshei Shem* from *Shoshanim LeDavid*).]

The mishnah stipulates that some leaves from the buried bundle protruded above the ground. This detail is included in order to overcome a technical problem with one of the subsequent rulings. It will be stated below that because the bundle is not considered planted, it may be retrieved even on the Sabbath, and no violation of the prohibition to uproot things on the Sabbath is incurred. However, if the bundle was covered over completely with earth, its retrieval would necessarily entail handling and moving earth — an activity forbidden Rabbinically on the Sabbath. Therefore, the mishnah constructs the case such that some leaves of the turnip bundle are exposed. In this way, the person can retrieve the stored bundle by grasping these leaves and easing the bundle out of its storage place. Since no earth is moved by hand, this procedure is permitted (*Rav; Rosh; Rash*).

כְּלָאִים אֵינוֹ חוֹשֵׁשׁ לֹא מִשּׁוּם כְּלְאַיִם, וְלֹא מִשּׁוּם
שְׁבִיעִית, וְלֹא מִשּׁוּם מַעַשְׂרוֹת, וְנִטָּלִים בְּשַׁבָּת.

יד אברהם

According to this explanation, as far as characterization of the stored bundle as "not planted" is concerned, there is no difference whether the bundle is entirely covered, or whether leaves jut out. Indeed, in the latter case one might have been inclined to regard the bundle as planted, on the grounds that in a normal transplant, the leaves are above ground. Despite this resemblance, the mishnah maintains that even then, because the person's intentions are not for planting and because by storing the turnips as a bundle he shows that he does not want the turnips to take root, the bundle is not considered planted.

This approach is at odds with a Geonic tradition which links the characterization of the stored turnips or radishes as "planted" or "not planted" to the situation of their bulbs, not their leaves (Rav Hai Gaon quoted by Ri ben Malki Tzedek, Rash, Tos. Shabbos 50b, and others; Rav Sherirah quoted by Piskei HaRid Shabbos 50b). When the bulb of the turnip or radish is fully buried, regardless of whether or not its leaves are exposed, it is considered planted (see Ritva to Shabbos 50b; Tos. Rid to Shabbos 113a). On the other hand, if part of the bulb is above ground, it is not considered planted, since this is not the way of planting. The Geonim had a variant text of the mishnah which omitted mention of leaves: "if part of them was exposed" (אִם הָיוּ מִקְצָתָן מְגֻלִּין), i.e. if part of the bulb of the turnip or radish was exposed. According to this reading, the mishnah need not be dealing with bundles of turnips and bundles of radishes — even individual turnips or radishes, which are placed in the ground such that part of the bulb is exposed, are not considered to be planted (Ramban and Ritva to Shabbos 50b).

אֵינוֹ חוֹשֵׁשׁ לֹא מִשּׁוּם כְּלְאַיִם, — he need not be concerned about kilayim,

Burying a bundle of turnips or radishes for storage is not considered planting and accordingly, it is not governed by prohibitions on planting in the vicinity of grapevines. It is therefore permitted to store such a bundle under a grapevine, even though planting there would be prohibited (Rav; Rambam Comm).

Moreover, even if the turnips or radishes generated new growths while in storage, these growths are not regarded as the forbidden product of an illegal planting in the vicinity of a grapevine (see Gen. Intro.). Since the bundle is not considered planted, any new growth is viewed as generated internally by the turnip or radish, and would occur even if the turnip or radish were stored on a shelf entirely out of the ground (see Sheviis 2:9). Since the growth is not influenced by proximity to the grapevine, it is not forbidden (Rav; Rosh; Rash; see Tos. Yom Tov).

We have assumed that the question of kilayim raised by the mishnah is due to the proximity of the bundle of turnips or radishes to the grapevine. According to some, turnips are regarded as a diverse kind with respect to radishes (Ravad to Hil. Kilayim 1:6; Ri ben Malki Tzedek to mishnah 5; see also Rash and Rosh to mishnayos 3 and 5, and see comm. above, mishnah 5). Thus, planting of turnips and radishes together would be forbidden. Nevertheless, storing them together in a fashion that is not regarded as planting is not considered a violation of the laws of kilayim.

There is a considerable controversy as to whether the mishnah's ruling applies even if the stored vegetables took root. It may be argued on the one hand that since storage does not resemble planting and the person does not want the vegetables to take root, any rooting can be disregarded (see Yerushalmi Maasros 5:2). On the other hand, if they strike roots, the vegetables ought to be viewed as growing from the ground and hence subject to the planting prohibitions. A full analysis of the various opinions may be found in Eglei Tal, Meleches Kotzer 12:24. See also Chazon Ish 3:13 and Derech Emunah 2:48, Beur HaHalachah 2:11, s.v. אינו חושש.

he need not be concerned about *kilayim*, nor about *sheviis*, nor about tithes, and they may be taken on the Sabbath.

YAD AVRAHAM

וְלֹא מִשּׁוּם שְׁבִיעִית, — *nor about sheviis,*

During the *shemittah* year,[1] it is forbidden to plant in the Land of Israel (*Lev.* 25:4). In addition, vegetables and the like which grew on their own during the seventh year are forbidden for consumption by Rabbinic decree (see *Gen. Intro.* to ArtScroll *Sheviis*). The mishnah here teaches that storing vegetables in the manner described is neither an infraction of the restriction on planting (*Rav; Rambam Comm.*), nor are any growths generated while in storage regarded as forbidden *shemittah* produce (*Rav; Rosh; Rash*).

וְלֹא מִשּׁוּם מַעֲשְׂרוֹת, — *nor about tithes,*

On retrieving the bundle of turnips from the ground, there is no new tithing obligation created. Only that which grows from the ground is subject to tithes (*Lev.* 27:30), and since this bundle is not "planted," it is not considered to be growing from the ground (*Rav; Rambam Comm.*).[2]

Alternatively, the case concerns turnips from the second year of the Sabbatical cycle which were owing in *maaser sheni* (the second tithe) and which were stored in the third year of the cycle and generated new growth. If this new growth is viewed as growing from the ground, it will be treated as third-

year produce and hence subject to *maaser ani* (poorman's tithe) rather than *maaser sheni*. However, because of the method of storage, the turnips are not regarded as planted, and hence the new growth is not nourished by the ground. As such, it is not third-year produce, but is instead treated as an extension of the second-year turnips themselves. Just as they are subject to *maaser sheni*, so too is the new growth (*Rosh; Rash; Ri ben Malki Tzedek*).

The assertion (of *Rash* et al.) — that with respect to the tithing obligation, new growth from the stored turnips or radishes is treated identically to the vegetables themselves — is not unanimously accepted. From *Rashi* (to *Shabbos* 51a, s.v. ולא), for example, it seems that even if a stored bundle of turnips was *tevel*, new growth during storage (when the turnips are not planted and are not growing from the ground) would not be *tevel* at all. This might explain why *Rav* omits *Rash's* explanation to this passage of the mishnah (cf. *Tos. Yom Tov*).

וְנִטָּלִים בְּשַׁבָּת. — *and they may be taken on the Sabbath.*

Since they are not growing from the ground, the removal of the bundle of turnips is not forbidden under the prohibition on detaching growing things on the Sabbath (i.e. harvesting). As for the Rabbinic prohibition on moving earth on

---

1. *Shemittah* — the Sabbatical year, occurring every seventh year, during which the land of Eretz Yisrael may not be cultivated. In addition, various restrictions apply to produce that grows wild during that year.

2. If a turnip which had already been tithed was then actually re-planted in the ground, it would seem from this that on being picked again later, it would again be subject to tithes independent of any new growth. However, from *Rashi* (*Shabbos* 51a) and *Tosafos* (*Shabbos* 50b) it appears that the issue in question is only any new growth that is generated while in storage. Thus, if a *chullin* (unsanctified produce from which *terumah* and *maaser* have been taken) turnip is replanted and adds growth, this new growth is *tevel*. [*Tevel* is produce from which *terumah* and *maaser* are owed. Until these dues are separated, it is forbidden for consumption.] If it is stored, as in our mishnah, and is thus not planted, new growth is not *tevel*. But in any case, the *chullin* turnip itself does not revert to *tevel* on being re-planted. This may also be the intention of *Rav* and *Rambam Comm.*

הַזּוֹרֵעַ חִטָּה וּשְׂעוֹרָה כְּאַחַת, הֲרֵי זֶה כִּלְאַיִם. רַבִּי יְהוּדָה אוֹמֵר: אֵינוֹ כִּלְאַיִם עַד שֶׁיְּהוּ שְׁתֵּי חִטִּים וּשְׂעוֹרָה, אוֹ חִטָּה וּשְׁתֵּי שְׂעוֹרִים, אוֹ חִטָּה, וּשְׂעוֹרָה וְכֻסֶּמֶת.

[א] **כָּל** סְאָה שֶׁיֵּשׁ בּוֹ רֹבַע מִמִּין אַחֵר, יְמַעֵט.

יד אברהם

the Sabbath, as long as the earth is not handled directly, no infraction is incurred. Since by grasping the exposed leaves, the turnips can be extracted from storage without handling earth, the bundles may be taken on the Sabbath (*Rav; Rambam Comm.; Rosh; Rash*).

In recording these laws in his code, *Rambam* (Hil. Shemittah 1:15; Hil. Shabbos 25:15) stipulates that if the turnips are stored such that leaves are exposed, then they are not considered planted. He does not mention that they must be stored in bundles. However, concerning *kilayim* (Hil. Kilayim 2:11), *Rambam* requires two conditions to be met if the turnips are to be regarded as not planted: (a) that leaves be exposed and (b) that the turnips be in a bundle.

Evidently, *Rambam* considered the exposure of the leaves to be inconsistent with the normal mode of planting (cf. *Rav Hai Gaon* as cited here by *Rosh* and by *Tos.* to *Shabbos* 50b; see *Chazon Ish* 3:13, s.v. מיהו and *Tos. Rid* to *Shabbos* 113a). It is thus a requisite condition in each case of the mishnah. The additional condition of bundles is needed only with respect to *kilayim*. There, in addition to ensuring that the stored turnips not be planted (accomplished according to *Rambam* by keeping leaves exposed), a person has to make sure that they do not even appear to be planted. This is because the prohibition of *kilayim* is concerned even with mere appearance of a forbidden mixture (see *Chazon Ish* 3:13, s.v. ר״מ).

הַזּוֹרֵעַ חִטָּה וּשְׂעוֹרָה כְּאַחַת, הֲרֵי זֶה כִּלְאַיִם. — *[If] someone sows a wheat grain and a barley grain together, this is kilayim.*

The Torah forbids sowing even a single seed of one species (e.g. wheat) together with a single seed of a different

kind (e.g. barley).

If wheat is *already* growing in a field, and a person plants a grain of barley right next to the wheat, there is some doubt as to whether this is forbidden by the Torah, or only Rabbinically. *Rambam* (Hil. Kilayim 3:9,10) makes it clear that even this is forbidden by the Torah (cf. *Kesef Mishneh* 4:16; see *Mishnah Rishonah*). Others disagree and assume the Torah's prohibition to apply only when the diverse kinds are planted simultaneously (see *Tos. Yom Tov; Shitah Mekubetzes* to *Bava Kamma* 55a; *Shenos Eliyahu, Peirush HaAroch* 3:5). A thorough survey of the different views may be found in *Derech Emunah* 1:1, *Beur HaHalachah* s.v. כאחד.

רַבִּי יְהוּדָה אוֹמֵר: אֵינוֹ כִּלְאַיִם עַד שֶׁיְּהוּ שְׁתֵּי חִטִּים וּשְׂעוֹרָה, אוֹ חִטָּה וּשְׁתֵּי שְׂעוֹרִים, אוֹ חִטָּה, וּשְׂעוֹרָה וְכֻסֶּמֶת. — *R' Yehudah says: It is not kilayim until there are two wheat grains and one barley grain, or a wheat grain and two barley grains, or a wheat grain, a barley grain and a spelt grain.*

R' Yehudah maintains that planting of *kilayim* must involve a minimum of three seeds: one, to characterize the place as a field, and the other two, to constitute the *kilayim*. He derives this from the verse (Lev. 19:19): שָׂדְךָ לֹא-תִזְרַע כִּלְאָיִם, *You shall not sow your field kilayim,* in which the term *field* is understood as land on which something is growing, not empty land. Accordingly, the verse prohibits sowing a mixture of two diverse kinds together with one's field. For example, if he sows two grains of wheat and one of barley, one grain of wheat is needed in order to characterize the spot as a field; the remaining mixture of a grain

[If] someone sows a wheat grain and a barley grain together, this is *kilayim*. R' Yehudah says: It is not *kilayim* until there are two wheat grains and one barley grain, or a wheat grain and two barley grains, or a wheat grain, a barley grain and a spelt grain.

1. **A**ny *se'ah* in which there is a quarter[-*kav*] of a different kind, he must reduce. R' Yose says:

of barley with a grain of wheat then constitutes the mixture of diverse kinds which it is forbidden to sow in one's field (*Rav* from first explanation of *Rosh*; *Rash*).

Alternatively, R' Yehudah assumes that the verb *to sow* used in the verse (*You shall not sow your field kilayim*) refers to a minimum of three seeds. Thus, the prohibited sowing is one involving at least three seeds (*Rosh*; *Rash*; *Ri ben Malki Tzedek*).

Rash writes that even R' Yehudah will concede that two seeds are sufficient to constitute *kilayim* if they are planted together within a square handbreadth (see

Hagahos R' Yechezkel Landau §3 and *Ri ben Malki Tzedek*). Apparently, this square handbreadth is surrounded on all sides by a crop, and as such is itself considered a field, even though it is bare. Accordingly, even one grain of barley planted there with one grain of wheat will be *kilayim*. A larger bald spot in a field does not count as part of a field, and hence R' Yehudah would require at least three seeds to make *kilayim*.

Alternatively, according to the second explanation of R' Yehudah above, even though forbidden sowing of *kilayim* refers to a minimum of three seeds, there is another form of illegal *kilayim* — namely, two seeds of diverse kind planted within a square handbreadth.

Chapter 2
1.

The prohibition on sowing together a mixture of diverse kinds does not state explicitly in what proportions a diverse kind must be present in order to constitute a forbidden mixture. For example, will a single grain of wheat mixed up with ten bushels of barley constitute a forbidden mixture which may not be sown until the grain of wheat is removed? The present mishnah formulates the guidelines needed to resolve this question.

כָּל סְאָה שֶׁיֶּשׁ בּוֹ רֶבַע מִמִּין אַחֵר, יְמַעֵט. —
Any se'ah in which there is a quarter[- kav] of a different kind, he must reduce.

If a *se'ah* of seed contains an admixture of a quarter-*kav* or more of a diverse kind of seed, it is forbidden to sow the mixture as is. A *se'ah* consists of six *kavs* or 24 quarter-*kavs*. Thus, the presence of a quarter-*kav* or more of foreign seed in a *se'ah* of seed means that the foreign seed constitutes one twenty-fourth or more of the mixture. The mishnah teaches that if a diverse kind accounts for one twenty-

fourth or more of a mixture of seed, the seed may not be sown until the concentration of the diverse kind is reduced to less than one twenty-fourth. This can be achieved either by removing some of the foreign seed from the mixture, or by adding to the major seed of the mixture. Once this has been accomplished, although some foreign seed is still present, it is permitted according to this Tanna to sow the seed (*Rav*; *Rosh*; *Rash*; *Rambam Comm.*).

In general, a forbidden item becomes

permitted through nullification if it becomes mixed with a large quantity of something permissible. Nevertheless, it is forbidden to deliberately mix a forbidden item together with something permitted in order to remove the prohibition. Following this premise, *Yerushalmi* questions how the mishnah can rule that a mixture of seed, which it is forbidden to plant, can be rendered permissible by reducing the concentration of the diverse kind. Is this not similar to deliberate nullification of a prohibited item?

Yerushalmi, as explained by *Rosh*, answers that the prohibition on deliberate nullification of a prohibited item applies only to something forbidden by the Torah. However, our mishnah is dealing with something forbidden only Rabbinically, as will now be explained. Under Torah law, if wheat for example was added to barley *for the purpose of planting a mixture*, then even a single grain of wheat is not nullified by a large quantity of barley, and the whole lot constitutes a forbidden mixture. If, however, the wheat was *not* introduced in order to plant a mixture, then the seed may be planted. This is because under Biblical law a minority component of a mixture is disregarded. Since the wheat was not mixed with the barley in order to plant a mixture, the wheat has no significance for the farmer wishing to plant barley. Accordingly, if it is outnumbered by the barley, it is indeed regarded as insignificant, and is nullified by the barley (see R' Yosef Engel, *Beis HaOtzar*, vol. 2, p. 83, s.v. והנני). Thus, on the Biblical level, the mixture is viewed as entirely barley; it is not considered a mixture and therefore it may be planted. However, in order to prevent confusion between such a permitted mixture and a forbidden one (in which the wheat was added for the purpose of planting), the Rabbis forbade planting all mixtures of seeds in which a diverse kind constituted more than one twenty-fourth. But since no one interested in planting a mixture would mix in less than one twenty-fourth of a diverse kind, the Rabbis did not interfere with the basic law for such low concentrations of foreign seed. Accordingly,

at concentrations of less than one twenty-fourth, the wheat was deemed nullified by the barley.

Now, the mishnah is dealing with a *se'ah* of wheat and barley which was not mixed for the purpose of planting a mixture. Thus, the prohibition on planting this *se'ah* of seed, consisting of five and three-quarters *kavs* of barley and a quarter *kav* of wheat, is only Rabbinical. However, a Rabbinical prohibition may be deliberately nullified. Accordingly, the mishnah rules that such a mixture may be deliberately rendered permitted for planting, either by adding barley or by removing wheat.

The above approach, which is apparently followed also by *Rav* (see especially *Rav* to *Shekalim* 1:1), is challenged by *Tos. Yom Tov*. It is impossible to say, argues *Tos. Yom Tov*, that the mixture is Biblically permitted due to the fact that the foreign seed is nullified. The mechanism of nullification in a mixture is valid only where the permitted component and the forbidden one are indistinguishable from each other. For example, if forbidden meat becomes mixed with a larger quantity of permitted meat, nullification is possible, since the forbidden meat is indistinguishable from the permitted meat. But if the forbidden meat was mixed with potatoes, even one thousand times its volume, the meat is not nullified and remains forbidden. Here as well, since barley is distinguishable from wheat, no nullification should be possible. Accordingly, the assertion that the mishnah's case involves no Biblical prohibition, due to nullification, is untenable.

To overcome this difficulty, *Tos. Yom Tov* argues that the mechanism utilized in permitting a mixture in which the proportion of the diverse kind has been reduced to less than one twenty-fourth is not nullification at all. Rather, *Tos. Yom Tov* posits that when a person is not interested in growing a mixture, the Torah does not prohibit its planting. Thus, even a one-to-one mixture of diverse seeds may be planted under Biblical law, as long as the farmer does not *want* to grow a mixture (e.g. he only needs wheat, but is not prepared to go through the tedious job of sifting out the barley). Following this

premise, *Tos. Yom Tov* argues that even when a person does not want both species in the mixture, planting it is nevertheless Rabbinically proscribed. However, the Rabbis only forbade the planting of mixtures where the diverse kind constituted at least one twenty-fourth. If it did not, this was not forbidden. Thus, the mishnah's case concerns a mixture of wheat and barley grain being planted by someone who was only interested in wheat. By reducing the concentration of barley, the person is not nullifying it — an impossibility since it is distinguishable — he is merely reducing the mixture to one which was not included in the Rabbinic prohibition.

According to both of the preceding explanations, if the mixture in the mishnah's case is planted *without* reducing the concentration of the diverse kind below one twenty-fourth, only a Rabbinic prohibition has been violated. However, *Rambam* (Hil. *Kilayim* 2:1) indicates that if a person planted a mixture of seeds containing twenty-three parts of barley to one part of wheat (i.e. the wheat was one twenty-fourth of the whole), then he has violated a Biblical prohibition (*Tos. R' Akiva*).

Apparently, *Rambam* understood that a field in which two species are growing in a mixture will only appear mixed if the minority component accounts for at least one twenty-fourth of the field. Assuming that the Torah's prohibition on sowing *kilayim* is in order to prevent a field from appearing mixed — see *Rambam Comm.* 3:1 and *Hil. Kilayim* 2:7 — it follows that a mixture of seeds which will produce a field that appears mixed will be forbidden to plant by the Torah. In particular, a mixture such as that of our mishnah in which the minority component is at least one twenty-fourth and will hence account for one twenty-fourth of the field is forbidden to plant under Torah law (*Toras Zeraim* p. 40; *Mikdash David* 61:2; *Chazon Ish* 4:11). [According to this explanation, the law that a single grain of wheat introduced intentionally into a heap of barley renders the heap forbidden to plant

— a law which *Rambam* (Hil. *Kilayim* 2:6) accepts — must be Rabbinic in nature, since the field grown from this heap will not appear mixed (*Mikdash David* 61:2).]

Alternatively, according to *Rambam*, any collection of seeds which is perceived as a mixture of more than one kind comes under the Torah's prohibition on sowing mixtures. When a quarter-*kav* of foreign seed is present, the collection is perceived as a mixture, and its planting is thus forbidden by the Torah. Otherwise, the collection is perceived as one variety of seed and is not forbidden for planting as a mixture (see *Teshuvos HaRashba* §259 and *He'aros beMishnayos Kilayim*, in *Collected Essays* from *Hadarom*, p. 147). [On this explanation, a single seed introduced *intentionally* is not inconsequential, and hence the collection is perceived as a mixture and forbidden by the Torah.]

רַבִּי יוֹסֵי אוֹמֵר: יָבֵר. — *R' Yose says: He must remove.*

R' Yose maintains that if a mixture of seeds includes a twenty-fourth part of a diverse kind, all of the diverse kind must be completely removed. It is insufficient in R' Yose's view merely to reduce the concentration of the diverse kind below one twenty-fourth, since this gives the impression that the person *wants* the remaining fraction to grow as a mixture. However, if to begin with the proportion of the foreign kind was less than one twenty-fourth, R' Yose agrees that then the seed can be planted as is, since the fraction of diverse kind in the mixture is tolerable (as above) and since nothing was done to indicate a desire to maintain a mixture (*Rav; Rosh; Rash*).

Rosh maintains that the *Tanna Kamma's* ruling, which permits planting the mixture once the proportion of foreign seed is reduced to less than one twenty-fourth, relates only to the terms under which the mixture may be planted. Even the *Tanna Kamma* agrees, however, that after the mixture has been reduced and planted, any foreign plants which sprout in the field must be totally

כלאים מִינִין. רַבִּי שִׁמְעוֹן אוֹמֵר: לֹא אָמְרוּ אֶלָּא מִמִּין
ב/א אֶחָד. וַחֲכָמִים אוֹמְרִים: כָּל שֶׁהוּא כִּלְאַיִם בִּסְאָה
מִצְטָרֵף לִרְבַע.

יד אברהם

eliminated, even if they constituted less than a twenty-fourth of the field (see also *Rav* to *Shekalim* 1:1). Most authorities disagree with *Rosh* and hold that even plants which sprouted must be reduced below ¹⁄₂₄, not totally eliminated (see *Derech Emunah* 2:7, *Beur HaHalachah*, s.v. עד and see below mishnah 5, s.v. אומרים לו).

בֵּין מִמִּין אֶחָד בֵּין מִשְּׁנֵי מִינִין. — *[This applies] whether it is of one kind and whether it is of two kinds.*

It makes no difference whether the quarter-*kav* of diverse seed is comprised of one species or many. For example, if 5 ³⁄₄ *kavs* (23 quarter-*kavs*) of wheat were mixed together with a ¹⁄₈ *kav* of barley and ¹⁄₈ *kav* of spelt, the barley and spelt combine to constitute a quarter-*kav* of diverse kinds. This minority component must be reduced (according to the *Tanna Kamma*) or eliminated (according to R' Yose). Even species which do not constitute *kilayim* with the predominant species in the mixture combine to create a quarter-*kav* which must be reduced or eliminated. For example, a *se'ah* consisting of 5³⁄₄ *kavs* of barley, ¹⁄₈ *kav* of oats and ¹⁄₈ *kav* of spelt may not be planted as is. Although oats do not constitute *kilayim* with barley (see mishnah 1:1), it combines with spelt (which is *kilayim* with barley) to constitute a quarter-*kav* of diverse seed which must be reduced or removed before planting (*Rav; Rosh; Rash; Rambam Comm.*).

In the latter case, in which oats and spelt are combined to make up the quarter-*kav*, it seems clear that R' Yose would require the total removal only of the spelt — the oats, which are not *kilayim* with barley, can be left. However, what about the previous case in which the quarter-*kav* is made up of two species, each of which is *kilayim* with the

majority species? Would the complete removal of one of the minority species be sufficient, since the remaining minority species would not be a quarter-*kav*? Or, would R' Yose maintain that once removal is necessitated, all of the diverse kinds must be eliminated? *Rosh* (following a variant text of *Yerushalmi*) assumes this question to be the subject of a difference of opinion between the two Talmuds: According to *Yerushalmi*, R' Yose considers removal of one of the components of the quarter-*kav* to be sufficient; according to *Bavli* (*Bava Basra* 94b), a removal of all the diverse kinds is needed. *Rosh*, however, concludes that even *Bavli* agrees that removing one of the components of the quarter-*kav* is sufficient. Thus, where ¹⁄₈ *kav* of barley and ¹⁄₈ *kav* of spelt make up a quarter-*kav* in a *se'ah* predominantly of wheat, R' Yose would require the complete elimination of either the spelt or the barley, but not both. Leaving the barley alone does not mean that the person *wants* to grow a mixture — he leaves it simply because its removal is tedious. Only if he begins to remove a species, and then leaves some behind, does it look (according to R' Yose) as if he *wants* the remainder. But here he has not removed any barley. Since nothing indicates that he *wants* the barley in the mixture, even R' Yose allows it to remain (*Tos. R' Akiva*).

רַבִּי שִׁמְעוֹן אוֹמֵר: לֹא אָמְרוּ אֶלָּא מִמִּין אֶחָד. — *R' Shimon says: They spoke only of one kind.*

R' Shimon rejects the notion that different kinds can be added together to make up the quarter-*kav* which will render the *se'ah* prohibited for planting. In his view, only a quarter-*kav* of one species renders a mixture forbidden (*Rav*). Thus, a *se'ah* of seed consisting of 5⁵⁄₈ *kavs* of wheat, and ¹⁄₈ *kav* each of barley, spelt, and beans, will not be forbidden for planting according to R' Shimon. Although the barley, spelt, and

2
1
and whether it is of two kinds. R' Shimon says: They spoke only of one kind. But the Sages say: Whatever is *kilayim* with the *se'ah* can be added together [to constitute] a quarter[-*kav*].

YAD AVRAHAM

beans together amount to three-eighths of a *kav* (1.5 quarter-*kavs*), R' Shimon maintains that we do not add together different species.

Yerushalmi explains that according to R' Shimon as much as half of the *se'ah* of seed can be made up of species which are *kilayim* with the major component of the *se'ah*. For example, as many as twenty-four species, each in quantities of ⅛ *kav*, could be mixed with three *kavs* of wheat. Since none of the minority components is by itself a quarter-*kav*, the *se'ah* may be planted, even though *half* of it consists of seeds which are *kilayim* with wheat!

However, if the combined quantity of the minority components of the *se'ah* exceeds three *kavs* — i.e. they account for more than half of the *se'ah* — then even R' Shimon agrees that the seed may not be planted as is (*Rosh*).

Note that in the above example we have assumed that each of the twenty-four minority species accounts for no more than ⅛. Since the *se'ah* contains three *kavs* of wheat, the ratio of wheat to each foreign variety is more than twenty-three to one. But if the quantity of wheat were not twenty-three times greater than any of the minority components, the mixture would be forbidden, even though the diverse kind in question was less than a quarter-*kav*. For example, consider a mixture containing 5⅝ *kavs* of wheat plus ⅛ *kav* of barley. [As it stands, the barley accounts for much less than one twenty-fourth of the mixture.] Into this mixture, there falls a quantity of lentils, slightly less than a quarter-*kav*. Now, the wheat *together* with the barley amounts to 5¾ *kavs*, which is more than twenty-three times the less than quarter-*kav* of lentils. But the wheat alone (22.5 quarter-*kavs*) is not sufficient to cancel the lentils (0.999 quarter-*kavs*). R' Shimon maintains that just as

different kinds can not be combined to make up a quarter-*kav* to disqualify a mixture, so too they can not be combined to validate one. Thus, in the present example, the wheat can *not* be combined with the barley to negate the effect of the lentils. Therefore, although the lentils are less than a quarter-*kav*, they remain significant, and the mixture may not be planted as is (*Rosh, Rash* from *Yerushalmi*; see *Tos. R' Akiva* and below, mishnah 2).

וַחֲכָמִים אוֹמְרִים: כָּל שֶׁהוּא כִּלְאַיִם בְּסָאָה מִצְטָרֵף לְרֹבַע — **But the Sages say: Whatever is kilayim with the se'ah can be added together [to constitute] a quarter-[kav].**

The Sages refer to a case such as the following: The majority component of the *se'ah* is barley, and this is mixed with oats and spelt which together exceed a quarter-*kav*. (However, neither the oats nor the spelt, on their own, are a quarter-*kav*.) Although oats and spelt are *kilayim* together, oats and barley are not (mishnah 1:1). Accordingly, the Sages maintain that the oats are ignored. In their opinion, only kinds which are *kilayim* with the predominant component of the *se'ah* can be included in the quarter-*kav* of foreign seed which disqualifies a *se'ah* for planting. But in the above example, oats which are not *kilayim* with barley (the major component of the *se'ah*) cannot be combined with spelt to make up the critical quarter-*kav* (*Rav; Rosh; Rash; Rambam Comm.*). The *Tanna Kamma* (above, s.v. בין) disputes this and rules that although oats are not *kilayim* with barley, they are added to the spelt to make up the critical quarter-*kav*, and the *se'ah* may not be planted as is. The halachah, however, follows the Sages (*Rav; Rambam, Hil. Kilayim* 2:2).

בַּמֶּה [ב] דְּבָרִים אֲמוּרִים? תְּבוּאָה בִתְבוּאָה, וְקִטְנִית בְּקִטְנִית, תְּבוּאָה בְּקִטְנִית, וְקִטְנִית בִתְבוּאָה. בֶּאֱמֶת אָמְרוּ: זֵרְעוֹנֵי גִנָּה שֶׁאֵינָן נֶאֱכָלִין מִצְטָרְפִין אֶחָד מֵעֶשְׂרִים וְאַרְבָּעָה בְּנוֹפֵל לְבֵית סְאָה. רַבִּי שִׁמְעוֹן אוֹמֵר: כְּשֵׁם שֶׁאָמְרוּ לְהַחְמִיר, כָּךְ אָמְרוּ לְהָקֵל. הַפִּשְׁתָּן

יד אברהם

2.

The present mishnah establishes the scope of the rule of the previous mishnah that a *se'ah* of seed (e.g. wheat) which includes a quarter-*kav* of a diverse kind (e.g. barley) may not be planted as is. A distinction is made between different classes of seeds, some which are governed by the above rule, and others for which a different rule applies.

בַּמֶּה דְּבָרִים אֲמוּרִים? תְּבוּאָה בִתְבוּאָה, וְקִטְנִית בְּקִטְנִית, תְּבוּאָה בְּקִטְנִית, וְקִטְנִית בִתְבוּאָה. — *With what are these things said? Grain in grain, legume in legume, grain in legume, legume in grain.*

Seeds (other than for trees) may be divided into two groups: (a) edible seeds, and (b) non-edible seeds. In Mishnaic usage, the first group is generally subdivided into grain (תְּבוּאָה) and legumes (קִטְנִיּוֹת). The term תְּבוּאָה, *grain*, refers specifically to the five principal varieties: wheat, barley, spelt, oats, and rye (*Nedarim* 55a; see above 1:1). The term קִטְנִיּוֹת, *legumes*, includes all other seeds which are eaten: for example, beans, peas, rice, sesame, etc. (*Rambam Comm.* and *Hil. Kilayim* 1:8; *Rosh*).

The mishnah thus states here that the rule of the first mishnah applies to any possible combination of edible seeds mixed with one another: one type of grain with another, one type of legume with another, grain in a mixture comprised primarily of legumes, and vice versa. Regardless of what the main component of the *se'ah* is — a grain or a legume — and regardless of whether the diverse kind mixed in is a grain or a legume, the critical concentration of a diverse kind which renders the mixture forbidden for planting is a quarter-*kav*

per *se'ah.* However, as will follow, the law when non-edible seeds are involved is different (*Rav; Rosh; Rash; Rambam Comm.*).

Rash (as explained by *Chazon Ish* 4:1) understands that the mention (in mishnah 1) of a *se'ah* containing a quarter-*kav* of some other kind is an illustration of the law when a diverse kind mixes with wheat. When the major component of a mixture of seeds is some species other than wheat, the mixture is forbidden for planting when an amount of seed which would be planted in a 2,500 square-cubit area contains a quarter-*kav* of diverse seed. This area, known as a *beis se'ah* (see *Eruvin* 23b), is the area in which a *se'ah* of wheat is normally planted. Thus, in order to determine whether or not a particular mixture of seeds may be planted, one must first ascertain what quantity of the predominant component of the mixture is needed to plant a *beis se'ah.* When a diverse kind is mixed with wheat, since a *se'ah* of wheat is planted in a *beis se'ah,* the proportion of the diverse kind which renders the mixture forbidden is a quarter-*kav* per *se'ah* (or one part in twenty-four), as stated in mishnah 1. If the main species is something which is planted at a rate of seven *kavs* per *beis se'ah,* then the proportion of a diverse kind which renders the mixture forbidden is a quarter-*kav* in seven *kavs* (or one part in twenty-eight). Similarly, if the main seed is one which is planted four *kavs* per *beis se'ah,* it will be rendered forbidden only at a concentration of one-six-

2
2

2. **W**ith what are these things said? Grain in grain, legume in legume, grain in legume, legume in grain. In truth, they said: Garden seeds which are not eaten combine to one twenty-fourth of what is sown in a *beis se'ah*. R' Shimon says: Just as they said to be stringent, so did they say to be lenient. Flax

YAD AVRAHAM

teenth (i.e. a quarter-*kav* in four *kavs*). Thus, the critical proportion varies from species to species depending on how much is needed to plant a *beis se'ah*. The quantity needed for a *beis se'ah* is divided by a constant — a quarter-*kav* — and this gives the concentration of a diverse kind which necessitates reduction. Our mishnah teaches that this rule, incorporating a constant quarter-*kav* regardless of the type of diverse seed present in a mixture, is only true where the seed was grain or legumes (i.e. it was edible). If the diverse seed was not edible, the rule changes as explained below.

בֶּאֱמֶת אָמְרוּ: זֵרְעוֹנֵי גִנָּה שֶׁאֵינָן נֶאֱכָלִין מִצְטָרְפִין אֶחָד מֵעֶשְׂרִים וְאַרְבָּעָה בְּנוֹפֵל לְבֵית סְאָה. — *In truth, they said: Garden seeds which are not eaten combine to one twenty-fourth of what is sown in a beis se'ah.*

Garden seeds is the term used to refer to seeds of plants, such as turnips and carrots, where the plant has an edible part, but the seeds *are not eaten*. The mishnah states that if a *se'ah* of seed (say, wheat) contains an admixture of garden seed equal to ¹⁄₂₄ of the amount of that garden seed which is sown in a *beis se'ah*, then the seed may not be planted until the proportion of garden seed is reduced. Consider, for example, a case of garden seeds which normally were planted at the rate of 1.5 *kavs* per *beis se'ah*. If one sixteenth of a *kav* of this seed (i.e. one twenty-fourth of the amount per *beis se'ah*) was mixed with 5¹⁵⁄₁₆ *kavs* of wheat, giving a total of a *se'ah*, the mixture may not be sown until the presence of garden seed is reduced. Thus, the garden seed renders the wheat forbidden at a mere concentration of ¹⁄₉₆. This minute quantity of garden seed,

which mixes with 5¹⁵⁄₁₆ *kavs* of any seed of diverse kind — whether grain, legume, or garden seed (see *Mishnah Rishonah*) — renders the *se'ah* of seed forbidden for planting until the concentration of the garden seed is reduced to below one ninety-sixth (*Rav; Rambam Comm.; Rashash*).

The phrase *in truth, they said* is explained by *Yerushalmi* as indicating a law received orally by Moshe at Mt. Sinai (see *Tos. Yom Tov*). Thus, the basis for the distinction made by the mishnah between the rule for admixture of grain or legumes (mishnah 1) and the rule for admixtures of garden seed is a *halachah leMoshe miSinai*.

Rambam Comm. explains the verb מִצְטָרְפִין, *combine*, used here as teaching that different species of garden seed can be combined to constitute the one twenty-fourth of what is sown in a *beis se'ah*. Thus, two points are being made here: One, instead of the quarter-*kav* used for grain and legumes, the critical quantity for garden seeds is a twenty-fourth of what is sown in a *beis se'ah*; and two, different kinds of garden seeds may be added together to reach the critical quantity and necessitate reduction.

רַבִּי שִׁמְעוֹן אוֹמֵר: כְּשֵׁם שֶׁאָמְרוּ לְהַחְמִיר, כָּךְ אָמְרוּ לְהָקֵל. — *R' Shimon says: Just as they said to be stringent, so did they say to be lenient.*

R' Shimon maintains that the law for garden seeds is not always more stringent than that for other seeds. When one twenty-fourth of what is sown in a *beis se'ah* equals less than a quarter-*kav*, the law for garden seed is indeed more stringent, since even less than a quarter-*kav* renders a *se'ah* of wheat, for example, forbidden. Nevertheless, if ¹⁄₂₂ of the

כלאים
ב/ג

בַּתְּבוּאָה מִצְטָרֶפֶת אֶחָד מֵעֶשְׂרִים וְאַרְבָּעָה בְּנוֹפֵל לְבֵית סְאָה.

[ג] **הָיְתָה** שָׂדֵהוּ זְרוּעָה חִטִּים, וְנִמְלַךְ לְזָרְעָה שְׂעוֹרִים — יַמְתִּין לָהּ עַד שֶׁתַּתְלִיעַ, וְיוֹפַךְ, וְאַחַר כָּךְ יִזְרַע.

יד אברהם

quantity normally planted in a *beis se'ah* is greater than a quarter-*kav*, then a mixture will be forbidden only if the garden seeds are present in the greater quantity. The mishnah proceeds to illustrate this with an example (*Rav; Rosh; Rash*).

Rambam Comm. understands R' Shimon's statement in this mishnah as referring back to his statement in the previous mishnah. There, R' Shimon argued that the quarter-*kav* of diverse seed in a *se'ah* which necessitates reduction must be comprised all of one kind. Elaborating on his position, R' Shimon adds here: Just as they said that two kinds are not added to make a quarter-*kav* to produce a stringent effect — viz. the disqualification of the mixture for planting as is — so too, they are not added to produce a lenient effect. For example, if 0.999 quarter-*kavs* of lentils were mixed with 22.5 quarter-*kavs* of wheat and 0.5 quarter-*kavs* of barley, the lentils constitute more than one part in twenty-four with respect to the wheat alone, but not with respect to the wheat combined with the barley (see comm. to mishnah 1, s.v. רבי שמעון).

Nevertheless, the wheat is not combined with the barley to annul the lentils, and the concentration of lentils must be reduced before this seed can be planted.

Thus, according to *Rambam*, R' Shimon here is not commenting on the scope of the "one twenty-fourth rule" given for garden seeds (i.e. does this apply only when the one twenty-fourth is less than a quarter-*kav* or even when it is more?); rather, R' Shimon is reacting to the second point made in the statement of the rule for garden seeds — viz. that they are combined (*Tos. Anshei Shem*; see *Tos. R' Akiva* to mishnah 1 [§8]).

הַפִּשְׁתָּן בַּתְּבוּאָה מִצְטָרֶפֶת אֶחָד מֵעֶשְׂרִים וְאַרְבָּעָה בְּנוֹפֵל לְבֵית סְאָה. — *Flax in grain*

combines to one twenty-fourth of what is sown in a *beis se'ah*.

The quantity of flaxseed normally sown in a *beis se'ah* is three *se'ahs* [i.e. three times as much as the quantity of wheat sown in a *beis se'ah*] (*Yerushalmi*; see *Meleches Shlomo*). Thus, one twenty-fourth of the quantity of flax sown in a *beis se'ah* is three quarter-*kavs*. This, then, is an example in which the rule for garden seeds is more lenient than the rule for grain and legumes. A grain (e.g. barley) mixed with wheat will disqualify a *se'ah* of the mixture for planting, with as little as a single quarter-*kav*. However, a garden seed such as flax does not render a *se'ah* of wheat forbidden until there are at least three quarter-*kavs* of flaxseed in the *se'ah* (*Rav; Rosh; Rash*).

According to *Rav's* explanation, the view that the law for garden seeds in a mixture can be more lenient than that for grain or legumes is R' Shimon's alone. The other *Tannaim* would contend that the one twenty-fourth rule for garden seeds applies only as long as this quantity is less than a quarter-*kav*. If, however, one twenty-fourth of what is sown in a *beis se'ah* is more than a quarter-*kav*, then a *se'ah* of wheat will be disqualified with only a quarter-*kav* of garden seed. In particular, a *se'ah* of wheat containing only a quarter-*kav* of flax would already be rendered forbidden [in contrast with R' Shimon's view that it is permitted unless it contains three quarter-*kavs*] (see *Chazon Ish* 4:2).

Rambam Comm., as explained above, understood R' Shimon as dealing with a different issue, such that the question of whether the garden-seed rule can be more lenient than the grain or legume rule has not yet been dis-

in grain combines to one twenty-fourth of what is sown in a *beis se'ah*.

3. **[I**f] his field was planted with wheat, and he reconsidered [and decided] to plant it with barley — he waits for it until it germinates, he turns [the soil], and afterwards he can plant.

YAD AVRAHAM

cussed. According to *Rambam, all* agree that indeed the one twenty-fourth rule for garden seed is applied even where this results in leniency with respect to the quarter-*kav* rule of mishnah 1. Thus, the example here, in which flax forbids a *se'ah* of wheat only where there is at least three quarter-*kavs* of flax in the *se'ah*, is unanimously agreed upon. [That this statement is not part of R' Shimon's can be inferred from the fact that it speaks of flax *combining* to make up the critical quantity needed to disqualify the *se'ah*. As understood

by *Rambam, combining* refers to adding together any diverse minority components of the *se'ah*. But according to R' Shimon (mishnah 1), such combining is not possible! (See *Tos. Anshei Shem.*) Obviously, this is not R' Shimon speaking, and as an anonymous statement it may be assumed to represent a consensus that when garden seeds are a minority component in a mixture of seeds, they disqualify according to one twenty-fourth of what is sown of them in a *beis se'ah* per *se'ah*, even if this is more than a quarter-*kav*.]

3.

The mishnah now considers the law when a farmer who has already planted wheat in a field decides to replant it with barley.

הָיְתָה שָׂדֵהוּ זְרוּעָה חִטִּים, וְנִמְלַךְ לְזָרְעָה — שְׂעוֹרִים — *[If] his field was planted with wheat, and he reconsidered [and decided] to plant it with barley —*
[If the wheat can be destroyed, and thus prevented from growing, planting of the barley is permitted. The first case considered is where the wheat has only just been sown, and has not yet begun to grow. In this case:]

יַמְתִּין לָהּ עַד שֶׁתַּתְלִיעַ, וְיוֹפַךְ, וְאַחַר כָּךְ יִזְרַע. — *he waits for it until it germinates, he turns [the soil], and afterwards he can plant.*
It takes approximately three days from the time of planting for wheat seeds to sprout roots (*Rosh,* from *Yerushalmi;* see *Nekudas HaKesef, Yoreh Deah* 293:1 and *Beur HaGra;* see also ArtScroll *Sheviis* 2:6, p. 55). Once this occurs, the infant plant is very fragile (see *Kilei Zeraim,* p. 204) and, if dislocated by a plow, will die. Accordingly, the mishnah

prescribes that the farmer wait until the wheat seed has begun to project roots, and then to plow through the field (*he turns [the soil]*). This plowing stops the wheat from growing, and afterwards the farmer can plant the field with barley (*Rav; Rosh; Rash*).

The mishnah's term for sending out roots, לְהַתְלִיעַ, is explained by *Rosh* as deriving from the word תּוֹלַעַת, meaning *worm,* and reflects the wormlike appearance of the infant root. *Aruch* (s.v. תלע), citing the verse (*Exodus* 16:20): *and [the manna] bred worms and rotted,* interprets הַתְלָעָה as decaying or decomposing. He explains that as part of its growth process, a seed decomposes and sends out roots (cf. *Rambam Comm.* and *Hil. Kilayim* 2:13).
From *Tosefta* (1:12) it appears that plowing the field *before* the wheat germinates is sufficient to permit planting barley. Moreover, three days from the time the wheat was planted, *Tosefta* appears to permit planting

אִם צָמְחָה, לֹא יֹאמַר: ,,אֶזְרַע וְאַחַר כָּךְ
אוֹפַךְ״; אֶלָּא, הוֹפֵךְ וְאַחַר כָּךְ זוֹרֵעַ.
כַּמָּה יְהֵא חוֹרֵשׁ? כְּתַלְמֵי הָרְבִיעָה. אַבָּא שָׁאוּל
אוֹמֵר: כְּדֵי שֶׁלֹּא יְשַׁיֵּר רֹבַע לְבֵית סְאָה.

יד אברהם

barley in the field as is, without taking any measures to destroy the wheat (see *Ravad* to *Hil. Kilayim* 2:13 and *Kesef Mishneh* ibid. 2:14). Apparently, *Tosefta* assumes that when a seed has been transformed into a root, and has not yet sprouted above ground, it is not considered a plant subject to the laws of *kilayim* (see *Rambam* and *Ravad, Hil. Kilayim* 2:12). Consequently, by waiting until the wheat seed (which *is* subject to the prohibition on planting mixtures) has been transformed into a root, the farmer can plant right over it [of course, when the wheat does break ground, it again qualifies as a plant and must then be removed from the field] (*Toras Zeraim*; see *Gilyon HaShas* to *Yerushalmi*, and see below, mishnah 5, s.v. לֹא). On the other hand, if the farmer does not wish to wait until the wheat seed has been transformed into a root, he has another option — to plow the field and then plant barley. Although plowing the wheat seed before it germinates does not kill it, such plowing demonstrates that the farmer does not want the wheat to grow. Assuming that such an expression of intent suffices to release the prohibition on planting *kilayim*, the *Tosefta* permits planting the field with barley even before three days have elapsed from the wheat planting, as long as before planting the barley, the farmer plows through the wheat seed (see *Chazon Ish* 4:26). *Ravad* (*Hil. Kilayim* 2:13) seems to have harmonized the *Tosefta's* opinion with the wording of the mishnah by means of a slight re-interpretation. By reading the word וְיוֹפֵךְ as "or he turns" (rather than, "and he turns"), the mishnah can be explained as counseling the same two paths prescribed in the *Tosefta*: namely, (a) to wait until the seed is transformed into a root (at which time no further measures are necessary), or else (b) to immediately plow the wheat seed (thus indicating disinterest with the wheat) (see notes of *R' Yitzchak Frankel* in *Shenos Eliyahu, Peirush HaAroch*; cf. *Chazon Ish* 4:26). [It is, however, unexplained why, unlike the *Tosefta*, the

mishnah (according to this last interpretation) lists these options out of order.]

אִם צָמְחָה, לֹא יֹאמַר: ,,אֶזְרַע וְאַחַר כָּךְ אוֹפַךְ״;
אֶלָּא, הוֹפֵךְ וְאַחַר כָּךְ זוֹרֵעַ. — *If it sprouted, he cannot say: "I will plant and afterwards turn [the soil]"; rather, he must turn [it] and afterwards plant.*

If the wheat has already broken ground by the time the farmer decides to replace it with barley, he must first plow through the field to destroy the wheat, and only then may he plant barley. On first glance, it is not clear why this ruling is formulated as if it is limited to the case where the wheat has already sprouted. After all, the same law is given above for wheat which has germinated but not yet broken ground! The point of the mishnah, however, is that plowing through wheat which has already emerged from the ground is far more destructive than plowing through a field planted with wheat seeds. Even though the person waits until the average germination time has passed before plowing, he has no way of knowing what percentage of the seeds has in fact already germinated and will thus be killed by plowing (see *Yerushalmi* that germination time varies with ground conditions, and see *Meleches Shlomo*). On the other hand, where the wheat has already broken ground, it is reasonable to assume that any remaining wheat seeds which have not broken ground will not do so (*Radbaz* to *Hil. Kilayim* 2:14). Furthermore, it can be safely assumed that all the plants which are plowed over will die (see *Tos. Yom Tov*). Since the wheat is already visible and thus not easily overlooked, it might have been thought that the farmer could be allowed to put off plowing the

If it sprouted, he cannot say: "I will plant and afterwards turn [the soil]"; rather, he must turn [it] and afterwards plant.

How much must he plow? Like the furrows of the rain. Abba Shaul says: So that there will not remain a quarter[-*kav*] per *beis se'ah*.

wheat until after he has sowed the barley. Accordingly, the mishnah states that even though the farmer states his intent to plow through the wheat after sowing the barley, he is forbidden to sow the barley until the wheat has actually been plowed through (*Tos. Yom Tov*).

We have assumed following *Tos. Tom Tov* that צָמְחָה in the mishnah means sprouting above ground. However, *Rosh* defines this as synonymous with עַד שֶׁתַּתְלִיעַ, *until it germinates*. According to this reading, the mishnah first states the rule that the farmer, on reconsidering his crop, must wait for germination of the wheat, must plow it through, and may only then plant barley. The mishnah then adds that the farmer may not delay the plowing of the germinating wheat until after he plants barley, not even if he explicitly declares his definite intent to do so.

Gra (*Shenos Eliyahu, Peirush HaAroch*; see also *Tif. Yisrael* and *Boaz*), following *Ravad's* explanation (above), notes that indeed prior to the emergence of the wheat above ground, it *is permitted* to sow the barley without first plowing through the wheat. Only with the emergence of the wheat, when it is again treated as a plant (and not merely as a root — see above), does planting barley, without first killing the wheat, become forbidden.

כַּמָּה יְהֵא חוֹרֵשׁ? כְּתַלְמֵי הָרְבִיעָה. — *How much must he plow? Like the furrows of the rain.*

The plowing of the wheat field carried out in order to permit re-planting the field with barley need not turn over the entire surface of the field (*Rav; Rambam Comm.*). As long as the furrows are spaced at intervals no greater than "the

furrows of the rain," it is sufficient, according to this *Tanna*.

It was common after the first rain to plow the fields in advance of planting (*Rav; Rosh; Rash; Ri ben Malki Tzedek*).[1] The furrows were separated such that the mound produced as one furrow was plowed would touch the mound produced as the next one was plowed (*Tosefta* 1:12; see *Chazon Ish* 4:25, s.v. תני). [This plowing gave the field a surface of alternating peaks and troughs, which enabled subsequent rainwater to be trapped in the field and seep into the ground, as well as prevented runoff of soil (*Kilei Zeraim*, pp. 209-210).]

The pattern created by this plowing after the first rain was known as "furrows of the rain," and the mishnah states that the furrows plowed in order to kill the wheat did not have to be more concentrated than the "furrows of the rain."

Although plowing at such intervals certainly left some wheat untouched, the first *Tanna* did not see this as an obstacle to planting the field with barley. Certainly this plowing destroys much of the wheat, and hence serves as a firm indication that the farmer does not want the wheat (*Chazon Ish* 4:24). If subsequently a significant amount of wheat turns up in the field, the farmer will remove it then (see below).

אַבָּא שָׁאוּל אוֹמֵר: כְּדֵי שֶׁלֹּא יְשַׁיֵּר רְבַע לְבֵית סְאָה. — *Abba Shaul says: So that there will not remain a quarter[-kav] per beis se'ah.*

A *beis se'ah*, it will be recalled, is an area of 2,500 square cubits in which a

---

1. *Rambam Comm.* understands "furrows of the rain" to have been plowed *before* the first rain, see there.

כלאים
ב/ד

[ד] זְרוּעָה וְנִמְלַךְ לְנוֹטְעָה, לֹא יֹאמַר: ,,אֶטַּע
וְאַחַר כָּךְ אוֹפַךְ,'' אֶלָּא הוֹפֵךְ
וְאַחַר כָּךְ נוֹטֵעַ.

נְטוּעָה וְנִמְלַךְ לְזָרְעָה, לֹא יֹאמַר: ,,אֶזְרַע וְאַחַר
כָּךְ אֲשָׁרֵשׁ''; אֶלָּא, מְשָׁרֵשׁ וְאַחַר כָּךְ זוֹרֵעַ. אִם
רָצָה, גּוֹמֵם עַד פָּחוֹת מִטֶּפַח, זוֹרֵעַ, וְאַחַר כָּךְ
מְשָׁרֵשׁ.

יד אברהם

se'ah of wheat is normally planted. Likewise, a beis rova (rova means quarter) is the area in which a rova-kav — i.e. a quarter-kav — would be planted. Since a quarter-kav is one twenty-fourth of a se'ah, a beis rova is one twenty-fourth of a beis se'ah. Abba Shaul states that although the entire surface need not be turned, nevertheless the total unturned area in a field the size of a beis se'ah may not exceed a beis rova, i.e., one twenty-fourth of 2,500 sq. cubits (104.16 sq. cu.). Thus, the farmer must be sure not to space the furrows so far apart that a total of a beis rova will be left unturned (Rav; Rambam Comm.).

According to the preceding interpretation, Abba Shaul would seem to be more stringent than the first Tanna. The first Tanna allows ''furrows of the rain'' even if the total unturned area exceeds a beis rova, while Abba Shaul does not.

Rosh, however, understands Abba Shaul as more lenient than the first Tanna. Evidently, in his view, ''furrows of the rain'' would normally leave less than a beis rova unturned, and Abba Shaul allows for them to be spaced at greater than usual intervals as long as the total unturned area does not equal a beis rova (see also second interpretation of Rash and see Chazon Ish 4:24-25). [When one takes into account that even in the turned part of the field not all the wheat seeds will be killed, it follows that according to Abba Shaul it is permitted to plant the barley even though more than a rova of wheat will grow! (Chazon Ish 24:5).]

An alternative suggestion of Rosh is that Abba Shaul allows the plowing of the wheat to be random, and as long as there are no patches the size of a beis rova left unturned, the barley may be planted. This is of course much more lenient than the first Tanna (see also Ri ben Malki Tzedek; and see R' Shlomo Sirilio for yet another interpretation).

4.

The previous mishnah considered the law for replacing one grain in a field with another. The present mishnah deals with replacing a grain field with a vineyard and vice versa.

זְרוּעָה וְנִמְלַךְ לְנוֹטְעָה, לֹא יֹאמַר: ,,אֶטַּע וְאַחַר כָּךְ אוֹפַךְ,'' אֶלָּא הוֹפֵךְ וְאַחַר כָּךְ נוֹטֵעַ — [If] it was sown and he decided to plant it, he cannot say: ''I will plant and afterwards turn [the soil]''; rather, he must turn [it] and afterwards plant.

A field was sown with grain, and the farmer then decided that he would prefer to grow grapes in this field, rather than grain (Rav; Rash). Since growing grapes

and grain together violates the laws prohibiting mixtures in vineyards (kilei hakerem), the farmer must first eradicate the grain in the field, and only then may he plant it with vines. Accordingly, he must wait until the grain seeds have germinated, at which point they are killed by plowing, and must then plow through the grain, as in the previous mishnah. Only afterwards may he plant

משניות / כלאים – פרק ב: כל סאה [40]

4. **[** If] it was sown and he decided to plant it, he cannot say: "I will plant and afterwards turn [the soil]"; rather, he must turn [it] and afterwards plant.

[If] it was planted and he decided to sow it, he cannot say: "I will sow and afterwards uproot"; rather, he must uproot and afterwards sow. If he wants, he can raze till less than a handbreadth, sow, and afterwards uproot.

YAD AVRAHAM

grapevines in the field (*Tos. Yom Tov;* see *Meleches Shlomo*).

The mishnah does not specify grains and grapevines and speaks instead in terms of sowing [זְרִיעָה] and planting [נְטִיעָה]. From a literal point of view, sowing could include seeds other than grains (e.g., legumes, garden seeds), and planting could include trees other than grapevines (*Rambam Comm.*). Indeed, it is not necessary to limit the mishnah's case exclusively to a field of grain. The same rule would apply to a field of beans which the farmer decided to convert to a vineyard (*Tos. Yom Tov*). However, as far as the connotation here of planting, it would seem that this must refer only to grapevines. This is because it is permitted to sow a mixture of tree and grain seeds, for example (*Rambam, Hil. Kilayim* 1:6), and only grafting between trees and other plants is forbidden (*Rambam, Hil. Kilayim* 1:5; see above, 1:7, s.v. ירק בירק). The only trees which may not be planted together with grains and the like are grapevines, and consequently the present mishnah, which forbids planting trees amongst grain, must be referring to grapevines (*Tif. Yis.; Chazon Ish* 4:27).

According to *Ravad* (*Hil. Kilayim* 1:6), sowing a mixture of trees and other seeds is forbidden. (*Chazon Ish* 3:11 explains that this is a Rabbinical prohibition.) Thus, following *Ravad*, planting trees other than grapevines together with grains or legumes, for example, is forbidden, and the mishnah here can be explained as referring to other trees as well (*Tif. Yis.; Chazon Ish* 4:27; see *Chazon Ish* 3:10,11). However, *Ravad's* view is not accepted in practice (*Derech Emunah* 1:35).

נְטוּעָה וְנִמְלַךְ לְזָרְעָהּ, לֹא יֹאמַר:,,אֶזְרַע וְאַחַר — כָּךְ אֲשָׁרֵשׁ", אֶלָּא, מְשָׁרֵשׁ וְאַחַר כָּךְ זוֹרֵעַ. — *[If] it was planted and he decided to sow it, he cannot say: "I will sow and afterwards uproot"; rather, he must*

uproot and afterwards sow.

[In this case the farmer wishes to convert a vineyard into a grain field. The mishnah states that before sowing, the farmer must first uproot the grapevines, and he cannot sow the grain first even though he explicitly declares an intention to remove the vines.]

The verb לשרש, *to uproot,* based on the noun שרש, meaning *root,* is used in this sense in *Psalms* 52:7 (*Rambam Comm.*). This illustrates a common peculiarity of Hebrew — that the same term is used for doing as well as undoing something (*Rishon LeTzion;* see also *Yad Avraham* to *Sheviis* 3:1).

אִם רָצָה, גּוֹמֵם עַד פָּחוֹת מִטֶּפַח, זוֹרֵעַ, וְאַחַר כָּךְ מְשָׁרֵשׁ. — *If he wants, he can raze till less than a handbreadth, sow, and afterwards uproot.*

The mishnah now teaches that razing the vines to less than a handbreadth from the ground, without fully uprooting them, is also sufficient to permit sowing. This is because a grapevine less than a handbreadth high does not come under the prohibition of *kilei hakerem* (*Radbaz* to *Hil. Kilayim* 6:6; *Mishnah Rishonah;* see *Rambam, Hil. Kilayim* 6:4, Mishnah *Sheviis* 1:8; *Chazon Ish* 4:27). Alternatively, this is because ordinarily such a vine does not regenerate (*Chazon Ish* 4:27). Thus, as long as the vines remain less than a handbreadth high, there is no need to uproot them. If, after sowing, the vines regenerated and started to produce shoots, they must be uprooted (*Chazon Ish* 4:27 from *Yerushalmi; Derech Emunah* 6:35).

As explained, razing the vines is normally equivalent to uprooting them and there

[ה] הָיְתָה שָׂדֵהוּ זְרוּעָה קַנְבּוֹס אוֹ לוּף, לֹא יְהֵא זוֹרֵעַ וּבָא עַל גַּבֵּיהֶם, שֶׁאֵינָן עוֹשִׂין אֶלָּא לִשְׁלֹשָׁה שָׁנִים. תְּבוּאָה שֶׁעָלָה בָהּ סְפִיחֵי אִסְטִיס, וְכֵן מְקוֹם הַגְּרָנוֹת שֶׁעָלוּ בָּהֶן מִינִין הַרְבֵּה, וְכֵן תִּלְתָּן שֶׁהֶעֱלָה מִינֵי צְמָחִים – אֵין מְחַיְּבִין אוֹתוֹ לְנַכֵּשׁ.

יד אברהם

would seem to be no requirement to uproot them, unless it turned out that razing did not stop their growth. However, *Radbaz* (to *Hil. Kilayim* 6:6) seems to have understood that in all events the vines must be uprooted. The mishnah here is lenient only in that razing entitles the person to delay the uprooting until later. [In the case of grains, reducing the stems to a height of less than a handbreadth does not release them from the prohibitions. Accordingly, unlike the case with vines, there is no alternative to plowing through the current grain crop and killing it (see *Radbaz* to *Hil. Kilayim* 6:6).]

5.

הָיְתָה שָׂדֵהוּ זְרוּעָה קַנְבּוֹס אוֹ לוּף, — *[If] his field was planted with caraway or arum,*

The precise definition of קַנְבּוֹס is unclear. Normally, the mishnah uses this with reference to hemp. However, in the present context this is unlikely, since hemp does not display the growth cycle which the mishnah associates with קַנְבּוֹס (*Tos. Yom Tov* from *R' Eliyahu of London*). *Rambam Comm.* has קרבס which he defines as caraway. This identification has support from *Yerushalmi* and has been adopted in the translation (see also *Ri ben Malki Tzedek* and *Kilei Zeraim*, pp. 220-221).[1]

What characterizes these two species is their vitality: Their growth is not inhibited by plowing over the germinated seed, and furthermore the root remains hardy and active for a period of three years. Because of these properties, the procedure prescribed in mishnah 3 — for a farmer who wishes to replant his field — letting the seeds germinate and then plowing through them — is not relevant to these species (*Rav; Rosh; Rash*; see *Tos. Yom Tov* and *Ri ben Malki Tzedek*).

According to *Ravad* (*Hil. Kilayim* 2:12), the case here involves a field planted with caraway or arum which has not yet grown. The issue in question is whether it is permitted to plant some other species in the field, on the assumption that the caraway or arum has decayed and will not grow.

According to *Rambam* (ibid.), the case assumes a field of caraway or arum which has been harvested. However, because the roots have been left in the ground, there remains a possibility that caraway or arum plants will regenerate. Consequently, these must be uprooted before anything else may be planted (see below).

לֹא יְהֵא זוֹרֵעַ וּבָא עַל גַּבֵּיהֶם, שֶׁאֵינָן עוֹשִׂין אֶלָּא לִשְׁלֹשָׁה שָׁנִים. — *he may not plant over them, since they do not produce for three years.*

Since the life cycle of these plants is so long, one can never assume that the seed has decayed merely because the plant has not appeared for a long time. Consequently, it is forbidden to plant anything else in the field (*Ravad* to *Hil. Kilayim* 2:12).

Rambam (*Comm.* and *Hil. Kilayim* 2:12)

---

1. New information based on material preserved in the *Genizah* suggests that the species intended by the mishnah is the colocasia (קְלְקָס; see *Plants and Animals of the Mishnah*, p. 148).

5. [If] his field was planted with caraway or arum, he may not plant over them, since they do not produce for three years.

Grain in which there arose aftergrowth of isatis, and similarly a place of threshing floors in which there arose many kinds, and similarly fenugreek which gave rise to varieties of plants — we do not obligate him to weed.

YAD AVRAHAM

had a version of the mishnah which read: *he may not plant over them "even though" they do not produce for three years.* The mishnah comes to dispel the notion that it is permitted to plant in a field in which there are live roots of a diverse species. *"Even though"* the roots will only produce in three years time, their presence in the field — albeit underground — makes it forbidden to plant another species until and unless these roots are removed. It follows that the implication of *Tosefta* (1:12) that roots are not governed by the laws of *kilayim* (see above, mishnah 3, s.v. יְמַתֵּין) is the subject of a dispute between *Rambam* and *Ravad. Rambam* assumes even roots to be included. For this reason he maintains that the roots of one species must be destroyed before planting another species over them (above mishnah 3), and for this reason the presence of roots of caraway or arum makes it forbidden to plant another species. As noted (mishnah 2:3, s.v. יְמַתֵּין; above, s.v. הַיְתָה and preceding paragraph), *Ravad* disputes both assertions and explains only seeds to be problematic, not roots (see *Toras Zeraim* to mishnah 3; cf. *Tif. Yis.*).

תְּבוּאָה שֶׁעָלָה בָּה סְפִיחֵי אִסְטִיס, — *Grain in which there arose aftergrowth of isatis,*

I.e. new isatis plants regenerated after the first crop was harvested. Alternatively, *aftergrowth* refers to isatis which grew from seeds that fell during the harvest (*Rav* from *Rambam Comm.;* see *Tos. Yom Tov*). Isatis is harmful to the grain crop, and in all likelihood would not be left there for long by the farmer. The question considered by the mishnah, especially in view of the fact that the isatis came up on its own, is whether there is a need to obligate its removal from the field.

וְכֵן מְקוֹם הַגְּרָנוֹת שֶׁעָלוּ בָּהֶן מִינִין הַרְבֵּה, וְכֵן תִּלְתָּן שֶׁהֶעֱלָה מִינֵי צְמָחִים — *and similarly a place of threshing floors in which there arose many kinds, and similarly fenugreek which gave rise to varieties of plants —*

A surface used as a threshing floor has to be smooth (*Rambam Comm.*). Consequently, it is undesirable to have any plants growing on such a surface (*Rav; Rosh*). Likewise, fenugreek intended for human consumption (*Rav; Rambam Comm.* and *Hil. Kilayim* 2:9) is adversely affected by weeds. Thus, no one would ordinarily leave weeds in a fenugreek patch for any length of time (*Rav; Rosh; Rash*).

Fenugreek was grown for human consumption, as well as for animal fodder. When grown for human consumption, the patches were arranged in well-defined rows; when it was grown for animals, no such care was exercised. Only the part of the plant used by humans is vulnerable to weeds, and therefore only fenugreek grown for human consumption would be regularly weeded. The part used for animals was unaffected by weeds, and a fenugreek crop intended for animals would therefore not be weeded (*Bava Kamma* 81a). Accordingly, the mishnah, which assumes that weeds will be removed from fenugreek, must be discussing a crop intended for humans, i.e. a fenugreek field arranged in orderly rows (*Rambam Comm.* and *Hil. Kilayim* 2:10).

אֵין מְחַיְּבִין אוֹתוֹ לְנַכֵּשׁ. — *we do not obligate him to weed.*

In all three of the preceding cases, a mixture of plants has arisen which is damaging either to the cultivated crop

אִם נִכֵּשׁ אוֹ כִּסַּח, אוֹמְרִים לוֹ: ,,עֲקֹר אֶת הַכֹּל
חוּץ מִמִּין אֶחָד."

[ו] הָרוֹצֶה לַעֲשׂוֹת שָׂדֵהוּ מֵשָׁר מֵשָׁר מִכָּל

יד אברהם

(grain or fenugreek) or is damaging to the site (a threshing floor). Ordinarily, a farmer is required to remove a diverse species from his field, even if the foreign plant arose on its own, provided that it constitutes at least ¹⁄₂₄ of the field (cf. *Rav, Shekalim* 1:1). The reason for this is that a diverse species in such a high concentration in a field creates suspicion that the farmer illegally planted it there. To dispel such suspicion, therefore, the Rabbis obligated a person to weed out the foreign invader (*Rambam, Hil. Kilayim* 2:7). In the cases of the mishnah, however, because the mixture is damaging, nobody will normally suspect the farmer of illegal planting. Accordingly, in these cases the Rabbis did *not obligate him to weed* out the diverse kind (*Rambam, Hil.Kilayim* 2:8; *Tosafos* to *Bava Kamma* 81a).

Rav follows *Rashi* (*Bava Kamma* 81a) who explains that the Rabbis did not *obligate* the farmer to eliminate the mixture of diverse kinds in the mishnah's cases, since the farmer will surely do so on his own. However, *Tosafos* reject this approach since it implies that a farmer who does not eliminate the mixture has not committed any transgression. Yet, in fact, it is illegal for a person to maintain *kilayim* in his field, even if he did not plant it, and even if it is damaging! Consequently, failure to eliminate the mixture would be tantamount to maintaining *kilayim* and would constitute an offense (see *Tos. Yom Tov*).

אִם נִכֵּשׁ אוֹ כִּסַּח, — *If he weeded or cut down,*

If the farmer removed *some* of the foreign species, but not all, then this is taken as an indication that he is satisfied with the presence of the remainder. Even if this is in fact not so, to remove only part of the mixture gives the impression

that the person wants to maintain *kilayim*, which is illegal (*Rav*). [As long as the farmer had not touched the foreign species at all, his failure to remove it would not be attributed to a desire to maintain it, but rather to some other reason such as laziness. However, once he removes some but leaves the rest, this is viewed as an indication that he wants the remainder where it is, even though it is damaging.]

Rash and *Rosh* (but cf. *Tos. HaRosh Moed Katan* 6a) explain that this statement of the mishnah refers only to the case of *a place of threshing floors in which there arose many kinds* (see also *Rambam, Hil. Kilayim* 2:7-10). In the other two cases of the mishnah, since the foreign species damages the farmer's crop, even the removal of only part of it does not indicate a desire to maintain the remainder. No one wants his crop damaged, and therefore the farmer will eventually remove the remainder as well. However, in the case of the *place of threshing floors*, the damage is to the place rather than to a crop. It is thus conceivable that a farmer might decide to relocate his threshing floor elsewhere and to use his former threshing place as farmland. Accordingly, if he removes only some of the plants that arise there, this is seen as an indication that he wants to maintain the remainder (cf. *Radbaz* to *Hil. Kilayim* 2:10 and *Meleches Shlomo*).

אוֹמְרִים לוֹ: ,,עֲקֹר אֶת הַכֹּל חוּץ מִמִּין אֶחָד." — *we say to him: "Uproot the whole except for one kind."*

[Since the present situation allows for suspicion that the farmer wishes to maintain *kilayim*, the mishnah requires him to remove all but one species from the field.]

Tos. Yom Tov questions why it is necessary to remove all presence of a foreign species. Why isn't it sufficient to reduce the presence of the foreign species to less than ¹⁄₂₄ as in mishnah 1?

2
6

If he weeded or cut down, we say to him: "Uproot the whole except for one kind."

6. [**I** f] someone wants to make his field into strips of

YAD AVRAHAM

It is of interest that *Rosh* (to mishnah 1; see also *Tos. HaRosh Moed Katan* 6a and *Perishas HaRosh Shekalim* 1:1) views our mishnah as a source for a fundamental distinction between the law for a mixture of seeds and the law for a mixture of plants in a field. In the former case, if the presence of a diverse kind in the mixture of seeds was one part in twenty-four, the Sages require the concentration of the diverse kind to be reduced below this level, whereas R' Yose requires it to be entirely removed (mishnah 1). In the present case, where *kilayim* arose in a field, all agree that it must be entirely eradicated and reduction of the foreign species to less than ¹/₂₄ does not suffice. Moreover, in the case of mishnah 1, if a person reduced his mixture of seeds in accordance with the view of the Sages and then planted it *legally*, if nonetheless the diverse kind occupied more than ¹/₂₄ of the field, he would be required to remove it from the field entirely. Obviously, *kilayim* growing in a field is dealt with more stringently than a mixture of seeds (see also *Rav, Shekalim* 1:1).

However, many authorities would seem to disagree and would equate the law in the case of attached *kilayim* in a field to that of a mixture of seeds: In both cases, an unacceptable presence of a foreign species would be dealt with by reducing the concentration of the diverse kind, not by eliminating it altogether (see e.g. *Rambam, Hil. Kilayim* 2:7; *Ritva* to *Moed Katan* 6a). However, this is only so where the requirement to remove the foreign species from the field was imposed in order to allay suspicion that the person had intentionally planted an illegal mixture. In such a case, reducing the presence of the foreign species to less than ¹/₂₄ of the fields suffices to show that it was not intentionally planted. In the present case, however, the problem is not that the person is suspected of having illegally *planted*; rather, he is suspected of illegally *maintaining* kilayim which arose on its own. This suspicion can only be removed if all of the foreign species is eliminated, and hence the mishnah rules that *we say to him: "Uproot the whole except for one kind"* (*Rambam, Hil. Kilayim* 2:8,10).

6.

The remainder of this chapter discusses various planting configurations which permit different crops to be planted within the same general area. The rationale at work is that each of these formations is visibly distinct from its surroundings and hence does not appear to be intermingled.

There is a fundamental dispute amongst the commentators as to the precise mechanism operating here. According to one school, barren spaces must be left between the planted formations and this separation allows each formation to be regarded as a distinct self-contained unit. Since within each such unit only one species is planted, the unit, which may be viewed as an independent field, is free of *kilayim*. The spacing between formations varies according to the particular shape and crop, and it is this spacing parameter on which the mishnah focuses. According to a second school, the shapes of these formations are by themselves distinctive, and allow two different crops to be grown in close proximity. On this approach, there is no need to leave a separation between formations, and the aim of the mishnah is to define the shapes and dimensions of these formations.

הָרוֹצֶה לַעֲשׂוֹת שָׂדֵהוּ מֵשָׂר מֵשָׂר מִכָּל מִין —
[If] someone wants to make his field into strips of every species —

I.e. he wants to divide his field into

strips which will each be planted with a different species (*Rav; Rosh; Rash*).

According to *Rav's* explanation (which follows *Rambam*), the mishnah

מִין – בֵּית שַׁמַּאי אוֹמְרִים: שְׁלֹשָׁה תְלָמִים שֶׁל
פָּתִיחַ. וּבֵית הִלֵּל אוֹמְרִים: מְלֹא הָעֹל הַשָּׁרוֹנִי.
וּקְרוֹבִין דִּבְרֵי אֵלּוּ לִהְיוֹת כְּדִבְרֵי אֵלּוּ.

does not specify any dimensions for these strips, but rather discusses the gap which must be left between them. [Nevertheless, *Chazon Ish* (5:18) maintains that the strips must be a minimum of six handbreadths wide.]

According to *Rash*, the mishnah deals exclusively with the dimensions of the planted strips. There is no requirement to distance the strips from one another.

We have followed the majority opinion in rendering מֶשֶׁר as *strip*. *Aruch* (s.v. משר) records a second interpretation which derives this word from a root meaning to soak (see *Numbers* 6:3) and explains it to mean an area which retains water. R' *Shlomo Sirilio* adopts this definition and explains that an area which the farmer surrounded with a small ridge for water retention was considered distinct from its surroundings. Thus, the mishnah is considering a field which was divided into numerous plots, each one delineated by a small water-retaining ridge (cf. *Kilei Zeraim*, p. 235).

בֵּית שַׁמַּאי אוֹמְרִים: שְׁלֹשָׁה תְלָמִים שֶׁל פָּתִיחַ. — Beis Shammai say: Three furrows of groundbreaking.

That is, the strips must be separated from one another by at least this amount (*Rav; Rambam Comm.*). Alternatively, this measure defines the width of the strips themselves such that even adjacent strips of the proper size may be planted with different species (*Rash*, first interpretation[1] of *Yerushalmi; Rosh*, first explanation; R' *Shlomo Sirilio; Gra, Shenos Eliyahu*).

Furrows of groundbreaking are fur-

rows made by plowing; the term פָּתִיחַ is derived from a verb found in *Isaiah* 28:24 ameaning *to plow* (*Rav; Rosh; Rash*). R' *Shlomo Sirilio* notes that the mishnah here speaks of *furrows of groundbreaking* in contrast with *furrows of the rain* of mishnah 3. The furrows of groundbreaking were produced by the first plowing in preparation for planting. Because the ground was still hard and dry at that time, the furrows of groundbreaking were even more widely spaced than the furrows of the rain which were the result of plowing after the first rainfall (see also *Kilei Zeraim*, pp. 209, 236; cf. *Meleches Shlomo*). In fact, *Ri ben Malki Tzedek* seems to understand the term פָּתִיחַ as meaning *wide open* (presumably from לפתוח, *to open*), a reference to the large spacing left between these furrows of groundbreaking. *Yerushalmi* indicates that three furrows of groundbreaking occupy two cubits (*Rav*).[2]

Rambam Comm. explains *furrows of groundbreaking* as cracks which develop naturally in the ground when it rains (see *Meleches Shlomo* from R' *Shlomo Sirilio* and see below, s.v. וקרובין).

וּבֵית הִלֵּל אוֹמְרִים: מְלֹא הָעֹל הַשָּׁרוֹנִי. — But Beis Hillel say: The full extent of the valley yoke.

The yoke used in lowlands[3] was larger than that used when plowing on an incline, and Beis Hillel use this larger yoke as a standard of measurement (*Rav; Rambam Comm.*). As the mishnah goes on to state, there is no substantial differ-

---

1. According to *Rash's* second interpretation of *Yerushalmi*, the mishnah indeed defines the width of the strips. However, *Yerushalmi* adds that these may not be planted adjacent to each other; rather, a gap of two cubits must be left between them.

2. According to *Rash's* second interpretation of *Yerushalmi*, the terms of the mishnah (*three furrows of groundbreaking, extent of the valley yoke*) are not explained.

3. We have rendered הָעֹל הַשָּׁרוֹנִי as *valley yoke* following *Rav* and *Rambam Comm. Rosh* takes שָׁרוֹן to be a place name (see also *Ri ben Malki Tzedek*).

every species — Beis Shammai say: Three furrows of groundbreaking. But Beis Hillel say: The full extent of the valley yoke. The opinion of these is close to being like the opinion of these.

ence between Beis Shammai and Beis Hillel, so that the *extent of the valley yoke* would also be approximately two cubits. *Yerushalmi* explains that the gaps between strips need not be two cubits wide

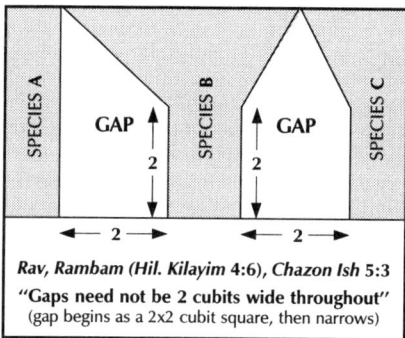

Rav, Rambam (Hil. Kilayim 4:6), Chazon Ish 5:3
"Gaps need not be 2 cubits wide throughout"
(gap begins as a 2x2 cubit square, then narrows)

throughout. Rather, as long as they start out as squares with sides of two cubits, the two edges may subsequently converge (see diagram above).

According to *Rash's* first interpretation of *Yerushalmi*, the strips of the mishnah are a minimum of two-by-two cubits (see diagram below). It is assumed that *the full extent of the valley yoke* is two cubits, that this defines both the minimum

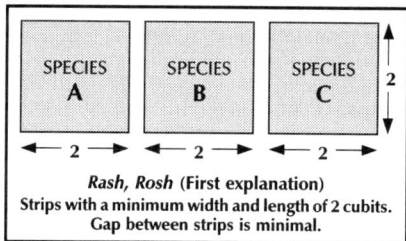

Rash, Rosh (First explanation)
Strips with a minimum width and length of 2 cubits.
Gap between strips is minimal.

length and width of the strips, and that no gap need be left between strips (see *Chazon Ish* 5:18).[1]

וּקְרוֹבִין דִּבְרֵי אֵלּוּ לִהְיוֹת כְּדִבְרֵי אֵלוּ. — *The opinion of these is close to being like the opinion of these.*

Ordinarily, whenever the opinion of Beis Shammai is more lenient than that of Beis Hillel, the matter is recorded in Tractate *Eduyos*. Since the present dispute is not listed there, this would indicate that the standard given here by Beis Hillel is somewhat smaller than that of Beis Shammai. Consequently, Beis Hillel's opinion is the more lenient (see *Tos. Yom Tov; Meleches Shlomo; Mishnah Rishonah*).

A similar dispute between Beis Shammai and Beis Hillel, upon which the mishnah comments *the opinion of these is close to being like the opinion of these*, may be found in *Sheviis* 1:1 (*Tos. R' Akiva*). [There, Beis Shammai set a time limit of *as long as it is good for the fruit*, while Beis Hillel say *until the festival of Shavuos*. That dispute is also not listed in *Eduyos*, and *Yerushalmi* (*Sheviis* 1:1) explains that this is because Beis Shammai's limit varies according to a natural phenomenon (rainfall). As such, it will sometimes be later than Beis Hillel's fixed limit (and hence more lenient) and sometimes earlier (and hence more stringent). It is of interest that according to *Rambam's* explanation of תְּלָמִים שֶׁל פֶּתִיחַ, the same argument may be applied to our mishnah. Here too, Beis Shammai refer to a natural phenomenon — the cracking of the ground by the rain. Since the spacing between such cracks would hardly be uniform, it is likely that this will sometimes be wider than

1. According to his second interpretation, the exact value of *the full extent of the valley yoke* is not known, but in any event the strips of this size must be separated by a gap of two cubits. From *Rash* it appears that the gaps must have a base and an altitude of two cubits; they need not start out as squares (see diagram).

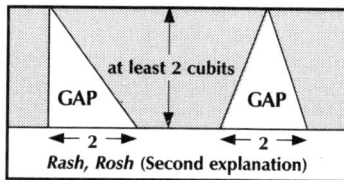

Rash, Rosh (Second explanation)

[ז] הָיָה רֹאשׁ תּוֹר חִטִּים נִכְנָס בְּתוֹךְ שֶׁל שְׂעוֹרִים – מֻתָּר, מִפְּנֵי שֶׁהוּא נִרְאֶה כְּסוֹף שָׂדֵהוּ.

שֶׁלּוֹ חִטִּים וְשֶׁל חֲבֵירוֹ מִין אַחֵר, מֻתָּר לִסְמוֹךְ לוֹ מֵאוֹתוֹ הַמִּין.

יד אברהם

Beis Hillel's fixed measure (*the full extent of the valley yoke*) and sometimes narrower. Accordingly, this dispute is not listed in *Eduyos*

where only those disputes in which Beis Shammai's view is consistently more lenient are recorded.]

7.

הָיָה רֹאשׁ תּוֹר חִטִּים נִכְנָס בְּתוֹךְ שֶׁל שְׂעוֹרִים – — *[If] a rosh tor of wheat protruded into a barley [field]* —

The expression תּוֹר רֹאשׁ, *rosh tor*, is somewhat obscure. *Rav* follows *Rambam Comm.* in explaining תּוֹר to be a triangular ornament (see *Song of Songs* 1:11), the points of which were called heads. This term was used in a borrowed sense with reference to corners in general, and consequently, the corner of a wheat field which protruded into a barley field would be known as a *rosh tor*.

According to the above explanation, it is not entirely clear that the case involves a corner of a wheat field that actually entered into a barley field. From *Rambam* (Hil. Kilayim 3:18) it seems that the tip of the wheat field touched the edge of the barley field, but did not actually penetrate into it [see diagram (A)] (*Tos. Anshei Shem*; see *Rambam Comm.*, *Kafich* ed.).

Rash, following *Ri ben Malki Tzedek*, relates תּוֹר to the word שׁוּרָה which means line.[1] Accordingly, *Rash* explains the case here as involving two fields side by side, one of wheat and the other of barley. The last row of the wheat field extends into the barley field, and this formation is what the mishnah refers to as תּוֹר רֹאשׁ [see diagram (B)].

Rosh has yet a different interpretation. After a farmer put down seed in his field, he would cover it by plowing (*Shabbos*

73b; see *Minchas Yitzchak* to *Tosefta* 2:2). This procedure, however, involved a certain difficulty. If a farmer plowed a furrow from east to west for example, as he approached the western edge of his field, he would make a U-turn in order to plow a parallel furrow from west to east. Occasionally, the farmer might make his U-turn only after crossing the edge of the field. Thus, seeds would be carried across the border of the field into the neighboring field. Now, *Rosh* defines the term רֹאשׁ תּוֹר as meaning the head of an ox (תּוֹר = שׁוֹר) and explains that the shape of the furrow formed at the U-turn resembles the head of an ox. Accordingly, the mishnah permits the farmer to cover his wheat seeds by plowing even though this might carry some wheat seeds into the neighboring barley field. Although the furrows actually protrude into the neighboring field, their continuity with their field of origin makes them distinct [see diagram (C)]. [It is of interest that *Rosh's* interpretation seems to have support in *Tosefta* 2:2.]

מֻתָּר, מִפְּנֵי שֶׁהוּא נִרְאֶה כְּסוֹף שָׂדֵהוּ. — *this is permitted, since it looks like the end of his field.*

Planting in a *rosh tor* formation is allowed, since it is clear that the barley and wheat were not planted together (*Rav*). Instead, it is obvious to the observer that the wheat which protrudes into the barley

1. It is common for שׁ to be interchanged with ת.

7. **[I**f] a *rosh tor* of wheat protruded into a barley [field] — this is permitted, since it looks like the end of his field.

[If] his [field] was wheat and his friend's was a different species, he is permitted to bring close to it that species.

YAD AVRAHAM

field was not planted as part of that field, but belongs instead to the neighboring wheat field. This is because *it looks like the end of his field* of wheat (*Rosh; Rash*).

Tos. Yom Tov contends that the lenient attitude evident in this mishnah is due to the fact that in the worst case it is only a Rabbinic prohibition that is involved, and not a Biblical one. This follows his position in mishnah 1:9 that under Torah law *only* simultaneously planting the seeds of two species *together* is forbidden. Accordingly, planting wheat next to an existing barley field is at most Rabbinically prohibited.

However, as explained in our commentary to mishnah 1:9, *Rambam's* position would seem to be otherwise. Consequently, the lenience reflected in this mishnah must be rooted in different considerations. In particular, even though planting of wheat next to already growing barley may be forbidden by the Torah, this is only so where the different kinds appear jumbled. But where one kind is visibly distinct from the other, such as here where the wheat is clearly associated with a separate field, there is no problem (*Rambam Comm.* 3:1).

שֶׁלּוֹ חִטִּים וְשֶׁל חֲבֵירוֹ מִין אַחֵר, מֻתָּר לְסָמוֹךְ לוֹ מֵאוֹתוֹ הַמִּין. — *[If] his [field] was wheat and his friend's was a different species, he is permitted to bring close to it that species.*

If Reuven's wheat field included an unplanted area adjacent to the border with Shimon's barley field, it is permitted for Reuven to plant this area with barley, and there is no need to leave a gap between the barley section of his field and the wheat section. Ordinarily, a person is not allowed to have more than one species growing in the same field without due separation. In the present case, however, the barley appears as though it is part of

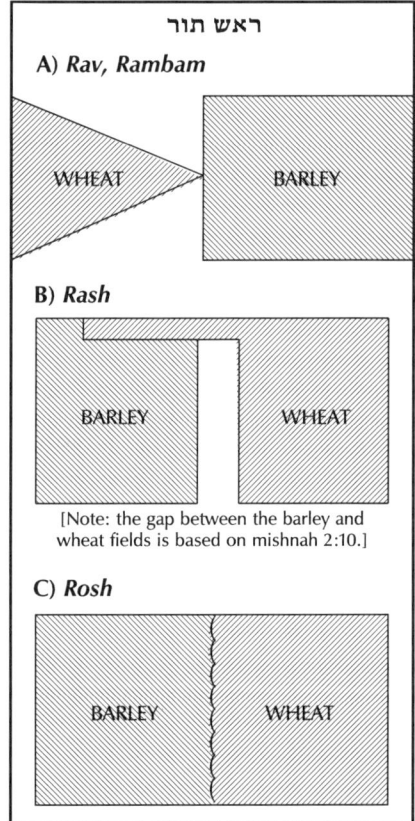

ראש תור

A) *Rav, Rambam*

WHEAT   BARLEY

B) *Rash*

BARLEY   WHEAT

[Note: the gap between the barley and wheat fields is based on mishnah 2:10.]

C) *Rosh*

BARLEY   WHEAT

Shimon's field, and not part of Reuven's. As Shimon's field, it would be permitted to be in close proximity with Reuven's (see below). Consequently, even though it is in fact in Reuven's field, the mere appearance of belonging to Shimon's field is sufficient to enable Reuven to plant barley in his own field and *bring it close to* his wheat (*Rav; Rash,* second explanation).

The barley which Reuven plants in his field

שֶׁלּוֹ חִטִּים וְשֶׁל חֲבֵירוֹ חִטִּים, מֻתָּר לִסְמוֹךְ לוֹ תֶּלֶם
שֶׁל פִּשְׁתָּן, וְלֹא תֶלֶם שֶׁל מִין אַחֵר. רַבִּי שִׁמְעוֹן אוֹמֵר:
אֶחָד זֶרַע פִּשְׁתָּן, וְאֶחָד כָּל הַמִּינִין. רַבִּי יוֹסֵי אוֹמֵר:
אַף בְּאֶמְצַע שָׂדֵהוּ מֻתָּר לִבְדֹּק בְּתֶלֶם שֶׁל פִּשְׁתָּן.

יד אברהם

must be continuous with the barley in Shimon's field, since otherwise it would not appear to be part of Shimon's field. According to *Rambam (Comm.* and *Hil. Kilayim* 3:16), this is what the mishnah means by *he is permitted to bring close to it* (i.e. to Shimon's barley field) *that species* (i.e. barley). That is, Reuven may plant barley right next to the wheat in his own field, provided that he brings the barley close to Shimon's barley (*Tos. Yom Tov; see Rosh*, second explanation).

The reason that Shimon's barley field may be immediately adjacent to Reuven's wheat field with no separation at all is explained by *Rambam (Hil. Kilayim* 3:16) as implied in Scripture.[1] The Torah (*Lev.* 19:19) states: *Your field you shall not sow* kilayim. This is understood to teach that a person cannot have two species growing without separation in his own field, but if one species is growing in his field and a second one is growing in his neighbor's, the two crops can be in close proximity. The present mishnah takes this idea even further and permits two species in close proximity in one person's field, provided that it appears as though the two crops are in separately owned fields.

Ri ben Malki Tzedek has another interpretation of the mishnah which corresponds to the first explanation given by *Rash* and *Rosh*. This is that the mishnah discusses the possibility of Reuven extending his wheat right up to the border between his property and Shimon's barley field. According to this explanation, the mishnah does not permit Reuven to plant barley in his own wheat field. It does, however, permit him to plant wheat in his own field right next to the barley in Shimon's field. The words of the mishnah are under-

stood as follows: *[If] his [field] was wheat and his friend's was a different species, he is permitted to bring close to it* (i.e. close to his friend's field) *that species* (i.e. wheat). *Rosh* notes, however, that the phrase *that species* does not seem to refer to the wheat of his own field.

שֶׁלּוֹ חִטִּים וְשֶׁל חֲבֵירוֹ חִטִּים, מֻתָּר לִסְמוֹךְ לוֹ — תֶּלֶם שֶׁל פִּשְׁתָּן, וְלֹא תֶלֶם שֶׁל מִין אַחֵר. *[If] his [field] was wheat and his friend's was wheat, it is permitted to bring close to it a furrow of flax, but not a furrow of a different species.*

Yerushalmi explains that the flax is being planted in order to test whether or not this particular field is suitable for flax growing. Strictly speaking, such planting should not be restricted by the laws of *kilayim* (see *Rambam, Hil. Kilayim* 3:17; *Rosh; Tos. Yom Tov*). However, an outside observer might not realize the purpose of the planting, so that to him two species in the same field would appear as a forbidden mingling of plants even though one species was planted merely as a test. To dispel such notions, the *Tanna Kamma* imposed three limitations on testing in fields with a different species already growing: (1) that such tests be conducted only with flax; (2) that the test planting not exceed a single furrow; and (3) that the test furrow be located at the edge of the field. In the *Tanna Kamma's* opinion, these precautions suffice to remove any suspicion that a violation has been committed. This is because a single furrow of flax is useless for any purpose other than testing (*Rambam Comm.* and

---

1. *Chazon Ish* (5:11) finds *Rambam's* reason to be difficult. He contends that *Ravad* rejects it and requires a separation even between fields belonging to different people. Moreover, he suggests a novel interpretation of both *Rash* and *Rosh* (and presumably *Rav* as well) according to which they too require a separation between diverse species growing in different people's fields!

[If] his [field] was wheat and his friend's was wheat, it is permitted to bring close to it a furrow of flax, but not a furrow of a different species. R' Shimon says: As with flax plants, so with all the species. R' Yose says: Even in the middle of his field he is permitted to check with a furrow of flax.

YAD AVRAHAM

Hil. Kilayim 3:16)[1] or, alternatively, because flax was harmful to grain and would not be planted near grain except as a test (Rosh). The requirement to locate the test furrow at the edge of the field was imposed as an additional precaution, since even a single furrow of flax could arouse suspicions if it were seen growing in the middle of a field of wheat.

Note that according to Rosh the Tanna Kamma's permission is based on the fact that flax damages grain. Presumably, then, to test a furrow of flax in a field with a crop not harmed by flax would not be permitted. According to Rambam, however, the permission is based on the fact that a single furrow of flax is useless except as a test. In that case, testing with flax should be permitted regardless of the other crop in the field.

It might also be noted that Rosh does not specify a single furrow of flax as the maximum test quantity. It is possible that in his opinion there is no such limitation, and the mishnah speaks of a furrow simply as an illustration.

רַבִּי שִׁמְעוֹן אוֹמֵר: אֶחָד זֶרַע פִּשְׁתָּן, וְאֶחָד כָּל הַמִּינִין. — R' Shimon says: As with flax plants, so with all the species.

Rav, following Rambam Comm., understands R' Shimon as forbidding testing with all species. Just as other species may not be tested in a field with another crop, so also flax may not be tested.

However, the bulk of the major commentators assume R' Shimon to be expressing a lenient opinion. Just as testing is permitted with flax — as stated by the Tanna Kamma — so too is it permitted with all species (Ri ben Malki Tzedek;

Rash; Rosh; R' Shlomo Sirilio; see Tif. Yis. and Mishnah Rishonah). Despite his lenience, however, R' Shimon agrees that a test furrow may only be planted at the edge of a field, and not in the middle (Rosh).

Rash explains that R' Shimon's lenience is due to the fact that the test furrow is planted on the border between fields belonging to two different people. Although a person cannot plant a test furrow at the edge of his field if he has another crop growing in the neighboring field, he may plant a test furrow at the edge of a field if the adjacent field is barren. Indeed, it is for this reason that the mishnah speaks of his ... and his friend's fields, since only when a test furrow will be sandwiched between two crops is there a question about its permissibility. However, if the test furrow will not be sandwiched, then all agree that it may be planted of any species (Chazon Ish 5:12; cf. Radbaz, Hil. Kilayim 3:17). Following this premise, R' Shimon argues that only sandwiching between two of a person's own crops will forbid planting a test furrow. But if a test furrow is located such that it is sandwiched by the owner's crop on one side and the neighbor's on the other, there are no restrictions. This is because another person's field does not count towards the forbidden "sandwich" and is thus regarded as though it were a barren field. But where a test furrow will be flanked on one side by a barren field, all testing is permitted. Accordingly, R' Shimon permits testing of all species in a furrow sandwiched on one side by the owner's field and on the other by the neighbor's field.

רַבִּי יוֹסֵי אוֹמֵר: אַף בְּאֶמְצַע שָׂדֵהוּ מֻתָּר לִבְדֹּק בְּתֶלֶם שֶׁל פִּשְׁתָּן. — R' Yose says: Even in the middle of his field he is permitted to

1. Rambam does not specify any size for the single furrow of flax. However, in Tosefta 2:4 two opinions are found. The Sages require the furrow to span the field from one end to the other, while R' Elazar and Abba Yose consider a fifty-cubit-long furrow as sufficient.

אֵין [ח] סוֹמְכִין לִשְׂדֵה תְבוּאָה חַרְדָּל וְחָרִיעַ.

יד אברהם

check with a furrow of flax.

R' Yose maintains that a furrow of flax even in the middle of one's field is not suspicious looking since everyone will realize that it has been planted merely in order to test the field. Accordingly, he permits checking with a furrow of flax anywhere in a field (*Rav; Rosh; Rash*). He agrees

with the *Tanna Kamma*, however, that testing is permitted only with flax (*Rosh*). Thus, according to R' Yose, it is permitted to plant a test furrow at the edge of a field or in the middle of a field even though the furrow will be "sandwiched" by another crop; however, as stated by the *Tanna Kamma*, such testing is limited to flax.

8.

אֵין סוֹמְכִין לִשְׂדֵה תְבוּאָה חַרְדָּל וְחָרִיעַ. — *It is not permitted [to grow] mustard or safflower close to a field of grain.*

Because these two plants damage grain, it is assumed that no farmer would allow a neighbor's safflower or mustard crop to come into close proximity with his own grain crop. Therefore, if a field contains mustard or safflower growing next to grain, an observer assumes that this was entirely the doing of one farmer. But in that case, the farmer will be suspected of illegally having *kilayim* in his field. Accordingly, the mishnah teaches that it is forbidden to grow mustard or safflower close to a field of grain (*Rav*).

Rav's explanation is vigorously challenged by *Tos. Yom Tov*. In the previous mishnah, two cases were considered in which it is permitted for a person to have more than one species growing within the same field. These are: (1) where the second species is the same as that in the neighbor's field and thus appears to be a continuation of the neighbor's crop; and (2) where the second species was planted along the edge of the field as a test. Now, in the latter case, the *Tanna Kamma* of the previous mishnah (whose view is accepted) permits testing only with flax and not with any other species. This implies that other species can never be grown inside a field of grain. Yet, according to *Rav* the present mishnah prohibits growing only mustard and safflower alongside grain, which implies that other species may be planted next to grain! On the other hand, to suppose that the case here involves mustard or safflower being planted where it appears to be a continuation of a neighbor's mustard

or safflower field is equally untenable. This is because the wording of the mishnah, *it is not permitted [to grow] mustard or safflower close to a field of grain* (rather than *his field of grain*), seems to mean that both the farmer's own field as well as his neighbor's field are grain fields (see *Rambam, Hil. Kilayim* 3:18 and see *Shoshanim LeDavid*). To overcome these objections, *Tos. Yom Tov* proposes that it is permitted for Reuven to plant a species inside Shimon's field which is different from Shimon's crop. He contends that the Torah only prohibits Shimon himself from planting two diverse crops in his field. However, Reuven is permitted to plant a diverse crop in Shimon's field. With reference to this, the mishnah states that although Reuven may plant a diverse species in Shimon's field, he cannot plant mustard or safflower in Shimon's grain field. This is because these plants would be assumed by the observer to have been planted next to the grain by Shimon himself, and thus create suspicion that Shimon has committed an infraction of the law. *Tos. Yom Tov* acknowledges, however, that this explanation of *Rav* seems strained.

A number of commentators suggest that *Rav* understood the mishnah as relating to the law that adjacent fields of different owners are not *kilayim* with each other (*Rambam, Hil. Kilayim* 3:16; see previous mishnah). Although in general the crop in one person's field does not restrict another person from planting whatever he wants in his own field, the case of mustard and safflower is different. This is because the normal assumption is that a person will not tolerate *someone else's* mustard or safflower next to his grain. Thus, if Reuven planted his field with grain, and if Shimon were then to plant his own

8. **I**t is not permitted [to grow] mustard or safflower close to a field of grain. However, it is permitted

YAD AVRAHAM

side of the border between their fields with mustard or safflower, the passerby would assume that both crops belong to Reuven, who would then be suspected of illegally growing *kilayim*. Consequently, the mishnah states that *it is not permitted [to grow] mustard or safflower close to* [someone else's] *field of grain* (see *Chiddushei R' Yoel Chasid, Beis David, Mishnas Chachamim*; see also *Tos. Anshei Shem* from *Radbaz*).

[It should be noted that *Tos. Yom Tov's* reasons for rejecting the possibility that the neighbor's adjacent field contained a mustard or safflower crop are not entirely convincing. Moreover, a close reading of *Rambam Comm.* would certainly seem to indicate that this indeed is the case of the mishnah. Accordingly, the law being considered is the earlier one in the previous mishnah, viz. that if Reuven's field contains one crop and Shimon's another, the gap between Shimon's crop and the border between the fields may be planted with Reuven's crop. Although this means that Shimon will have two diverse species growing side-by-side in the same field, this is permitted, since the observer will assume that the second species is part of Reuven's field, and between fields of two owners there is no *kilayim*. The present mishnah adds one qualification: If Reuven's field is mustard or safflower and Shimon's is grain, Shimon may not plant mustard or safflower next to his grain as if a continuation of Reuven's mustard or safflower. This is because these varieties damage grain and would not be tolerated so close by, unless planted by the same person. Consequently, the observer will realize that the mustard or safflower belongs to Shimon, the owner of the grain, and thus the permissive mechanism employed by the previous mishnah (that the observer will assume the second species to belong to the neighbor) is not present. Accordingly, the mishnah teaches that *it is not permitted [to grow] mustard or safflower close to a field of grain*, as a continuation of the neighbor's mustard or safflower field (see *Chiddushei R' Eliyahu Guttmacher*).]

Rosh has a different interpretation of the mishnah based on the assumption that mustard or safflower do *not* damage

grain. The setting of the mishnah is where Reuven and Shimon have adjacent grain fields, and the issue in question is whether or not it is permitted, say, for Reuven to plant a furrow of mustard or safflower along the border between the fields. In the previous mishnah it was taught that a test furrow of flax could be planted there. However, that was because a single furrow of flax is useless and because flax damages grain (see previous mishnah). Thus, planting a furrow of flax between grain fields is obviously for testing and is not prohibited by the laws of *kilayim*. However, a similar furrow of mustard or safflower will not be automatically assumed to be a test, since even a single furrow of these species is useful and since these do not damage grain. Thus, an observer will not realize that they have been planted there as a test and will instead suspect the farmer of having committed an infraction. Accordingly, the mishnah outlaws planting even a single furrow of mustard or safflower between one person's grain field and his neighbor's.

According to *Rosh's* explanation, the first law of our mishnah is merely an illustration of the law already stated in the previous mishnah that *it is permitted to bring close to it a furrow of flax, but not a furrow of a different species*. It is recorded here as a preface to the novel second law of our mishnah, that *it is permitted [to grow] mustard or safflower close to a field of greens* (*Kesef Mishneh* to *Hil. Kilayim* 3:18 from *Mahari Korkus*; *Tif. Yis., Boaz* §8).

R' Yehosef Ashkenazi, quoted by *Meleches Shlomo*, suggests another approach to the relationship between our mishnah and the previous one. He contends that the setting for the present mishnah is a field of grain which is not adjacent to any other field. In such a case, he argues, planting a test furrow of any species will be permitted at the edge of the field, since only where a test furrow is sandwiched between two crops are there any restrictions (see previous mishnah from *Chazon Ish* 5:12). However, mustard or safflower cannot be

אֲבָל סוֹמְכִין לְשָׂדֶה יְרָקוֹת חַרְדָּל וְחָרִיעַ.
וְסוֹמֵךְ לַבּוּר, וְלַנִּיר, וְלַגָּפָה, וְלַדֶּרֶךְ, וְלַגָּדֵר

יד אברהם

tested even in such a situation and this is the law stated here by the mishnah. Thus, the previous mishnah concerns planting test furrows in between two fields and this is forbidden for all species but flax, while the present mishnah concerns planting a test furrow at the edge of a field which is not adjacent to any other crop, and this is permitted except with mustard or safflower. [R' Yehosef does not suggest any reasons for the stringency in the case of mustard or safflower (see *Kilei Zeraim*, p. 259).]

אֲבָל סוֹמְכִין לְשָׂדֶה יְרָקוֹת חַרְדָּל וְחָרִיעַ. — *However, it is permitted [to grow] mustard or safflower close to a field of greens.*

Mustard and safflower do not damage greens and hence a person does not care if someone else's mustard or safflower plants are close to his own greens. Accordingly, if the grain of the preceding case is substituted by greens, it is permitted to have safflower or mustard next to it since an observer will assume the mustard or safflower to belong to someone other than the owner of the greens (*Rav*).

Rosh, as above, assumes the opposite — i.e. that mustard and safflower *do* damage greens. Because of this, a furrow of mustard or safflower between two fields of greens is treated just like a furrow of flax between two fields of grain. In both cases, because the test furrow damages the main crop, the purpose of its planting is apparent to all and is thus not suspicious. It is therefore permitted.[1]

וְסוֹמֵךְ לַבּוּר, וְלַנִּיר, — *It is permitted to*

grow [a diverse kind] close to a barren spot, to plowed terrain,

If any of these phenomena interrupt a field, it is permitted to plant a different species on each side of the interruption (*Rosh; Rambam, Hil. Kilayim* 3:15; see *Rav, Rash, Ri ben Malki Tzedek*).

Rambam Comm. relates this part of the mishnah to the previous discussion concerning mustard or safflower. Although it was stated above that mustard or safflower cannot be brought close to grain, this does not apply if the two are separated by any of the phenomena listed here. According to this explanation, it would seem that the present rule cannot be generally applied to permit planting different species on opposite sides of such interruptions. See also *Meleches Shlomo*.

The *barren spot* and *plowed terrain*[2] are both unplanted areas. *Rav* (following *Rosh, Rash,* and *Ri ben Malki Tzedek*) stipulates that to constitute a valid interruption, these must be at least a *beis rova* in size.[3] This is the separation required by mishnah 10, below, between two fields of grain; between two fields of greens, a separation of six handbreadths suffices. The point of our mishnah is that regardless of whether the separation between the species is barren land or plowed land which will eventually be used for planting, an empty slot of sufficient size constitutes a separation enabling planting of different species on opposite sides (*Chazon Ish* 6:5).

Rambam (Comm. and *Hil. Kilayim* 3:15) specifies no dimensions for the *barren spot* etc. of the mishnah. Possibly in his opinion it

---

1. *Rambam* (*Hil. Kilayim* 3:18), according to the standard texts, seems to agree with *Rosh* in viewing mustard and safflower as damaging to greens but not to grain. However, in his *Comm.*, *Rambam* states the reverse. Many authorities suggest a textual emendation of the wording in *Hil. Kilayim* to make it consistent with the position in the commentary, and it should be noted that such a correction would appear to have support from *Mahari Beirav* and *Radbaz* who refer to *Rambam Comm.* in their commentaries to *Hil. Kilayim* 3:18, yet fail to note any discrepancy between the two!

2. It was common to revitalize a field by plowing it regularly over a period of time during which it was intentionally left unplanted. See *Tosefta, Bava Metzia* 9:7 (*Kilei Zeraim*, p. 269).

3. I.e. approximately ten-and-a-half by ten-and-a-half cubits. See above, mishnah 1.

[to grow] mustard or safflower close to a field of greens.
It is permitted to grow [a diverse kind] close to a
barren spot, to plowed terrain, to a stone wall, to a road,

YAD AVRAHAM

is permitted to plant diverse species on opposite sides of these phenomena even if they do not satisfy the spacing criteria of mishnah 10. This suggests an important distinction between planting on opposite sides of a gap intentionally left unplanted (the rule of mishnah 10), and planting on opposite sides of the various phenomena listed in our mishnah. Leaving unplanted spaces as prescribed in mishnah 10 makes it permissible for the borders between fields of different species to approach each other beyond the separation; things planted on opposite sides of the separators of our mishnah cannot approach each other beyond the separator. That is, the diverse species can be brought close to the separator, but not to each other (see *Rambam, Hil. Kilayim* 3:9, 16 and *Chazon Ish* 6:16, 5:3; cf. *Tif. Yis.* and see below, mishnah 10). The reason for this distinction is that leaving a gap unplanted because it is not suitable for planting does not show that the farmer views the crops on opposite sides of the gap as belonging to distinct fields. Directly opposite the gap, different species may be grown since they do not appear mixed when so positioned. But, beyond the gap there is nothing to indicate that they are separate fields, and hence they cannot be brought close together. On the other hand, if arable soil is left untilled, it is clear that this is an intentional gap that has been left in order to define the fields. Accordingly, even beyond the space the borders of the fields can approach one another [see diagram].

Radbaz (Hil. Kilayim 3:15) reads בור of the mishnah as בור, i.e. a pit. He explains that a pit must be four handbreadths wide and ten handbreadths deep to constitute an interruption, but this is not specified by the mishnah since these are the standard dimensions of a pit. Additionally, *Radbaz* maintains that the *plowed terrain* refers to a four-handbreadth-wide strip, and not to the *beis rova* of mishnah 10.

וְלַגָּפָה, וְלַדֶּרֶךְ, — *to a stone wall, to a road,*

If either a stone wall or a road divides a field in two, it is permitted to plant one species on one side and a different species

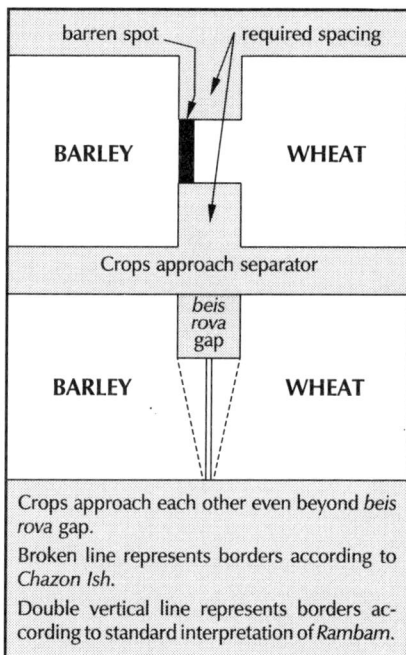

Crops approach each other even beyond *beis rova* gap.

Broken line represents borders according to *Chazon Ish.*

Double vertical line represents borders according to standard interpretation of *Rambam.*

on the other side (*Rav; Rosh; Rash*).

Rav (following *Rosh, Rash,* and *Ri ben Malki Tzedek*) defines גָּפָה as a wall constructed of stones which rest on each other without cement (cf. *Rambam Comm.* to *Peah* 6:2 and *Rashi* to *Bava Metzia* 25b).

The term דֶּרֶךְ is understood as referring even to a private road (*Rav; Rash*), which is normally four cubits wide (*Rosh;* see *Peah* 2:1). Certainly a public road which is sixteen cubits wide (see *Peah* ibid.) would also count as a separator (*Ri ben Malki Tzedek; R' Shlomo Sirilio; Tif. Yis.*).

Tif. Yis. (§55) contends that the uncemented *stone wall* of the mishnah, unlike the cemented *wall* mentioned below, does not need to be ten handbreadths high. This is because an uncemented wall will normally be much thicker than a cemented wall (cf. *Derech Emunah* 3:79 from *Chazon Ish*).

שֶׁהוּא גָבֹהַּ עֲשָׂרָה טְפָחִים, וְלֶחָרִיץ שֶׁהוּא עָמֹק עֲשָׂרָה וְרָחָב אַרְבָּעָה, וְלָאִילָן שֶׁהוּא מֵסֵךְ עַל הָאָרֶץ, וְלַסֶּלַע שֶׁהוּא גָבֹהַּ עֲשָׂרָה וְרָחָב אַרְבָּעָה.

[ט] הָרוֹצֶה לַעֲשׂוֹת שָׂדֵהוּ קָרַחַת קָרַחַת מִכָּל מִין, עוֹשֶׂה עֶשְׂרִים וְאַרְבָּעָה קָרָחוֹת לְבֵית סְאָה — מִקָּרַחַת לְבֵית רֹבַע — וְזוֹרֵעַ בְּתוֹכָהּ כָּל מִין שֶׁיִּרְצֶה. הָיְתָה

יד אברהם

וְלָאִילָן שֶׁהוּא מֵסֵךְ עַל הָאָרֶץ, וְלַסֶּלַע שֶׁהוּא גָבֹהַּ עֲשָׂרָה וְרָחָב אַרְבָּעָה. — *to a tree which covers the ground, and to a rock ten high and four wide.*

If the branches of a tree reach to within three handbreadths of the ground, they count as a wall and separate the area under the branches from that outside them. Accordingly, it is permitted to plant one species under the branches, and another outside them (*Rav; Rosh; Rash*).

A rock which is ten handbreadths high is the optimal divider. The mishnah lists it

וְלַגָּדֵר שֶׁהוּא גָבֹהַּ עֲשָׂרָה טְפָחִים, — *to a wall ten handbreadths high,*

This is a regular cemented wall (*Tif. Yis.*). The mishnah specifies the height as ten handbreadths but makes no mention of the length or thickness of the wall. *Rash* (s.v. ולסלע) argues that the length of the wall must be at least four handbreadths, but its thickness can be minimal.

From many of the classical commentaries, as well as the Parma ms. of *Rav*, it is clear that their texts of the mishnah read: *to a road, to a stone wall, to a wall ten handbreadths high* (i.e. the order of the list is changed so that *stone wall* and *wall* are adjacent). This would suggest that the qualification *ten handbreadths high* refers to the uncemented *stone wall* as well (cf. *Tif. Yis.* §55).

וְלֶחָרִיץ שֶׁהוּא עָמֹק עֲשָׂרָה וְרָחָב אַרְבָּעָה, — *to a ditch which is ten [handbreadths] deep and four wide,*

Even if the ditch is several cubits long, it constitutes a separation only if it is four handbreadths wide (*Rosh; Rash*). Unlike a wall, a ditch narrower than four handbreadths does not appear to separate (*Tos. Yom Tov*, s.v. ולסלע; see *Rosh*). Although walls have no width requirements in order to constitute separators, they must be at least four handbreadths long (*Rash*). Presumably, a ditch must also be at least four handbreadths long in order to count as a separator (see *Tziyun HaHalachah* 3:165).

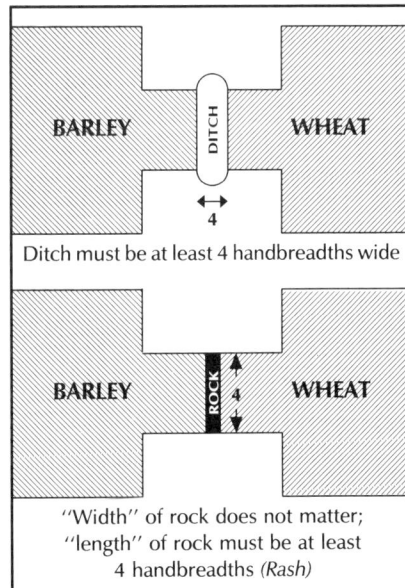

Ditch must be at least 4 handbreadths wide

"Width" of rock does not matter; "length" of rock must be at least 4 handbreadths (*Rash*)

to a wall ten handbreadths high, to a ditch which is ten [handbreadths] deep and four wide, to a tree which covers the ground, and to a rock ten high and four wide.

9. **[** **I**f] someone wants to make his field into squares of every species, he can make twenty-four squares in a *beis se'ah* — each square is a *beis rova* — and he can plant inside it any species he wants. [If] there were

YAD AVRAHAM

explicitly to stress that even this must be *four* [handbreadths] *wide* if it is to function as a separator in the context of *kilayim* (*Rav; Rosh; Rash*).

The phrase *four wide* used above concerning *a ditch* refers to the dimension which is perpendicular to the edges of the crops (see diagram facing page). It is not entirely clear what its meaning is in the present context. *Rash* explains that the *length* of the rock (i.e. the dimension parallel to the edges of the facing crops) must be four handbreadths just as in the case of a wall. Similarly, the width is treated no differently than the width of a wall and hence has no restrictions. According to *Rash* then, the phrase *four wide* is used differ-

ently here than above. On the other hand, *Tos. Yom Tov* quotes *R' Eliyahu of London* who assumes that here too the dimension addressed is the width of the rock. He maintains that man-made walls can serve as separators even if they are of minimal width since they were constructed for this purpose. But, a natural "wall," such as *the rock* under discussion, is not considered a separator unless it is four handbreadths wide. In his view, the phrase *four wide* has the same meaning throughout our mishnah. The various merits of each approach have been extensively discussed by the commentators. See especially *Tos. R' Akiva; Tif.Yis., Boaz* §10 and *Ohr Gadol* to 2:8 and to 4:4.

9.

הָרוֹצֶה לַעֲשׂוֹת שָׂדֵהוּ קָרַחַת קָרַחַת מִכָּל מִין, — *[If] someone wants to make his field into squares of every species,*

A cleared square of land is referred to by the mishnah as קָרַחַת (*Rav* from *Rash* and *Rambam Comm.*). In the mishnah's case, a person has a square field of fifty-by-fifty cubits (i.e. a *beis se'ah*) which he wishes to divide into square (or almost square — see below) patches, each planted with a different species. These patches are still referred to as קָרַחַת even after planting (*Tos. Yom Tov*).

עוֹשֶׂה עֶשְׂרִים וְאַרְבָּעָה קְרָחוֹת לְבֵית סְאָה — מִקְּרַחַת לְבֵית רֹבַע — וְזוֹרֵעַ בְּתוֹכָה כָּל מִין שֶׁיִּרְצֶה. — *he can make twenty-four squares in a beis se'ah — each square is a beis rova — and he can plant inside it any species he wants.*

I.e. a field with an area of a *beis se'ah*

can be broken up into twenty-four squares each with an area of a *beis rova*, and each of these squares can then be planted with a different species.

A *beis se'ah* is an area of 2,500 sq. cubits, and if a field of this size is square it will have sides of fifty cubits. A *beis rova* is an area equal to $\frac{1}{24}$ of a *beis se'ah* (approximately 104.2 sq. cubits). A square *beis rova* would have sides of approximately 10.2 cubits. It can readily be seen that a square with sides of fifty cubits cannot be broken down into twenty-four squares.

To overcome this problem, *Tos. Yom Tov* suggests that the קָרַחַת of the mishnah is not actually a square, but rather a rectangle of length 12.5 cubits and width 8.33 cubits. Arranging such rectangles in four rows of six produces a

קָרַחַת אַחַת אוֹ שְׁתַּיִם, זוֹרְעָם חַרְדָּל. שָׁלֹשׁ, לֹא
יִזְרַע חַרְדָּל, מִפְּנֵי שֶׁהִיא נִרְאֵית כִּשְׂדֵה
חַרְדָּל. דִּבְרֵי רַבִּי מֵאִיר. וַחֲכָמִים אוֹמְרִים: תֵּשַׁע
קָרָחוֹת מֻתָּרוֹת, עֶשֶׂר אֲסוּרוֹת. רַבִּי אֱלִיעֶזֶר בֶּן

יד אברהם

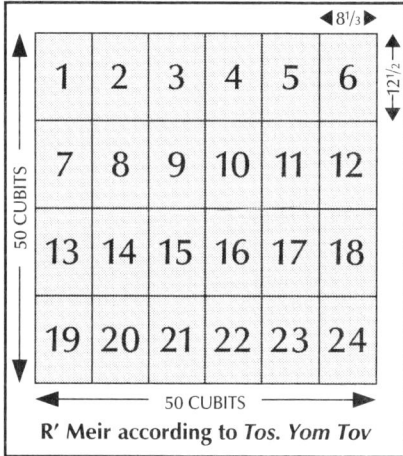

◀ 8¹/₃ ▶					
1	2	3	4	5	6
7	8	9	10	11	12
13	14	15	16	17	18
19	20	21	22	23	24

50 CUBITS / 50 CUBITS / 12½

R' Meir according to Tos. Yom Tov

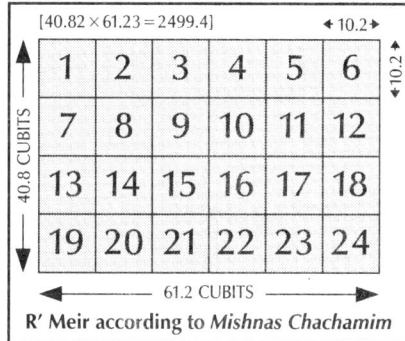

[40.82 × 61.23 = 2499.4]   ◀ 10.2 ▶

1	2	3	4	5	6
7	8	9	10	11	12
13	14	15	16	17	18
19	20	21	22	23	24

40.8 CUBITS / 61.2 CUBITS / 10.2

R' Meir according to Mishnas Chachamim

square *beis se'ah* (see diagram). It is difficult, however, to see why such rectangles would be described as squares (see *Rav* and *Rambam Comm.; Ri ben Malki Tzedek, Rash, Rosh* make no specification that the patches be square).

An alternative explanation is proposed by *Mishnas Chachamim* (see also *Chazon Ish* 6:8, s.v. והנה אין, and *Kilei Zeraim*, p. 282). Noting that *Rambam Comm.* to mishnah 2 (quoted there by *Tos. Yom Tov*) explains that any area of 2,500 sq. cubits *regardless of its shape* is referred to by the mishnah as a *beis se'ah*, he maintains that the קָרַחַת of the mishnah does in fact refer to square patches as emphasized by *Rav* and *Rambam Comm.* However, the *beis se'ah* referred to here by the mishnah is not a square *beis se'ah*, but rather a rectangular one. If squares with sides of 10.2 cubits (i.e. with an area of a *beis rova*) are arranged in four rows of six for example, the result will be a rectangle with an area of a *beis se'ah* (see diagram, next column).

Whatever the exact arrangement, the point of the mishnah is that in R' Meir's opinion, these patches can be planted with different species and no distancing or separations are required between them. In his opinion, the square shape of each patch serves to define it as distinct (*Rav; Rambam Comm.*). Additionally, the *beis rova* size of each patch is sufficiently large for each patch to be viewed as an independent field, and not merely as part of a larger field (*Rosh*; see also *Tif. Yis.* §61 and *Chazon Ish* 6:8).

הָיְתָה קָרַחַת אַחַת אוֹ שְׁתַּיִם, זוֹרְעָם חַרְדָּל. שָׁלֹשׁ, לֹא יִזְרַע חַרְדָּל, מִפְּנֵי שֶׁהִיא נִרְאֵית כִּשְׂדֵה חַרְדָּל. דִּבְרֵי רַבִּי מֵאִיר. — *[If] there were one or two squares, he can plant them with mustard. [If there were] three, he cannot plant [them] with mustard, because it looks like a field of mustard. This is the opinion of R' Meir.*

If a person has one or two bald adjacent squares inside his field of grain, he can plant them with mustard. If he has three such adjacent squares, he cannot plant them with mustard. Although R' Meir ordinarily regards a square *beis rova* as distinctive, he does not allow three or more such squares of mustard inside a grain field. This is because that much mustard is sufficient to be regarded as a full field of

one or two squares, he can plant them with mustard. [If there were] three, he cannot plant [them] with mustard, because it looks like a field of mustard. This is the opinion of R' Meir. But the Sages say: Nine squares are permitted, ten are forbidden. R' Eliezer ben

YAD AVRAHAM

mustard and so the impression created is that a mustard field has been planted inside a grain field (*Rav; Rosh; Rash*).

Rambam Comm. understands this statement by R' Meir as continuing the discussion of twenty-four squares in a *beis se'ah*. When R' Meir permits as many as twenty-four different species within a *beis se'ah*, this is because no single species can be said to characterize the *beis se'ah* as a whole. Thus, each individual square is viewed independently, and is not seen as *kilayim* with any other. However, if one species would be present in sufficient quantities to constitute a field of that species, then all the other squares would be viewed as *kilayim* with that field. Although R' Meir permits independent *beis rova* squares to be *adjacent* to one another, he does not permit a square of one species to be planted adjacent to a field of another (see *Rambam Comm.* 3:1). Now, ordinarily, three adjacent *beis rovas* of any crop are not viewed as an entire field of that crop. However, this is not true of mustard. Because of the limited quantities in which mustard was normally planted, even three adjacent *beis rova* squares constituted a field of mustard. Accordingly, R' Meir adds a qualification to his opening remarks, viz. that of the twenty-four squares in the *beis se'ah*, the farmer must be careful not to plant three adjacent ones with mustard (see *Tos. Anshei Shem* s.v. היתה).

וַחֲכָמִים אוֹמְרִים: תֵּשַׁע קְרָחוֹת מְתָּרוֹת, עֶשֶׂר אֲסוּרוֹת. — *But the Sages say: Nine squares are permitted, ten are forbidden.*

The Sages dispute R' Meir's contention that planted *beis rova* squares of different species can be adjacent. In their opinion, the planted squares must be equidistant from each other in a regular array, and

must be separated by unplanted squares approximately equal in size to the planted ones. These criteria allow for nine *beis rova* squares (with sides of 10.2 cubits) to fit into a *beis se'ah* (see following diagram). The distance between planted squares in any given row is 9.7 cubits, and this is also the distance between the planted rows (*Rav; Rambam Comm.*).

Rash (apparently followed by *Rosh*) has a slight variation on the above explanation. In his view, the planted *beis rovas* must be separated by empty areas also equaling a *beis rova* (see *Rash* to mishnah 8, s.v. סומך). However, this necessitates distributing the nine planted *beis rovas* in an area *larger* than the *beis se'ah* allotted by the mishnah (see *R' Shlomo Sirilio* and see *Kilei Zeraim*, p. 288).

Tos. Yom Tov questions why the Sages limit the number of planted squares to nine. By taking advantage of the *rosh tor* formation encountered in mishnah 7, it should be possible to plant as many as thirteen different species without contravening the laws for spacing between species (see diagram).

Tos. Yom Tov apparently understands the

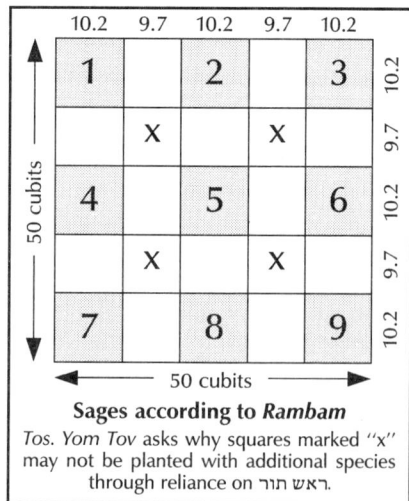

Sages according to *Rambam*

Tos. Yom Tov asks why squares marked "x" may not be planted with additional species through reliance on ראש תור.

יַעֲקֹב אוֹמֵר: אֲפִילוּ כָּל שָׂדֵהוּ בֵּית כּוֹר, לֹא יַעֲשֶׂה
בְּתוֹכָה חוּץ מִקָּרַחַת אַחַת.

[י] **כָּל** שֶׁהוּא בְּתוֹךְ בֵּית רֹבַע עוֹלֶה בְּמִדַּת בֵּית

יד אברהם

crux of the dispute between R' Meir and the Sages as relating to the spacing laws. R' Meir, either because he does not require spacing at all between planted areas of a given size or because he considers a square to be a distinctive shape and thus equivalent to spacing, does not require any spacing between squares here. The Sages, on the other hand, disagree with R' Meir's perspective on *beis rova* squares and they do require spacing. In that case, their arrangement of the planted squares is merely the result of correct application of the spacing laws, and hence, argues *Tos. Yom Tov*, one needs to explain why the *rosh tor* law does not apply.

However, from *Rambam Comm.* it appears that the Sages' positioning of the planted squares is not generated by the general spacing laws. On the contrary, according to *Rambam* the gap between planted squares here is only a square with sides of 9.7 cubits, not the *beis rova* square required by the spacing laws of mishnah 10! Evidently, the Sages permit specifically this array of nine squares of different species distributed inside a *beis se'ah* on the grounds that the equidistant spacing throughout the array makes the planted squares distinct. As long as this pattern is intact, the Sages do not insist on the normal spacing laws. But additional planted squares which destroy the pattern necessitate the spacing laws to be applied throughout the *beis se'ah*. Accordingly, additional squares cannot be added using the *rosh tor* mechanism, as this destroys the pattern (*Mishnas Chachamim*).

A different arrangement based on *Yerushalmi* (and adopted in the main by the later commentaries on *Yerushalmi*) is that proposed by *Ri ben Malki Tzedek*. A fifty-by-fifty-cubit *beis se'ah* is divided into twenty-five squares of ten-by-ten cubits, arranged in five rows of five squares. Planted squares are permitted to touch other planted squares at their corners (see above, mishnah 7) but not along

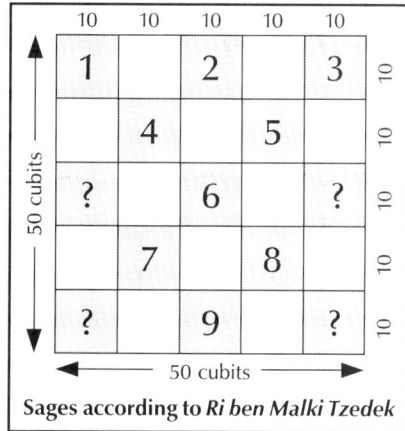

Sages according to **Ri ben Malki Tzedek**

their sides (see diagram). [It is not entirely clear why this approach does not permit planting of the squares marked with a question mark in the diagram (see *R' Shlomo Sirilio* and see *Pnei Moshe*). However, this seems to be the only arrangement which satisfies *Yerushalmi*'s description of the planted squares as an array of "three, two, one, two, one."]

Gra (*Shenos Eliyahu, Peirush HaAroch* and *Beurei HaGra* to *Yerushalmi*) understands the Sages as agreeing with R' Meir as far as permitting squares of different species to be adjacent (see diagram). Their dispute relates

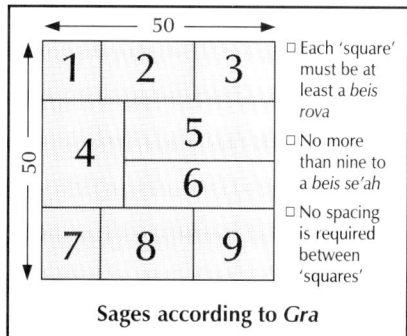

- Each 'square' must be at least a *beis rova*
- No more than nine to a *beis se'ah*
- No spacing is required between 'squares'

Sages according to **Gra**

Yaakov says: Even if his entire field is a *beis kor*, he cannot make in it more than one square.

10. **A**ll that is within a *beis rova* is counted in the measure of a *beis rova*. The work area of a

merely to the maximum number of different species which can be planted inside a limited area (i.e. a *beis se'ah*) without appearing like *kilayim*. The Sages maintain that more than nine species within a *beis se'ah* is not tolerable, and hence they state: *Nine squares are permitted, ten are forbidden.*[1]

רַבִּי אֱלִיעֶזֶר בֶּן יַעֲקֹב אוֹמֵר: אֲפִילוּ כָל שָׂדֵהוּ בֵּית כּוֹר, לֹא יַעֲשֶׂה בְתוֹכָה חוּץ מִקְּרַחַת אַחַת. — *R' Eliezer ben Yaakov says: Even if his entire field is a beis kor, he cannot make in it more than one square.*

A *beis kor* is equal to thirty *beis se'ahs*, i.e. 75,000 sq. cubits (*Rav; Rambam Comm.*). R' Eliezer ben Yaakov maintains that it is never permitted to grow more than a single square of a second species inside a field, regardless of the size of the field (*Rambam Comm.*). Presumably, the one square which R' Eliezer does permit cannot be entirely contained inside the larger crop, but can only be adjacent to it (*R' Shlomo Sirilio*). R' Eliezer's reasoning is not known (*Rav*).

10.

This mishnah, as understood by most of the early commentators, deals with the spacing laws: that is, the rules for the separation which must be left unplanted between different species. According to a second approach, however, there is no need to leave a separation between fields of different species, provided that the fields are a certain minimum size and shape.

כָּל שֶׁהוּא בְתוֹךְ בֵּית רֹבַע עוֹלֶה בְמִדַּת בֵּית רֹבַע. — *All that is within a beis rova is counted in the measure of a beis rova.*

If a *beis rova* which is left unplanted in order to separate two fields of different grains, for example, contains untillable sections, this does not matter. Even water-filled crevices which are totally unsuited for planting can be included in the *beis rova* (*Rav; Rosh; Rash; Ri ben Malki Tzedek; see Bava Basra 103a*).

Presumably, the crevices referred to by *Rav* et al. are not ten handbreadths deep and four wide. If they were, there would be no need for them to be counted as part of a *beis rova* separation, since they would independently

serve as separators, as taught in mishnah 8 (*Mishnah Rishonah*; see *Ri ben Malki Tzedek* who speaks of *small* crevices).

[Alternatively, the mishnah has to teach that even a ditch which is ten deep and four wide can be included in the measure of a *beis rova*. This is because the barriers listed in mishnah 8 are not as effective separators as the *beis rova* discussed here. The barriers listed in mishnah 8 allow planting of different species only directly opposite themselves, while the *beis rova* of our mishnah serves as an indicator that the two *fields* planted on opposite sides of it are entirely separate. Consequently, the borders of the fields beyond the *beis rova* separation may in fact be adjacent (see *Rambam, Hil. Kilayim* 3:9,15 and see above mishnah 8, s.v. וסומך).]

1. At first glance, *Gra's* explanation would seem to conflict with *Yerushalmi* which states that according to "the Rabbis" — presumably, a reference to the Sages of the mishnah — the planted squares of the mishnah may not be adjacent. However, it is likely that *Gra* understood "the Rabbis" to be a reference to *Amoraim* who contest *R' Chizkiya's* interpretation of the view of the Sages of the mishnah given earlier. *Gra* adopts *R' Chizkiya's* interpretation; that of "the Rabbis" conforms to the standard interpretation of the Sages' opinion.

רֹבַע. אֲכִילַת הַגֶּפֶן, וְהַקֶּבֶר, וְהַסֶּלַע עוֹלִין בְּמִדַּת
בֵּית רֹבַע.
תְּבוּאָה בִּתְבוּאָה — בֵּית רֹבַע; יָרָק בְּיָרָק —

יד אברהם

אֲכִילַת הַגֶּפֶן, וְהַקֶּבֶר, וְהַסֶּלַע עוֹלִין בְּמִדַּת בֵּית
רֹבַע. — *The work area of a grapevine, a grave, or a rock are counted in the measure of a beis rova.*

The area within six handbreadths of a grapevine which is needed when working the vine is referred to as אֲכִילַת הַגֶּפֶן, lit. *the area consumed by a grapevine* (*Rav; Rosh; Rash; Tos. Yom Tov*). *Yerushalmi* explains that the *Tanna* of our mishnah is R' Yishmael who maintains that it is permitted to plant within the work area surrounding a single grapevine. Since this area could be planted, the farmer's failure to do so reflects his conscious decision to leave it unplanted in order to mark off the two neighboring fields as separate. However, the space occupied by the grapevine itself cannot be included in the *beis rova*. This space cannot be planted and anything planted there becomes forbidden for use. Accordingly, leaving it unplanted does not indicate that it has been left as a marker and it can hence not be figured into the *beis rova*.

According to the accepted law, planting even within the work area of a single grapevine is forbidden (*Yoreh Deah* 296:21,31). It should therefore follow from the above that in fact even the work area around a vine is not included in the calculation of the *beis rova* separator (*Radbaz to Hil. Kilayim 4:3; Mareh HaPanim*).

Rash mentions a second interpretation of אֲכִילַת הַגֶּפֶן according to which the term ought to be translated as *a consumed grapevine.*[1] This is a grapevine which has withered and died leaving only roots in the ground. It is not clear why the mishnah saw a need to mention this case. Additionally, this explanation does not seem consistent with *Yerushalmi*.

In addition to *the work area of a grapevine*, the mishnah explicitly mentions *a grave or a rock* as examples of areas which are included in the calculation

of a *beis rova* separator. Although planting over a grave is forbidden (*Yerushalmi*), the grave in question is unmarked (*Meleches Shlomo*) and hence an observer, unaware of the presence of a grave, will assume that it has been deliberately left unplanted as a marker. Accordingly, it can be included in the *beis rova*. The *rock* listed by the mishnah is smaller than the *ten [handbreadths] high and four wide* rock of mishnah 8. Although it can not serve as an independent divider, it can be included in the calculation of a *beis rova* (*Rav; Rosh; Rash*). [Presumably, a rock of this small size is not especially noticeable and is perceived by the observer as tillable soil which was intentionally left unplanted as a marker.]

[It was suggested above that there is a difference between the effectiveness of a *beis rova* separation and the separation effected by the items listed in mishnah 8, in that the former permits the borders of the different species to become adjacent beyond itself, whereas the latter permits the different species to approach only opposite the separator but not beyond it. In that case, the mishnah could even be discussing a rock which is *ten high and four wide* located inside a *beis rova*. On its own, the rock would only permit the species to approach opposite itself. As part of a *beis rova* separation, however, the different species would not approach the rock, but beyond it they could be adjacent.]

תְּבוּאָה בִּתְבוּאָה — בֵּית רֹבַע; — *Grain with grain — a beis rova;*

If a person's field was planted, say, with wheat, and he wanted to plant some barley inside the wheat, he could do so if he adhered to the following rules: (a) he left an unplanted gap of a *beis rova* be-

---

1. *Meleches Shlomo* brings this explanation in the name of *R' Yitzchak the Tosafist.*

grapevine, a grave, or a rock are counted in the measure of a *beis rova.*

Grain with grain — a *beis rova;* greens with greens —

YAD AVRAHAM

tween the different grains; (b) he did not surround the barley with wheat on all four sides (*Rav; Rosh; Rash;* see diagram). [The latter condition stems from

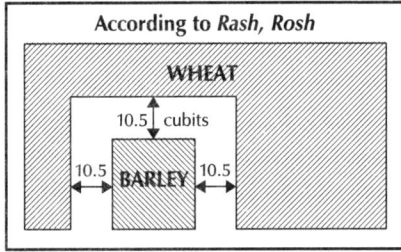

According to *Rash, Rosh*

WHEAT

10.5 cubits

10.5 **BARLEY** 10.5

Yerushalmi and is not recorded explicitly by *Rambam;* see however *Kesef Mishneh* to *Hil. Kilayim* 3:9.]

Rambam (*Comm.* and *Hil. Kilayim* 3:9) explains the case as involving a field of one grain next to which one wishes to plant a field of another grain. If the person leaves an unplanted *beis rova* square somewhere along the border between the fields, this is permitted (see diagrams).[1]

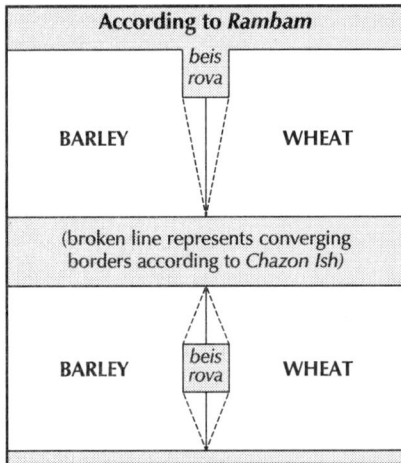

According to *Rambam*

beis rova

BARLEY   **WHEAT**

(broken line represents converging borders according to *Chazon Ish*)

beis rova

BARLEY   **WHEAT**

[*Rav, Rosh* and *Rash* would seem to require the fields to be separated along the entire border.]

Despite possible minor technical differences, all the above commentators assume that the mishnah's reference to *beis rova* refers to the size of the separation which must be left between fields of different grains. A radically different approach is taken by *R' Shlomo Sirilio* and *Gra* (see especially *Shenos Eliyahu, Peirush HaAroch* to mishnah 6). According to them, the mishnah does *not* require any separation between fields of different species provided that the fields are large enough to stand out on their own. Small planted patches of different grains can not be adjacent, as they would appear to be all mixed up. However, large fields of different grains can be adjacent, since their size makes them distinct. Accordingly, the mishnah states that the minimum size which fields of different grains must be in order to permit them to be adjacent is a *beis rova.* As for the initial statement of the mishnah — *All that is within a beis rova is counted in the measure of a beis rova* — this, too, refers to the planted field and not to an unplanted separation. The point of the statement is that although the field must be at least a *beis rova* in size to qualify for adjacency to a field of another grain, the entire *beis rova* need not be actually planted, and various obstructions can also be reckoned into the field when measuring it to see if it is a *beis rova.*

[It should be noted that R' Meir, who in mishnah 9 permits twenty-four *beis rova* squares planted with different species in a

1. Beyond the *beis rova* square, it seems from *Rambam* that the borders between the two fields can be adjacent (*Tif. Yis.*). However, *Chazon Ish* (5:3) maintains that the borders beyond the *beis rova* may converge as in the case of *strips* in mishnah 6. They may not, however, be adjacent in his opinion.

שִׁשָּׁה טְפָחִים.

תְּבוּאָה בְּיָרָק, יָרָק בִּתְבוּאָה — בֵּית רֹבַע. רַבִּי אֱלִיעֶזֶר אוֹמֵר: יָרָק בִּתְבוּאָה — שִׁשָּׁה טְפָחִים.

[יא] **תְּבוּאָה** נוֹטָה עַל גַּבֵּי תְבוּאָה, וְיָרָק עַל גַּבֵּי יָרָק, תְּבוּאָה עַל גַּבֵּי יָרָק, יָרָק עַל גַּבֵּי תְבוּאָה — הַכֹּל מֻתָּר חוּץ מִדְּלַעַת יְוָנִית. רַבִּי מֵאִיר אוֹמֵר: אַף הַקִּשּׁוּת וּפוֹל הַמִּצְרִי. וְרוֹאֶה אֲנִי אֶת דִּבְרֵיהֶן מִדְּבָרַי.

יד אברהם

single beis se'ah, is understood by Rash and Rosh (to mishnah 6) as maintaining that no separation is required between beis rova fields of different grains. Thus, the dispute between the two schools above (i.e. Rav, Rosh, Rash, Ri ben Malki Tzedek and Rambam on one side, R' Shlomo Sirilio and Gra on the other) is, according to the first school, the subject of a dispute between Tannaim.]

יָרָק בְּיָרָק — שִׁשָּׁה טְפָחִים. — greens with greens — six handbreadths.

If a person wishes to plant two fields with different species of greens adjacent to each other, he must leave an unplanted square of six-by-six handbreadths somewhere along the border between the two fields (Rav to mishnah 3:3, s.v. רוחב; Rambam Comm. and Hil. Kilayim 3:10). [We have followed Rambam in describing the separation as a square located somewhere along the border. It is possible that Rav, Rosh and Rash require the borders to be six handbreadths apart along their entire length.]

Note that the six-handbreadth separation between different species of greens refers to fields of greens. The separation required between small patches of greens is much less and is discussed in the next chapter (Rav, Rosh, Rash to 3:1, Rav and Rambam Comm. to 3:3).

R' Shlomo Sirilio and Gra explain that a patch of greens which is six-by-six handbreadths is considered a distinct

field and may be adjacent to another such field of a different species of greens.

תְּבוּאָה בְּיָרָק, יָרָק בִּתְבוּאָה — בֵּית רֹבַע. — Grain with greens, greens with grain — a beis rova.

[The separation required between two fields, one of greens and one of grain, is a beis rova.]

Rav, Rosh, and Rash, following Yerushalmi, point out that the fields in question are square in shape. But if a person wishes to plant a row of greens inside a field of grain, for example, it suffices for the separation to be ten-and-a-half cubits (the length of a beis rova) by six handbreadths (see Mishnah Rishonah). Rambam (Hil. Kilayim 3:12) gives a smaller separation for this case (Tos. R' Akiva; see Mareh HaPanim 2:8, s.v. כהדא).

רַבִּי אֱלִיעֶזֶר אוֹמֵר: יָרָק בִּתְבוּאָה — שִׁשָּׁה טְפָחִים. — R' Eliezer says: Greens with grain — six handbreadths.

The separation between a field of greens and a field of grain need not be a beis rova square, according to R' Eliezer. Instead, it suffices for it to be six handbreadths wide by the length of a beis rova, which is ten-and-a-half cubits (Rav; Rosh; Rash; see Tos. Yom Tov).

Again, R' Shlomo Sirilio and Gra explain the issue in dispute between the Tanna Kamma and R' Eliezer to be the size of a field of greens needed to permit it to be

2
11

six handbreadths.

Grain with greens, greens with grain — a *beis rova*. R'
Eliezer says: Greens with grain — six handbreadths.

11. **G**rain leaning over grain, greens [leaning] over
greens, grain [leaning] over greens, [and] greens
[leaning] over grain — all is permitted except for Greek
gourd. R' Meir says: Also chatemelon and Egyptian bean.
But I see their opinion better than mine.

YAD AVRAHAM

planted adjacent to a field of grain. Moreover, *R' Shlomo Sirilio* contends that R'
Eliezer disputes only the case of *greens
with grain* (cf. *Meleches Shlomo*). If a
person wanted to introduce greens into a
field of grain, he could do so if the greens
were planted in a six-handbreadth *square*.
If he wanted to introduce grain into a field
of greens, he could do so only if he planted
the grain in a square *beis rova* (see diagram).

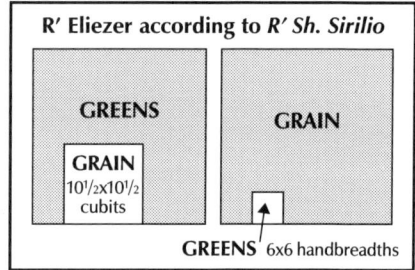

R' Eliezer according to R' Sh. Sirilio

GREENS

GRAIN

GRAIN
10½x10½
cubits

GREENS 6x6 handbreadths

11.

The previous mishnah completed the treatment of the regulations governing proximity of fields of different species. The mishnah now considers the law when fields are
planted in full compliance with the rules, but the different species nevertheless mingle.

תְּבוּאָה נוֹטָה עַל גַּבֵּי תְבוּאָה, וְיָרָק עַל גַּבֵּי יָרָק,
תְּבוּאָה עַל גַּבֵּי יָרָק, יָרָק עַל גַּבֵּי תְבוּאָה – הַכֹּל
מֻתָּר חוּץ מִדְּלַעַת יְוָנִית. — *Grain leaning
over grain, greens [leaning] over greens,
grain [leaning] over greens, [and] greens
[leaning] over grain — all is permitted except for Greek gourd.*

Two fields of different species were
planted according to the separation rules,
but the plants had long stems and thus
reached across the separation. Although
this results in one species leaning on another, it is permitted with all plants except
for Greek gourd. The latter generates a
long stalk with large leaves, and when it
comes into contact with other plants it en-
tangles itself more than any other species.
Because of this, an appearance of *kilayim*
is created and hence such mingling is disallowed (*Rav; Rosh; Rash; Rambam
Comm.*).

Two fields, one of wheat and the other of

barley, must be separated by a *beis rova*
(mishnah 10). How can these grains ever lean
on each other across such a large separation?
To resolve this problem, *Tif. Yis.* points out
that the *beis rova* separation must be left
somewhere along the border, but beyond it
the borders of the two fields can be adjacent.
Accordingly, it is not necessary to posit
extraordinary grain in order to conjure up the
mishnah's situation (see also *Chazon Ish* 6:20).
[Note, however, that *Rav, Rosh*, and *Rash*
clearly refer to the stalks of grain as being so
long as to mingle across the separation. This
would seem to suggest that in their view, the
borders between the fields must be separated
by a *beis rova* (i.e. ten-and-a-half cubits)
along their entire length (see above mishnah
10 and *Mishnas R' Nosson* from *Rash* 3:3).]

רַבִּי מֵאִיר אוֹמֵר: אַף הַקִּשּׁוּת וּפוֹל הַמִּצְרִי. וְרוֹאֶה
אֲנִי אֶת דִּבְרֵיהֶן מִדְּבָרַי. — *R' Meir says:
Also chatemelon and Egyptian bean. But
I see their opinion better than mine.*

R' Meir reports the opinion he received

כלאים **[א] עֲרוּגָה** שֶׁהִיא שִׁשָּׁה טְפָחִים עַל שִׁשָּׁה

ג/א טְפָחִים, זוֹרְעִים בְּתוֹכָהּ חֲמִשָּׁה

זְרְעוֹנִים, אַרְבָּעָה בְּאַרְבַּע רוּחוֹת הָעֲרוּגָה וְאֶחָד

בָּאֶמְצַע.

יד אברהם

from his teachers, even though he concedes that the opinion of the *Tanna Kamma* seems more reasonable (*Tif. Yis., Mishnah Rishonah*). R' Meir's tradition was that even varieties such as chatemelon and Egyptian bean, which grow less extensively than Greek gourd, are still not permitted to become entangled with plants from another legally planted field. Since however, no violation was committed in the planting of the two species, and the concern here is merely to dispel even an impression of *kilayim*, R'

Meir agrees that it is sufficient to exercise stringency only with the Greek gourd which tends to become more entangled than any other species (*Tif. Yis.*).

Ri ben Malki Tzedek indicates that any plant which has become entangled with Greek gourd becomes forbidden for use. This seems odd since it is clearly stated (mishnah 8:1) that only *kilayim* of the grapevine creates a prohibition on use (*R' Shlomo Sirilio*). However, it is of interest that a similar position seems to be held by *Rashbam* (*Bava Basra* 94a, s.v. כל סאה; see *Tos.* loc. cit.).

Chapter 3

1.

This chapter deals with the planting of *small* quantities of different greens (see mishnah 2) within *small* areas. The opening mishnah considers a special arrangement known as an עֲרוּגָה, *patch*, in which many different species may be planted provided that certain rules are followed. There is considerable confusion amongst the commentators as to exactly what these rules are, and the problem is compounded by the fact that the Talmudic discussion of this mishnah is exceedingly obscure. (Part of the mishnah recurs in *Shabbos* 9:2 and is dealt with by the *Gemara Shabbos* 84b ff. as well as by *Yerushalmi*.)

Our commentary will attempt to portray and simplify some of the more representative approaches to this mishnah, taking our lead from *Rav* whose treatment of this mishnah is uncharacteristically extensive.[1] It will be assumed throughout that the reader is familiar with certain basic arithmetic formulae used to determine the areas of triangles, squares and circles. Likewise, knowledge of the Pythagorean theorem is taken for granted.

עֲרוּגָה שֶׁהִיא שִׁשָּׁה טְפָחִים עַל שִׁשָּׁה טְפָחִים, זוֹרְעִים בְּתוֹכָהּ חֲמִשָּׁה זְרְעוֹנִים — *If a patch is six handbreadths by six handbreadths, one may plant within it five varieties,*

Five different varieties of greens may be planted within a single square patch measuring six-by-six handbreadths.

The mishnah (*Shabbos* 9:2) infers this

from a verse in *Isaiah* 61:11 in which allusions can be found to the idea that as many as five different species may be planted within a small area. It is not clear, however, that this represents the *maximum* number of species which can be planted within a six-by-six patch. *Rash* indeed maintains that (according to this

1. *Gra*, consistent with his approach to mishnah 2:10, explains the mishnah here on the assumption that no distancing is required between species (see *Shenos Eliyahu* at length).

1. [I]f a patch is six handbreadths by six handbreadths, one may plant within it five varieties, four on the four sides of the patch and one in the middle.

Tanna) the verse teaches that more than five species may not be planted within a six-by-six patch, as this would constitute an intolerable confusion of species. However, *Rambam Comm.*, following *Ri Migash* (responsum 26), indicates that this is not the maximum number at all. In principle, this *Tanna* would also permit more than five species within a six-by-six patch. The reason that he mentions only five varieties has to do with practical considerations which will be explained below.

A description of the precise arrangement of the different varieties within the patch follows. What should be noticed at this point is that regardless of their arrangement, it is impossible for there to be a six-handbreadth gap between the different greens if they are all to be squeezed into a six-by-six patch. Clearly, the law stated by mishnah 2:10 that *greens with greens* must be separated by six handbreadths is not applicable here. That law refers to *fields* of greens and hence deals with larger quantities. Here, however, the question concerns very small quantities and so a different set of spacing rules applies (*Rav; Rosh; Rash; Rambam Comm.*).

אַרְבָּעָה בְּאַרְבַּע רוּחוֹת הָעֲרוּגָה וְאֶחָד בָּאֶמְצָע. — *four on the four sides of the patch and one in the middle.*

I.e. a different species may be planted on each of the four sides of the patch, and a fifth species in the middle.

Rambam Comm. explains the layout of the species to be based on the *rosh tor* formation encountered in mishnah 2:7. The only unplanted gaps in the patch are those spots which cannot be fit into such a formation. There are actually two different ways to implement this system, the main difference between them being that one arrangement leaves the corners of the patch unplanted, while the other has them planted. These two arrangements are shown in diagram A and B. [It is clear from *Rambam Comm.* that an arrangement such as that shown in diagram C which contains *six* species in a six-by-six patch would also be acceptable to this *Tanna*. However, that arrangement utilizes only 18 sq. handbreadths of the available planting space of 36 sq. handbreadths, while the five-species arrangements (diagrams A,B) utilizes 24 and 27 sq. handbreadths, respectively (*Rashash*; see below).]

Rash assumes that within a six-by-six

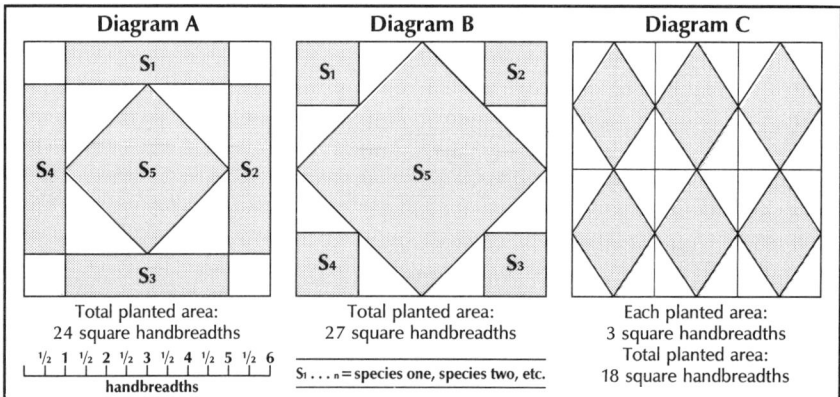

Diagram A	Diagram B	Diagram C
Total planted area: 24 square handbreadths	Total planted area: 27 square handbreadths	Each planted area: 3 square handbreadths Total planted area: 18 square handbreadths

½ 1 ½ 2 ½ 3 ½ 4 ½ 5 ½ 6
handbreadths

S₁ . . . ₙ = species one, species two, etc.

הָיָה לָהּ גְּבוּל גָּבֹהַּ טֶפַח, זוֹרְעִין בְּתוֹכָהּ שְׁלֹשָׁה
עָשָׂר, שְׁלֹשָׁה עַל כָּל גְּבוּל וּגְבוּל וְאֶחָד בָּאֶמְצַע.
לֹא יִטַּע רֹאשׁ הַלֶּפֶת בְּתוֹךְ הַגְּבוּל, מִפְּנֵי שֶׁהוּא
מְמַלְאֵהוּ.

יד אברהם

patch the law of *rosh tor* is not operative (see *Shabbos* 85b). Additionally, he assumes that greens of different species must be separated by at least one-and-a-half handbreadths, this being the radius throughout which a plant draws nourishment. Thus, a plant of one species is not permitted to be within this radius of a plant of a different species. Application of these rules results in the layout depicted in diagram D. Under this arrangement, the *one in the middle* is a single seed of a fifth species.

It is easy to construct a case in which nine different species separated from each other by the required one-and-a-half handbreadths fit into a six-by-six patch (see diagram E). *Rambam Comm.* explains that the *Tanna* of the mishnah did not mention this since under this arrangement the total planted area is only nine square handbreadths. In the *rosh tor* construction using five species, however, the total planted area is 24 or 27 square handbreadths. Accordingly, although the *Tanna* agrees that the nine-species arrangement is permissible, he selects the case which maximizes the use of the available space in the patch.

On the other hand, *Rash* maintains that the *Tanna* would not permit such a case. Al-though the spacing rules are indeed satisfied under the arrangement of diagram E, nevertheless the concentration of more than five different species within a six-by-six patch is unacceptable. In the opinion of *Rash*, it is never permitted to have more than five species in a six-by-six patch according to this *Tanna*, and this is why the *Tanna* speaks of only five species in the patch.

[It is of interest that in his code, *Rambam* (*Hil. Kilayim* 4:9) also adopts the idea that more than five species within a six-by-six patch are prohibited.]

הָיָה לָהּ גְּבוּל גָּבֹהַּ טֶפַח, זוֹרְעִין בְּתוֹכָהּ שְׁלֹשָׁה
עָשָׂר, שְׁלֹשָׁה עַל כָּל גְּבוּל וּגְבוּל וְאֶחָד בָּאֶמְצַע.
— *[If] it has a border a handbreadth high, one may plant in it thirteen [varieties], three on each border and one in the middle.*

The border was a clay strip which framed the six-by-six patch (*Rav* to mishnah 2). From *Yerushalmi*, it emerges that the border was not only a handbreadth high as stated in the mishnah, but also a handbreadth wide. The resultant area was thus eight-by-eight handbreadths (*Rav; Rosh; Rash*).

The mishnah states that in such a situ-

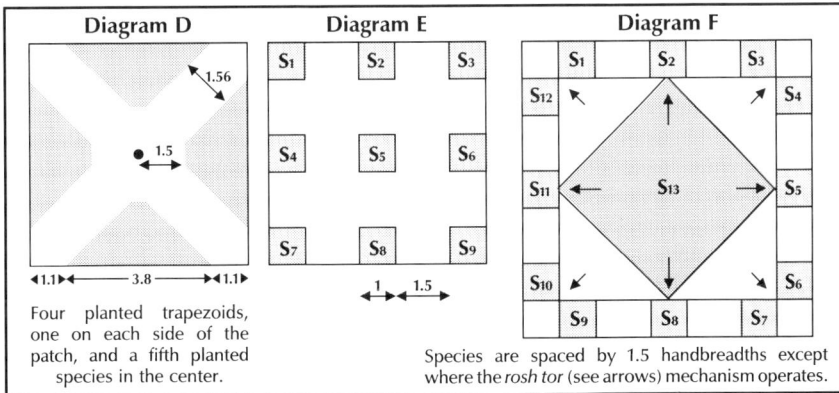

Diagram D

1.56

1.5

◄1.1►◄——— 3.8 ——►◄1.1►

Four planted trapezoids, one on each side of the patch, and a fifth planted species in the center.

Diagram E

S₁	S₂	S₃
S₄	S₅	S₆
S₇	S₈	S₉

1 ◄—► 1.5

Diagram F

S₁	S₂	S₃
S₁₂		S₄
S₁₁	S₁₃	S₅
S₁₀		S₆
S₉	S₈	S₇

Species are spaced by 1.5 handbreadths except where the *rosh tor* (see arrows) mechanism operates.

3
1
[If] it has a border a handbreadth high, one may plant in it thirteen [varieties], three on each border and one in the middle.

It is not permitted to plant a head of turnip inside the border, since it fills it up.

ation it is permitted to plant as many as thirteen different species within the eight-by-eight square. This may be accomplished by planting twelve species on the border and one in the middle. According to *Rambam Comm.*, the layout is that depicted in diagram F. Again, *Rambam* employs the *rosh tor* mechanism in order to construct the case. The resultant arrangement has three different species on each side of the border, and a thirteenth species in the middle. It is readily seen that the total planted area is 30 square handbreadths.

Rash, consistent with his view that the *rosh tor* mechanism is not operative inside a patch, has a different construction which is depicted in diagram G. In this plan, in order to accommodate the requirement that different species be separated by one-and-a-half handbreadths, the species planted on the border cannot all be present in identical quantities. [*Rosh* shares *Rash's* basic assumptions, but slightly modifies the layout described by *Rash* so that the width of each species planted on the border is the same (⁷⁄₈ of a handbreadth). The species planted in the

corners can occupy no more than a square with sides of ⁷⁄₈ of a handbreadth, while those in between can occupy rectangles with a width of ⁷⁄₈ of a handbreadth and a length of one handbreadth (see diagram H). *Rav* cites *Rosh's* plan.]

[The reason that the *Tanna* limits the number of species planted in the middle to one will be discussed below in the treatment of R' Yehudah's opinion. Similarly, the reason that the height of the border is specified will be discussed below.]

Rosh, quoted by *Rav*, points out that a plan such as that depicted in diagram I also satisfies the spacing rules while enabling as many as sixteen species to be planted on the border. He contends, however, that to do so would be forbidden since such a high concentration of different species constitutes too great a confusion.

לֹא יִטַּע רֹאשׁ הַלֶּפֶת בְּתוֹךְ הַגְּבוּל, מִפְּנֵי שֶׁהוּא מְמַלְּאֵהוּ. — *It is not permitted to plant a head of turnip inside the border, since it fills it up.*

The term *head of turnip* is explained by *Tos.* (*Chullin* 99b) to mean turnip roots (i.e. the bulb-shaped part which is eaten). It is not entirely clear why the turnip is

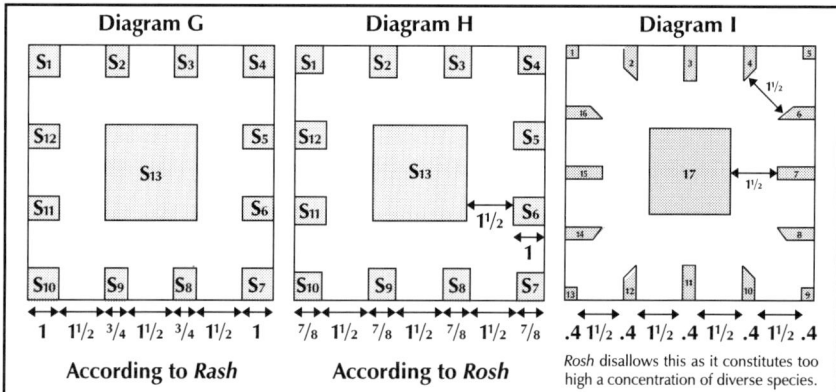

Diagram G	Diagram H	Diagram I
According to *Rash*	According to *Rosh*	*Rosh* disallows this as it constitutes too high a concentration of diverse species.

singled out more than other plants which also grow extensively. It is also unclear whether the restriction here also applies to planting a head of turnip inside a six-by-six square (see *Tos. Yom Tov*, *Mishnah Rishonah*, and *Chazon Ish* 8:10). *Rav*, following *Rosh*, writes that the filling up of the border by the turnip head makes it impossible to plant three different species on each side. *Rambam* (*Hil. Kilayim* 4:12) indicates that even planting turnip seeds is forbidden lest the plant eventually fill up the border (see *Chazon Ish* 8:10).

רַבִּי יְהוּדָה אוֹמֵר: שִׁשָּׁה בָּאֶמְצַע. — *R' Yehudah says: Six in the middle.*

After some initial wavering, *Yerushalmi* concludes that R' Yehudah is referring to the case of a six-by-six patch surrounded by a border with height and width each a handbreadth. In his opinion, it is permitted to plant eighteen different species in such a patch — twelve on the border and another *six in the middle*. There is considerable controversy, however, as to whether R' Yehudah's position is disputed by the *Tanna Kamma*.

Rambam Comm. understands that the *Tanna Kamma* would also agree that this may be done. Although the *Tanna Kamma* only mentions *one in the middle*, this is not to exclude other possibilities. According to *Rambam*, *Yerushalmi* discusses why the *Tanna* specifies only *one in the middle* when he could just as well have specified *six in the middle* like R' Yehudah. Although *Yerushalmi* leaves this question unanswered, it is clear from the discussion that in principle the *Tanna Kamma* also agrees that in such a case six species may be planted in the middle (*Chazon Ish* 8:1, s.v. הי"ב). The arrangement of the six species in the middle again utilizes the *rosh tor* mechanism and is depicted in diagram J.

The standard versions of *Yerushalmi* record an inquiry questioning why the *Tanna Kamma* does not count *six* in the middle. This

text is challenged by *Rash* and others on the grounds that at most the first *Tanna* could have counted *five* in the middle, since in the standard six-by-six patch discussed at the start of this mishnah, the *Tanna Kamma* allowed only five different species. There seems to be no reason now for allowing more just because this patch is surrounded by a border! Accordingly, *Rash* emends the text so that it asks why the *Tanna* does not count *five* in the middle (see also *Rosh* and *Tos. Yom Tov*).

However, it is clear from *Rambam Comm.* that he accepted the standard text (*Tos. Yom Tov*). According to his approach, however, the text is not problematic. It will be recalled that in *Rambam's* opinion (in his commentary), the *Tanna Kamma's* mention of five species in the standard patch was only because this enables maximum use of the available planting space in the patch. But, in fact, the *Tanna* does not view five species as a limit. Similarly, it will be observed that both R' Yehudah's eighteen-species arrangement and the *Tanna Kamma's* thirteen-species arrangement use exactly the same area for planting. Since in terms of efficient use of the planting space there seems to be no advantage to the *one in the middle* system over the *six in the middle* one, *Yerushalmi* questions why the *Tanna* does not in fact count six in the middle.

[In his code (*Hil. Kilayim* 4:9), *Rambam* accepts the notion that in a standard patch, five species constitutes a limit. Nevertheless, he rules that in a bordered patch, eighteen species may be planted, twelve on the sides and six in the middle (ibid. 4:12). Evidently, the

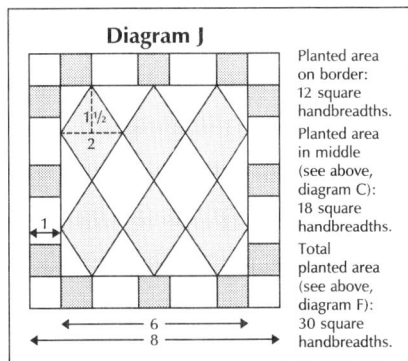

Diagram J

Planted area on border: 12 square handbreadths.
Planted area in middle (see above, diagram C): 18 square handbreadths.
Total planted area (see above, diagram F): 30 square handbreadths.

YAD AVRAHAM

presence of a border somehow serves to cancel the five-species limit (see *Tos. Yom Tov* and *Chazon Ish* 8:1).]

Rash cannot accept *Rambam's* explanation since it involves the *rosh tor* configuration which, according to *Rash*, does not apply inside a patch. This would seem to create an enormous problem, since without using the *rosh tor* configuration, it is necessary to space all species one-and-a-half handbreadths from each other. But if the middle species are to be distanced one-and-a-half handbreadths from the border, this leaves only three square handbreadths of planting space in the middle (see diagrams G,H). It can readily be seen that to satisfy the spacing rules within such a limited area, the only way to plant six different species is if each species is planted in lines no wider than a single seed! (see diagram K).

To overcome this problem, *Rash* postulates: (1) that according to R' Yehudah, the spacing between greens of different species needs to be only a single handbreadth (rather than the one-and-a-half handbreadths of the *Tanna Kamma*), and (2) that the one handbreadth *height* of the border counts like a handbreadth space. Additionally, R' Yehudah agrees

with the *Tanna Kamma* that in an area of less than six-by-six handbreadths, only a single species may be planted. Assuming these premises, it follows that the species planted in the middle do not need to be distanced horizontally from the border. Thus, according to R' Yehudah, there is a full six-by-six square available for planting in the middle. The consequent arrangement of the *six in the middle* is shown in diagram L.

According to the *Tanna Kamma*, the available space in the middle is five-by-five handbreadths (since in addition to the handbreadth of height there is another half-handbreadth of spacing needed). *Rash* assumes that the *Tanna Kamma* does not allow even five species to be planted in the middle, and certainly not six. This is because the verse in *Isaiah* 61 teaches that five species distributed throughout a six-by-six square is tolerable, but multiple species in less than this area is not acceptable. Since according to the *Tanna Kamma* there are only five square handbreadths available in the middle, these must be planted with only one species, as depicted in diagram M.

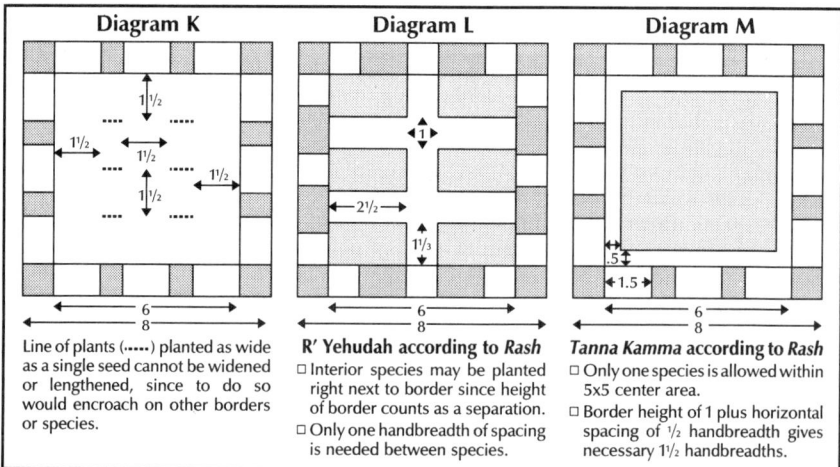

Diagram K	Diagram L	Diagram M
Line of plants (·····) planted as wide as a single seed cannot be widened or lengthened, since to do so would encroach on other borders or species.	**R' Yehudah according to *Rash***	**Tanna Kamma according to *Rash***

R' Yehudah according to *Rash*
□ Interior species may be planted right next to border since height of border counts as a separation.
□ Only one handbreadth of spacing is needed between species.

Tanna Kamma according to *Rash*
□ Only one species is allowed within 5x5 center area.
□ Border height of 1 plus horizontal spacing of ½ handbreadth gives necessary 1½ handbreadths.

כָּל [ב] מִין זְרָעִים אֵין זוֹרְעִים בָּעֲרוּגָה, וְכָל מִין יְרָקוֹת זוֹרְעִין בָּעֲרוּגָה.
חַרְדָּל וַאֲפוּנִים הַשּׁוּפִין מִין זְרָעִים. אֲפוּנִים הַגַּמְלָנִים מִין יָרָק.
גְּבוּל שֶׁהָיָה גָבֹהַּ טֶפַח וְנִתְמָעֵט כָּשֵׁר, שֶׁהָיָה כָּשֵׁר מִתְּחִלָּתוֹ.

יד אברהם

2.

This mishnah discusses the scope of the laws of the previous mishnah concerning planting many species within small patches. Additionally, the mishnah considers other situations in which a variety of species may be planted within close proximity of each other.

כָּל מִין זְרָעִים אֵין זוֹרְעִים בָּעֲרוּגָה, וְכָל מִין יְרָקוֹת זוֹרְעִין בָּעֲרוּגָה. — *No types of zeraim may be planted in a patch, but all types of greens may be planted in a patch.*

The law permitting five different species to be planted within a six-by-six patch, or thirteen different species within an eight-by-eight patch, applies only to greens since these are normally planted in small patches. It does not apply to the class of vegetables known as *zeraim* since these are normally planted in larger areas which can be called fields. Because of this, the presence of many species of *zeraim* within a small patch looks like *kilayim* (*Rav; Rambam Comm.;* see *Mishnah Rishonah*). Alternatively, the difference between greens and *zeraim* is that the latter draw much more nourishment from the ground than do the former. Accordingly, *zeraim* cannot be packed into the small-patch arrangements of the previous mishnah in which the different species are spaced according to a small standard radius of nourishment per plant (*Rav; Rosh; Rash; Ri ben Malki Tzedek;* see also *Rashi to Pesachim* 39b).

Rambam (*Hil. Kilayim* 1:8,9) explains that both greens and *zeraim* are subsets of a larger category of plants known as garden seeds (see

mishnah 2:2). The term garden seeds includes all plants whose seeds are not eaten. Of these, some are normally planted in small patches and known as greens, while others are planted in fields and known as *zeraim*. Thus, according to *Rambam*, not all garden seeds may be planted in a six-by-six patch.

One early authority (*Chiddushei Kilayim LeTalmid HaRashba*) suggests that plants which are grown for their leaves are known as greens, while those which are grown for their fruit are known as *zeraim*. A plant grown for its leaves would thus be eligible for planting in a six-by-six patch even if it was normally planted in large fields. A similar approach is adopted by *R' Shlomo Sirilio*, who argues that plants whose stems or roots are eaten are regularly plucked even before they form seeds and are hence referred to as greens (this green being the color of the leafy part of the plant). Grains and legumes in which the seeds are consumed are referred to as *zeraim*, literally *seeds* (see also *Gra, Shenos Eliyahu* here and *Peah* 1:4). Accordingly, all plants with seeds which are not eaten (i.e. those which *Rambam* calls garden seeds) are classed as greens and may be planted in a six-by-six patch.

חַרְדָּל וַאֲפוּנִים הַשּׁוּפִין מִין זְרָעִים. אֲפוּנִים הַגַּמְלָנִים מִין יָרָק. — *Mustard and smooth beans are types of zeraim. Large beans are types of greens.*[1]

1. Actually *Rambam* distinguishes between the terms מִין יָרָק, *type of greens*, of our mishnah and the term יָרָק, *greens*. Only the former have inedible seeds and are characterized by being

2. **N**o types of *zeraim* may be planted in a patch, but all types of greens may be planted in a patch. Mustard and smooth beans are types of *zeraim*. Large beans are types of greens.

A border which was a handbreadth high and was reduced is acceptable, since it was acceptable at the start.

The translation of אֲפוּנִים הַשּׁוּפִין as *smooth beans* follows *Rav* (from *Rosh*, *Rash and Rambam Comm.*). Alternatively, שׁוּפִין may be defined as small (*Rav*, *Meleches Shlomo* from *Aruch*). The term גַּמְלָנִים is generally assumed to mean large and is derived from the Aramaic usage of camels (גמלים) as a symbol for all things large (*Rambam Comm.*). *Talmid HaRashba* explains גַּמְלָנִים as covered with camel-like humps, in contrast with the *smooth beans* mentioned first.

According to *Rambam* that *zeraim* refers to plants grown in fields, the listing of mustard as a type of *zeraim* needs some explanation, since above (mishnah 2:9) it was stated that mustard is *not* normally planted in large fields. Presumably, although mustard was not planted in full-size fields, it was not planted in small patches either (*Tos. Yom Tov*; see also *Peah* 3:2 and *Derech Emunah, Beur HaHalachah* 1:9, s.v. והחרדל and 4:13, s.v. מיני ירקות). *Chazon Ish* (5:15, s.v. והנה) entertains the possibility that mustard is actually considered a type of greens, but for the purposes of the law of patches it was treated like *zeraim*.

Rosh notes that אֲפוּנִים are generally classed as legumes (i.e. קְטְנִיוֹת), since it is the seed of the plant which is eaten. Whatever definition is used for *greens*, all agree that plants with edible seeds such as beans are *not* greens. Evidently, the assertion of the mishnah that אֲפוּנִים הַגַּמְלָנִין, the large variety of these beans, are viewed as *greens* must be understood within the specific context of the laws of patches. That is, for the purposes of the present law, even though technically these beans are not greens, they are

treated like greens. Thus, the point of the mishnah is that all *greens* can be planted in the six-by-six patches of the previous mishnah, while not all *zeraim* are eligible. Some *zeraim* such as *large beans*, however, are exceptions and can be planted in such patches (see also *Chiddushei Kilayim LeTalmid HaRashba*).

גְּבוּל שֶׁהָיָה גָבֹהַּ טֶפַח וְנִתְמָעֵט כָּשֵׁר, שֶׁהָיָה כָּשֵׁר מִתְּחִלָּתוֹ. —*A border which was a handbreadth high and was reduced is acceptable, since it was acceptable at the start.*

The border around a six-by-six patch may be planted with twelve different greens, as explained in the previous mishnah, provided that it is one handbreadth high and one wide. If it satisfied these requirements when it was planted, but later eroded and was reduced to less than a handbreadth, the plants may be left in place. No new plants may be added to it in its current condition, but whatever was planted when it was the proper size may be left there, and this is not viewed as illegal maintenance of *kilayim* (*Rav; Rosh*).

Similarly, the five-square-handbreadths area planted inside the border (see above, diagram M) may be left intact. Although these must be separated by one-and-a-half handbreadths from the border, and although one handbreadth of the necessary one-and-a-half is accounted for by the height of the border, this is only required at the time of planting. If the height of the border is subsequently reduced, the plants already in the patch may be left as is (*Rash*).

Rambam Comm. explains that a border which is one handbreadth high and wide serves as a separator between small

planted in small patches. The term יְרֶק is a more general term including even leguminous plants whose seeds are edible. The rule of mishnah 2:11 above refers to יֶרֶק, and therefore applies even to legumes [see *Eretz Chemdah* 2:2:7 pg. 287 ff.].

כלאים
ג/ג

הַתֶּלֶם וְאַמַּת הַמַּיִם שֶׁהֵם עֲמֻקִים טֶפַח, זוֹרְעִים לְתוֹכָן שְׁלֹשָׁה זֵרְעוֹנִין, אֶחָד מִכָּאן וְאֶחָד מִכָּאן וְאֶחָד בָּאֶמְצַע.

[ג] הָיָה רֹאשׁ תּוֹר יָרָק נִכְנָס לְתוֹךְ שְׂדֵה יָרָק אַחֵר, מֻתָּר, מִפְּנֵי שֶׁהוּא נִרְאֶה כְּסוֹף שָׂדֵהוּ.

הָיְתָה שָׂדֵהוּ זְרוּעָה יָרָק, וְהוּא מְבַקֵּשׁ לִטַּע בְּתוֹכָהּ שׁוּרָה שֶׁל יָרָק אַחֵר – רַבִּי יִשְׁמָעֵאל אוֹמֵר: עַד שֶׁיְּהֵא הַתֶּלֶם מְפֻלָּשׁ מֵרֹאשׁ הַשָּׂדֶה וְעַד רֹאשׁוֹ.

יד אברהם

patches of greens. Thus, a patch of onions can be planted next to a patch of lettuce for example, either by spacing them one-and-a-half handbreadths apart, or by separating them with a border which is a handbreadth high and wide (see also *Rambam Comm.* to mishnah 1). The present mishnah teaches that the proper dimensions of the separating border are critical only at the time of planting. If subsequently the dimensions are reduced, there is no need to uproot the plants which were planted right next to the border (cf. *Rambam, Hil. Kilayim* 4:14).

הַתֶּלֶם וְאַמַּת הַמַּיִם שֶׁהֵם עֲמֻקִים טֶפַח, זוֹרְעִים לְתוֹכָן שְׁלֹשָׁה זֵרְעוֹנִין, אֶחָד מִכָּאן וְאֶחָד מִכָּאן וְאֶחָד בָּאֶמְצַע. — *[If] a furrow or water channel is one handbreadth deep, one may plant inside it three species, one over here and one over here and one in the middle.*

If a person has a furrow or a dried-up water channel suitable for planting, he can plant one species of greens on one edge, a second species on the opposite edge, and a third inside the furrow or channel. However, the walls of the furrow or channel do not count as the separation between species of greens, and conse-

quently, it is necessary to leave the requisite one-and-a-half handbreadth gap between species.[1] Although the mishnah's mention of the depth of the furrow or channel would seem to indicate that the sides of the channel *do* serve as separators between the species on the floor of the channel and those on the edges, this is in fact not so. The reason the mishnah speaks of planting on the floor of a channel or furrow is to stress that even then other species may be planted the required distance away on the edges of the depression. Although it might be argued that the plants inside the channel appear to be overshadowed by the plants at ground level on the edges, and hence such an arrangement should be forbidden, the mishnah teaches that even this is permitted (*Rav; Rosh; Rash*).

Rash writes that the width of the furrow or channel must be at least six handbreadths. It is not clear why this must be so, and both *Rosh* and *Rav* make no mention of such a requirement.

Rambam (*Hil. Kilayim* 4:4) apparently understands that the depth of the channel or furrow constitutes a separation between the species planted on the floor of the depression and those planted on the

1. The walls are included in this calculation of 1.5 handbreadths. If the walls are one handbreadth high, the species on the surface need to be distanced only an additional half-handbreadth (*Chazon Ish* 9:8).

3

3

If a furrow or water channel is one handbreadth deep, one may plant inside it three species, one over here and one over here and one in the middle.

3. [I f] a *rosh tor* of greens entered into a field of a different [type of] greens, this is permitted since it appears like the end of his field.

If his field was planted with greens, and he wants to plant inside it a row of a different [type of] greens — R' Yishmael says: [Not] until the furrow reaches from one end of the field to the other. R' Akiva says: A length

YAD AVRAHAM

surface at the edges. The point of the mishnah is that when one species is planted on the floor of a channel, others can be planted on the edges even though the horizontal separation between the

species is less than one-and-a-half handbreadths. However, the depth of the channel must be at least one handbreadth (*Mahari Korkus* ibid.; see also *R' Shlomo Sirilio*).

3.

After its opening statement regarding the *rosh tor* formation in the context of greens, the present mishnah discusses the regulations for planting a *row* of one species of greens in a *field* of another species of greens.

הָיָה רֹאשׁ תּוֹר יָרָק נִכְנָס לְתוֹךְ שָׂדֶה יָרָק אַחֵר, מֻתָּר מִפְּנֵי שֶׁהוּא נִרְאֶה כְּסוֹף שָׂדֵהוּ. — [If] a *rosh tor of greens entered into a field of a different [type of] greens, this is permitted since it appears like the end of his field.*

The *rosh tor* formation was encountered and explained in mishnah 2:7. There it was presented in connection with grain, while here it is mentioned concerning greens. *Mishnah Rishonah* suggests that the mishnah's point is that the *rosh tor* formation permits even a patch of greens (which are normally planted in small patches) which enters a full field of a plant which normally is planted in fields. This is indicated by the wording of the mishnah: *into a field of a different [type of] greens.* The *rosh tor* mechanism does not permit a patch of one greens to come into contact with a patch of different greens (see *Shabbos* 85b-86a and esp. *Rashi* to 86a, s.v. התם; see also *Tos. Yom Tov* above, 2:9, and *Rambam, Hil. Kilayim* 4:11).

הָיְתָה שָׂדֵהוּ זְרוּעָה יָרָק, וְהוּא מְבַקֵּשׁ לִטַּע בְּתוֹכָהּ שׁוּרָה שֶׁל יָרָק אַחֵר — [If] *his field was planted with greens, and he wants to plant inside it a row of a different [type of] greens —*

Rambam Comm. to mishnah 7 below explains that the term *row* refers to a line of plants arranged in single file. Accordingly, the mishnah considers the possibility of planting such a row inside a field of another species. From *Rash*, however, it appears that *row* is not a technical term, but simply refers to a rectangular formation which can contain a number of parallel rows of plants. The entire formation is referred to as a *row.*

רַבִּי יִשְׁמָעֵאל אוֹמֵר: עַד שֶׁיְּהֵא הַתֶּלֶם מְפֻלָּשׁ מֵרֹאשׁ הַשָּׂדֶה וְעַד רֹאשׁוֹ. — R' *Yishmael says: [Not] until the furrow reaches from one end of the field to the other.*

There are two significantly different systems for understanding the various opinions expressed by the mishnah. The entire matter revolves around the mean-

יד אברהם

ing of the term תֶּלֶם, *furrow*, used here by R' Yishmael: According to one school, this refers to the row of greens (which the farmer wants to plant in his field of a different species of greens); according to another, this refers to an unplanted separator which sets apart the row from the field.[1]

Ri ben Malki Tzedek understands *the furrow* here to correspond to the planted row. That is, according to R' Yishmael, it is permitted to run a single row of one species right through a field of another species provided that the row reaches from one end of the field to the other. The field is thus effectively cut into two by the row. *Yerushalmi* (as understood by *Ri ben Malki Tzedek*) proves that the width of the row must be six handbreadths. Additionally, the different species must be separated from each other by a gap of six handbreadths as required by the spacing laws of mishnah 2:10 (*Rash*). Despite the spacing gap, it is still necessary for the planted row to span the field. Otherwise, the *row of a different [type of] greens* would not constitute an entity unto itself; rather, it would be viewed as an integral part of the larger field. But in that case two species of greens will be growing in the same field, which is forbidden.

Thus, according to this approach, the point of the mishnah here is that for a configuration such as a row, the six-handbreadth spacing of mishnah 2:10 alone is not sufficient to separate it from a field. In addition to the spacing, the planted area itself must satisfy certain length and width requirements. According to R' Yishmael, the requirement is that the row be six handbreadths wide, and stretch from one end of the field to the other (see diagram A).

Rambam Comm. understands *the furrow* to refer to the gap which must be left

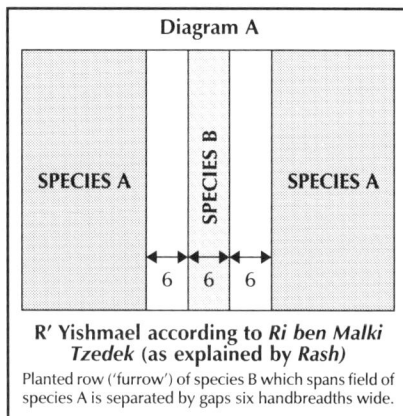

Diagram A

SPECIES A   SPECIES B   SPECIES A

6   6   6

R' Yishmael according to *Ri ben Malki Tzedek* (as explained by *Rash*)
Planted row ('furrow') of species B which spans field of species A is separated by gaps six handbreadths wide.

between the row of one species and the field of another. In his view, the six-handbreadth separation called for in mishnah 2:10 is required only between fields; but between a row and a field (as in the present case), even a furrow serves as a separation. The term furrow refers to the groove cut by a plough (*Rambam Comm.* to mishnah 2:2), not to the ridge (cf. *Meleches Shlomo* to mishnah 2:2). The furrow serves as a divider between greens as long as its width equals its depth (*Yerushalmi* as understood by *Rambam Comm.*). Additionally, the furrow must be at least one handbreadth deep (*Rambam Comm.* to mishnah 1). R' Yishmael's statement that the furrow must extend מֵרֹאשׁ הַשָּׂדֶה וְעַד רֹאשׁוֹ is apparently understood by *Rambam* to mean: from one end of the field until *its* end, where *end* refers to the end of the *row* of greens, not the end of the field. Thus, as understood by *Rambam*, R' Yishmael allows a single *row* of greens to be separated from a field of other greens by a mere furrow; however, the furrow must extend the full length of the row (see diagram B).

רַבִּי עֲקִיבָא אוֹמֵר: אֹרֶךְ שִׁשָּׁה טְפָחִים וְרֹחַב מְלֹאוֹ. — *R' Akiva says: A length of six*

1. As *Tos. Yom Tov* already points out, *Rav's* explanation is difficult to understand, and accordingly, reference will be made to the proponents of each approach, rather than to *Rav*.

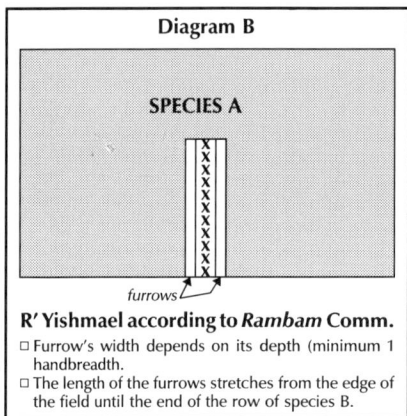

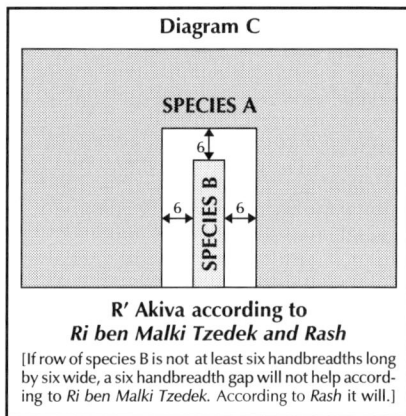

of six handbreadths and a width equal to its fullness.

Diagram B	Diagram C

R' Yishmael according to *Rambam* Comm.

□ Furrow's width depends on its depth (minimum 1 handbreadth.

□ The length of the furrows stretches from the edge of the field until the end of the row of species B.

R' Akiva according to
Ri ben Malki Tzedek and Rash

[If row of species B is not at least six handbreadths long by six wide, a six handbreadth gap will not help according to *Ri ben Malki Tzedek*. According to *Rash* it will.]

handbreadths and a width equal to its fullness.

The phrase *equal to its fullness* is somewhat obscure. *Rav* (from *Rash* and *Ri ben Malki Tzedek*) explains this to mean the full width of the standard furrow, i.e. six handbreadths (see *Tos. Yom Tov* and *Tif. Yis.*). Alternatively, he quotes *Rambam Comm.* who understands the *fullness* of the furrow to mean its depth. That is, the width of the furrow must equal its depth. *Ravad* (*Hil. Kilayim* 3:12) explains it to mean the size of the yoke used in plowing the furrow. However it is understood, it is evident from *Yerushalmi* that both R' Akiva and R' Yishmael agree on the width of the furrow, and their disagreement is only with respect to its length.

According to *Ri ben Malki Tzedek*, in order for a planted row to stand out inside a big field, it must span the field in R' Yishmael's opinion, while in R' Akiva's opinion it is sufficient for the row to have sides of at least six handbreadths. A planted row of six-by-six handbreadths is not considered insignificant in contrast with the field, and hence the standard six-handbreadth separation is effective (see diagram C).

Rash notes that according to *Ri ben Malki Tzedek* it follows that if the planted row is not six handbreadths long and six handbreadths wide, then the six-handbreadth spacing will not work. This conflicts with a statement in *Tosefta* 2:8 which indicates that even a single plant can be permissibly located inside a field of a different species as long as they are spaced six handbreadths apart. Because of this and other problems, *Rash* accepts the approach that the mishnah is legislating regarding the gap to be left between the row and the field, and not regarding the shape of the row.[1] In his view, the square of six-by-six handbreadths referred to by R' Akiva is the minimum gap which is needed even if only a single plant is introduced into the field. For larger patches, such as a row, the six-handbreadth separation must be maintained throughout the entire border between the row and the field (see diagram C).

According to *Rambam*, the six-handbreadth spacing is entirely unnecessary in order to set a row apart from a field, and a furrow is just as good. Unlike R' Yishmael who required the furrow to extend the full length of the planted row, R' Akiva maintains that it is enough for the furrow to be six handbreadths long

---

1. *Rosh*, however, explains the mishnah like *Ri ben Malki Tzedek* as dealing with the planted row.

רַבִּי יְהוּדָה אוֹמֵר: רֹחַב כִּמְלֹא רֹחַב הַפַּרְסָה.

[ד] **הַנּוֹטֵעַ** שְׁתֵּי שׁוּרוֹת שֶׁל קִשּׁוּאִין, שְׁתֵּי שׁוּרוֹת שֶׁל דְּלוּעִים, שְׁתֵּי שׁוּרוֹת שֶׁל פּוֹל הַמִּצְרִי — מֻתָּר. שׁוּרָה שֶׁל קִשּׁוּאִים, שׁוּרָה שֶׁל דְּלוּעִים, שׁוּרָה שֶׁל פּוֹל הַמִּצְרִי — אָסוּר.

יד אברהם

(see diagram D). [This is sufficient to mark off the row as a separate entity, so that beyond the six-handbreadth-long furrow, the borders between the row and the field can be adjacent (see *Rambam, Hil. Kilayim* 3:9-10 and 4:6).]

רַבִּי יְהוּדָה אוֹמֵר: רֹחַב כִּמְלֹא רֹחַב הַפַּרְסָה. — *R' Yehudah says: A width the full width of a foot.*

In R' Yehudah's opinion, the furrow need not be wider than the width of a foot. This equals a handbreadth, but R' Yehudah preferred to refer to a foot's width rather than to a handbreadth in order to allude to his source — a verse in *Deut.* 11:10. The Torah speaks there of watering a garden of greens with one's foot, and this is taken by R' Yehudah as an indication that between greens there must be enough room left to place one's foot. Thus, in contrast with R' Akiva who requires the furrow to be six handbreadths wide (according to *Rash* and *Ri*

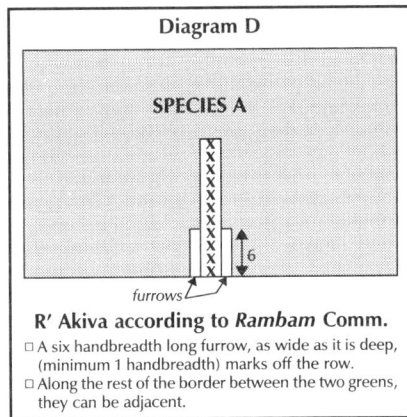

Diagram D

SPECIES A

furrows

6

R' Akiva according to *Rambam* Comm.

□ A six handbreadth long furrow, as wide as it is deep, (minimum 1 handbreadth) marks off the row.
□ Along the rest of the border between the two greens, they can be adjacent.

ben Malki Tzedek), or as wide as it is deep (according to *Rambam Comm.*), R' Yehudah maintains that it is sufficient for the furrow to be a single handbreadth wide. The halachah, however, follows R' Akiva's opinion (*Rav; Rambam Comm.*).

4.

According to *Rambam Comm.*, the previous mishnah taught that between a *field* of greens and a *row* of a different species of greens, a furrow suffices as a separator, and it is not necessary to leave any wide gap. In R' Akiva's opinion, which the halachah follows (*Rambam, Hil. Kilayim* 3:12), the furrow needs to be six handbreadths long, but its width only needs to equal its depth, even if this is as little as a single handbreadth.

Thus, two different sorts of separators are available when dealing with greens: (1) Between *fields* of different greens, a gap of six-by-six handbreadths must be left (mishnah 2:10; *Rambam, Hil. Kilayim* 3:10); (2) between a *row* of one type of greens and a *field* of another, a narrow six-handbreadth-long furrow suffices (mishnah 3:3; *Rambam, Hil. Kilayim* 3:12).

The present mishnah legislates for the case where a *row* of one species of greens is planted next to a *row* of another species of greens. As understood by *Rambam* (who

R' Yehudah says: A width the full width of a foot.

4. **[I**f] someone plants two rows of melons, two rows of gourds, [and] two rows of Egyptian bean — [this is] permitted.

A row of melons, a row of gourds, [and] a row of Egyptian bean — [this is] forbidden.

YAD AVRAHAM

is followed here by *Rav*),[1] it is assumed that between *rows* of different greens, R' Akiva's narrow furrow separation is sufficient. However, with certain varieties this separation is not effective between single rows of different species, but only between pairs of rows. It is these varieties on which the mishnah here focuses.

הַנּוֹטֵעַ שְׁתֵּי שׁוּרוֹת שֶׁל קִשּׁוּאִין, שְׁתֵּי שׁוּרוֹת שֶׁל דְּלוּעִים, שְׁתֵּי שׁוּרוֹת שֶׁל פּוֹל הַמִּצְרִי — מֻתָּר. — *[If] someone plants two rows of melons, two rows of gourds, [and] two rows of Egyptian bean — [this is] permitted.*

These three varieties tend to spread extensively (*Shabbos* 85b; see mishnah 2:11). Consequently, single rows separated by narrow furrows intermingle, and the different species do not appear distinct (see preface). However, pairs of rows separated by such a furrow do stand out as distinct entities, and hence such an arrangement is permitted (*Rav; Rambam Comm.*).

שׁוּרָה שֶׁל קִשּׁוּאִים, שׁוּרָה שֶׁל דְּלוּעִים, שׁוּרָה שֶׁל פּוֹל הַמִּצְרִי — אָסוּר. — *A row of melons, a row of gourds, [and] a row of Egyptian bean — [this is] forbidden.*

The excessive spreading and entanglement which marks the growth of these species creates an impression of confusion when single rows are separated by only a furrow. To the observer, it appears as though the different species were planted all at once illegally. Consequently, even though a furrow is effective in separating between double rows of these species, it does not separate between single rows (*Rav; Rambam Comm.*).

An alternative interpretation of this mishnah assumes that the separation between the species here is not accomplished by means of

a furrow. Rather, the mechanism at work here is that encountered in the following mishnah: pointing the plants of different species in opposite directions. As will be seen there, two different species can be planted close together provided that they can be trained in opposite directions. Similarly, the rows of melons, gourds, and Egyptian bean can be planted adjacent to one another provided that the plants all point in opposite directions. Clearly, in an arrangement of double rows this is possible to accomplish: The two rows in each pair can be trained towards each other. However, with single rows the middle row cannot be oriented away from both of the outside rows (see diagram). Consequently, the mishnah states

double rows			single rows		
melons	gourds	E. beans	melons	gourds	E. beans

Ri MiGash: In single rows of these three species there is no direction in which to point the plants of the middle row so as to avoid the outside rows.

that these species may be grown adjacently in double rows, but not in single rows (*Responsa Ri MiGash* §26; *Otzar HaGeonim*

1. In contrast with his commentary to the previous mishnah, *Rav* explicitly states in this mishnah that a furrow serves as a separator.

כלאים
ג/ה
שׁוּרָה שֶׁל קִשּׁוּאִים, שׁוּרָה שֶׁל דְּלוּעִים, שׁוּרָה
שֶׁל פּוֹל הַמִּצְרִי, וְשׁוּרָה שֶׁל קִשּׁוּאִים — רַבִּי
אֱלִיעֶזֶר מַתִּיר, וַחֲכָמִים אוֹסְרִין.

[ה] **נוֹטֵעַ** אָדָם קִשּׁוּת וּדְלַעַת לְתוֹךְ גּוּמָא
אַחַת, וּבִלְבַד שֶׁתְּהֵא זוֹ נוֹטָה לְצַד
זֶה וְזוֹ נוֹטָה לְצַד זֶה [וְנוֹטֶה שֵׂעָר שֶׁל זוֹ לְכָאן

יד אברהם

(responsa) to *Shabbos* 85a).

Another approach to the mishnah is evident from *Rosh, Rush,* and *Ri ben Malki Tzedek.* This is that no differentiation whatsoever is necessary between double rows of melons, gourds, or Egyptian beans. Double rows of these species are inherently distinctive and when planted alongside each other need no separations. Single rows, however, do not stand out, and hence these may not be planted side by side (see *Chazon Ish* 8:12).[1]

שׁוּרָה שֶׁל קִשּׁוּאִים, שׁוּרָה שֶׁל דְּלוּעִים, שׁוּרָה
שֶׁל פּוֹל הַמִּצְרִי, וְשׁוּרָה שֶׁל קִשּׁוּאִים — רַבִּי
אֱלִיעֶזֶר מַתִּיר, וַחֲכָמִים אוֹסְרִין. — *A row of melons, a row of gourds, a row of Egyptian bean, and a row of melons — R' Eliezer permits, but the Sages forbid.*

The case in question involves four rows: two outer rows, both of melons, and two inner rows, one of gourds and one of Egyptian bean. R' Eliezer argues that the two rows of melons characterize the place as a *field* of melons. Accordingly, the single rows of gourds and Egyptian bean are viewed as single rows planted inside a larger field. But between rows and fields, a furrow serves as a separator (see preface). The Sages counter that since the rows of melons are not adjacent, they do

not constitute a field of melons. Accordingly, the whole arrangement is treated as a collection of single rows. But as stated above, between single rows of these species, a furrow is not an effective separator. Accordingly, the Sages forbid such an arrangement to be separated by furrows (*Rav; Rambam Comm.*).

As mentioned above, *Rash, Rosh,* and *Ri ben Malki Tzedek* explain that the mishnah's rulings here have nothing to do with the capacity of a furrow to serve as a separator. In their opinion, the question under discussion is: When do rows of these species — i.e. melons, gourds, and Egyptian beans — constitute intrinsically distinctive entities which need no separation? Now, above it was taught that if there were *three* adjacent rows each with a different one of these species, then none are distinctive and the whole arrangement is considered *kilayim*. In such a situation, no single row can be said to be an intrinsically distinct unit because it is overwhelmed by the presence of a majority of rows of different species. But, *two* rows (e.g. one of melons and one of gourds) would be allowed to be adjacent without any separation. Because neither row dominates the arrangement, each can be said to be intrinsically distinctive and

1. In the previous mishnah, *Rosh* and *Ri ben Malki Tzedek* fail to mention explicitly any separation between the row and field discussed there. This would seem to suggest that there as well they regard a row as distinctive, and not in need of any separation between it and a field (see also *Rosh* to mishnah 2:10 and *Mishnah Rishonah* ibid., end of s.v. ירק בתבואה). However, *Rash* clearly assumes that those who explain the furrow of mishnah 3 to be the planted row still require it to be separated by six handbreadths from the field.

משניות / כלאים – פרק ג: ערוגה **[80]**

A row of melons, a row of gourds, a row of Egyptian bean, and a row of melons — R' Eliezer permits, but the Sages forbid.

5. **A** person may plant a melon and a gourd in the same hole, provided that this one leans to this side and this one leans to this side [and the hair of this

YAD AVRAHAM

independent. R' Eliezer argues that the arrangement here of four rows should be treated like two sets of two rows. The first set which contains one row of melons and one row of gourds should be permitted, since two single rows of these species are regarded as distinctive and need no separation. Similarly, the row of Egyptian bean and the row of melons which make up the second set should be permitted.

Since the rows can be grouped in twos, R' Eliezer maintains further that each two rows can be viewed as a separate field which needs nothing to mark it off from the adjacent field, as taught in the first case of this mishnah. The Sages, however, do not accept these arguments, and treat the arrangement like the single rows of the second case of the mishnah. Accordingly, *the Sages forbid.*

5.

The mishnah now discusses a technique for separation which permits even melons and gourds to be grown in close proximity. *Chazon Ish* (7:23, 8:5, 9:10) maintains that this technique, namely, directing the plants in opposite directions, is effective only with greens. With grains, this method is not acceptable. Additionally, even with greens, this method only works in cases where otherwise it would be necessary to leave only a one-and-a-half-handbreadth gap. If a larger gap would ordinarily be required (e.g. the six-by-six gap between two fields of greens), the method described here is ineffective.

נוֹטֵעַ אָדָם קִשּׁוּת וּדְלַעַת לְתוֹךְ גּוּמָא אַחַת, וּבִלְבַד שֶׁתְּהֵא זוֹ נוֹטָה לְצַד זֶה וְזוֹ נוֹטָה לְצַד זֶה — *A person may plant a melon and a gourd in the same hole, provided that this one leans to this side and this one leans to this side*

It is permitted to grow plants of different species in the same small hole provided that the plants are trained in opposite directions. This is permissible even with melons and gourds despite their tendency to spread and entangle (as seen in the preceding mishnayos). It goes without saying that this technique is effective with other greens that do not have this tendency (*Rav; Rambam Comm.*).

Tosafos (*Shabbos* 85b, s.v. איתביה) disagree. In their opinion, this technique is

allowed only for a combination of gourds with melons, or gourds with Egyptian bean. But melons and Egyptian beans may not be planted in the same hole since these cannot be separated by training them in different directions (see also *Tos. HaRosh* and *Meiri* to *Shabbos* 85b and see *Sefer HaYashar LeRabbeinu Tam* (Schlezinger ed.) §267).

Chazon Ish (2:4, 9:10) suggests that only plants which are already large enough to be trained over the edge of the hole may be planted in close proximity inside the hole. This is because such plants may already be pointed in opposite directions as soon as they are planted in the hole. However, to plant seeds of different species inside the same hole, with the intent of directing the plants in opposite directions once they grow, would be forbidden.

כלאים
ג/ו

וְשֵׂעָר שֶׁל זוֹ לְכָאן, שֶׁכָּל מַה שֶׁאָסְרוּ חֲכָמִים לֹא גָזְרוּ אֶלָּא מִפְּנֵי מַרְאִית הָעָיִן].

[ו] הָיְתָה שָׂדֵהוּ זְרוּעָה בְצָלִים, וּמְבַקֵּשׁ לִיטַע בְּתוֹכָהּ שׁוּרוֹת שֶׁל דְּלוּעִים — רַבִּי יִשְׁמָעֵאל אוֹמֵר: עוֹקֵר שְׁתֵּי שׁוּרוֹת וְנוֹטֵעַ שׁוּרָה אַחַת וּמַנִּיחַ קָמַת בְּצָלִים בִּמְקוֹם שְׁתֵּי שׁוּרוֹת וְעוֹקֵר שְׁתֵּי שׁוּרוֹת וְנוֹטֵעַ שׁוּרָה אַחַת.

יד אברהם

[וְנוֹטֶה שֵׂעָר שֶׁל זוֹ לְכָאן וְשֵׂעָר שֶׁל זוֹ לְכָאן, שֶׁכָּל מַה שֶׁאָסְרוּ חֲכָמִים לֹא גָזְרוּ אֶלָּא מִפְּנֵי מַרְאִית הָעָיִן]. — [and the hair of this leans to here and the hair of this leans to here, for all that the Rabbis prohibited was decreed only because of suspicious appearance].

The body of this mishnah appears to have become corrupted through the inadvertent intrusion of a commentator's gloss into the text (see *Shinuyei Nuschaos* and *Meleches Shlomo*). This accounts for the statement *the hair of this leans to here and the hair of this leans to here*, which is nothing but a reformulation of the preceding statement *this one leans to this side and this one leans to this side*, and is absent from most early manuscripts (*Shinuyei Nuschaos*). [The term *hair* means the foliage produced by the plant — see *Peah* 2:3 (*Tos. Yom Tov*).] Likewise, the phrase *for all that the Rabbis prohibited was decreed only because of suspicious appearance* is absent from most early copies of the mishnah (see *Ri ben Malki Tzedek*).

Whatever the true origin of this phrase, it seems to indicate that the issue here in the mishnah involves Rabbinic law alone. That is, because the prohibitions involved in the case of the mishnah are merely Rabbinical, and because the Rabbis only forbade cases which have a suspicious appearance, the present case was permitted. Training the plants in opposite directions removes suspicion of illegal mixed planting and hence this technique was permitted by the Rabbis (*Rav; Rash; Ri ben*

Malki Tzedek). *Gra* (*Shenos Eliyahu, Peirush HaAroch*) explains that only when two species are sown simultaneously is the Torah prohibition on planting *kilayim* violated. The mishnah's case, however, involves a situation in which a second species is introduced into a hole in which another species is already growing. This type of mixing of species is normally Rabbinically forbidden because it allows for suspicion that the species were simultaneously and hence illegally planted. However, since directing the plants in opposite directions eliminates such suspicions, it was permitted (see also *Tos. Yom Tov* 1:8, s.v. הרי).

Rambam (whose text of the mishnah omits this line which refers to Rabbinic prohibitions) seems to understand that the mechanism described here by the mishnah overcomes a Biblical prohibition. In his opinion, to plant two species in close proximity may be Biblically forbidden, even though they are not planted simultaneously (see *Kesef Mishneh* to *Hil. Kilayim* 5:1 and *Tif. Yis., Boaz* 2:9). Nevertheless, the Torah only prohibits a planting in which the different species *appear* to be intermingled. If the species are clearly defined, then this is not forbidden. Accordingly, the mishnah teaches that training the plants in opposite directions eliminates any appearance of confusion and hence is permitted (*Chazon Ish* 2:10; see *Rambam Comm.* 3:1 and *Hil. Kilayim* 3:5 and 4:16; and see *Rabbeinu Chananel, Shabbos* 85b).

leans to here and the hair of this leans to here, for all that the Rabbis prohibited was decreed only because of suspicious appearance].

6. **[**If] his field was planted with onions, and he desired to plant inside it rows of gourds — Rabbi Yishmael says: He uproots two rows and plants one row and leaves standing onions in place of two rows and uproots two rows and plants one row.

YAD AVRAHAM

6.

The present mishnah considers the procedure for introducing rows of gourds into a field of onions. As understood by *Rav* (following *Rambam Comm.*), there are two problems which must be overcome. Firstly, the gourds and onions must be separated. As will be seen, there is a difference of opinion as to whether or not the furrow of mishnah 3 is effective in the present case. Secondly, the rows of gourds must not be associated with each other in such a way as to constitute a *field* of gourds. Independent rows of gourds can grow inside a *field* of onions without constituting *kilayim*; a *field* of gourds cannot. As will be seen, the rows of gourds are not regarded as constituting a *field* as long as they are separated from each other by a certain amount.

הָיְתָה שָׂדֵהוּ זָרוּעָה בְּצָלִים, וּמְבַקֵּשׁ לִטַּע בְּתוֹכָהּ שׁוּרוֹת שֶׁל דְּלוּעִים — — *[If] his field was planted with onions, and he desired to plant inside it rows of gourds —*

A person wishes to introduce rows of gourds into his onion field. At first glance this would seem to be the same case already encountered in mishnah 3: *[If] his field was planted with greens, and he wants to plant inside it a row of different greens.* However, here special care must be taken to insure that the rows of gourds do not become a *field* of gourds (see preface). Moreover, according to Rabbi Yishmael, even single rows of gourds are treated more stringently than single rows of other greens inside a field of a different green (*Rav; Rambam Comm.*).

Rash (following *Ri ben Malki Tzedek* and followed by *Rosh*) has a different approach to the mishnah than *Rav* and *Rambam*. In his view, the mishnah's concern is simply how to prevent the gourds from mingling with the onions. There is no consideration whatever of the relationship between the rows of gourds. According to *Rash*, mishnah 4

taught that the furrow separation of mishnah 3 is not adequate when dealing with single rows of gourds. Moreover, the rule of mishnah 4 that double rows of gourds are distinctive and may be planted adjacent to other species without any separation (according to *Rash*) does not apply in this case. Double rows might only be distinctive relative to other species planted in double rows, not relative to an entire field of another species. Furthermore, there is a difference between planting in an empty field and planting in an already planted one. In the former case, which corresponds to the situation in mishnah 4, two rows of gourds can be adjacent to two rows of another green; in the latter case, that of the present mishnah, one species must be uprooted to make space for another and the law is therefore more stringent (*Tos. Yom Tov*; see *Mishnah Rishonah*).

רַבִּי יִשְׁמָעֵאל אוֹמֵר: עוֹקֵר שְׁתֵּי שׁוּרוֹת וְנוֹטֵעַ שׁוּרָה אַחַת וּמַנִּיחַ קָמַת בְּצָלִים בִּמְקוֹם שְׁתֵּי שׁוּרוֹת וְעוֹקֵר שְׁתֵּי שׁוּרוֹת וְנוֹטֵעַ שׁוּרָה אַחַת. — *Rabbi Yishmael says: He uproots two rows and plants one row and leaves standing onions in place of two rows and uproots two rows and plants one row.*

The width of a row is four cubits, so

רַבִּי עֲקִיבָא אוֹמֵר: עוֹקֵר שְׁתֵּי שׁוּרוֹת וְנוֹטֵעַ
שְׁתֵּי שׁוּרוֹת וּמַנִּיחַ קָמַת בְּצָלִים בִּמְקוֹם שְׁתֵּי
שׁוּרוֹת וְעוֹקֵר שְׁתֵּי שׁוּרוֹת וְנוֹטֵעַ שְׁתֵּי שׁוּרוֹת.

יד אברהם

that uprooting two rows of onions clears a strip eight cubits wide. If such clearings are made in an onion field eight cubits apart, the result will be a field consisting of eight-cubit-wide strips of standing onions separated by eight-cubit-wide clearings. If the middle four cubits of each clearing are then planted with a row of gourds, then each row of gourds will be separated from the nearest row of onions by two cubits, and the rows of gourds themselves will be separated from each other by twelve cubits (see diagram A). In R' Yishmael's opinion, this two-cubit gap between the gourds and the onions is essential, since the furrow separator of mishnah 3 is not effective here. Similarly, the twelve-cubit distance between rows of gourds is imperative in order to preserve the character of the gourd plantings as single unrelated rows, rather than as one united field (see preface).

Thus, if someone wishes to plant rows of gourds inside his onion field, R' Yishmael prescribes the following procedure: *He uproots two rows* of onions, thus clearing a strip eight cubits wide, *and plants one row* of gourds within the clearing. *Yerushalmi* cites Shmuel who explains that the row of gourds is planted in the middle four cubits of the clearing,

so that a two-cubit gap is left on each side. *And leaves standing onions in place of two rows*, an eight-cubit-wide stretch, *and uproots two rows and plants one row* beyond the stretch of standing onions; another eight-cubit-wide clearing is made, and in the middle of it another row of gourds is planted. This pattern can be continued endlessly (*Rav; Rambam Comm.*).

Ri ben Malki Tzedek, Rash, and *Rosh* interpret R' Yishmael's words differently based on the premise that a four-cubit-wide "work area" must be left for each species. Thus, *he uproots two rows*, making an eight-cubit-wide clearing, *and plants one row* of gourds along the far edge of the clearing. This row of gourds is thus separated from the onions by eight cubits — four cubits of work area for the gourds and another four for the onions. He then *leaves standing onions in place of two rows*. There is no minimum width for the standing onions. This phrase simply means that the onions beyond the eight-cubit gap may lean in the direction of the gap and this does not affect it. The standing onions thus "point" into the *place of two rows*, i.e. the eight-cubit clearing. He then *uproots two rows and plants one row*, i.e. another eight-cubit-wide clearing is made on the other side of the standing onions, and at its far edge another row of gourds may be planted. In this arrangement, there are eight cubits between the gourds and the onions, and the rows of gourds them-

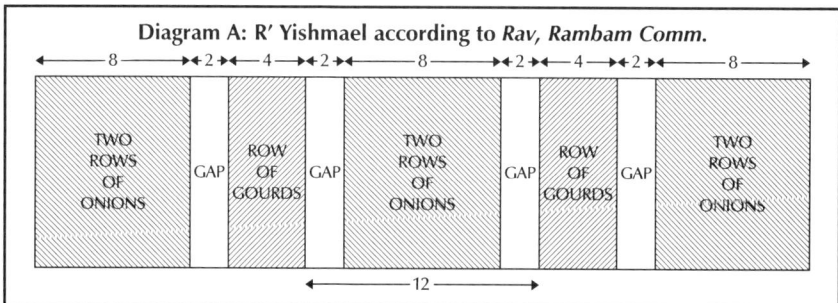

Diagram A: R' Yishmael according to *Rav, Rambam Comm.*

Rabbi Akiva says: He uproots two rows and plants
two rows and leaves standing onions in place of two
rows and uproots two rows and plants two rows.

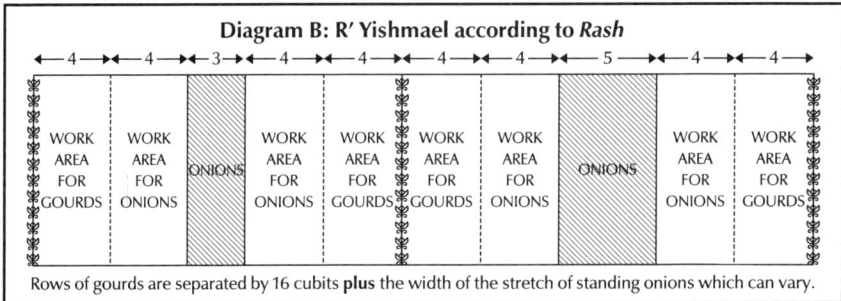

Diagram B: R' Yishmael according to *Rash*

←—4—→ ←—4—→ ←—3—→ ←—4—→ ←—4—→ ←—4—→ ←—4—→ ←——5——→ ←—4—→ ←—4—→

| WORK AREA FOR GOURDS | WORK AREA FOR ONIONS | ONIONS | WORK AREA FOR ONIONS | WORK AREA FOR GOURDS | WORK AREA FOR GOURDS | WORK AREA FOR ONIONS | ONIONS | WORK AREA FOR ONIONS | WORK AREA FOR GOURDS |

Rows of gourds are separated by 16 cubits **plus** the width of the stretch of standing onions which can vary.

selves are at least sixteen cubits apart (see
diagram B). [As will be seen below, some of
the work areas can be eliminated if the
gourds are pointed away from the onions,
and the distance between the rows of gourds
can then be reduced to twelve cubits.]

רַבִּי עֲקִיבָא אוֹמֵר: עוֹקֵר שְׁתֵּי שׁוּרוֹת וְנוֹטֵעַ שְׁתֵּי
שׁוּרוֹת וּמַנִּיחַ קָמַת בְּצָלִים בִּמְקוֹם שְׁתֵּי שׁוּרוֹת
— וְעוֹקֵר שְׁתֵּי שׁוּרוֹת וְנוֹטֵעַ שְׁתֵּי שׁוּרוֹת.
*Rabbi Akiva says: He uproots two rows
and plants two rows and leaves standing
onions in place of two rows and uproots
two rows and plants two rows.*

R' Akiva disagrees with R' Yishmael
on two counts. First of all, in R' Akiva's
opinion there is no need to leave two
cubits between the onions and gourds —
the furrow of mishnah 3 is sufficient to
separate them. Secondly, the distance
between rows of gourds can be as little as
eight cubits without the rows being
viewed as constituting a field of gourd.
Thus, R' Akiva advises: *He uproots two
rows and plants two rows* — i.e. he
plants gourds in the entire eight cubits
which he has cleared, *and leaves standing onions in place of two rows* — i.e. he
leaves eight cubits of standing onions. He
then *uproots two rows and plants two
rows* — i.e. he replaces eight cubits of
onions with gourds. The gourds must be
separated from the onions by a furrow,
but otherwise no gaps need to be left.

The rows of gourds themselves are separated by eight cubits of standing onions
(*Rav; Rambam Comm.*; see diagram C).

[It is not entirely clear what R' Akiva
would hold if a person planted single
rows of gourds, rather than double rows.
Perhaps he permits the use of a furrow as
a separator only between double rows of
gourds and onions, but not between
single rows (see mishnah 4). On the other
hand, it is possible that he mentions two
rows simply to parallel R' Yishmael and
to teach that the entire eight-cubit clearing called for by R' Yishmael may be
planted with gourds (*Tos. Anshei
Shem*).]

Rash, Rosh, and *Ri ben Malki Tzedek*
explain that R' Akiva disagrees with R'

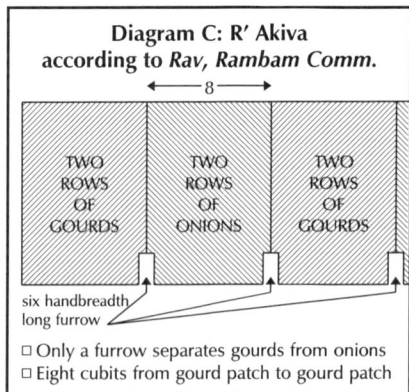

**Diagram C: R' Akiva
according to *Rav, Rambam Comm.***

←——8——→

| TWO ROWS OF GOURDS | TWO ROWS OF ONIONS | TWO ROWS OF GOURDS |

six handbreadth
long furrow

□ Only a furrow separates gourds from onions
□ Eight cubits from gourd patch to gourd patch

וַחֲכָמִים אוֹמְרִים: אִם אֵין בֵּין שׁוּרָה לַחֲבֶרְתָּהּ שְׁתֵּים עֶשְׂרֵה אַמָּה, לֹא יְקַיֵּם אֶת הַזֶּרַע שֶׁל בֵּינָתַיִם.

[ז] **דְּלַעַת** בְּיָרָק כְּיָרָק. וּבִתְבוּאָה, נוֹתְנִין לָהּ בֵּית רֹבַע.

יד אברהם

Yishmael on one point: that according to R' Akiva, a single row of gourds does not need its own work area, while according to R' Yishmael, a single row of gourds must be separated from the onions by two work areas, one for the onions and one for the gourds. Thus, in Rabbi Akiva's opinion, a single row of gourds must be separated from the onions by only four cubits, the work area left for the onions. According to R' Akiva, only when there are two rows of gourds do they need their own work area. Thus, only when planting two rows of gourds must eight cubits be left between the gourds and the onions. R' Akiva therefore states: *he uproots two rows —* an eight-cubit-wide clearing — *and plants two rows* at one end of the clearing, *and leaves standing onions in place of two rows —* i.e. he leaves standing onions on the other side of the clearing which can point into the clearing. The separation between gourds and onions is eight cubits, the same as required by R' Yishmael. The process is then repeated — i.e. *he uproots two rows and plants two rows,* giving sixteen cubits, plus the width of the standing stretch of onions, as the distance between gourd patches (see diagram D).

וַחֲכָמִים אוֹמְרִים: אִם אֵין בֵּין שׁוּרָה לַחֲבֶרְתָּהּ שְׁתֵּים עֶשְׂרֵה אַמָּה, לֹא יְקַיֵּם אֶת הַזֶּרַע שֶׁל בֵּינָתַיִם. — *But the Sages say: If there are*

not twelve cubits between one row [of gourds] and the next, he may not retain the plants in the middle.

The Sages agree with R' Yishmael that twelve cubits must separate individual rows of gourds if they are not to be viewed collectively as a gourd field. They do not, however, accept his position that a furrow is not effective in separating a row of gourds from onions. In the Sages' view, introducing a row of gourds into an onion field is no different than introducing any other greens into that field. Just as in the latter case a furrow suffices as a separation (mishnah 3), so too in the present case. Thus, no gap other than the furrow need be left between the gourds and the onions. Because the distance between rows of gourds must be twelve cubits, there must be at least three standing rows of onions between rows of gourds (*Rav; Rambam Comm.;* see diagram E).

Rash, Rosh, and *Ri ben Malki Tzedek* explain that the Sages require twelve cubits between rows of gourds in addition to the space taken up by the standing onions. It is assumed that the rows of gourds which

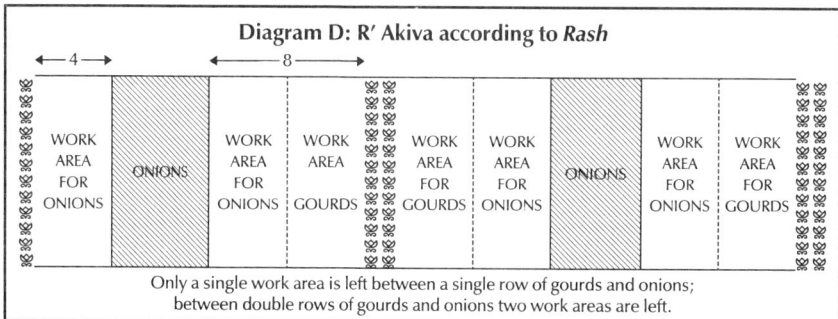

Diagram D: R' Akiva according to *Rash*

Only a single work area is left between a single row of gourds and onions;
between double rows of gourds and onions two work areas are left.

But the Sages say: If there are not twelve cubits between one row [of gourds] and the next, he may not retain the plants in the middle.

7. **G**ourd in greens is like greens. But in grain, we give it a *beis rova*.

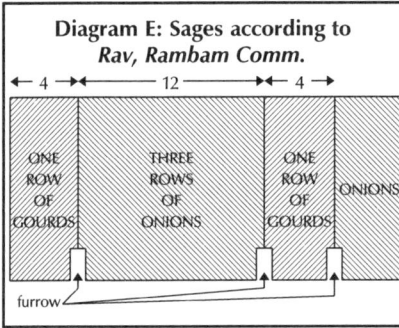

Diagram E: Sages according to Rav, Rambam Comm.

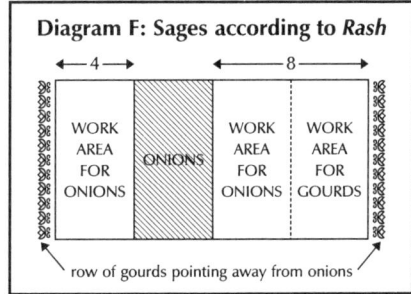

Diagram F: Sages according to *Rash*

sandwich the standing onions are pointing away from the onions. In that case, ordinarily it should be sufficient to leave work areas on either side of the onions, and it should not be necessary to leave work areas for the gourds. However, the Sages maintain that on one side of the onions two work areas must be left (see diagram F). If the outside gourd rows are pointing towards the onions, then two work areas must be left on both sides of the onions. In that case, there will be sixteen cubits between the rows of gourds (see diagram B, above). This is the same as R' Yishmael's opinion. The difference between the Sages and R' Yishmael occurs in the case in which the outside gourds are pointing away from the onions. The Sages distribute

the twelve-cubit separation unevenly — i.e. one work area on one side of the onions, two work areas on the other. R' Yishmael leaves six cubits on each side (see diagram G).

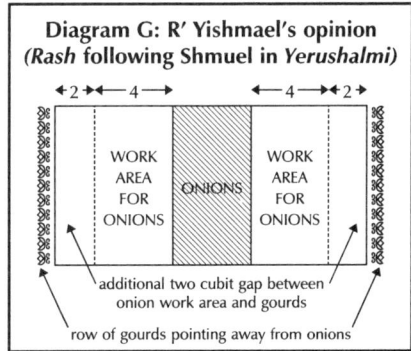

Diagram G: R' Yishmael's opinion (*Rash* following Shmuel in *Yerushalmi*)

7.

This mishnah deals with the Greek gourd. In mishnah 2:11 it was taught that of all those vines which tend to spread and entangle, the Greek gourd is the most prolific. Because of this, it is dealt with more stringently in certain cases than other gourds and melons, as will be seen again in the coming mishnah (*Rav; Rosh; Rash*). [*Rambam* does not specify that the gourd mentioned in this mishnah is the Greek gourd. See however *Mahari Korkus* to *Hil. Kilayim* 3:14 that *Rambam* also accepts this.]

דְּלַעַת בְּיָרָק כְּיָרָק. וּבִתְבוּאָה, נוֹתְנִין לָהּ בֵּית רֹבַע. — *Gourd in greens is like greens. But in grain, we give it a beis rova.*

If someone wants to plant a single

Greek gourd plant next to other greens, he must leave a six-handbreadth gap. This is the work area of greens, so that in this case the Greek gourd is treated like

הָיְתָה שָׂדֵהוּ זְרוּעָה תְּבוּאָה, וּבִקֵּשׁ לִטַּע
לְתוֹכָהּ שׁוּרָה שֶׁל דְּלוּעִין, נוֹתְנִין לָהּ לַעֲבוֹדָתָהּ
שִׁשָּׁה טְפָחִים. וְאִם הִגְדִּילָה, יַעֲקֹר מִלְּפָנֶיהָ. רַבִּי
יוֹסֵי אוֹמֵר: נוֹתְנִין לָהּ עֲבוֹדָתָהּ אַרְבַּע אַמּוֹת.
אָמְרוּ לוֹ: הֲתַחְמִיר זוֹ מִן הַגֶּפֶן? אָמַר לָהֶן:
מָצִינוּ שֶׁזּוֹ חֲמוּרָה מִן הַגֶּפֶן, שֶׁלְּגֶפֶן יְחִידִית נוֹתְנִין
לָהּ עֲבוֹדָתָהּ שִׁשָּׁה טְפָחִים, וְלִדְלַעַת יְחִידִית
נוֹתְנִין לָהּ בֵּית רֹבַע.

יד אברהם

greens. However, if planting a Greek gourd next to grain, the gap which must be left is equal to the work area of grain, viz. a *beis rova* (*Rav*; *Rosh*; *Rash*; see *Meleches Shlomo*).

[In mishnah 2:10 a six-handbreadth separation was prescribed between two *fields* of greens (see mishnah 3:1, s.v. ערוגה). *Chazon Ish* (6:1:29-30 and 9:1) argues that a single plant of one species of greens needs to be separated from a field of another species of greens only by the radius throughout which it draws nourishment. This is one-and-a-half or three handbreadths, and not six handbreadths. However, from *Rav*, *Rosh*, and *Rash* here, it seems that the case of *gourd in greens* involves a *single* Greek gourd plant (*Meleches Shlomo* states this explicitly), and that the six-handbreadth separation is the one encountered in connection with greens in mishnah 2:10. This would suggest that even between a single specimen of one species of greens and a field of another, the six-handbreadth separation is required. The matter, however, needs further study.]

Rambam (*Comm*. and *Hil. Kilayim* 3:10) explains the case here of *gourd in greens* as referring to a *field* of gourds next to a field of greens. Just as any two fields of different greens must be separated by a square of six handbreadths (mishnah 2:10), so too a field of gourds must be separated from a field of other greens by such a square. Thus, *gourd in greens is like greens*.

הָיְתָה שָׂדֵהוּ זְרוּעָה תְּבוּאָה, וּבִקֵּשׁ לִטַּע לְתוֹכָהּ שׁוּרָה שֶׁל דְּלוּעִין, נוֹתְנִין לָהּ לַעֲבוֹדָתָהּ שִׁשָּׁה טְפָחִים. — *[If] his field was planted with grain, and he wished to plant inside it a*

row of gourds, we give it for its work six handbreadths.

In the previous case, the mishnah discussed a single gourd plant in grain and required a *beis rova* separation; here, it discusses a *row* of gourds in grain. A row of gourds is considered more distinctive than a single gourd plant and for this reason it is sufficient to leave a gap only six handbreadths wide between a row of gourd and a grain field. *Tosefta* (2:13) adds that the separation here must be ten-and-a-half cubits long (*Rav*; *Rosh*; *Rash*).

Rambam, who explained the previous case of gourd in grain as involving a *field* of gourds next to a grain field, understands the present case as teaching that a *row* is treated more leniently than a *field*. Thus, instead of a *beis rova* separation, a six-handbreadth separation suffices (*Rambam Comm*. and *Hil. Kilayim* 3:13). [*Rambam* fails to specify any length for this separation. See *Radbaz* and *Mahari Korkus* to *Hil. Kilayim* 3:13; see also *Derech Emunah* 3:66.]

וְאִם הִגְדִּילָה, יַעֲקֹר מִלְּפָנֶיהָ. — *If it grew large, he must uproot in front of it.*

If the gourds grew large and their branches spread into the six-handbreadth gap, then those branches which penetrated the six-handbreadth zone must be removed (*Rav*, *Rambam Comm*., Vilna ed.). Alternatively, if the branches and leaves of the gourd reached the grain and became entangled with it, the grain in front of the gourd must be

3
7

[If] his field was planted with grain, and he wished to plant inside it a row of gourds, we give it for its work six handbreadths. If it grew large, he must uproot in front of it. R' Yose says: We give it for its work four cubits.

They said to him: Do you treat this more stringently than the grapevine? He said to them: We find that this is stricter than the grapevine, because for a single grapevine we give for its work six handbreadths, while for a single gourd [plant] we give a *beis rova*.

removed to prevent further entanglement (*Rambam, Hil. Kilayim* 3:13; *Rosh*).

רַבִּי יוֹסֵי אוֹמֵר: נוֹתְנִין לָהּ עֲבוֹדָתָהּ אַרְבַּע אַמּוֹת. — *R' Yose says: We give it for its work four cubits.*

R' Yose maintains that the row of gourds must be separated from the grain by four cubits (*Rav; Rambam Comm.*). This is a very stringent position and is challenged by the Sages in what follows.

אָמְרוּ לוֹ: הֲתַחֲמִיר זוֹ מִן הַגֶּפֶן? — *They said to him: Do you treat this more stringently than the grapevine?*

Kilayim involving grapevines is more stringent than other forms of *kilayim*, as evidenced by the fact that it creates a prohibition on benefit (*Tos. Yom Tov* from mishnah 8:1). Accordingly, one would expect that the separation required between a *row* of gourds and grain should be no greater than that needed between a *row* of grapevines and grain. Yet, in mishnah 4:5 it is taught that according to Beis Hillel a *row* of grapevines must be separated from grain by six handbreadths. And here, R' Yose requires a four-cubit separation (which is the gap required between a vineyard and grain). He is therefore challenged by the Sages: *Do you treat this* [i.e. gourds] *more stringently than the grapevine?* (*Rav; Rosh; Rash*).

Rambam Comm. understands the Sages' question to be based on the separation required between a *single* grapevine and grain. The law is that if a person has a field of grain and he wishes to plant a single

grapevine next to it, then he needs to leave a gap of six handbreadths. Accordingly, argue the Sages, if a person has a field of grain and he wants to plant a gourd next to it, he should not need to leave a gap greater than six handbreadths. Although the case of our mishnah deals with a *row* of gourds, and not with a *single* gourd, there should be no difference between them since a row is simply a collection of single gourds arranged single file. Consequently, R' Yose is challenged to explain how it is that he is more stringent with gourds than with grapevines.

Rambam assumes an equivalence between a single plant and a row. This is disputed by *Rav* (et al.) who explains the previous case of the mishnah — *in grain, we give it a beis rova* — as dealing with a single gourd plant next to a field of grain.

It should also be noted that according to *Rambam*, the case here specifically involves a row of gourds to be planted next to an *existing* field of grain. As will be seen below, in *Rambam's* opinion there is a difference between the case in which a gourd is to be planted next to an existing grain field and the reverse case in which grain is to be planted next to an existing gourd plant.

אָמַר לָהֶן: מָצִינוּ שֶׁזּוֹ חֲמוּרָה מִן הַגֶּפֶן, שֶׁלְּגֶפֶן יְחִידִית נוֹתְנִין לָהּ עֲבוֹדָתָהּ שִׁשָּׁה טְפָחִים, וְלִדְלַעַת יְחִידִית נוֹתְנִין לָהּ בֵּית רֹבַע. — *He said to them: We find that this is stricter than the grapevine, because for a single grapevine we give for its work six handbreadths, while for a single gourd [plant] we give a beis rova.*

R' Yose counters that although *kilayim* involving grapes is stricter than other forms of *kilayim*, nevertheless this does not mean that the spacing required

רַבִּי מֵאִיר אוֹמֵר מִשּׁוּם רַבִּי יִשְׁמָעֵאל: כָּל שְׁלֹשָׁה דְלוּעִין לְבֵית סְאָה, לֹא יָבִיא זֶרַע לְתוֹךְ בֵּית סְאָה.

רַבִּי יוֹסֵי בֶּן הַחוֹטֵף אֶפְרָתִי אָמַר מִשּׁוּם רַבִּי יִשְׁמָעֵאל: כָּל שְׁלֹשָׁה דְלוּעִין לְבֵית כּוֹר, לֹא יָבִיא זֶרַע לְתוֹךְ בֵּית כּוֹר.

יד אברהם

between gourds and grain cannot be larger than that required between grapes and grain. This is because the spacing laws are a function of the growth properties of a species, not the severity of the prohibition. And because the gourd plant grows more extensively than does the grapevine, it requires a greater separation. For this reason we find that the spacing required between a single gourd plant and grain is larger than that required between a single grapevine and grain. The single gourd requires a *beis rova* separation, as stated at the beginning of this mishnah, whereas the single grapevine needs only a six-handbreadth separation (see mishnah 6:1). Just as in the case of a single plant next to grain, the spacing required for a gourd is greater than that required for a grapevine, so also in the case of a row, the spacing for gourds is greater than that for grapevines (*Rav; Rosh; Rash*).

R' Yose points to the case of a single gourd in grain as an example in which gourd is treated more stringently than a grapevine. According to *Rav* (et al.), this case is in fact the earlier case of our mishnah: *gourd . . . in grain . . . a beis rova*. However, *Rambam* (as noted above) explains that ruling with reference to a *field* of gourds next to a field of grain. Moreover, it seems clear that according to *Rambam*, the separation required between a single gourd plant and a field of grain should be identical to the separation required between a row of gourds and a field of grain — i.e. six handbreadths. This is because, as noted above, *Rambam* maintains that there is no difference between a row and a single plant. However, above it is stated that a row

of gourds next to grain must be spaced six handbreadths (or four cubits according to R' Yose), while here R' Yose refers to an apparently unanimous ruling that a single gourd must be given a *beis rova*! Clearly the case here involving a single gourd is *not* equivalent to the earlier case involving a row.

The resolution of all this would seem to be that above, the situation discussed by the mishnah is one in which *his field was planted with grain, and he wished to plant inside it a row of gourds*. That is, the grain was already growing in the field, and only then did he decide to plant a row of gourds inside it. Since the grain came first, it is sufficient to leave a small six-handbreadth gap between the grain and the gourd, and if the gourds grow out of control *he must uproot in front of it*.

Here, however, R' Yose is pointing to a case in which a single gourd plant was already growing, and now the farmer desired to plant grain nearby. Since the gourd came first and since gourds tend to grow extensively, the entire radius throughout which the gourd might spread is considered the growing area of the gourd. Indeed, it is likely that the gourd has already spread over a large area. In that case, to plant grain nearby would look like planting *kilayim* and consequently the grain must be planted outside this area (see *Mahari Korkus* and *Ohr Same'ach* to Hil. Kilayim 4:3). Accordingly, R' Yose states that where a single gourd is already growing in an area, it is given a *beis rova*, and any grain to be planted must be planted a *beis rova* away. This is agreed to by all, and since someone who wants to plant grain near an already growing single grapevine needs to distance the grain only six handbreadths, it serves as an example in which the spacing between gourds and grain is greater than that between grapevines and grain.

R' Yose thus argues that just as we find in

R' Meir says in the name of R' Yishmael: If there are three gourd plants per *beis se'ah*, he may not bring [other] seed into the *beis se'ah*.

R' Yose ben HaChotef Efrosi said in the name of R' Yishmael: [If] there are three gourd plants per *beis kor*, he may not bring [other] seed into the *beis kor*.

YAD AVRAHAM

the case in which the gourd or grapevine preceded the grain that the spacing between the gourd and the grain is greater than that between the grapevine and grain, so too this spacing can be greater in the case in which the grain came first. Consequently, in such a case it is feasible for the separation to be four cubits (*Rambam Comm.* and *Hil. Kilayim* 4:3, 3:13; see *Radbaz, Mahari Korkus* and *Ohr Same'ach* loc.cit.; cf. *Chazon Ish* 9:12).

רַבִּי מֵאִיר אוֹמֵר מִשּׁוּם רַבִּי יִשְׁמָעֵאל: כָּל שְׁלֹשָׁה דְלוּעִין לְבֵית סְאָה, לֹא יָבִיא זֶרַע לְתוֹךְ בֵּית סְאָה. — *R' Meir says in the name of R' Yishmael: If there are three gourd plants per beis se'ah, he may not bring [other] seed into the beis se'ah.*

R' Meir disputes the law stated by the *Tanna Kamma* above that a single gourd plant inside a field of grain must be distanced by only a *beis rova*. Instead, he quotes R' Yishmael to the effect that a single gourd plant is given a third of a *beis se'ah* (*Rav*). Since a *beis se'ah* contains twenty-four *beis rova's*, a third of a *beis se'ah* is eight times the spacing required by the *Tanna Kamma*.

Rambam Comm. assumes that R' Meir is referring to a case in which a person wished to plant grain next to an already-growing gourd plant. In such a case, R' Yose indicated that the grain must be separated by a *beis rova*. R' Meir considers this separation too small and requires the grain to be planted a third of a *beis se'ah* away. Thus, if there were three gourd plants distributed evenly throughout a *beis se'ah*, no grain could be planted anywhere within the *beis se'ah*.

רַבִּי יוֹסֵי בֶּן הַחוֹטֵף אֶפְרָתִי אָמַר מִשּׁוּם רַבִּי יִשְׁמָעֵאל: כָּל שְׁלֹשָׁה דְלוּעִין לְבֵית כּוֹר, לֹא יָבִיא זֶרַע לְתוֹךְ בֵּית כּוֹר. — *R' Yose ben HaChotef Efrosi said in the name of R' Yishmael: [If] there are three gourd plants per beis kor, he may not bring*

[other] *seed into the beis kor.*

The *Tanna* R' Yose ben HaChotef Efrosi is not mentioned elsewhere in the Mishnah (*Rambam Comm., Introduction to the Mishnah*). He is credited here with a different version of R' Yishmael's opinion than that reported above by R' Meir. *Yerushalmi* explains that the two versions represent R' Yishmael's earlier and later opinions (*Rosh; Rash; Ri ben Malki Tzedek;* cf. standard versions of *Yerushalmi* and see *Mareh HaPanim*, s.v. שתחלתו). At first, he had maintained that a third of a *beis se'ah* was a sufficient separation. Later, he decided that only a third of a *beis kor* would suffice. A *beis kor* equals thirty *beis se'ahs*, so that a third of a *beis kor* equals ten *beis se'ahs* — thirty times larger than his original opinion. According to his later position, if there were three gourd plants distributed throughout an area of 75,000 sq. cubits (a *beis kor*), no grain could be planted within the entire *beis kor* (*Rambam Comm.*).

The separations required by R' Yishmael are enormous. A third of a *beis se'ah* amounts to an area of 833.3 sq. cubits and is contained by a square with sides of almost 29 cubits. A third of a *beis kor* is a square with sides of just over 158 cubits and an area of 25,000 sq. cubits! It is difficult to see why R' Yishmael was so stringent.

In an attempt to reduce somewhat the severity of R' Yishmael's position, *Tif. Yis.* suggests that R' Yishmael referred exclusively to the case of *three* gourd plants growing within a given area (i.e. a *beis se'ah* or a *beis kor*). For a single gourd plant, however, R' Yishmael would agree with the *Tanna Kamma* that only a *beis rova* separation is needed. Additionally, *Tif. Yis.* proposes that the separations here are not a full *third of a*

[א] קָרַחַת הַכֶּרֶם – בֵּית שַׁמַּאי אוֹמְרִים:
עֶשְׂרִים וְאַרְבַּע אַמּוֹת. וּבֵית הַלֵּל
אוֹמְרִים: שֵׁשׁ עֶשְׂרֵה אַמָּה.
מְחוֹל הַכֶּרֶם – בֵּית שַׁמַּאי אוֹמְרִים: שֵׁשׁ עֶשְׂרֵה
אַמָּה. וּבֵית הַלֵּל אוֹמְרִים: שְׁתֵּים עֶשְׂרֵה אַמָּה.
וְאֵיזוֹ הִיא קָרַחַת הַכֶּרֶם? כֶּרֶם שֶׁחָרַב מֵאֶמְצָעוֹ.

יד אברהם

beis se'ah or a full *third of a beis kor*, but only half of these amounts. The separations here are to be calculated on the assumption that the gourd plant is centered within the specified area. Thus, a third of a *beis se'ah* separation does not mean a 29-cubit separation, but only a 14.5-cubit separation. Similarly, the third of a *beis kor* separation would be "only"

79 cubits, rather than 158.

Finally, it should be noted that according to *Rambam* (see above), the issue in question only arises when the gourds came first. If gourds were to be introduced into an existing field of grain, even R' Yishmael would agree that a six-handbreadth (or, according to R' Yose, a four-cubit) separation suffices.

Chapter 4

1.

The incidental mention of *kilayim* of grapevines in the last mishnah of the previous chapter is now followed by an extensive treatment of this topic. The next four chapters of the tractate are devoted to the laws of *kilei hakerem* — illegal mixtures in a vineyard.

The first mishnayos of this chapter deal with spacing laws — i.e. the gap which must be left in order to legally plant grain or greens in a vineyard. As a general rule, foreign seed[1] must be distanced four cubits from a vineyard and six handbreadths from a single grapevine. A vineyard consists of at least five vines arranged in a particular formation (see mishnah 4:6).

Ordinarily, as long as the appropriate gaps are left, there are no limits on how much or how little of the foreign species may be planted. However, when the area available for planting is sandwiched in between two vineyards, foreign planting is forbidden there unless the area for planting is large enough to constitute a distinct field. The following mishnah considers such a scenario.

קָרַחַת הַכֶּרֶם — *The clearing of a vineyard* —

[The mishnah explains below that this refers to an area within a vineyard which has been cleared of vines. If grain or greens are to be planted in this clearing, the planting area must constitute an independent field in order to be considered separate and distinct from the surrounding vineyards. The dispute which

follows as to the minimum size of the clearing is a direct outgrowth of a dispute regarding the dimensions of a distinct and separate field.]

בֵּית שַׁמַּאי אוֹמְרִים: עֶשְׂרִים וְאַרְבַּע אַמּוֹת. וּבֵית הַלֵּל אוֹמְרִים: שֵׁשׁ עֶשְׂרֵה אַמָּה. — *Beis Shammai say: twenty-four cubits. But Beis Hillel say: sixteen cubits.*

There must be at least twenty-four cubits (according to Beis Shammai) or

---

1. In general, grain and greens constitute *kilayim* in a vineyard. This is discussed in greater detail below, mishnah 5:8 and mishnah 7:7.

1. The clearing of a vineyard — Beis Shammai say: twenty-four cubits. But Beis Hillel say: sixteen cubits.

The perimeter of a vineyard — Beis Shammai say: sixteen cubits. But Beis Hillel say: twelve cubits.

And what is the clearing of a vineyard? A vineyard which has been destroyed in its middle. If there

YAD AVRAHAM

sixteen cubits (according to Beis Hillel) between the vines on one side of the clearing and those on the opposite side, in order to plant within the clearing. Both schools agree that a work area four cubits wide must be left along the edge of the vineyard. This work area was considered part of the vineyard and was needed to make room for the oxen and wagons used during the vintage and plowing. No foreign planting whatsoever can be done within this work area. Beyond this work area, planting is permitted only if there is an area large enough to constitute a distinct field. Because of the sandwiching by the vineyard on the opposite side, any area smaller than that of a field would be viewed as part of the overall vineyard. As part of the vineyard, foreign planting would constitute *kilayim* and would be forbidden.

Now, in Beis Shammai's opinion, an area of eight cubits across counts as a distinct field. When sandwiched between two vineyards, however, a patch must be large enough to contain *two* such fields for planting to be permitted. Up to eight cubits from the edge of each vineyard — i.e. from the edge of the work area of the vineyard — is considered peripheral to that vineyard. Therefore, only an eight-cubit-wide area outside *each* vineyard is considered distinct. If the planting area between two vineyards is only ten cubits across, for example, this will be viewed as five more cubits on the periphery of each vineyard. Only if the planting area is at least sixteen cubits across does it contain enough planting area for two eight-cubit fields, each of which is distinct and

independent of the adjacent vineyard. Thus, according to Beis Shammai, the clearing must be at least twenty-four cubits across, four cubits at each end as a work area for the vines, and an additional sixteen cubits as a foreign planting area.

In Beis Hillel's opinion, a field is only four cubits across. Therefore, an eight-cubit-wide area for planting is sufficient for two independent fields between the two vineyards. A clearing of sixteen cubits is sufficient to permit foreign planting — a work area of four cubits at each end, and an additional eight-cubit planting area (*Rav; Rosh; Rash*).

Note that the measurements given for the clearing are for one dimension. If the clearing is surrounded by the vineyard on all four sides, the clearing will have to be sixteen cubits by sixteen cubits so that no planting is considered peripheral to the surrounding vineyards (*Rav; Rosh; Rash*).

מְחוֹל הַכֶּרֶם – בֵּית שַׁמַּאי אוֹמְרִים: שֵׁשׁ עֶשְׂרֵה אַמָּה. וּבֵית הִלֵּל אוֹמְרִים: שְׁתֵּים עֶשְׂרֵה אַמָּה. — *The perimeter of a vineyard — Beis Shammai say: sixteen cubits. But Beis Hillel say: twelve cubits.*

[The perimeter of a vineyard is the empty area between a vineyard and its surrounding wall. It is discussed in mishnah 2 below.]

וְאֵיזוֹ הִיא קָרַחַת הַכֶּרֶם? כֶּרֶם שֶׁחָרַב מֵאֶמְצָעוֹ. — *And what is the clearing of a vineyard? A vineyard which has been destroyed in its middle.*

The *clearing of a vineyard* debated by Beis Shammai and Beis Hillel above refers to a clearing which has been created in the *middle* of a vineyard. The clearing is flanked on at least two sides by vine-

אִם אֵין שָׁם שֵׁשׁ עֶשְׂרֵה אַמָּה, לֹא יָבִיא זֶרַע לְשָׁם. הָיוּ שָׁם שֵׁשׁ עֶשְׂרֵה אַמָּה, נוֹתְנִין לוֹ עֲבוֹדָתוֹ, וְזוֹרֵעַ אֶת הַמּוֹתָר.

[ב] **אֵיזֶה** הוּא מְחוֹל הַכֶּרֶם? בֵּין כֶּרֶם לַגָּדֵר. אִם אֵין שָׁם שְׁתֵּים עֶשְׂרֵה אַמָּה, לֹא יָבִיא זֶרַע לְשָׁם. הָיוּ שָׁם שְׁתֵּים עֶשְׂרֵה אַמָּה,

yards (*Rav; Rosh; Rash*; see below, mishnah 4:8, s.v. רבי אליעזר). [If the clearing is not surrounded by vineyards, but merely by individual vines, then the laws for spacing between foreign species and individual vines apply, and foreign planting is permitted even if the clearing is not sixteen cubits across.]

If the clearing was not created by uprooting existing vines, but instead the vineyard was initially planted with a large gap left unplanted in the middle, it is not clear whether the laws for a vineyard clearing apply. In the latter case, since the site of the clearing never was planted with vines, perhaps it is not automatically viewed as peripheral to the vineyard (see *Rambam, Hil. Kilayim* 7:4 and *Ravad* to *Hil. Kilayim* 7:3; see also *Derech Emunah* 7:57, *Beur HaHalachah* 7:11, s.v. כרם שחרב כו׳; *Tos. Anshei Shem*).

אִם אֵין שָׁם שֵׁשׁ עֶשְׂרֵה אַמָּה, לֹא יָבִיא זֶרַע לְשָׁם. — *If there are not sixteen cubits*

there, he may not bring [other] seed there.

This anonymous statement is consistent with the view of Beis Hillel stated above that a vineyard clearing is sixteen cubits across (*Rav; Rambam Comm.*). Above, the mishnah presented the different opinions regarding the size of a vineyard clearing, without detailing the ramifications. Here, the mishnah states that if the clearing is not of the required size, it is forbidden to plant in it any foreign seed.

הָיוּ שָׁם שֵׁשׁ עֶשְׂרֵה אַמָּה, נוֹתְנִין לוֹ עֲבוֹדָתוֹ, וְזוֹרֵעַ אֶת הַמּוֹתָר. — *[If] there were sixteen cubits there, we give it its work area, and he may plant the rest.*

If the clearing is of the proper dimensions, then it is permitted to plant foreign seed there provided that the four-cubit work areas of the vineyards on each side of the clearing are left unplanted (*Rav; Rosh; Rash; Rambam Comm.*).

2.

The mishnah now defines *the perimeter of the vineyard* and explains its practical significance. The explanation is given in terms of Beis Hillel's opinion (in mishnah 1) that the vineyard perimeter is twelve cubits.

אֵיזֶה הוּא מְחוֹל הַכֶּרֶם? בֵּין כֶּרֶם לַגָּדֵר. — *What is the perimeter of the vineyard? [The area] between the vineyard and the wall.*

The empty space left between the end of the vineyard and its surrounding wall is known as the *perimeter of the vineyard* (*Rav; Rosh; Rash; Rambam Comm.*).

The etymology of the term מְחוֹל is not

certain. *Rav* cites *Jeremiah* 31:12 where it occurs in the sense of a dance circle. Likewise, the space at the perimeter of the vineyard, which encircles the vineyard, is called מְחוֹל (see also *Ri ben Malki Tzedek*). It should be noted, however, that the laws regarding this perimeter apply even if the space does not completely encircle the vineyard and exists only on one side (*Yerushalmi, Tos. Yom*

are not sixteen cubits there, he may not bring [other] seed there. [If] there were sixteen cubits there, we give it its work area, and he may plant the rest.

2. **W**hat is the perimeter of the vineyard? [The area] between the vineyard and the wall. If there are not twelve cubits there, he may not bring seed there. [If]

Tov). *R' Moshe Zaccutto* (quoted by *Tos. Anshei Shem*) notes that the mishnah *Taanis* 4:8 speaks of dancing in the vineyards and uses the term חוֹלוֹת for dancing. He therefore suggests that the area between the edge of the vineyard and the surrounding wall was called מָחוֹל because of the dances held there. *Rambam Comm.* relates the term to the root מחל which means *abandon* or *forgo*. The area between the vineyard and the wall is not planted, and as an abandoned area it is known as מְחוֹל. [*Shoshanim LeDavid* suggests that according to *Rambam* the word should be read מָחוֹל הַכֶּרֶם.]

אִם אֵין שָׁם שְׁתֵּים עֶשְׂרֵה אַמָּה, לֹא יָבִיא זֶרַע לְשָׁם. — *If there are not twelve cubits there, he may not bring seed there.*

Ordinarily it is permitted to plant foreign seed outside a vineyard provided that the planting is four cubits away from the edge of the vineyard. However, if the vineyard is enclosed by a wall, then it is forbidden to plant between the wall and the edge of the vineyard as long as the distance between the vineyard and the wall is not twelve cubits. Thus, if the *perimeter of the vineyard* is not twelve cubits, *he may not bring seed there* even if he distances the seed more than four cubits from the edge of the vineyard.

The *Gemara* (*Eruvin* 93a) explains that anything planted between a vineyard and a wall which is less than twelve cubits away from the edge of the vineyard will be viewed as planted within the vineyard, which is forbidden. Only a planting area which is perceived to be distinct from the vineyard can be planted, and within the wall only a four-cubit

planting area can qualify as distinctive. Thus, unless four cubits are available for foreign planting, any planting will be regarded as insignificant and will be forbidden as peripheral to the vineyard.

Since the work area of a vineyard extends to four cubits beyond the edge of the vineyard, no foreign planting can take place there. Similarly, an area four cubits wide along the length of a wall was normally left as a passageway and not used for planting, since walking near the wall firmed up the ground there and strengthened the foundations of the wall (see *Bava Basra* 22b; *Tos. Yom Tov*). Because of this, even if the person was to plant it, this area would not be regarded as a planting area and would hence not be viewed as distinct from the vineyard. Therefore, if only eight cubits, for example, separated the vineyard from the wall, no planting would be allowed. Within four cubits of the vineyard, planting encroaches illegally on the work area of the vineyard; within four cubits of the wall, planting is not viewed as part of a distinct planting area. Thus, the only way for planting between the wall and the vineyard to take place is if there are at least four cubits between the end of the vineyard's four-cubit work area and the four-cubit passageway along the base of the wall. If there are not four cubits there, then again the planting would not be viewed as belonging to a planting area distinct and separate from the vineyard, and it would be forbidden. I.e. *if there are not twelve cubits from the vineyard to the wall, he may not bring seed there* (*Rav; Rosh; Rash*).

כלאים נוֹתְנִין לוֹ עֲבוֹדָתוֹ, וְזוֹרֵעַ אֶת הַמּוֹתָר.

[ג] **רַבִּי** יְהוּדָה אוֹמֵר: אֵין זֶה אֶלָּא גֶּדֶר הַכֶּרֶם. וְאֵיזֶה הוּא מְחוֹל הַכֶּרֶם? בֵּין שְׁנֵי הַכְּרָמִים.

יד אברהם

The mishnah follows the opinion of Beis Hillel in mishnah 1, who define the prohibition on planting within the walled perimeter of the vineyard as *twelve cubits*. According to Beis Shammai there, a perimeter of up to sixteen cubits may not be planted. Since Beis Shammai view only an eight-cubit planting area as significant and distinct (see mishnah 1), they require four cubits of work area plus *eight* cubits of planting area plus four cubits of passageway before the walled perimeter of a vineyard may be planted.

הָיוּ שָׁם שְׁתֵּים עֶשְׂרֵה אַמָּה, נוֹתְנִין לוֹ עֲבוֹדָתוֹ, וְזוֹרֵעַ אֶת הַמּוֹתָר. — *[If] there were twelve cubits there, we give it its work area, and he may plant the remainder.*

If there were twelve cubits between the wall and the vineyard, then it is permitted to plant all of the area within the wall as long as no planting is done within the four-cubit work area of the vineyard.

In certain contexts, a ditch of appropriate dimensions is equivalent to a wall (see e.g. mishnah 2:8). What about in connection with the laws of the *perimeter of a vineyard*? If a vineyard is bounded by a ten-handbreadth-deep ditch, does this make planting between

the ditch and the vineyard forbidden unless the two are twelve cubits apart? Some authorities assume that it does (*R' Shlomo Sirilio*), while others disagree (*Radbaz to Hil. Kilayim 7:14, Mishnah Rishonah*). [Those who assume that a ditch does not prohibit planting within the perimeter explain that the twelve-cubit distance between the wall and the vineyard is based on the assumption that a four-cubit strip along the base of a wall is generally left as a passageway, so that the ground there will be firmed by the people treading upon it. Since this consideration is not relevant to a ditch, it is argued that the law was not said concerning a ditch. It should be noted, however, that this explanation of the four-cubit strip is not stated explicitly by the *Gemara* with regard to the perimeter of a vineyard (see *Eruvin* 93a and *Yerushalmi*), nor is it mentioned explicitly by *Rambam*. On the other hand, those who maintain that this law applies even in the case of a ditch argue that since a ditch is generally treated like a wall, the law applies even though the underlying reason for this rule is not present in the case of a ditch (see *Derech Emunah* 7:67, *Beur HaHalachah* 7:15, s.v. פחות מעשרה טפחים).]

3.

The present mishnah continues the discussion of מְחוֹל הַכֶּרֶם.

— רַבִּי יְהוּדָה אוֹמֵר: אֵין זֶה אֶלָּא גֶּדֶר הַכֶּרֶם. *Rabbi Yehudah says: This is none other than the wall of a vineyard.*

Rabbi Yehudah maintains that the area between a vineyard and its wall is *not* what is meant by the term מְחוֹל, and that this area is known instead as גֶּדֶר הַכֶּרֶם, *the wall of a vineyard*. In his opinion, planting between a vineyard and its wall was never specially prohib-

ited, and even if there are, for example, only six cubits between the vineyard and its wall, the two cubits next to the wall may be planted (*Rav; Rash; Ri ben Malki Tzedek*). [The four cubits next to the vineyard may of course not be planted since these constitute the work area of the vineyard.]

The example given above of a case in which there are six cubits between the vineyard and its wall is taken from *Rav*. The same would hold true if there were only four-and-a-half cubits — that is, the half-cu-

there were twelve cubits there, we give it its work area, and he may plant the remainder.

3. **R'** Yehudah says: This is none other than the wall of a vineyard. But what is the perimeter of a vineyard? Between two vineyards.

YAD AVRAHAM

bit beyond the four cubits of the vineyard's work area may be planted (*Tos. Yom Tov*; see *Tos. Anshei Shem*). Thus, the area which R' Yehudah refers to as the *wall of the vineyard* would seem to be treated no differently than any area around a vineyard which may be planted, except for the four cubits of the vineyard's work area. *Rashash* finds this difficult, however, since in that case, why give the area between the vineyard and its wall a special name (see also *Mishnah Rishonah*)? He therefore suggests that R' Yehudah disputes only the contention of the *Tanna Kamma* that between a vineyard and a wall it is forbidden to plant unless there are *twelve* cubits. In R' Yehudah's opinion, there is no need to discount a four-cubit strip along the base of the wall, and therefore it is sufficient to have *eight* cubits to permit planting. That is, R' Yehudah agrees that it is forbidden to plant between a vineyard and its wall unless a significant four-cubit-wide strip is available for foreign planting, but he contends that a four-cubit-wide strip along the base of the wall counts as a legitimate planting area. Accordingly, he disputes the need for twelve cubits and maintains that eight is sufficient. But if there are less than eight cubits between the vineyard and the wall, he also agrees that planting will be forbidden. The same approach to R' Yehudah is evident from *Rosh*, as *Rashash* himself points out.

וְאֵיזֶה הוּא מְחוֹל הַכֶּרֶם? בֵּין שְׁנֵי הַכְּרָמִים. — *But what is the perimeter of a vineyard? Between two vineyards.*

R' Yehudah agrees that there is an area in which it is forbidden to plant unless there are twelve cubits, and it is this area alone which is referred to as the *perimeter of a vineyard*. This is the area left unplanted between two vineyards.

Apparently, R' Yehudah distinguishes

between an area from which vines were cleared (the *clearing of a vineyard* of mishnah 1) and an unplanted area between vineyards which never contained vines. In the former case, planting is forbidden unless there are sixteen cubits available (following Beis Hillel of mishnah 1), whereas in the latter case — which R' Yehudah refers to as the *perimeter of a vineyard* — twelve cubits is sufficient to permit planting (*Rav* from *Rambam Comm.*).

Rambam Comm. writes that according to the *Tanna Kamma*, who defines מְחוֹל הַכֶּרֶם, *perimeter of the vineyard*, as the area between the vineyard and its wall, an area left unplanted between two vineyards is treated identically to an area inside a vineyard from which vines were cleared. Both come under the category of a קְרַחַת הַכֶּרֶם, *vineyard clearing*, and planting is permitted only if there are sixteen cubits available. *Beur HaGra* (*Yoreh Deah* 296:69) points to *Tosefta Kilayim* 3:2 as *Rambam's* source. [However, *Chazon Ish* (*Yoreh Deah, Dinei Kilei HaKerem* §11) maintains that according to the *Tanna Kamma*, the area left unplanted between vineyards[1] is treated like the area outside the vineyard, which may be planted beyond the four-cubit work area (see *Derech Emunah* 7:62, *Tziyun HaHalachah* 7:132, *Beur HaHalachah* 7:21, s.v. שביל at length).]

Yerushalmi indicates that in R' Yehudah's opinion, the difference between a *vineyard clearing* and *the perimeter of a vineyard* has to do with the alignment of the rows in the two vineyards. *Rash* and *Rosh* understand that when the rows of the two vineyards are parallel to each other, then a space between them is

---

1. At least in the case in which the vineyards are not aligned, as explained below.

treated as a *clearing* (see diagram A).

Diagram A

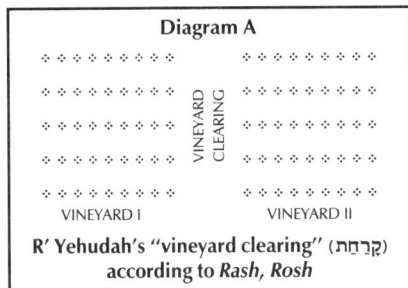

VINEYARD CLEARING

VINEYARD I   VINEYARD II

**R' Yehudah's "vineyard clearing" (קָרַחַת)
according to *Rash, Rosh***

When the rows are perpendicular to each other, the space between them is considered a *perimeter* (see diagram B). Alter-

---

Diagram B

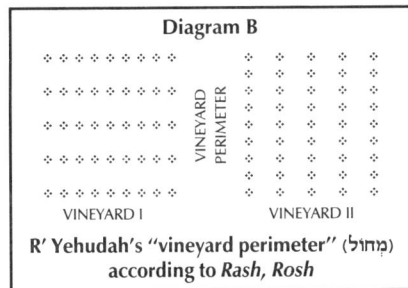

VINEYARD PERIMETER

VINEYARD I   VINEYARD II

**R' Yehudah's "vineyard perimeter" (מְחוֹל)
according to *Rash, Rosh***

---

natively, *R' Shlomo Sirilio, Pnei Moshe* and *Gra* (*Shenos Eliyahu, Peirush HaAroch*) explain that a *perimeter* is the space between two vineyards aligned such that the rows of each are arranged in the same direction (e.g. north-south) but are not on the same line (see diagram C).

Diagram C

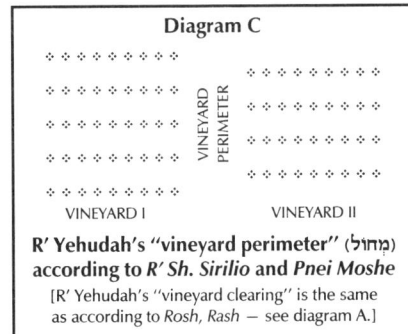

VINEYARD PERIMETER

VINEYARD I   VINEYARD II

**R' Yehudah's "vineyard perimeter" (מְחוֹל)
according to *R' Sh. Sirilio* and *Pnei Moshe***
[R' Yehudah's "vineyard clearing" is the same
as according to *Rosh, Rash* — see diagram A.]

Rosh explains that according to R' Yehudah the four-cubit work area which is left at the

edge of a vineyard is needed in order to provide room for the oxen team pulling the plow to reverse direction (see also *Rosh* to mishnah 1). After plowing between rows A and B of vineyard I (see diagram D), the plow enters the

---

Diagram D

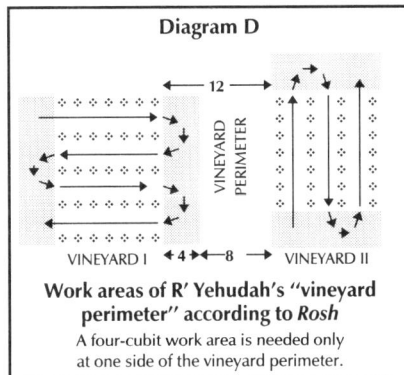

VINEYARD PERIMETER

VINEYARD I   VINEYARD II

**Work areas of R' Yehudah's "vineyard
perimeter" according to *Rosh***
A four-cubit work area is needed only
at one side of the vineyard perimeter.

---

work area, reverses direction, and returns to plow between rows B and C. It follows that it is not necessary to leave a work area on all four sides of a vineyard, but only on those sides where it will be necessary for a plow to execute a U-turn (see *Tos. Anshei Shem*). Accordingly, assuming *Rosh's* construction of R' Yehudah's *vineyard perimeter* (diagram B), the side of vineyard II which borders on the vacant area between vineyards I and II does not need a four-cubit work area. Consequently, R' Yehudah maintains that if the vineyards are separated by only twelve cubits, the area may be planted. In the case of a *vineyard clearing* the vineyards on opposite sides of the clearing both need four-cubit work areas. When the required eight-cubit planting area is added to this (see mishnah 1 and *Eruvin* 93a), the total separation needed before planting is sixteen cubits (see diagram E). In the present case of a *vineyard perimeter*, however, only one of the vineyards needs a four-cubit work area on the side adjacent to the perimeter, so that together with the required eight-cubit planting area, a total separation of only twelve cubits is sufficient to permit planting (see diagram D).

According to *R' Shlomo Sirilio's* interpretation of R' Yehudah, the difference between a *perimeter of a vineyard* and a *clearing of a vineyard* is whether the vineyards on either side of the vacant space look like a continuation of one another or not (see diagram E). In

YAD AVRAHAM

Diagram E

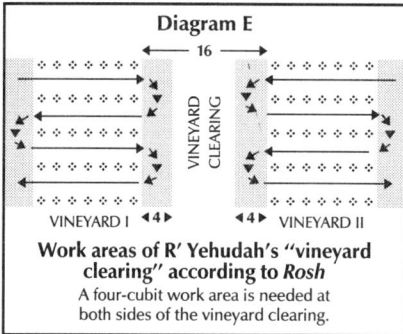

**Work areas of R' Yehudah's "vineyard
clearing" according to *Rosh***
A four-cubit work area is needed at
both sides of the vineyard clearing.

a *vineyard clearing* situation, the rows of the
vineyard on one side of the clearing look like
a direct continuation of the rows of the vineyard on the other side. Because of this, the
clearing itself appears to be part of the vineyard, and hence only an eight-cubit planting
area is large enough to seem independent of
the vineyards. In a *vineyard perimeter* situation, however, there is no clear continuity between the vineyards (see diagram C). The two
vineyards do not appear related to each other,
and hence the intervening space is viewed as
a separation between two distinct vineyards
rather than an interruption in a single vineyard. Accordingly, a planting area of four cubits is deemed distinct from either of the surrounding vineyards.

אֵיזֶה הוּא גָדֵר? — *What is a wall?*
The *Tanna* of mishnah 2 referred to a
wall incidentally in order to define מְחוֹל
הַכֶּרֶם. The mishnah now elaborates on the
characteristics a wall must have in order to
serve as a barrier between a vineyard on
one side and foreign planting on the other.
Just as in mishnah 2:8 it is taught that a
wall serves as a separator between different varieties of seed, so too, a wall can
serve as a separator between grapevines
and foreign seed. If the wall satisfies the
criteria of a separating wall, it is permitted
to plant vines on one side of the wall and
foreign seed on the other, even though
there are not four cubits between them.
Accordingly the mishnah asks: *What is a
wall?* (*Rav; Rash; Rambam Comm.*).
Rosh explains that the question of the
mishnah here relates to the four-cubit-

wide strip which was left along the base of
a wall as a passageway and which necessitated that there be twelve cubits between
a vineyard and its wall to permit planting
(see mishnah 2). Only if the wall around
the vineyard satisfied the criteria outlined
here was such a passageway normally left
and were twelve cubits needed to permit
planting. [The same approach is evident
from *Rambam, Hil. Kilayim* 7:14.]
We stated above that when a wall separates
the vines from the foreign seed, there is no
need to leave four cubits between them. This
is, in fact, the position of *Rambam* (*Hil. Kilayim* 7:15) and is followed here by *Rav.*
However, *Rambam Comm.* (based on *Tosefta*
4:1) adds that by Rabbinic enactment it is required to leave four cubits between the vines
and the wall. Effectively then, even if the foreign seed is planted right against one side of
the wall, it will still be four cubits away from
the vines. In his Code, *Rambam* makes no
mention of such an enactment and appears to
have interpreted the *Tosefta* differently (see
Kesef Mishneh and *Radbaz* to *Hil. Kilayim*
7:25; see also *Sheyarei Minchah* and *Kometz
Minchah* to *Tosefta Kilayim* 4:1).

שֶׁהוּא גָבֹהַּ עֲשָׂרָה טְפָחִים. — *[That] which is
ten handbreadths high.*
For a wall to count as a separator, it
must be ten handbreadths high. If it is not
this high, then foreign seed may not be
planted within four cubits of the vineyard, even though the vineyard is on the
other side of the wall (*Rav; Rosh; Rash;
Rambam Comm.*).
Rosh maintains that the wall which defines
the perimeter of a vineyard in mishnah 2 must
be ten handbreadths high. Only then must
there be at least twelve cubits between the
vineyard and the wall for foreign planting to
be permitted. But if a wall which is less than
ten handbreadths high surrounds a vineyard,
then the area between the vineyard and its
wall may be planted even though the distance
between them is not twelve cubits. *Rambam*
(*Hil. Kilayim* 7:14) adds that if a wall is ten
handbreadths high, but is not four handbreadths wide, it does not create a vineyard
perimeter. Even if the distance between the
vineyard and such a wall is only four-and-a-

וְחָרִיץ שֶׁהוּא עָמֹק עֲשָׂרָה וְרָחָב אַרְבָּעָה.

[ד] **מֶחֱצַת** הַקָּנִים — אִם אֵין בֵּין קָנֶה לַחֲבֵירוֹ שְׁלֹשָׁה טְפָחִים, כְּדֵי שֶׁיִּכָּנֵס הַגְּדִי, הֲרֵי זוֹ כִמְחִצָּה.

וְגָדֵר שֶׁנִּפְרַץ — עַד עֲשָׂרָה אַמּוֹת, הֲרֵי הִיא כְפֶתַח; יָתֵר מִכֵּן, כְּנֶגֶד הַפִּרְצָה אָסוּר.

יד אברהם

half cubits, the half-cubit along the wall, which is outside the four-cubit work area, may be planted. This would suggest that *Rambam* reads the words *four wide* at the end of the mishnah as applying to the wall as well as the ditch (*Radbaz* to *Hil. Kilayim* 7:14). However, when discussing a wall acting as a separator (*Hil. Kilayim* 7:15; see also *Hil. Kilayim* 3:15), *Rambam* does not appear to require any minimum width. *Mareh HaPanim* (*Yerushalmi* 4:1, s.v. לא) therefore suggests that *Rambam's* source for requiring a ten-handbreadth height and a four-handbreadth width in the case of the wall of a vineyard perimeter is *not* from our mishnah (but from a discussion in *Eruvin* 93a).

וְחָרִיץ שֶׁהוּא עָמֹק עֲשָׂרָה וְרָחָב אַרְבָּעָה. — *And a ditch [is that] which is ten deep and four wide.*

Having entered into a discussion of the requisite dimensions for a wall to be a separator, the mishnah now continues to detail the dimensions of another separator, namely, a ditch (*Rav; Rambam Comm.*). Alternatively, the wall discussed till now is the wall of a *vineyard perimeter*. Since, however, a wall also functions as a separator, the mishnah now goes on to discuss separators in general. It begins this discussion with the

case of a ditch, and returns in the next mishnah to the case of a wall (*Rosh*).

Concerning a ditch, the mishnah teaches that in order to act as a separator it must be ten handbreadths deep and four handbreadths wide. Although for a wall to act as a separator there are no restrictions on its thickness (*Chiddushei R' Yoel Chasid;* see *Tos. Yom Tov* 2:8 and *Ohr Gadol* 2:8 and 4:4), a ditch only serves to separate between species if it is difficult to cross. Thus, it only separates if the distance from the edge of the ditch where the grapes are planted to the edge where the foreign seed is planted is at least four handbreadths (*Chiddushei R' Yoel Chasid*).

No length requirements are stipulated for a wall or ditch to act as separators. *Rash* (to mishnah 2:8), drawing on *Eruvin* 16a, maintains that a separator must run for at least four handbreadths. [A wall must therefore be ten handbreadths high and four long to be a separator, but its thickness does not matter; a ditch must be ten deep, four long and four across.] *Ritva* (*Eruvin* 16a) considers a wall of only three handbreadths length as sufficient to be a separator (see *Tos. R' Akiva* and *Ohr Gadol* to mishnah 4:4; *Derech Emunah* 7:78; and see below, mishnah 4:4, end of s.v. ואם).

4.

After momentarily digressing to record the law of a ditch as a separator, the mishnah now returns to its discussion of a wall as a separator.

מֶחֱצַת הַקָּנִים — *A partition of sticks* — [I.e. a fence, consisting of upright sticks or poles, which surrounds a vineyard.]

אִם אֵין בֵּין קָנֶה לַחֲבֵירוֹ שְׁלֹשָׁה טְפָחִים, כְּדֵי שֶׁיִּכָּנֵס הַגְּדִי, הֲרֵי זוֹ כִמְחִצָּה. — *if there are not three handbreadths between one*

And a ditch [is that] which is ten deep and four wide.

4. **A** partition of sticks — if there are not three handbreadths between one stick and the next, enough room for a goat to enter, then this is a partition.

A wall that has been broken — up to ten cubits, this is like an opening; more than this, it is forbidden [to plant] opposite the breach.

YAD AVRAHAM

stick and the next, enough room for a goat to enter, then this is a partition.

As long as the spaces between sticks are not larger than three handbreadths, the spaces are regarded as closed (*Yerushalmi*) and the sticks are viewed as connected to each other (*Rambam Comm.*). Thus, when sticks are placed less than three handbreadths apart, they constitute an effective partition and it is permitted to plant grapevines on one side of the partition and foreign seed on the other (*Rav; Rosh; Rash*). The rule that less than three handbreadths is considered closed was orally received by Moses at Sinai (*Tos. Yom Tov; Rambam Comm.* from *Shabbos* 96a) and is of general application (*Rav; Rosh; Rash*). Nevertheless, if goats could easily fit through such holes, then these sticks could hardly be considered an effective partition. The mishnah thus adds that a gap of less than three handbreadths is *not* wide enough for a goat to fit through with ease: *If there are not three handbreadths between one stick and another* then there is not *enough room for a goat to enter*. This fact, coupled with the law that items (in this case, sticks or poles) separated by less than three handbreadths are considered connected, enables the mishnah to assert: *this is a partition* (*Rashi* to *Eruvin* 16a, s.v. צריך; *Rambam Comm.*; see *Rav*).

◆§ When a wall serves as a partition (e.g. between grapevines and greens), it is permitted to plant not only opposite the solid

wall but even opposite the entrances and exits. Although the greens planted opposite an entrance are not separated by a physical barrier from the grapevines, the entranceway is viewed as a continuation of the wall. This reasoning holds true only because the entranceway is not so large as to disrupt the continuity of the wall. If, however, an opening in a wall is large enough to be considered an interruption of the wall, then the wall is not viewed as continuing through the opening. In such a case, since the opening is not part of a wall, it is not permitted to plant opposite it. The mishnah now provides parameters with which to determine when a break in a wall is considered a continuation of the wall, and when it is not.

וְגָדֵר שֶׁנִּפְרַץ — עַד עֲשָׂרָה[1] אַמּוֹת, הֲרֵי הִיא כְּפֶתַח; — *A wall that has been broken — up to ten cubits, this is like an opening;*

A break of up to ten cubits wide is treated like an entrance and is regarded as a continuation of the wall. Accordingly, it is permitted to plant foreign seed opposite such a break just as if a physical barrier existed there (*Rav; Rosh; Rash*).

יָתֵר מִכֵּן, כְּנֶגֶד הַפִּרְצָה אָסוּר. — *more than this, it is forbidden [to plant] opposite the breach.*

If a break in the wall is wider than ten cubits, it is no longer viewed as a continuation of the wall but is considered instead an interruption of the wall. As such, any planting opposite such a break must be distanced by the requisite four cubits

1. The text is obviously corrupted and should read עֶשֶׂר אַמּוֹת, since אַמָּה is feminine.

כלאים
ד/ה

נִפְרְצוּ בּוֹ פְּרָצוֹת הַרְבֵּה — אִם הָעוֹמֵד מְרֻבֶּה עַל הַפָּרוּץ, מֻתָּר. וְאִם הַפָּרוּץ מְרֻבֶּה עַל הָעוֹמֵד, כְּנֶגֶד הַפִּרְצָה אָסוּר.

[ה] **הַנּוֹטֵעַ** שׁוּרָה שֶׁל חָמֵשׁ גְּפָנִים — בֵּית שַׁמַּאי אוֹמְרִים: כֶּרֶם. וּבֵית הִלֵּל אוֹמְרִים: אֵינוֹ כֶּרֶם עַד שֶׁיְּהוּ שָׁם שְׁתֵּי שׁוּרוֹת.

יד אברהם

from the vineyard within the wall (*Rav; Rash*). Nevertheless, the standing parts of the wall continue to function as separators, so that opposite the standing parts of the wall no distancing is required (*Rash*).

נִפְרְצוּ בּוֹ פְּרָצוֹת הַרְבֵּה — אִם הָעוֹמֵד מְרֻבֶּה עַל הַפָּרוּץ, מֻתָּר. — [If] many breaches have been made in it — if the standing [part] is greater than the breached, it is permitted.

The rule above that a break which is greater than three handbreadths, but less than ten cubits, is considered an entrance-way in the wall refers to a single such opening in the wall. But if many such breaches have been made in the wall, the law depends on whether the majority of the wall is standing (*Tos. Yom Tov; Rash*). If the total length of the standing parts of the wall is greater or equal to the total length of all the breaks in the wall, the breaks are treated like openings and it is permitted to plant opposite them (*Tos. Yom Tov, Rambam Comm.*). In both cases, it is permitted to plant opposite the breaks without any special distancing.

וְאִם הַפָּרוּץ מְרֻבֶּה עַל הָעוֹמֵד, כְּנֶגֶד הַפִּרְצָה אָסוּר. — But if the breached [part] is greater than the standing [part], opposite the breach it is forbidden.

If the total length of the breaks exceeds that of the standing segments of the wall, the breaks are no longer treated as openings in a continuous wall, but are instead regarded as disruptions in the wall. Accordingly, it is forbidden to plant opposite the breaches without the necessary distancing. On the other hand, it is permitted to plant opposite the standing remnants of the wall, as long as these are at least four handbreadths long (*Rav; Rosh; Rash*).

If a standing remnant of the wall is not four handbreadths long, it no longer functions as a separator, so that planting of a foreign species opposite it would require the standard four-cubit distancing from the vineyard (*Rav; Rosh; Rash*). R' Akiva Eiger, basing himself upon *Eruvin* 16a, contends that according to the conclusion of the *Gemara* there, a standing segment of wall only three handbreadths in length still functions as a separator. Although this is indeed the way the *Gemara* is understood by *Ritva* and others (see *Tos. R' Akiva*), it is not the only interpretation. A number of commentators have shown that the position endorsed here by *Rav*, namely that only a four-handbreadth segment is a separator, is not inconsistent with the *Gemara's* conclusion (see e.g. *Tiferes Yerushalayim, Ohr Gadol, Chazon Ish* 6:6, 11:8; see also *Tif. Yis., Boaz* §2).

5.

In connection with the laws of *kilayim* involving grapevines, there is a difference between a single vine and a vineyard. For example, planting a foreign species near a single vine is permitted if it is six handbreadths away (mishnah 3:7); planting near a vineyard is permitted only four cubits away from the vineyard. To constitute a

4
5
[If] many breaches have been made in it — if the standing [part] is greater than the breached, it is permitted. But if the breached [part] is greater than the standing [part], opposite the breach it is forbidden.

5. [I f] someone plants a row of five grapevines — Beis Shammai say: [It is] a vineyard. But Beis Hillel say: It is not a vineyard until there are two rows there.

YAD AVRAHAM

vineyard, there must be a minimum number of vines, and these must be arranged in conformity with certain patterns. The coming mishnayos deal with the definition of a vineyard.[1] First the mishnah discusses the minimum number of vines or rows needed to constitute a vineyard (present mishnah), then the mishnah discusses the configuration of the vines in a vineyard (mishnayos 6,7), and finally the mishnah discusses the dimensions of the vineyard (mishnayos 8,9).

הַנּוֹטֵעַ שׁוּרָה שֶׁל חָמֵשׁ גְּפָנִים – בֵּית שַׁמַּאי אוֹמְרִים: כֶּרֶם. וּבֵית הִלֵּל אוֹמְרִים: אֵינוֹ כֶּרֶם עַד שֶׁיְּהוּ שָׁם שְׁתֵּי שׁוּרוֹת. — *[If] someone plants a row of five grapevines — Beis Shammai say: [It is] a vineyard. But Beis Hillel say: It is not a vineyard until there are two rows there.*

Beis Shammai maintain that a single row qualifies as a vineyard provided that it consists of at least five vines.[2] Beis Hillel disagree. In their opinion, a single row, no matter how many vines it contains, can never be considered a vineyard (*Rambam, Hil. Kilayim* 7:1). Rather, it is treated like a collection of single vines from each of which a foreign planting must be distanced by six handbreadths. According to Beis Hillel, a collection of grapevines does not constitute a vineyard *until there are two rows there*. For such an arrangement, the law is that planting within four cubits of it is forbidden (*Rav; Rosh; Rash; Rambam Comm.*).

How many vines must Beis Hillel's two rows contain in order to qualify as a vineyard? *Rosh* explains that Beis Hillel also assume a minimum of five vines, and that these must be arranged such that one row consists of three vines while the other consists of two. This requirement is based on the discussion of a five-vine vineyard in the next mishnah, which according to *Rosh* is arranged in two rows — one row of three vines and another row of two vines. An arrangement in which one row has four vines while the other has only one is not a vineyard.

Rambam (Hil. Kilayim 7:2) maintains that a row must contain a minimum of three vines (see *Kesef Mishneh* loc. cit.). Accordingly, Beis Hillel's two rows contain a minimum of six vines, three per row. Although the next mishnah does indeed discuss a five-vine vineyard, that vineyard, according to *Rambam*, does not consist of only two rows (see next mishnah).

1. *Tosafos (Bava Basra* 37b, s.v. אינו), apply the definition of vineyard developed here to other laws in which the Torah uses the term כֶּרֶם (vineyard). [The Torah uses this term in *Deut.* 22:9 where the prohibition on *kilayim* involving grapes is presented.] In particular, *Tosafos* refer to the military exemption given to someone who has planted a vineyard (*Deut.* 20:6). Additionally, according to some, the law of כֶּרֶם רְבָעִי (vintage of the fourth year) is modeled on this definition of כֶּרֶם (see *Shulchan Aruch, Yoreh Deah* 294:7; see also *Tif. Yis., Boaz* §3).

2. R' Moshe Zaccutto suggests that the number five is alluded to by the word הַכֶּרֶם (*Deut.* 22:9), which may be read as, ה (*hei*) (which has a numerical value of five) equals a כֶּרֶם (*Tos. Anshei Shem*).

לְפִיכָךְ, הַזּוֹרֵעַ אַרְבַּע אַמּוֹת שֶׁבַּכֶּרֶם — בֵּית
שַׁמַּאי אוֹמְרִים: קִדֵּשׁ שׁוּרָה אַחַת. וּבֵית הִלֵּל
אוֹמְרִים: קִדֵּשׁ שְׁתֵּי שׁוּרוֹת.

יד אברהם

לְפִיכָךְ, הַזּוֹרֵעַ אַרְבַּע אַמּוֹת שֶׁבַּכֶּרֶם — בֵּית
שַׁמַּאי אוֹמְרִים: קִדֵּשׁ שׁוּרָה אַחַת. וּבֵית הִלֵּל
אוֹמְרִים: קִדֵּשׁ שְׁתֵּי שׁוּרוֹת. — *Therefore, [if]
someone plants [within] the four cubits of
a vineyard — Beis Shammai say: He has
condemned one row. But Beis Hillel say:
He has condemned two rows.*

The Torah (*Deut.* 22:9) states that *kilayim* in a vineyard results in the prohibition for use of both the foreign seed and
the vineyard (see mishnah 8:1, s.v. וְאָסוּרִין
בַּהֲנָאָה). The term used by the Torah to indicate a prohibition on use is תִּקְדַּשׁ, and
this root is used by the mishnah as well
when discussing the prohibition for use
resulting from *kilayim* of a vineyard
(*Rambam Comm.*). The present mishnah
discusses the condemnation of the vineyard when foreign seed is planted outside
the vineyard; mishnah 5:5 discusses the
law when foreign seed is planted inside
the vineyard (*Tos. Yom Tov*).

The disagreement between Beis Shammai and Beis Hillel regarding the definition of a vineyard has application in the
event that foreign seed was illegally
planted within the four-cubit work area
surrounding a vineyard. All agree that the
resulting prohibition encompasses only
the minimum vineyard. However, exactly
which and how many vines are included
depends on the definition of vineyard.

According to Beis Shammai, *he has
condemned one row*. Since in their opinion one row constitutes a vineyard, only
one row of the vineyard becomes prohibited. If the foreign planting was to the east
of the vineyard, for example, then only
the easternmost row of the vineyard will

be condemned. Beis Hillel, on the other
hand, maintain that the two easternmost
rows of the vineyard will be included in
the prohibition. Since in their view a minimum vineyard consists of two rows, the
prohibition on use likewise encompasses
two rows (*Rav; Rambam Comm.*).[1]

From *Rav* and *Rambam Comm.* it would
appear that regardless of how many vines are
found in the row nearest the foreign seed, the
entire row is condemned. Furthermore, no
limits are set as to how much foreign seed is
needed to generate this prohibition. Thus, if a
vineyard is made up of twenty rows each
containing twenty vines, and even a small
amount of foreign seed is planted somewhere
within the four-cubit work area on the east
side of the vineyard, all twenty vines of the
easternmost row will be condemned according to Beis Shammai (and all forty vines of
the two easternmost rows according to Beis
Hillel). Although five vines is the minimum
number of vines needed to constitute a
vineyard, all the vines of a row are part of the
same vineyard. Accordingly, the *kilayim*
between the vineyard and the foreign
seed involves the entire row. Similarly, two
whole rows belong to the same vineyard
according to Beis Hillel, and both are condemned as a consequence of the *kilayim* (see
diagram A).

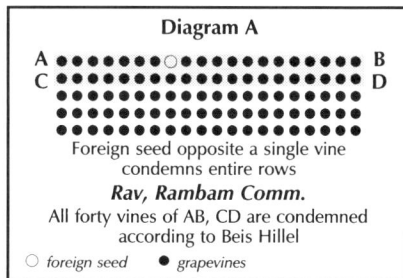

Diagram A

A ●●●●●●●○●●●●●●●●●●●● B
C ●●●●●●●●●●●●●●●●●●●● D
●●●●●●●●●●●●●●●●●●●●
●●●●●●●●●●●●●●●●●●●●

Foreign seed opposite a single vine
condemns entire rows
Rav, Rambam Comm.
All forty vines of AB, CD are condemned
according to Beis Hillel

○ *foreign seed*   ● *grapevines*

---

1. Beis Shammai's position regarding condemnation of vines is atypically more lenient than
Beis Hillel's. This dispute is in fact recorded in *Eduyos* 5:2 where it is listed among the disputes
in which Beis Shammai is more lenient than Beis Hillel (see *Tos. Yom Tov* ibid.).

4
5 Therefore, [if] someone plants [within] the four cubits of a vineyard — Beis Shammai say: He has condemned one row. But Beis Hillel say: He has condemned two rows.

Rosh, following *Yerushalmi,* maintains that according to Beis Shammai only the five-vine row immediately opposite the foreign seed is forbidden. However, it is not known with certainty *which* five-vine row is forbidden. Do we assume that the foreign seed is planted opposite the midpoint of the five-vine row? Or perhaps the vine which it faces is the endpoint of the row? And if the latter, in which direction is the row drawn? Out of doubt, all three possibilities must be taken into account. To illustrate, imagine a vineyard consisting of five rows of ten vines each (diagram B; vines are specified by two

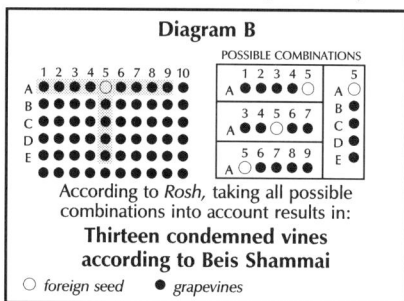

Diagram B

According to *Rosh,* taking all possible combinations into account results in:
Thirteen condemned vines according to Beis Shammai
○ *foreign seed* ● *grapevines*

co-ordinates: row and column, where row is a letter and column a number). Now, consider the case in which greens are planted opposite vine A/5. If the row of five prohibited vines is found in row A, it might be any of the following combinations: A/1-5, A/2-6, A/3-7...A/5-9. On the other hand, the prohibited vines might be on the same line as the illegally planted greens and would then consist of A-E/5. It can readily be seen that out of doubt thirteen vines must be treated as forbidden as indicated in diagram B.[1] According to Beis Hillel, only three vines from one row and two from another should strictly speaking become prohibited. But again, all the different possibilities for the five condemned vines must be considered.

The result is that according to Beis Hillel as well, there are thirteen vines which are condemned (see diagram C). [Note,

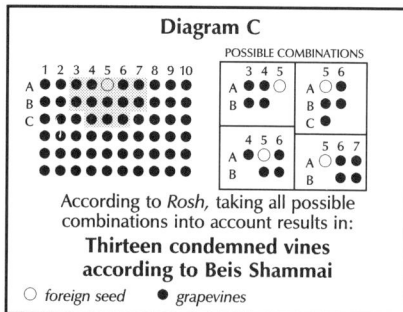

Diagram C

According to *Rosh,* taking all possible combinations into account results in:
Thirteen condemned vines according to Beis Shammai
○ *foreign seed* ● *grapevines*

however, that the thirteen vines prohibited according to Beis Shammai are not the same thirteen vines prohibited according to Beis Hillel.]

Rambam (Hil. Kilayim 6:3) has a different system for determining which vines are forbidden. According to him, Beis Hillel would forbid those vines in the two rows closest to the foreign seed which are opposite the foreign seed. In addition, vines in these two rows, which are opposite a four-cubit extension from each end of the foreign seed, are also forbidden (see diagram D). *Rambam's* source for this, however, is unclear (*Ravad* and *Mahari Korkus* to *Hil. Kilayim* 6:3).

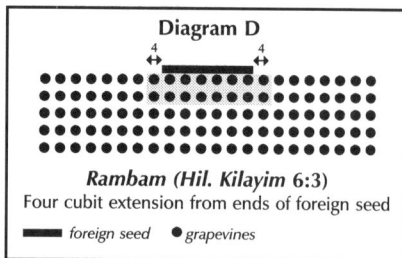

Diagram D

Rambam (Hil. Kilayim 6:3)
Four cubit extension from ends of foreign seed
▬▬ *foreign seed* ● *grapevines*

1. Note that diagonal rows are not considered as possible candidates for the forbidden vineyard. See however *Derech Emunah* 6:3, *Beur HaHalachah,* s.v. לכל רוח, that according to *Ri ben Malki Tzedek* diagonal rows are also taken into account.

[ו] **הַנּוֹטֵעַ** שְׁתַּיִם כְּנֶגֶד שְׁתַּיִם, וְאַחַת יוֹצְאָה זָנָב, הֲרֵי זֶה כֶּרֶם. שְׁתַּיִם כְּנֶגֶד שְׁתַּיִם וְאַחַת בֵּינָתַיִם, אוֹ שְׁתַּיִם כְּנֶגֶד שְׁתַּיִם וְאַחַת בָּאֶמְצַע, אֵינוֹ כֶּרֶם עַד שֶׁיְּהוּ

יד אברהם

6.

The following mishnah discusses the configuration in which five vines constitute a vineyard. The mishnah does not yet discuss the dimensions of the vineyard. The acceptable distance between rows in a vineyard is dealt with later in the chapter (mishnayos 8 and 9), and for the present purposes it is sufficient to assume that the rows are between four and eight cubits apart.

The mishnah is also relevant for Beis Shammai who state in the previous mishnah that five vines in a single row constitute a vineyard. This is because Beis Shammai agree that even five vines which are not in a single row constitute a vineyard, provided that they are arranged in the pattern described here (*Meleches Shlomo*).

When the status of vineyard is conferred upon an arrangement of vines, this means that: (a) planting outside the arrangement must be distanced by four cubits; and (b) planting within the vineyard is forbidden (see below, mishnah 8).

הַנּוֹטֵעַ שְׁתַּיִם כְּנֶגֶד שְׁתַּיִם, וְאַחַת יוֹצְאָה זָנָב, הֲרֵי זֶה כֶּרֶם. — *[If] someone plants two opposite two, and one protruding like a tail, this is a vineyard.*

Rav, Rosh, Rash, and *Ri ben Malki Tzedek* explain this to be an arrangement consisting of two rows, one with three vines and the other with two. The vines of the two-vine row are directly opposite adjacent vines in the three-vine row, so that the third vine of that row protrudes like a tail (see diagram A).

Rabbeinu Nosson Av HaYeshivah explains the configuration described by the mishnah as follows: Two vines are planted corresponding to the forelegs of an animal, two more are planted corresponding to the hind legs of an animal, and one more is planted resembling the tail of an animal. This description suggests the arrangement shown in diagram B, which is the same as that in *Rambam Comm.* (and see *Rambam, Hil. Kilayim* 7:7). *Tos. Yom Tov* writes that a visitor from Safed reported to him that the vineyards in the Holy Land were indeed planted according to the plan depicted by *Rambam.*

As noted above, the classification of an arrangement of vines as a vineyard results in the requirement to distance foreign planting by four cubits from the border of the vineyard. It is not entirely clear, however, how the border is drawn from the vine which protrudes like a tail. According to *Rash* and others, this very question is debated by *Yerushalmi* where Shmuel maintains that the border is drawn as shown in diagram A. The shape of the vineyard is thus trapezoidal. *R' Yochanan,* however, assumes that the border is rectangular. An imaginary vine is posited in row one (which has two vines) opposite the "tail" of row two (which has three). This imaginary vine forms the fourth corner of the rectangle (see diagram A). [The fictional vine assumed by *R' Yochanan* may be central to the classification of this arrangement as a vineyard — see below.]

שְׁתַּיִם כְּנֶגֶד שְׁתַּיִם וְאַחַת בֵּינָתַיִם, — *Two opposite two and one in between,*

Rav explains this as an arrangement in which two vines are planted opposite another two, and a fifth vine is planted opposite the space separating the others. This arrangement, which the mishnah states is not a vineyard, seems to be the very arrangement shown in diagram B, which according to *Rambam* is a vine-

6. **[I**f] someone plants two opposite two, and one protruding like a tail, this is a vineyard.

Two opposite two and one in between, or two opposite two and one in the middle, is not a vineyard until there

Diagram A	Diagram B	Diagram C
row one: Ⓐ Ⓑ	"forelegs" "hindlegs" ● ●	Ⓐ Ⓑ
row two: Ⓒ Ⓓ Ⓔ	"tail" ●	Ⓒ Ⓔ Ⓓ
"Two (A,B) opposite two (C,D) and one (E) protruding like a tail" following *Rav* (et al)	● ●	
---- border according to *Shmuel*	Five vine vineyard according to	"Two opposite two (A,B/C,D) and one in between (E)"
..... border according to *R' Yochanan*	*Rabbeinu Nosson Av HaYeshivah, Ri MiGash* and *Rambam Comm.*	as understood by *Rambam, Rash* et al.

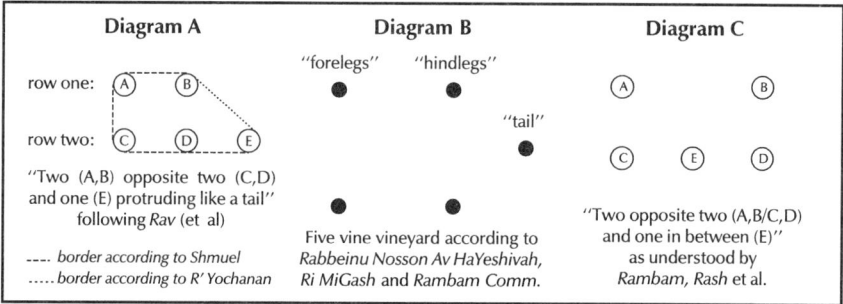

yard (*Tos. Yom Tov*).

Rambam Comm., Rosh, Rash,[1] and *Ri ben Malki Tzedek,* however, all explain *two opposite two and one in between* to be a two-rowed arrangement in which one row has two vines and the other has three, and the two vines of the two-vine row are located opposite the two outside vines of the three-vine row (see diagram C).

It is not clear how *Rambam* classifies the two-rowed arrangement of diagram A which according to *Rav* (et al.) is a vineyard. From *Hil. Kilayim* 7:7, it would appear that *Rambam* does not consider it a vineyard (*Aruch HaShulchan, Yoreh Deah* 296:52,57; see *Derech Emunah, Beur HaHalachah* 7:7, s.v. או שלש). [Perhaps this is because *Rambam* maintains that an arrangement of two rows must have at least six vines to count as a vineyard (see *Hil. Kilayim* 7:2 and previous mishnah; see also mishnah 8 below).]

[Likewise, the status of *Rambam's* vineyard configuration (diagram B) in the eyes of *Rosh, Rash* and *Ri ben Malki Tzedek*[2] is unclear. It may be argued that in their view, the rows of a vineyard must in principle contain

at least three vines. The novelty of the present mishnah is that if the third vine of one row is missing, legal fiction allows us to act as though it were present and located opposite the third vine of the neighboring row. If one row is complete — i.e. it has three vines — the neighboring row which has only two can be regarded as complete as long as the arrangement has a "tail" (see *Yerushalmi*). But if neither row has the full three vines (as is the case in the plan adopted by *Rambam*), then this legal device cannot be used. If this is so, then *Rosh* (et al.) would not count *Rambam's* five-vine arrangement as a vineyard.]

Tos. Yom Tov (s.v. עד) assumes that *each* of the major schools above disqualifies the arrangement of the other from being a vineyard. (See, however, *Derech Emunah, Beur HaHalachah* 7:7, s.v. או שלש.)

אוֹ שְׁתַּיִם כְּנֶגֶד שְׁתַּיִם וְאַחַת בָּאֶמְצַע, אֵינוֹ כֶּרֶם — *or two opposite two and one in the middle, is not a vineyard*

Rav, following all the other major commentators (*Rosh, Rash, Ri ben Malki Tzedek,* and *Rambam Comm.*), explains this as a quincuncial arrangement in which four vines are at the corners of a

1. In the Vilna ed. of *Rash*, the wording is identical to that of *Rosh* and states clearly that the case is an arrangement of two rows (diagram C). However, in the recently published Paris manuscript, the wording in *Rash* is exactly the same as in *Rav*.

2. *Rav's* opinion on this question would seem to be clear, since as noted he explains the case of *one in between* as diagram A. Thus, *Rav* would disqualify *Rambam's* five-vine vineyard. The same is true for *Rash* according to the newly published manuscript edition (see previous footnote).

שְׁתַּיִם נֶגֶד שְׁתַּיִם וְאַחַת יוֹצְאָה זָנָב.

[ז] **הַנּוֹטֵעַ** שׁוּרָה אַחַת בְּתוֹךְ שֶׁלּוֹ, וְשׁוּרָה אַחַת בְּתוֹךְ שֶׁל חֲבֵירוֹ, וְדֶרֶךְ הַיָּחִיד וְדֶרֶךְ הָרַבִּים בָּאֶמְצַע, וְגָדֵר שֶׁהוּא נָמוּךְ

יד אברהם

Diagram D

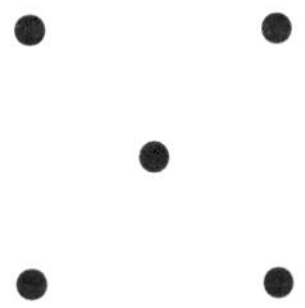

"Two opposite two and
one in the middle"

Diagram C

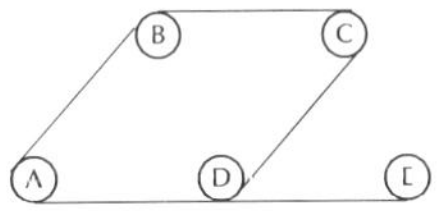

ABCD is a parallelogram
not a square or rectangle.

A is not "opposite" B; D is not "opposite" C.
Although E might be viewed as a "tail,"
this arrangement does not count as a vineyard.

square or rectangle and a fifth vine is at the middle (see diagram D).

The mishnah rules that the latter two arrangements do not qualify as vineyards. Accordingly, they are treated as a collection of single vines for which the rule is that foreign planting is permissible as long as it is six handbreadths away from every vine (*Rambam, Hil. Kilayim 7:7*).

עַד שֶׁיְּהוּ שְׁתַּיִם נֶגֶד שְׁתַּיִם וְאַחַת יוֹצְאָה זָנָב. — *until there are two opposite two and one protruding like a tail.*

This is seemingly nothing more than a restatement of the opening line of the mishnah and would appear to be redundant. *Tos. Yom Tov* suggests that the mishnah's point here is to stress that only one of the arrangements shown in diagram A and diagram B can be a vineyard. According to *Rav*, who views diagram A as a vineyard, the mishnah teaches here that diagram B is not; according to *Ram-*

bam, who views diagram B as a vineyard, the mishnah teaches that diagram A is not.

R' Shlomo Sirilio and *Mishnah Rishonah* suggest that the mishnah's point is that both conditions of the configuration must be satisfied if it is to be counted as a vineyard. Not only is it critical that the fifth vine *protrude like a tail*, but also that the other four vines be arranged *two opposite two*. The four vines in a *two opposite two* arrangement must describe a square or a rectangle (*Chazon Ish 10:20*, s.v. וא"ת; *Derech Emunah 7:36*). An arrangement such as that shown in diagram E, which has a fifth vine *protruding like a tail* but in which the other four vines describe a parallelogram, is not a vineyard. A five-vine arrangement is not a vineyard *until there are* both *two opposite two* (forming a square or rectangle) and *one protruding like a tail*.

7.

Having established that two rows constitute a vineyard, the mishnah now teaches that these two rows need not belong to the same person.

הַנּוֹטֵעַ שׁוּרָה אַחַת בְּתוֹךְ שֶׁלּוֹ, וְשׁוּרָה אַחַת בְּתוֹךְ שֶׁל חֲבֵירוֹ, — *[If] someone plants one row within his own property, and there is one row within his neighbor's property,*

A person plants a row of vines in his own field across from his neighbor's row of vines. [It is clear from *Yerushalmi* that the vines within the neighbor's property

are two opposite two and one protruding like a tail.

7. **[**I**f]** someone plants one row within his own property, and there is one row within his neighbor's property, and there is a private road or a public road in the middle, or a wall which is lower

belong to the neighbor. The words וְשׁוּרָה אַחַת בְּתוֹךְ שֶׁל חֲבֵרוֹ must therefore be translated as: *and "there is" one row within his neighbor's property*, and not as: *and "he plants" one row within his neighbor's property* (*Tos. Anshei Shem* from *R' Moshe Zaccutto;* cf. *Mishnah Rishonah*).]

Rav and *Rash*, consistent with their view that two rows, one of three vines and the other of two, make a vineyard, describe the present case as involving such an arrangement. According to *Rambam*, who holds that such an arrangement is not a vineyard, the case here concerns two complete rows of three vines or more each. The issue in question by the mishnah is whether two rows belonging to different owners can be combined and viewed as a vineyard.

וְדֶרֶךְ הַיָּחִיד וְדֶרֶךְ הָרַבִּים בָּאֶמְצַע, — *and there is a private road or a public road in the middle,*

Even though the two rows of vines are separated by a road, they still combine to form a vineyard. Although with respect to *kilei zeraim* it was taught that even a four-cubit-wide private road is considered a separator which permits planting of diverse species on opposite sides of the road (mishnah 2:8), nevertheless trees — in particular, grapevines — are not separated by a road (*Rash* from *Peah* 2:3). Accordingly, despite the fact that the two rows of vines here are on opposite sides of a road, they are considered united in the same vineyard. However, this is so only if the road is not eight cubits wide. But if the road is eight cubits wide, the rows do not constitute a vineyard, since two rows do not consti-

tute a vineyard if they are more than eight cubits apart (*Rav* from mishnah 8; see *Rambam, Hil. Kilayim* 7:5).

Rav evidently assumes that all *Tannaim* of mishnayos 8 and 9 agree that two rows cannot be a vineyard if they are eight or more cubits apart. However, *Rosh* (to mishnah 9) understands the *Tanna Kamma* of mishnah 9 as allowing up to sixteen cubits between rows of a vineyard, even a vineyard consisting of only two rows. Accordingly, the road mentioned here might be up to sixteen cubits wide without preventing the combination of the two rows of vines into a vineyard.

Rambam Comm. writes that the דֶּרֶךְ הָרַבִּים, *public road,* of our mishnah is sixteen cubits wide. Although this is the way the Mishnah defines this term elsewhere (*Bava Basra* 6:7; see also *Peah* 2:1, *Bava Kamma* 6:4), it is difficult to see how this can be its meaning here. Certainly, everyone agrees that a sixteen-cubit separation prevents rows from being combined into a vineyard (see below mishnayos 8 and 9)! Furthermore, *Rambam* himself (*Comm.* to mishnah 9, *Hil. Kilayim* 7:2-4) maintains that even an eight-cubit separation prevents combination. *Ohr Same'ach* (*Hil. Kilayim* 7:5) resolves this difficulty by pointing out that a public road need not be sixteen cubits wide throughout its entire length. Rather, as long as it is sixteen cubits wide at its entrance and is traveled by the public, it is considered a public road even though it narrows somewhere in the middle. Accordingly, the case of the mishnah indeed refers to a public road which is sixteen cubits wide — it is this wide at its entrance, but between the rows of vines under discussion it is narrower. It is thus possible for *Rambam* (*Hil. Kilayim* 7:5) to speak of a public road which separates the two rows of vines, yet at the same time to specify (ibid.) that the distance between the rows is less than eight cubits.

מֵעֲשָׂרָה טְפָחִים, הֲרֵי אֵלּוּ מִצְטָרְפוֹת. גָּבְהַּ מֵעֲשָׂרָה
טְפָחִים, אֵינָן מִצְטָרְפוֹת. רַבִּי יְהוּדָה אוֹמֵר: אִם
עֵרְסָן מִלְמַעְלָה, הֲרֵי אֵלּוּ מִצְטָרְפוֹת.

[ח] **הַנּוֹטֵעַ** שְׁתֵּי שׁוּרוֹת — אִם אֵין בֵּינֵיהֶן
שְׁמוֹנֶה אַמּוֹת, לֹא יָבִיא זֶרַע לְשָׁם.

יד אברהם

וְגָדֵר שֶׁהוּא נָמוּךְ מֵעֲשָׂרָה טְפָחִים, הֲרֵי אֵלּוּ
מִצְטָרְפוֹת. — *or a wall which is lower than
ten handbreadths, then these [rows]
combine.*

Although the rows belong to different
owners, and although they are separated
by a road or by a low wall, the rows are
viewed as constituting a single vineyard.
Thus, planting must be distanced four
cubits (*Rav*) and, assuming the distance
between the rows to be less than eight
cubits, planting between the rows is
entirely forbidden (*Rambam Comm.* and
Hil. Kilayim 7:3-5).

In the mishnah's case in which a row of
vines belonging to Reuven combines with a
row belonging to Shimon to form a vineyard,
if Shimon, for example, plants foreign seed
within four cubits of the vineyard, the wheat
will be rendered forbidden for benefit. Although R' Shimon states below (mishnah 7:4)
that Reuven's vine cannot cause condemnation of Shimon's wheat, here, it is the combination of Reuven's vine and Shimon's vine
that causes the condemnation of the wheat.
Accordingly, even R' Shimon will agree
(*Rav; Rosh; Rash;* see also *Mishnas Nechemiah* ch. 10).

גָּבְהַּ מֵעֲשָׂרָה טְפָחִים, אֵינָן מִצְטָרְפוֹת. — *[If the
wall is] higher than ten handbreadths,
[the rows] do not combine.*

Even if the wall is exactly ten hand-

breadths high, the rows do not combine.
The mishnah speaks of *higher than ten
handbreadths* merely to stress that even
then the ruling of R' Yehudah which follows will apply. The mishnah does not
mean to imply that a wall exactly ten
handbreadths high does not separate (*Tos.
Yom Tov;* cf. *Rashash*).

This rule corresponds to that for a wall
separating between diverse species (above
2:8, 4:3). Similarly, trees of the same species which are separated by a wall ten
handbreadths high are viewed as belonging to separate fields with respect to the
laws of *peah* (*Peah* 2:1). Thus, two rows of
grapevines on opposite sides of a wall ten
handbreadths high or more *do not combine.*

רַבִּי יְהוּדָה אוֹמֵר: אִם עֵרְסָן מִלְמַעְלָה, הֲרֵי אֵלּוּ
מִצְטָרְפוֹת. — *R' Yehudah says: If he intertwined them above, then they combine.*

If he raised the vines from each side of
the wall to the top of the wall, so that the
vines from one side of the wall became intertwined with the vines from the other,
the wall no longer counts as a divider, and
the rows combine to form a vineyard
(*Rav; Rosh; Rash; Rambam Comm.;* see
Peah 2:3 and mishnah 6:1 below). The halachah does not follow R' Yehudah (*Rambam Comm.*).

8.

In the preceding mishnayos the configuration and the minimum number of vines
and rows needed to constitute a vineyard have been discussed. Now, the mishnah
addresses the spacing between rows of a vineyard — that is, the maximum distance
possible between rows if they are to be considered part of one vineyard.

[*Rav's* interpretation of this mishnah is problematic. Although it evidently derives
from *Rambam Comm., Rav* incorporates into his commentary certain elements of the

than ten handbreadths, then these [rows] combine. [If the wall is] higher than ten handbreadths, [the rows] do not combine. R' Yehudah says: If he intertwined them above, then they combine.

8. **[I**f] someone plants two rows [of vines] — if there are not eight cubits between them, he may not bring [foreign] seed there.

YAD AVRAHAM

approach of *Rash* and *Rosh* which seem inconsistent with *Rambam Comm*. Moreover, recent commentators have challenged *Rav's* understanding of *Rambam Comm.* (see *Chazon Ish* 10:13, *Eretz Chemdah* pp. 245, 249). In view of these difficulties, *Rav's* explanation of this mishnah has not been given its customary priority.]

הַנּוֹטֵעַ שְׁתֵּי שׁוּרוֹת – אִם אֵין בֵּינֵיהֶן שְׁמוֹנֶה אַמּוֹת, לֹא יָבִיא זֶרַע לְשָׁם. — *[If] someone plants two rows [of vines] — if there are not eight cubits between them, he may not bring [foreign] seed there.*

Rash and *Rosh* explain that the *two rows* mentioned by the mishnah contain between them at least five vines, the minimum number of vines needed for a vineyard. The point of the mishnah is that unless certain spacing rules are adhered to, the required number and configuration of vines is not sufficient by itself to make a vineyard. In particular, a two-row arrangement is only a vineyard if the two rows are within eight cubits of each other; if there are eight cubits or more between the two rows, they are not combined and do not form a vineyard. When two rows are close enough to each other to form a vineyard, no foreign planting is permitted between them, and outside the rows planting is only allowed at a distance of four cubits. When they do not form a vineyard, planting is permitted even between the rows at a distance of only six handbreadths from the vines.

Rav, apparently following *Rambam Comm.* (but cf. *Chazon Ish* 10:13, *Eretz Chemdah* pp. 245, 249), explains that the mishnah here is discussing two rows of two vines each, i.e. a four-vine vineyard. Although from

mishnah 6 above it seems that less than five vines do *not* constitute a vineyard, that is only with respect to the law that foreign planting must be distanced by four cubits from the outside of a vineyard. But with respect to planting *inside* a vineyard, our mishnah teaches that even *if someone plants two rows* of only two vines each, and *there are not eight cubits between* the rows, *he may not bring foreign seed there.* Thus, if the two rows of two are less than eight cubits apart, it is forbidden to plant *between* them, but outside the rows it is permitted to plant as little as six handbreadths away (*Tos. Yom Tov; Tos. Anshei Shem; Tif. Yis.*).

Rav's basis for explaining the case here as involving two rows of two has been explained as follows. It will be recalled from mishnah 1 that a clearing of up to sixteen cubits in a vineyard may *not* be planted.[1] If the case here involved a normal vineyard (two full rows of three vines each, or the protruding-tail arrangement of mishnah 6), how can the mishnah permit planting within a gap between rows of only eight cubits? Planting in the space between rows of a vineyard should be no more lenient than planting in a vineyard clearing, and should be forbidden in a space of less than sixteen cubits!

On the other hand, if the present case involves a two-by-two arrangement, which is not really a vineyard, the prohibition on planting between the rows is not as serious as when planting between rows of a real vineyard, and this would account for the extra le-

---

1. Although the rule of mishnah 1 was explained as applying only when the clearing is flanked by vineyards (see there s.v. ואיזו), *Rambam Comm.*, which is followed here by *Rav*, makes no such requirement (see below, s.v. רבי אליעזר).

הָיוּ שָׁלֹשׁ – אִם אֵין בֵּין שׁוּרָה לַחֲבֶרְתָּהּ
שֵׁשׁ עֶשְׂרֵה אַמָּה, לֹא יָבִיא זֶרַע לְשָׁם. רַבִּי
אֱלִיעֶזֶר בֶּן יַעֲקֹב אוֹמֵר מִשּׁוּם חֲנִינָא בֶּן חֲכִינַאי:
אֲפִילוּ חָרְבָה הָאֶמְצָעִית, וְאֵין בֵּין שׁוּרָה
לַחֲבֶרְתָּהּ שֵׁשׁ עֶשְׂרֵה אַמָּה, לֹא יָבִיא זֶרַע לְשָׁם,

יד אברהם

niency displayed in this case. Accordingly, *Rav* assumes the case in question to be a four-vine arrangement, which is not really a vineyard (see *Mishnah Rishonah* and *Shoshanim LeDavid*).

הָיוּ שָׁלֹשׁ – אִם אֵין בֵּין שׁוּרָה לַחֲבֶרְתָּהּ שֵׁשׁ עֶשְׂרֵה אַמָּה, לֹא יָבִיא זֶרַע לְשָׁם. — *[If] there were three [rows] — if there are not sixteen cubits between one row and the next, he may not bring [foreign] seed there.*

Although two rows are considered unrelated if they are separated by only eight cubits, three or more rows are unrelated only when they are spaced apart by sixteen cubits or more. If they are within sixteen cubits of one another, they are counted together to form a vineyard.[1] By distributing his vines over three rows, the grower shows that he regards the entire area as one large vineyard. As such, the spaces between rows are no worse than vineyard clearings which, as taught in mishnah 1, are prohibited to plant when they are less than sixteen cubits (*Rash; Rosh*). [As will be seen below, however, the law for clearings in a three-row vineyard is not identical in all respects with the law for clearings in a vineyard with more numerous rows.]

There are two very different interpretations of *Rav's* approach to this case of the mishnah. According to the first interpretation (advanced by *Mishnas Chachamim*), *Rav* explained the case here as involving three complete rows. According to the second (advanced by *Mishnah Rishonah*), *Rav* saw the case here as involving three rows of two vines each. According to the first interpretation of

Rav, the mishnah first dealt with the special case of two rows of two vines each. Now the mishnah considers the law for planting between rows of a real vineyard. [The same law applies to two full rows — i.e. two rows of three vines each or the protruding-tail arrangement — since this arrangement is also a real vineyard. The reason the mishnah deals with a three-row vineyard will be explained below.] The mishnah states that when the spacing between rows is less than sixteen cubits, it is not permitted to plant between the rows. If the space between rows is sixteen cubits or more, the rows are not considered to be related to one another, and as single rows they do not constitute a vineyard (according to Beis Hillel of mishnah 5). In such a situation, it would be permitted to plant between the rows at a distance of only six handbreadths from the vines.

The mishnah chooses a three-row field in order to distinguish between two cases: one in which the rows were originally planted up to sixteen cubits apart, and one in which the clearing was created by uprooting a middle row. The mishnah's ruling forbidding planting between rows up to sixteen cubits apart applies only where the three rows were initially spaced in this manner. However, a clearing created inside a three-row vineyard by removing the middle row is not treated as a vineyard clearing, where planting is forbidden. For example, if the rows were seven cubits apart to begin with, then removal of the middle row will leave the two outer rows separated by fourteen cubits. Although even two rows are combined up to sixteen cubits apart, that is only if they are planted as such to begin with. If they must combine across a clearing which has been created by removal of vines, then they are only united to form a vineyard

1. According to one opinion in *Rash*, the sixteen cubits mentioned here refer to the distance between the two outside rows of a three-row vineyard, and not to the distance between one row and the next (*Tos. R' Akiva*). In the interests of simplicity, this view has not been expounded.

[If] there were three [rows] — if there are not sixteen cubits between one row and the next, he may not bring [foreign] seed there. R' Eliezer ben Yaacov says in the name of Chanina ben Chachinai: Even if the middle [row] is destroyed, and there are not sixteen cubits between one row and the next, he may not bring seed there,

YAD AVRAHAM

in the event that a real vineyard remains on at least one side of the vineyard. But if the clearing is bounded by single rows as in the present example of a three-row vineyard, then on no side is there a real vineyard (following Beis Hillel of mishnah 5).

It follows that a vineyard clearing which may not be planted if it is less than sixteen cubits is only one which is bounded by a vineyard; if it is not bounded by a vineyard, then even less than sixteen cubits of clearing severs the connection between the vines on opposite sides of the clearing and these are treated like individual vines (Rav as understood by Mishnah Chachamim).[1]

The alternative interpretation of Rav's approach assumes that here too the mishnah is discussing rows consisting of two vines each. Three rows of two vines each are combined over spacings of up to sixteen cubits and are thus treated differently than two rows of two which combine only up to eight cubits. The reason for the additional stringency in the case of three rows of two is that this looks more like a real vineyard. In a real vineyard, the law of a vineyard clearing forbids planting in gaps of up to sixteen cubits. Likewise, unless these are sixteen cubits or greater, the spaces between the rows in an arrangement of three rows of two vines each may not be planted (Mishnah Rishonah and Shoshanim LeDavid). [According to this explanation the mishnah here does not deal at all with the acceptable distance between rows of real vineyards, and this is left for the next mishnah. The difficulty with this approach is that Rav (end of s.v. בין) indicates that if an interior row

is removed from a four-row arrangement, then what remains will contain at least one vineyard. Now, if the discussion here concerns two-vine rows, then what will remain after removing a row is two rows of two on one side and one row of two on the other. But two rows of two are only combined if they are within eight cubits of each other (as Rav derives from the first part of the mishnah), yet Rav (ibid.) is explicitly discussing rows which were planted up to sixteen cubits apart!]

רַבִּי אֱלִיעֶזֶר בֶּן יַעֲקֹב אוֹמֵר מִשׁוּם חֲנִינָא בֶּן חֲכִינָאי: אֲפִילוּ חָרְבָה הָאֶמְצָעִית, וְאֵין בֵּין שׁוּרָה לַחֲבֶרְתָּהּ שֵׁשׁ עֶשְׂרֵה אַמָּה, לֹא יָבִיא זֶרַע לְשָׁם,
— R' Eliezer ben Yaacov says in the name of Chanina ben Chachinai: Even if the middle [row] is destroyed, and there are not sixteen cubits between one row and the next, he may not bring seed there,

If the middle row of a three-row vineyard is removed and the remaining two outer rows are not sixteen cubits apart, the area between them may not be planted. This seems to be the law of the vineyard clearing discussed in mishnah 1. However, Yerushalmi (4:1) maintains that the law of the vineyard clearing applies only where the clearing is bounded on at least one side by a vineyard. Following on this premise, Yerushalmi questions the view advanced here by R' Eliezer ben Yaacov which applies the law of a vineyard clearing to a three-row vineyard. When the middle row is removed, what remains are

1. The difficulty with this explanation is obvious. Since two rows combine over sixteen cubits, what does it matter that the space between two rows is the result of removal of vines? Even after the middle row of a three-row vineyard is removed, as long as the outer rows are within sixteen cubits of each other, they should combine, and hence the area between them should be bona fide vineyard, forbidden for planting. This problem is heightened by the fact that an area in which vines already had grown is viewed by some Tannaim as more stringent in terms of the prohibition on planting than an area in which no vines had grown. Nowhere is it considered more lenient!

יד אברהם

two single rows on opposite sides of the clearing, and a single row according to Beis Hillel does not constitute a vineyard!

To resolve this difficulty, *Yerushalmi* contends that R' Eliezer ben Yaacov follows Beis Shammai's opinion that a single row (of at least five vines) does constitute a vineyard (see mishnah 5). Thus, removal of the middle row of a three-row vineyard still leaves the clearing bounded by vineyards. Although Beis Shammai maintain that a clearing is forbidden for planting unless it is twenty-four cubits across (mishnah 1), R' Eliezer ben Yaacov accepts Beis Hillel's position on that matter. Accordingly, removal of the middle row from a three-row vineyard creates a clearing bounded by vineyards and the clearing is therefore subject to the law of vineyard clearings. Planting within it is forbidden unless the clearing is sixteen cubits across (*Rash; Rosh*).

According to this approach, the *Tanna Kamma* maintains that a single row does not constitute a vineyard and hence differs with R' Eliezer ben Yaacov. In that *Tanna's* opinion, the clearing created by removal of the middle row from a three-row vineyard is *not* considered a vineyard clearing since it is not bounded by vineyards. Instead, it is evaluated according to the rules for the combining of two rows: if the two rows are less than eight cubits apart, the area between them may not be planted. If they are eight or more cubits apart, then planting is permitted even between the rows at a distance of six handbreadths from the vines (*Rash; Rosh;* see also *Rav,* s.v. בין).

[Above (mishnah 1) it was indicated that a vineyard clearing must be bounded on at least *two* sides by a vineyard (see ibid. s.v. ואיזו היא). This is indeed the impression received from *Yerushalmi* 4:1 and accords with the theoretical basis for the sixteen-cubit limit given there by *Rav, Rosh,* and *Rash.* In the present mishnah, however, all these authorities speak of a vineyard clearing in a four-row vineyard. But

if an interior row is removed from such a vineyard, the remainder consists of a two-row vineyard on one side and a single row, which is not a vineyard, on the other. This would suggest that even a clearing which is bounded on only one side by a vineyard is included in the law of the vineyard clearing. See, however, *R' Shlomo Sirilio* who omits mention of a four-row vineyard and see *Ri ben Malki Tzedek.* The matter requires further study.]

Rambam Comm. makes no mention of R' Eliezer ben Yaacov's dependence on the opinion of Beis Shammai that a single row counts as a vineyard. Evidently *Rambam* does not require a clearing to be bounded by a vineyard in order to come under the law of mishnah 1 (*Mishnah Rishonah*). R' Eliezer ben Yaacov's point is that since the area from which the vines were removed had previously been considered a vineyard, this status is not easily revoked. Thus, although two rows which are planted together will constitute a vineyard only if they are within eight cubits of each other, two rows which are the remnant of a three-row vineyard will still combine up to sixteen cubits. [It can be shown that this approach is consistent with an alternative opinion in *Yerushalmi* 4:6 (see *Pnei Moshe,* s.v. ר' יהודה).]

Rav follows *Rambam Comm.* in terms of the crux of R' Eliezer ben Yaacov's argument. If *Rav* understands the *Tanna Kamma's* case of a three-row vineyard as involving three full rows (as per *Mishnas Chachamim*), then his explanation of R' Eliezer ben Yaacov is as explained above according to *Rambam Comm.*

If he understands the *Tanna Kamma* as referring to three rows of two vines each (*Mishnah Rishonah*), then the issue in question is how stringently should such a case be dealt with. The *Tanna Kamma* forbids planting between the rows if they are within sixteen cubits of each other, since such an arrangement might be confused with a real vineyard. But since it is not in fact a real vineyard, they do not prohibit planting inside it when all that is left is two rows which will not be confused with a real vineyard. R' Eliezer ben Yaacov, however, is stricter: Even though the remain-

even though had they been planted [thus] to begin with,
it would have been permitted with eight cubits.

ing two rows have only two vines each, he treats them like the remains of a real vineyard. Just as a clearing made inside a real vineyard of three full rows may not be planted, so too, the clearing made inside an arrangement of two-vine rows may not be planted (*Mishnah Rishonah*).

שֶׁאֵלּוּ מִתְּחִלָּה נִטְעָן, הֲרֵי זֶה מֻתָּר בִּשְׁמוֹנֶה אַמּוֹת. — *even though had they been planted [thus] to begin with, it would have been permitted with eight cubits.*

R' Eliezer ben Yaacov appears to be saying that unlike a clearing between two rows which resulted from the removal of the middle row of a three-row vineyard (which may not be planted unless it is sixteen cubits across), an area between two rows which has never been planted with vines may be planted with foreign seed if it is eight cubits across. However, according to our assumption above that R' Eliezer ben Yaacov follows Beis Shammai's view that a single row is a full vineyard, this cannot be true. Since planting must be distanced four cubits from a vineyard, it follows that planting between two rows of vines must be distanced four cubits from each row. But in that case, a gap of precisely eight cubits is *not* sufficient to allow planting, since any spot within the gap will be within four cubits of one of the rows!

To resolve this problem, *Yerushalmi* suggests a number of solutions. One is that the mention here of eight cubits is not precise and that really planting would be allowed only in a gap of slightly more than eight cubits (*Rash; Tos. R' Akiva*). [The planting would be allowed in the center of the gap where it is four cubits from each row.]

Another suggestion is to reinterpret R' Eliezer ben Yaacov's words: *had they been planted [thus] to begin with, it would have been permitted with eight cubits*. He does not mean that *had* a vineyard *been planted* with only two rows *to begin with*, then a gap of eight cubits

would be permitted to plant in. Such a reading would mean that he is discussing two rows planted eight cubits apart. Rather, he means that *had* two rows *been planted sixteen cubits* apart *to begin with*, then the *middle* eight cubits of that gap would be permitted to plant. [This would be permitted since the middle segment of the gap is four cubits from each of the single-row vineyards.] However, now that the clearing was created by removal of the middle row of a three-row vineyard, the entire clearing is forbidden for planting. Thus, R' Eliezer ben Yaacov is stricter with a site which once supported vines (i.e. a clearing) than with a site that did not (*Rosh;* cf. *Pnei Moshe*, s.v. ר' יהודה בן פזי בשם ר' יוחנן).

Rambam Comm. assumes that R' Eliezer ben Yaacov does not follow Beis Shammai's view that a single row constitutes a vineyard. The statement that *it would have been permitted with eight cubits* may thus be taken at face value: If two rows are planted eight cubits apart, they do not combine to form a vineyard, and the area between them may be planted, as long as the planting is distanced six handbreadths from any vines. Since single rows do not constitute vineyards, there is no need to distance any planting four cubits from each row. The moment the gap between two rows is large enough to prevent the rows from being combined into a single vineyard, it may be planted. As stated at the start of the mishnah, this gap is eight cubits. R' Eliezer ben Yaacov's point is that although two rows eight cubits apart are considered separate, and hence the area between them is not vineyard and may be planted, the area between two rows which remains after the middle row of a three-row vineyard is removed may not be planted unless it is sixteen cubits across. Since this area once supported grapevines, it does not lose its classification as a vineyard unless the two outer rows are separated by sixteen cubits. [*Rav* appears to follow *Rambam's* explanation. If R' Eliezer ben Yaacov is discussing full rows (as per *Mishnas Chachamim*) rather than two-vine rows (as per *Mishnah Rishonah* and *Shoshanim LeDavid*), the refer-

[ט] **הַנּוֹטֵעַ** אֶת כַּרְמוֹ עַל שֵׁשׁ עֶשְׂרֵה אַמָּה,
שֵׁשׁ עֶשְׂרֵה אַמָּה... ,, מֻתָּר לְהָבִיא
זֶרַע לְשָׁם. אָמַר רַבִּי יְהוּדָה: מַעֲשֶׂה בְּצַלְמוֹן
בְּאֶחָד שֶׁנָּטַע אֶת כַּרְמוֹ עַל שֵׁשׁ עֶשְׂרֵה, שֵׁשׁ
עֶשְׂרֵה אַמָּה... ,, וְהָיָה הוֹפֵךְ שְׂעַר שְׁתֵּי שׁוּרוֹת
לְצַד אַחַת וְזוֹרֵעַ אֶת הַנִּיר, וּבַשָּׁנָה הָאַחֶרֶת הָיָה
הוֹפֵךְ אֶת הַשֵּׂעָר לְמָקוֹם אַחֵר וְזוֹרֵעַ אֶת הַבּוּר,
וּבָא מַעֲשֶׂה לִפְנֵי חֲכָמִים וְהִתִּירוּ. רַבִּי מֵאִיר

יד אברהם

ence to an earlier mention in the mishnah of the fact that eight cubits constitutes a separation between two rows is difficult to understand, since according to *Rav* the earlier statement in the mishnah dealt with two-vine rows.]

9.

הַנּוֹטֵעַ אֶת כַּרְמוֹ עַל שֵׁשׁ עֶשְׂרֵה אַמָּה, שֵׁשׁ עֶשְׂרֵה אַמָּה... ,, מֻתָּר לְהָבִיא זֶרַע לְשָׁם. — [If] someone plants his vineyard sixteen cubits, sixteen cubits ..., it is permitted to bring seed there.

The mishnah discusses a vineyard in which each row is sixteen cubits away from the next row (*Rav*; *Rash*; *Rambam Comm.*). In such a case, it is permitted to plant between the rows at a distance of six handbreadths from each row (*Rav*). Because of the large gap between them, the rows are not combined to form a vineyard (in the halachic sense), and there is no need to remove planting four cubits from the vines. Since six handbreadths equals one cubit, it follows that of the sixteen cubits between rows, fourteen may be planted (*Rash*).

The opening statement of the mishnah would seem to be nothing more than a positive reformulation of the law taught in the previous mishnah. There it was taught that if there are *not* sixteen cubits between rows in a vineyard of three rows or more, then planting between them is *prohibited*. Here, it is stated that if there *are* sixteen cubits between rows, then planting between them is *permitted*. If this is so, then the ruling here relates only to a case involving three rows or more. But in a case of two rows, the *Tanna* of our mishnah

would agree with the *Tanna* of the previous mishnah that even if the area between the two rows is only eight cubits, it may be planted (*Meleches Shlomo*).

Rosh, however, writes that the ruling of this mishnah conflicts with the opinion given in the previous mishnah that when there are only two rows, a separation of eight cubits may be planted. Evidently, *Rosh* understood that the *Tanna* of this mishnah does not differentiate between a two-row vineyard and a multi-row vineyard: in all cases, only a separation between rows of at least sixteen cubits may be planted (see *Derech Emunah* 7:3, *Beur HaHalachah*, s.v. ובין).

אָמַר רַבִּי יְהוּדָה: מַעֲשֶׂה בְּצַלְמוֹן בְּאֶחָד שֶׁנָּטַע אֶת כַּרְמוֹ עַל שֵׁשׁ עֶשְׂרֵה, שֵׁשׁ עֶשְׂרֵה אַמָּה... ,, וְהָיָה הוֹפֵךְ שְׂעַר שְׁתֵּי שׁוּרוֹת לְצַד אַחַת וְזוֹרֵעַ אֶת הַנִּיר, וּבַשָּׁנָה הָאַחֶרֶת הָיָה הוֹפֵךְ אֶת הַשֵּׂעָר לְמָקוֹם אַחֵר וְזוֹרֵעַ אֶת הַבּוּר, — R' Yehudah said: It happened in Tzalmon that a certain individual planted his vineyard sixteen [cubits], sixteen cubits ... And he used to turn the branches of two rows towards the same area and plant the plowed area, and the following year he would turn the branches to the other side and plant the barren area,

R' Yehudah relates a story which supports the position of the *Tanna Kamma* (*Tos. Yom Tov*; see *Rashi* to *Gittin* 74b,

9. [I**f] someone plants his vineyard sixteen cubits, sixteen cubits ..., it is permitted to bring seed there. R' Yehudah said: It happened in Tzalmon that a certain individual planted his vineyard sixteen [cubits], sixteen cubits ... And he used to turn the branches of two rows towards the same area and plant the plowed area, and the following year he would turn the branches to the other side and plant the barren area, and the story came before the Sages and they permitted [it]. R' Meir**

YAD AVRAHAM

s.v. מאי תנא). It once happened in a place called Tzalmon that a certain individual planted vines over a large area, leaving sixteen cubits between each row. He wanted to sow the areas between the rows with foreign seed, but in order to prevent the soil from becoming depleted, he did not want to sow the same areas each year (see *Bava Basra* 29a). He therefore devised a plan to leave the gaps between rows fallow on alternate years by planting only every other gap in a given year. The following year he would sow the areas which had been left barren the previous year and leave barren the areas which had been sown the previous year. Now the law is that even when foreign seed is planted the requisite distance from the trunk of a grapevine, it is nevertheless forbidden to plant under the branches of the vine (mishnah 7:3). If the vines were to grow extensively this would severely limit the space available for foreign planting, since planting under the branches would be forbidden regardless of how far the spot was from the trunk of the vine. To overcome this problem and to maxi-

mize his available space, the person used to train the vines of rows which bounded the areas left fallow into those areas. One year, he might leave spaces a, c, e, etc., barren (see diagram). He would therefore train the vines in rows 1 and 2 towards each other and hence into the area left fallow, and so also with rows 3 and 4, and so on. The following year he would leave spaces b, d, f, etc., barren and would train the vines which bounded these spaces into these spaces. In this way the vines were all concentrated in the barren areas and the areas to be planted — i.e. the *plowed areas* — were completely free of foliage and were fully available for foreign planting. The person then distanced his foreign planting six handbreadths from the rows and planted the remaining fourteen cubits of the gap (*Rav; Rosh; Rash*).

וּבָא מַעֲשֶׂה לִפְנֵי חֲכָמִים וְהִתִּירוּ. — *and the story came before the Sages and they permitted [it].*

The Sages approved of the person's action. This shows that when a gap of sixteen cubits is left between rows, the

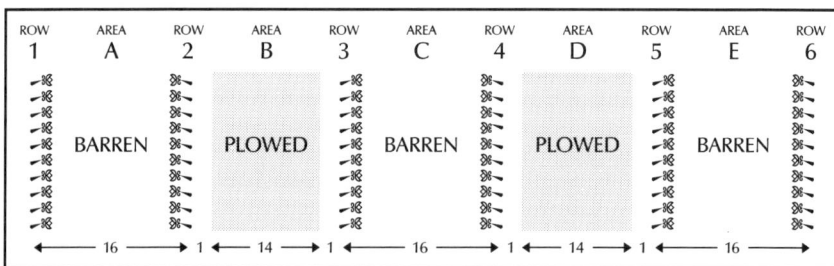

ROW	AREA	ROW	AREA	ROW	AREA	ROW	AREA	ROW	AREA	ROW
1	A	2	B	3	C	4	D	5	E	6
	BARREN		PLOWED		BARREN		PLOWED		BARREN	

←— 16 —→ 1 ←— 14 —→ 1 ←— 16 —→ 1 ←— 14 —→ 1 ←— 16 —→

כלאים
ה/א

וְרַבִּי שִׁמְעוֹן אוֹמְרִים: אַף הַנּוֹטֵעַ אֶת כַּרְמוֹ עַל שְׁמוֹנֶה, שְׁמוֹנֶה אַמּוֹת . . . ,, מֻתָּר.

[א] **כֶּרֶם** שֶׁחָרַב – אִם יֶשׁ בּוֹ לְלַקֵּט עֶשֶׂר גְּפָנִים לְבֵית סְאָה וּנְטוּעוֹת כְּהִלְכָתָן,

יד אברהם

rows do not combine to form a vineyard and it is permitted to plant between them, as in fact stated by the first *Tanna* of this mishnah (*Rav; Rosh; Rash*).

As understood by *Rav* et al., the story merely proves the statement of the *Tanna Kamma* of our mishnah. *Rambam Comm.*, however, understands that the story teaches something new. Ordinarily, even if a gap between rows is permitted for planting, the planting must be distanced six handbreadths from the rows. The present story teaches that if the branches of the vines are trained away from the area which is planted, then no distancing whatsoever is required (see above mishnah 3:5). Thus, according to *Rambam*, by training his vines away from the areas to be planted, the person made the *entire* sixteen cubits available for planting and it is this that the Sages permitted.

Rashbam (*Bava Basra* 82b) understands that the sixteen-cubit gap required for planting is measured from the tips of the branches of one row to the tips of the branches of the next row. Thus, if there are exactly sixteen cubits between the trunks of the vines in each row, and the branches point towards each other, the distance between branches will be less than sixteen cubits and planting in the gap between these rows will be forbidden. According to *Rashbam*, the story of the mishnah teaches that only by training the branches away from the gap was it permitted to plant the gap at all. Had the person not done this, the gap between branches would not have equaled sixteen cubits, and no foreign planting would have been permitted. [*Rav, Rosh*, and *Rash*, however, disagree and make it clear that the training of the branches was done merely to permit planting in those spaces which would otherwise have been under the branches of the vines. But the spaces

which would not have been under the branches could anyway have been planted because of the sixteen cubits between the trunks.]

רַבִּי מֵאִיר וְרַבִּי שִׁמְעוֹן אוֹמְרִים: אַף הַנּוֹטֵעַ אֶת כַּרְמוֹ עַל שְׁמוֹנֶה, שְׁמוֹנֶה אַמּוֹת . . . ,, מֻתָּר. — *R' Meir and R' Shimon say: Even if someone plants his vineyard eight [cubits], eight cubits . . ., it is permitted.*

R' Meir and R' Shimon say that it is permitted to plant between the rows of a vineyard even if the rows are only eight cubits apart. In their opinion, the prohibition on planting a gap of less than sixteen cubits (mishnah 4:1) applies only to a clearing which was created by removal of vines. But gaps left between rows to begin with are permitted for foreign planting even if they are only eight cubits across (*Rav; Rambam Comm.*). Thus, according to R' Meir and R' Shimon, if a person plants even a multi-row vineyard such that the rows are eight cubits apart, he is permitted to plant foreign seed in the gaps. He needs to distance this planting six handbreadths from the rows of vines as is the requirement when planting near a single vine, and the remaining six cubits[1] of the gap may be completely planted (*Rav; Rosh; Rash*). The halachah follows R' Meir and R' Shimon (*Rav; Rambam Comm.*).

Although spacing of eight cubits between rows suffices to permit planting between the rows, *Rambam* (*Hil. Kilayim* 7:4) maintains that any planting *outside* the vineyard must be distanced by four cubits. The basis for this distinction appears to be a statement in *Yerushalmi* 7:2 (*Mareh HaPanim* 4:6, s.v. אמר

---

1. *Rambam Comm.*, consistent with his interpretation of the story related by R' Yehudah, adds that if the vines which border the eight-cubit gap between rows are trained away from the gap, then the entire eight cubits may be planted with foreign seed (see *Mishnah Rishonah*).

and R' Shimon say: Even if someone plants his vineyard
eight [cubits], eight cubits . . ., it is permitted.

1. [**I**f] a vineyard was destroyed — if there are [still]
to be found in it ten vines per *beis se'ah* and
they are planted in the correct configuration, this is

YAD AVRAHAM

ר' זעירא and 7:2, s.v. הדא, *Beur HaGra, Yoreh Deah* 296:54), but it nevertheless is difficult to understand. If such an arrangement is considered a vineyard, then planting inside it should be altogether forbidden. If it is not, then planting outside it should be allowed six

handbreadths away and there should be no need to leave the four-cubit work area characteristic of vineyards (see *Hasagos HaRavad* loc. cit.). The matter requires further study (*Kesef Mishneh*; see also *Tos. Yom Tov* and *Tos. Anshei Shem*).

Chapter 5

1.

In mishnah 4:1 the law for a vineyard clearing was discussed. If the clearing extends sixteen cubits or more, planting within it is permitted, as long as the planting is at least four cubits from the surrounding vines.

The topic of the present mishnah is a *destroyed vineyard*. Unlike the vineyard clearing *which has been destroyed in its middle* (mishnah 4:1), a *destroyed vineyard* is one in which the removal of vines is not limited to the interior of the vineyard. It might have been expected that the greater level of destruction of this vineyard would make it less of a vineyard, and hence more lenient with regard to planting it with foreign seed. In fact, as will be seen below, the prohibition on planting foreign seed in the destroyed areas of a destroyed vineyard is more stringent than the prohibition on planting in the clearing of a vineyard clearing.

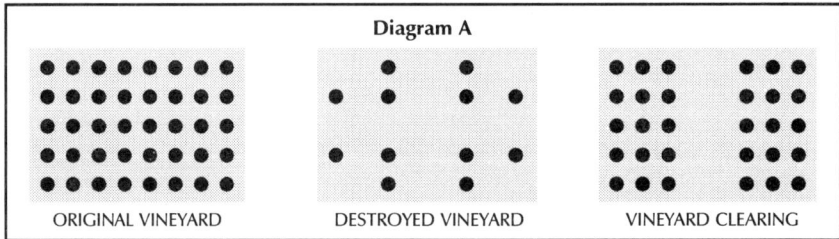

Diagram A

ORIGINAL VINEYARD   DESTROYED VINEYARD   VINEYARD CLEARING

כֶּרֶם שֶׁחָרַב — *[If] a vineyard was destroyed* —

The difference between a destroyed vineyard and a vineyard clearing is that the latter is restricted to the interior of the vineyard [so that it is bounded, at least on two sides,[1] by complete rows of vines]. In a destroyed vineyard, however, the clearing penetrates even the outer rows of the vineyard, so that it is not bounded by complete rows (*Rav; Ri ben Malki Tze-*

dek from *Yerushalmi*; see diagram A).

אִם יֵשׁ בּוֹ לְלַקֵּט עֶשֶׂר גְּפָנִים לְפָנִים לְבֵית סָאָה וּנְטוּעוֹת כְּהִלְכָתָן, —*if there are [still] to be found in it ten vines per beis se'ah and they are planted in the correct configuration,*

As will be recalled, a *beis se'ah* is 2,500 square cubits. This area must still contain at least ten vines in order to qualify as a vineyard. In addition, the vines form the correct configuration, which means *two*

---

1. See *Radbaz* to *Hil. Kilayim* 7:11, *Mareh HaPanim* 4:1, s.v. קרחת.

הֲרֵי זֶה נִקְרָא כֶּרֶם דַּל. כֶּרֶם שֶׁהוּא נָטוּעַ עִרְבּוּבְיָא — אִם יֵשׁ בּוֹ לְכַוֵּן שְׁתַּיִם נֶגֶד שָׁלֹשׁ, הֲרֵי זֶה כֶּרֶם; וְאִם

יד אברהם

opposite two plus one protruding like a tail (mishnah 4:6). If these surviving vines are not sixteen cubits or more apart, nor less than four cubits from one another, they are referred to by the mishnah as *planted in the correct configuration*, and they constitute a vineyard as will be explained (*Rav; Rosh; Rash*).

According to *Rash* and *Rosh*, all ten vines are part of such a formation. The distribution of the surviving vines is shown in diagram B for a vineyard which

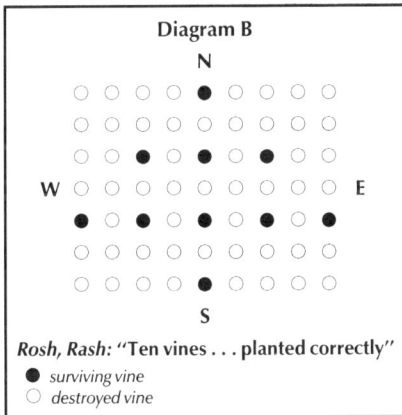

Diagram B

N

W   E

S

Rosh, Rash: "Ten vines . . . planted correctly"

● *surviving vine*
○ *destroyed vine*

originally contained 63 vines arranged in seven rows of nine vines each. Of the ten vines which survive, four are on the outer rows (one per side) and six are aligned in two rows of three vines each in the interior of the vineyard. It can readily be seen that each of the vines can be viewed as belonging to a configuration in which there are *two opposite two plus one protruding like a tail.* [Note that the *tail* is positioned according to the interpretation of *Rash* and *Rosh* to mishnah 4:6.]

From *Rambam* (*Hil. Kilayim* 7:8), how-

ever, it appears that as long as five of the vines can be fit into a protruding tail formation, then all ten vines are together considered a vineyard[1] (*Tif. Yis.; Mishnah Rishonah*).

The spacing limitation given by *Rav, Rosh* and *Rash*, namely, that the surviving vines cannot be sixteen cubits apart, is not stated in the mishnah nor is it mentioned by *Rambam* or *Shulchan Aruch* (*Tif. Yis.*). As will be seen below, the novelty of the mishnah is that even areas of the vineyard which are no longer situated between vines are still treated as vineyard if the surviving vines satisfy the conditions of the mishnah (ten per *beis se'ah*, planted correctly). According to *Rav et al.* the mishnah does *not* contain novelties with respect to the combination of vines. Thus, just as vines do not combine across a vineyard clearing of sixteen cubits, so too the vines here cannot be combined if they are sixteen or more cubits apart. When they are not this far apart and hence can be combined, they preserve the status of vineyard even in those areas no longer between vines (cf. *Mishnah Rishonah*). According to *Rambam*, however, it seems that even if the surviving vines are spread across large distances, as long as they satisfy the configuration and density conditions of the mishnah, they combine to preserve the status of vineyard throughout the *beis se'ah* (*Tos. Anshei Shem*).

הֲרֵי זֶה נִקְרָא כֶּרֶם דַּל. — *this is called a "poor vineyard."*

The entire *beis se'ah* retains its status as a vineyard so that foreign planting is forbidden throughout it (*Rambam, Hil. Kilayim* 7:8, *Rosh*). *Rosh* (following his understanding of *planted in the correct configuration* shown in diagram B) explains that foreign planting was prohibited throughout the entire *beis se'ah*, since on each side of the *beis se'ah* there re-

---

1. *Rambam* (*Hil. Kilayim* 7:8) states also that if six of the vines are aligned in two rows of three opposite three, all the vines constitute a vineyard (see *Mahari Korkus*).

5

1

called a "poor vineyard."

[If] a vineyard was planted chaotically — if it is possible to align two opposite three, then this is a vineyard;

YAD AVRAHAM

mains a vineyard configuration (protruding tail) and since on each of the four outer rows at least one vine survives. Although the *beis se'ah* no longer contains a high quantity of vines — i.e. it is "poor" in vines (*Yerushalmi*) — it remains classified as a vineyard. For this reason it is referred to as a *poor vineyard* (*Rav; Rambam Comm.*).

A *vineyard clearing* would seem to be less of a disruption of a vineyard than that caused when *a vineyard is destroyed*. Yet, a vineyard clearing remains classified as a vineyard only when it is less than sixteen cubits across. But if it is sixteen cubits across, even if it is surrounded on all sides by vineyards, planting it with foreign seed is permitted (mishnah 4:1). In contrast, no part of the *beis se'ah* of a destroyed vineyard may be planted with foreign seed, even if it is more than sixteen cubits from the nearest vine. Although the original vineyard has been drastically diminished (destroyed), its entire original area remains classified as a vineyard!

The explanation of this apparent paradox would seem to be rooted in the difference between the orderliness of the vineyard-clearing situation compared with the chaos of the destroyed-vineyard situation. In the former, the clearing does not penetrate the outer rows of the vineyard. It is thus always bounded by vines which can be said to define its limits. As a delimited area, it can be viewed as distinct from the surrounding vines so that with appropriate distancing, planting it may be permitted. The cleared areas of a destroyed vineyard are not delimited by any vines. On the contrary, they permeate the entire vineyard without any regular definable pattern. This lack of definition makes it impossible to speak of the clearing separately from the vineyard, and hence as long as a remnant of the vineyard remains, the entire *beis se'ah* may not be planted (see *Mishnah Rishonah*).

[*Chazon Ish* (10:8) has a novel interpretation of this mishnah. If ten vines grow in an area of 2,500 square cubits, then it may be said that each vine draws nourishment from 250 square cubits. Assuming that the radius

of a circle with this area is approximately 9 cubits, *Chazon Ish* contends that the spacing between vines may not exceed 18.25 cubits. That is, as long as the distance between two vines is not greater than their combined radii of nourishment, the vines can be said to belong to the same vineyard. Moreover, *Chazon Ish* entertains the possibility that it is *permitted* to plant foreign seed inside a *poor vineyard* just as with a *vineyard clearing*. The designation of such a vineyard as a vineyard is merely in order to require distancing of four cubits from the outer vines, rather than the six-handbreadth gap required when dealing with individual vines.]

כֶּרֶם שֶׁהוּא נָטוּעַ עִרְבּוּבְיָא — *[If] a vineyard was planted chaotically* —

I.e. the vines were not planted in neatly arranged parallel rows but rather without any apparent pattern (*Rav; Rosh; Rash; Rambam Comm.*; see below from *Tif. Yis.*).

אִם יֵשׁ בּוֹ לְכַוֵּן שְׁתַּיִם נֶגֶד שָׁלֹשׁ, הֲרֵי זֶה כֶּרֶם; *if it is possible to align two opposite three, then this is a vineyard;*

If it is possible to find, among all the vines growing, five vines which are aligned *two opposite three*, then the entire haphazard collection of vines is deemed a vineyard. To determine whether vines form a straight row, a string is tied to the trunk of one of the vines and pulled taut. The trunks of the other vines must touch the string simultaneously if they are to be counted as part of the same row. Note that the row is defined by the position of the trunks and not the branches. Even if the branches are aligned, the vines do not form a row if the trunks are not aligned (*Rav; Rosh; Rash*).

The wording *two opposite three* strongly suggests the two-row formation which *Rav*, *Rosh*, and *Rash* understand to be the protruding-tail formation (see 4:6 diagram A). If *Rambam* does not consider that formation to constitute a vineyard (see 4:6), then he must

[ב] **כֶּרֶם** שֶׁהוּא נָטוּעַ עַל פָּחוֹת פָּחוֹת מֵאַרְבַּע אַמּוֹת, רַבִּי שִׁמְעוֹן אוֹמֵר: אֵינוֹ כֶּרֶם. וַחֲכָמִים אוֹמְרִים: כֶּרֶם, וְרוֹאִין אֶת הָאֶמְצָעִיּוֹת כְּאִלּוּ אֵינָן.

יד אברהם

explain that here too the formation referred to has the "tail" opposite the space between the other four vines (see 4:6 diagram B), and the mishnah's language is not precise (see *Radbaz* to *Hil. Kilayim* 7:9). Alternatively, *Rambam* agrees that in the case of the chaotic vineyard, since there are many vines present, even a *two opposite three* formation suffices (*Sheyarei Minchah* to *Tosefta* 3:6 from *Chasdei David*).

וְאִם לָאו, אֵינוּ כֶּרֶם. — *if not, it is not a vineyard.*

If no such pattern can be found among the vines, they do not constitute a vineyard. The consequences of being classified a vineyard have already been encountered in chapter 4: (a) foreign planting is generally forbidden between vines of a vineyard unless the conditions for a vineyard clearing are satisfied (cf. *Rambam, Hil. Kilayim* 7:2); and (b) foreign planting must be distanced four cubits from the outside of a vineyard. If vines do not constitute a vineyard — as in the present case — foreign planting need be distanced only six handbreadths (see *Rambam Comm.* and *Hil. Kilayim* 7:9).

רַבִּי מֵאִיר אוֹמֵר: הוֹאִיל וְהוּא נִרְאֶה כְּתַבְנִית הַכְּרָמִים, הֲרֵי זֶה כֶּרֶם. — *R' Meir says: Since it resembles the structure of vineyards, it is a vineyard.*

It is not clear in what way a chaotically planted vineyard resembles *the structure of vineyards*. *Tif. Yis.* indicates that R' Meir is referring to a situation in which the vines *are* planted in rows, but the vines of different rows are not aligned. Thus, in one direction the vineyard can be seen as a collection of parallel rows of vines, but from the other it appears confused (see diagram C). Nevertheless, since the vineyard is composed of rows, it resembles *the structure of vineyards* according to R' Meir and is hence treated

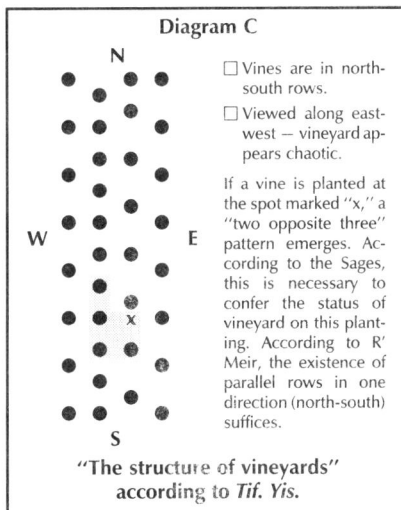

Diagram C

N

□ Vines are in north-south rows.

□ Viewed along east-west — vineyard appears chaotic.

If a vine is planted at the spot marked "x," a "two opposite three" pattern emerges. According to the Sages, this is necessary to confer the status of vineyard on this planting. According to R' Meir, the existence of parallel rows in one direction (north-south) suffices.

W ······ E

x

S

"The structure of vineyards" according to *Tif. Yis.*

like a vineyard. Planting within four cubits of its outer edge is forbidden, as is planting between rows. Only if a clearing which extends sixteen cubits is created inside it will planting inside it be permitted (*Rav* as understood by *Tos. Anshei Shem;* cf. *Mishnah Rishonah*).

From *Tif. Yis.* it emerges that for the *Tanna Kamma* a vineyard with parallel rows in one direction only, which does not have five vines that fit into a two opposite three pattern, is not considered a vineyard. Evidently, it is necessary that a vineyard be arranged so that it forms parallel lines on both a horizontal and a vertical axis. Otherwise, it is considered chaotic. [Note however that the early commentators make no mention of such a requirement.]

An interesting interpretation of R' Meir's statement is offered by R' Chanoch Albek. He suggests that R' Meir is referring to the *two opposite three* arrangement, which is necessary in order to confer vineyard status on a chaotic planting of vines. According to the *Tanna Kamma*, it is necessary to *align* two op-

2. [**I**f] a vineyard is planted with less than four cubits [between rows], R' Shimon says: It is not a vineyard. But the Sages say: [It is] a vineyard, and we view the interior [vines] as if they are not [present].

YAD AVRAHAM

posite three. That is, the pattern consists of a tail appended to a right-angled quadrilateral. According to R' Meir, however, any quadrilateral would suffice as the body of the protruding-tail arrangement, provided that the two-vine row was parallel to the three-vine row (see diagram D). The parallelism of the two rows of the two opposite three arrangement resembles *the structure of vineyards* and hence enables the entire collection of vines to be considered a vineyard. According to R' Meir, then, a chaotic vineyard would be one that has no parallel rows in any direction.

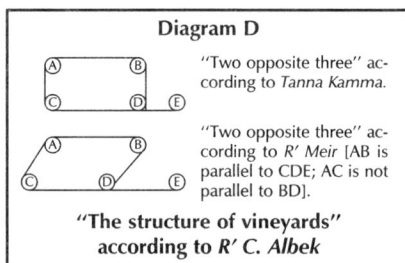

Diagram D

"Two opposite three" according to *Tanna Kamma.*

"Two opposite three" according to R' Meir [AB is parallel to CDE; AC is not parallel to BD].

"The structure of vineyards" according to R' C. Albek

[See also *Maseches Kilayim im Beurim* for yet another explanation.]

2.

כֶּרֶם שֶׁהוּא נָטוּעַ עַל פָּחוֹת מֵאַרְבַּע אַמּוֹת, — *[If] a vineyard is planted with less than four cubits [between rows],*

The rows of the vineyard are separated one from another by less than four cubits (*Rav; Rosh; Rash; Rambam Comm.*). When rows are planted this closely together, it is not possible to plow with oxen between them (*Rav; Rosh*). [As noted in the commentary to mishnah 4:1, the four-cubit work area of a vineyard is determined by the space needed for the oxen and plow (*Tos. Yom Tov*).] *Rambam Comm.* writes that in such crowded conditions the vines do not have enough room to grow properly (*Rambam Comm.*).[1]

The mishnah (here and in mishnah 1) speaks of a vineyard which *was planted,* rather than of planting a vineyard (see e.g. mishnah 4:9). This is because the arrangements under discussion here are not normal. It might happen that a vineyard was planted in this way, but it is not likely that a person would plant his vineyard in this manner by design. Accordingly, the passive form is used (*Tos. Anshei Shem* from R' Moshe Zaccutto).

רַבִּי שִׁמְעוֹן אוֹמֵר: אֵינוֹ כֶרֶם. — *R' Shimon says: It is not a vineyard.*

R' Shimon says that since the rows cannot be plowed, the vines do not constitute a vineyard, and foreign planting needs to be distanced only six handbreadths from the vines (*Rav; Rosh*).

Eretz Chemdah (p. 248) notes that *Rambam* (*Hil. Kilayim* 7:2) indicates that in the case of two rows of vines within four cubits of each other, all the vines are viewed collectively as part of a single grapevine. If so, then although outside the vines foreign planting will be permitted at a distance of only six handbreadths, between the vines no planting at all will be allowed.

וַחֲכָמִים אוֹמְרִים: כֶּרֶם, וְרוֹאִין אֶת הָאֶמְצָעִיוֹת כְּאִלּוּ אֵינָן. — *But the Sages say: [It is] a vineyard, and we view the interior [vines] as if they are not [present].*

The Sages maintain that intervening rows can be disregarded. For example, in a five-row arrangement, where the distance between rows is, say, three cubits, rows number one, three, and five can be counted as a vineyard since these rows are six cubits apart. The intervening rows,

1. *Eretz Chemdah* (p. 246-7) suggests that according to *Rambam's* reasoning a gap of four cubits should be required between vines of the same row. See *Meiri* to *Bava Basra* 83a and *Mahari Korkus* to *Hil. Kilayim* 7:2.

[ג] **חָרִיץ** שֶׁהוּא עוֹבֵר בַּכֶּרֶם עָמֵק עֲשָׂרָה
וְרָחָב אַרְבָּעָה, רַבִּי אֱלִיעֶזֶר בֶּן
יַעֲקֹב אוֹמֵר: אִם הָיָה מְפֻלָּשׁ מֵרֹאשׁ הַכֶּרֶם וְעַד
סוֹפוֹ, הֲרֵי זֶה נִרְאֶה כְּבֵין שְׁנֵי כְרָמִים, וְזוֹרְעִים
בְּתוֹכוֹ. וְאִם לָאו, הֲרֵי הוּא כְגַת.

יד אברהם

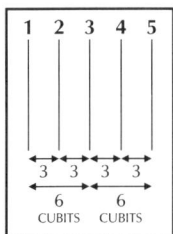

```
1  2  3  4  5
```
(diagram with measurements: 3 3 3 3; 6 CUBITS, 6 CUBITS)

two and four, can be ignored (see diagram).

In contrast with R' Shimon, the Sages maintain that people will plant row after row in close proximity, intending the rows which can survive as a vineyard and those which cannot as firewood. Thus, the intervening rows are viewed as firewood and do not interfere with the combination of the outer rows into a vineyard (*Rav; Rosh; Rash*).

In the previous mishnah, *Rav* (following *Rosh* and *Rash*) stipulates that in order for the surviving vines of a destroyed vineyard to constitute a vineyard, they must be spaced at least four cubits apart. Although at first glance this requirement would seem to be based on R' Shimon's opinion (*Tos. Yom Tov* to mishnah 1), it is possible that in that case the Sages would also concur. This is because the mishnah there specifies that a minimum of ten vines distributed within a *beis se'ah* must remain. Now, if ten vines are arranged within four cubits of each other, it is true that the Sages do not see this as preventing their classification as a vineyard. However, this is only because the intervening vines are viewed *as if they are not present*. But in the case of the preceding mishnah, if some of the vines are regarded as absent, the quota of ten vines is not satisfied! Accordingly, even the Sages will agree in the case of mishnah 1 that the vines may not be within four cubits of each other if they are to constitute a vineyard (*Chiddushei*

R' Yoel Chasid; Tos. Chadashim; Mishnas Chachamim; Rashash to mishnah 1).

It must be noted, however, that the contention that the Sages view the intervening vines as absent is not unanimously agreed. *Rambam Comm.* following *Yerushalmi* writes that it is permitted to train the intervening vines over foreign seed, since these vines which are destined for firewood are looked upon as mere wood and not grapevines. This would suggest that these intervening vines are regarded as absent for all intents and purposes. However, in his Code, *Rambam* makes no mention of such a law despite the fact that he records the assertion of the mishnah that *we view the interior vines as if they are not [present]*. Assuming that in his Code he is of the opinion that these vines are not regarded as non-existent, he would not permit them to be trained on foreign seed (*Tos. Yom Tov* to mishnah 1, *Chazon Ish* 11:14). Indeed, *Rosh* writes explicitly that although the interior vines are ignored, this is only with respect to designating the outer vines as a vineyard. The outer vines generate a prohibition on planting foreign seed which extends to four cubits in accordance with the law for vineyards; the interior vines prohibit planting only up to six handbreadths away. Accordingly, the mishnah might better be rendered: *we view the interior [vines] as if they are not [part of the vineyard]*. We do not view them as non-existent, merely as not part of the vineyard (*Mishnah Rishonah*). It has been shown that this alternative approach accords with a second opinion expressed in *Yerushalmi* (see *Derech Emunah* 7:16, *Tziyun HaHalachah* 7:29; see *Maseches Kilayim im Beurim* 7:2).

3.

The investigation of the circumstances in which foreign planting in a vineyard is permitted is continued. The coming mishnah discusses foreign planting in a ditch, a vat, or a lookout which are located in a vineyard.

3. [I]f] a ditch which passes through a vineyard is ten [handbreadths] deep and four wide, R' Eliezer ben Yaacov says: If it stretches from one end of the vineyard to the [other] end, then it looks like it is between two vineyards, and it is permitted to plant inside it. But if not, then it is like a winepress.

YAD AVRAHAM

חָרִיץ שֶׁהוּא עוֹבֵר בַּכֶּרֶם עָמֹק עֲשָׂרָה וְרָחָב אַרְבָּעָה, — *[If] a ditch which passes through a vineyard is ten [handbreadths] deep and four wide,*

[Above it was taught that a ditch of these dimensions (*ten [handbreadths] deep and four wide*) constitutes a divider between a vineyard and its surroundings, which allows planting foreign seed on the other side of the ditch across from the vineyard (mishnah 4:3 and see also mishnah 2:8). Our mishnah considers the status of the ditch itself: Is the ditch considered an independent realm in which foreign planting is permitted, or not? The case addressed concerns a ditch which cuts through a vineyard, leaving the ditch surrounded by vines on two sides.]

רַבִּי אֱלִיעֶזֶר בֶּן יַעֲקֹב אוֹמֵר: אִם הָיָה מְפֻלָּשׁ מֵרֹאשׁ הַכֶּרֶם וְעַד סוֹפוֹ, הֲרֵי זֶה נִרְאֶה כְּבֵין שְׁנֵי כְּרָמִים, וְזוֹרְעִים בְּתוֹכוֹ. — *R' Eliezer ben Yaacov says: If it stretches from one end of the vineyard to the [other] end, then it looks like it is between two vineyards, and it is permitted to plant inside it.*

If the ditch reaches from one end of the vineyard to the other, thereby bisecting the vineyard, *it is permitted to plant inside it.* In such a situation the ditch looks like a barrier between two vineyards which is part of neither, and hence it constitutes an independent realm which may be planted (see *Rav; Rosh; Rash*).

The expression בֵּין שְׁנֵי כְּרָמִים, *between two vineyards*, was encountered in mishnah 4:3 where R' Yehudah identifies the unplanted area *between two vineyards* with מְחוֹל הַכֶּרֶם. According to R' Yehudah, the area between two vineyards must be at least twelve cubits across for planting in it to be permitted. It was explained in the commentary there (s.v. וְאֵיזֶה)

that according to the *Tanna Kamma* of mishnah 4:2, who disputes R' Yehudah's position, the area between vineyards is treated like a *vineyard clearing* which may be planted only if it is sixteen cubits across (*Rambam Comm.* ibid.).

In both opinions, a substantial distance was required between two vineyards before any planting was permitted.

But the language of the present mishnah seems to imply that the area *between two vineyards* is viewed as independent of both vineyards. The distinction between the two cases seems to be that when the empty space is on the same level as the vineyards, it does not appear separate from the vineyards unless it is very large. On the other hand, a ditch such as that of the mishnah, which bisects the vineyard, appears separate from the vineyard. Accordingly, it is classified as *between two vineyards,* i.e. outside of both of them, and may be planted. There is no need for planting on the bottom of the ditch to be distanced four cubits from the edge of the vineyards, since the wall of the ditch functions like a divider which obviates the need for such distancing (*Beur HaHalachah* 7:20, s.v. כבין).

וְאִם לָאו, הֲרֵי הוּא כְּגַת. — *But if not, then it is like a winepress.*

If any of the conditions specified by the mishnah are not satisfied, then the ditch is treated like a vineyard winepress. Thus, if the ditch is less than ten handbreadths deep, even though it is four across and bisects the vineyard, it may not be planted. Similarly, if it is less than four handbreadths across, even though it is deep enough and bisects the vineyard, or if it does not stretch from one end of the vineyard to the other, even though it is both deep enough and wide enough, it is treated like a winepress in a vineyard. R' Eliezer ben Yaacov sides with the Sages immediately below, who forbid planting

וְהַגַּת שֶׁבַּכֶּרֶם עֲמֻקָה עֲשָׂרָה וְרֹחַב אַרְבָּעָה, רַבִּי
אֱלִיעֶזֶר אוֹמֵר: זוֹרְעִים בְּתוֹכָהּ. וַחֲכָמִים אוֹסְרִים.
שׁוֹמֵרָה שֶׁבַּכֶּרֶם גְּבֹהָה עֲשָׂרָה וּרְחָבָה אַרְבַּע,
זוֹרְעִין בְּתוֹכָהּ. וְאִם הָיָה שֵׂעָר כּוֹתֵשׁ, אָסוּר.

[ד] **גֶּפֶן** שֶׁהִיא נְטוּעָה בַּגַּת אוֹ בַנֶּקַע, נוֹתְנִין
לָהּ עֲבוֹדָתָהּ וְזוֹרֵעַ אֶת הַמּוֹתָר.

יד אברהם

in a vineyard wine-press. He therefore compares a ditch which does not satisfy the mishnah's conditions to a winepress in a vineyard — both seem like distinct entities but are not considered to occupy a distinct and separate realm from the vineyard and therefore may not be planted (*Rav; Rosh; Rash*).

The ditch which fails to bisect the vineyard, and hence may not be planted, is not necessarily contained entirely within the vineyard and surrounded by vines on all four sides (see diagram). Even if it stretches from

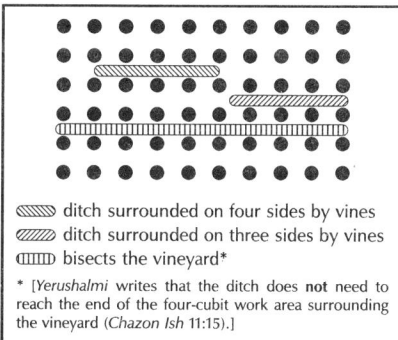

⬛ ditch surrounded on four sides by vines
⬛ ditch surrounded on three sides by vines
⬛ bisects the vineyard*

* [*Yerushalmi* writes that the ditch does **not** need to reach the end of the four-cubit work area surrounding the vineyard (*Chazon Ish* 11:15).]

one end of the vineyard to the middle of the vineyard, so that it is surrounded by vines on only three sides, it is still treated like a winepress in a vineyard and may not be planted (*Rav; Rosh; Rash;* see *Mishnah Rishonah*).

וְהַגַּת שֶׁבַּכֶּרֶם עֲמֻקָה עֲשָׂרָה וְרֹחַב[1] אַרְבָּעָה, רַבִּי אֱלִיעֶזֶר אוֹמֵר: זוֹרְעִים בְּתוֹכָהּ. וַחֲכָמִים אוֹסְרִים. — *And [if] a winepress in a vineyard is ten deep and four wide, R' Eliezer*

says: [It is permitted] to plant inside it. But the Sages forbid [this].

The winepress was a large pit in which the grapes were pressed and the wine collected. Although it was ten handbreadths deep and four wide, it did not bisect the vineyard. Rather, it was located along the edge of the vineyard and thus was surrounded on only three sides by vines (*Mishnah Rishonah*). R' Eliezer considers the fact that it was surrounded on only three sides by vines as sufficient to permit the winepress to be planted with foreign seed. The Sages disagree (*Rav; Rosh; Rash;* see *Mishnah Rishonah*). [Assuming that each of the other conditions specified by the mishnah for planting in a ditch are as critical as the condition that the ditch bisect the vineyard, R' Eliezer ben Yaacov (above) maintains that just as a winepress may not be planted even though it lacks only one of the mishnah's conditions (it does not stretch from one end of the vineyard to the other), so too a ditch which lacks any of the mishnah's other conditions may also not be planted.]

שׁוֹמֵרָה שֶׁבַּכֶּרֶם גְּבֹהָה עֲשָׂרָה וּרְחָבָה אַרְבַּע,[2] זוֹרְעִין בְּתוֹכָהּ. — *[If] the lookout in a vineyard is ten high and four wide, planting inside it [is permitted].*

The lookout was a high mound in the vineyard from which a watchman could see far and wide (*Rav; Rosh; Rash; Rambam Comm.*). If it was ten handbreadths high and had a surface four handbreadths square (*Chazon Ish* 11:16), the lookout was considered independent realm which could be planted with foreign seed. Even the Sages, who forbid foreign planting in the previous case of a

1. The text should read וּרְחָבָה, the feminine form, rather than וְרֹחַב (*Shinuyei Nuschaos*).

2. The text should read אַרְבָּעָה, the masculine form, since it refers to handbreadths which are masculine. The feminine form אַרְבַּע is used with reference to cubits (*Shinuyei Nuschaos; Chazon Ish* 11:16; cf. *Shenos Eliyahu*).

5
4

And [if] a winepress in a vineyard is ten deep and four wide, R' Eliezer says: [It is permitted] to plant inside it. But the Sages forbid [this].

[If] the lookout in a vineyard is ten high and four wide, planting inside it [is permitted]. But if branches were intertwined [above it], it is forbidden.

4. [I]f] a grapevine is planted inside a winepress or a hole, [we] give it its work area and plant the remainder.

winepress, permit it on the lookout. Although a winepress descends below the surface of the vineyard, nevertheless at its top it is level with the vineyard. Consequently, assuming the airspace of the vineyard to extend to ten handbreadths above the ground of the vineyard, the winepress is contained within the airspace of the vineyard. The planting on the lookout, however, is more than ten handbreadths above the ground and is thus outside the airspace of the vineyard (*Rav; Rosh; Rash;* see *Meleches Shlomo*). Alternatively, a winepress is surrounded by the vines above it and hence appears to be contained within the vineyard to a greater extent than a lookout, which rises above the vines to a level of its own (*Ri ben Malki Tzedek* and *Rash*).

The statement of the mishnah that planting *inside* the lookout is permitted really means that planting *on top of it* is permitted (*Meleches Shlomo; Mishnah Rishonah*). Indeed, many versions of the mishnah have בְּרֹאשָׁה, *on its top*, rather than בְּתוֹכָה, *inside it*. See *Shinuyei Nuschaos, Meleches Shlomo* and *Tos. Anshei Shem*.

וְאִם הָיָה שֵׂעָר כּוֹתֵשׁ, אָסוּר. — *But if branches were intertwined [above it], it is forbidden.*

If the vines reached above the lookout and intertwined over it, planting on top of it is no longer permitted (*Rav; Rosh; Rash*). From *Rambam* (*Hil. Kilayim* 7:22) it appears that even if the vines are intertangled above the top of the lookout, as long as they do not touch the lookout,

planting on it is permitted. This is provided that the foreign plants are not directly beneath a branch of the vine (*Derech Emunah, Tziyun HaHalachah* 7:262 from *Beur HaGra, Yoreh Deah* 296:70).

The term שֵׂעָר כּוֹתֵשׁ is encountered in *Peah* 2:3 (see ArtScroll *Yad Avraham Commentary* ibid.), where it is also used with reference to the entanglement of branches. [The term שֵׂעָר, literally *hair*, is used by the mishnah to refer to foliage (see e.g. mishnah 4:9). In mishnah 4:7, however, R' Yehudah uses the verb עִרְסָן to refer to entanglement. *Rash* suggests that the latter term is used for entanglement produced through human intervention, whereas שֵׂעָר כּוֹתֵשׁ refers to entanglement which came about naturally (*Tos. Yom Tov*).

Ri ben Malki Tzedek (followed by *Rash* and *Rosh*) mentions a fundamentally different interpretation, based on one version of *Yerushalmi*, according to which the term שֵׂעָר כּוֹתֵשׁ has nothing to do with entanglement of vines. Rather, it refers to earth which forms part of a mound (here) or a wall (in *Peah* 2:3) which tends to crumble and blow away.

[Presumably, the term שֵׂעָר is related to סְעָרָה which means *gale*. The term כּוֹתֵשׁ means to *crush* or *pound*.] The point of the mishnah is that if the top of the lookout is not durable and will be eroded by a pounding wind, then its present height of ten handbreadths cannot be relied upon to permit planting on it. The lookout is treated as though it does not have the proper dimensions and planting is therefore forbidden (*Tos. R' Akiva*).

4.

גֶּפֶן שֶׁהִיא נְטוּעָה בַּגַּת אוֹ בַנֶּקַע, נוֹתְנִין לָהּ עֲבוֹדָתָהּ וְזוֹרֵעַ אֶת הַמּוֹתָר. — *[If] a grapevine is planted inside a winepress*

or a hole, [we] give it its work area and plant the remainder.

Normally, the work area of a single

רַבִּי יוֹסֵי אוֹמֵר: אִם אֵין שָׁם אַרְבַּע אַמּוֹת, לֹא יָבִיא זֶרַע לְשָׁם.

יד אברהם

grapevine, within which no foreign seed may be planted, is six handbreadths (mishnah 6:1). But it might have been thought that when a vine occupies a confined space, such as a winepress pit or a hole in the ground, that the entire confined space is viewed as the domain of the vine. In that case, planting foreign seed anywhere within the confined space would be forbidden since it appears to be within the domain of the vine. The *Tanna Kamma* of our mishnah dispels such notions by stating that except for the standard six-handbreadth work area ordinarily considered the domain of a vine, the remainder of the confined space is *not* the domain of the vine and may hence be planted with foreign seed. Thus, although the vine and the foreign seed share the same confined space, this does not have the appearance of *kilayim* and is permitted (*Rav*).

Yerushalmi (as understood by *Rosh, Rash,* and *Ri ben Malki Tzedek*) states that the hole under discussion by the mishnah is from 3 to 4 handbreadths wide. (Its length depends on the dispute between the Sages and R' Yose.) Assuming that the vine is located in the hole such that it is equidistant from the sides, then the distance between the vine and the walls of the hole is 1.5 to 2 handbreadths. If foreign seed is planted at ground level, it must be distanced an additional 4.5 to 4 handbreadths from the edge of the hole in order to complete the required six-handbreadth distancing from the vine (see diagram A). *Yerushalmi* assumes that when the six-handbreadth spacing from a vine is arrived at by combining the distance from the

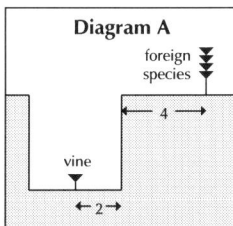

Diagram A

foreign species

vine

← 2 →

← 4 →

vine at the floor of the hole with the distance at ground level from the edge of the hole, then the ground-level spacing must be at least four

handbreadths. If the hole is wider than four handbreadths, the distance between the vine and the wall will be greater than two handbreadths, so that less than four handbreadths are needed on ground level to complete the requisite six handbreadths. But because such combinations are allowed only if the ground level component is at least four handbreadths, planting on ground level must still be distanced four handbreadths from the edge of the hole. Thus, in such a case, the

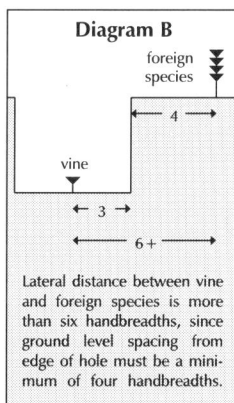

Diagram B

foreign species

vine

← 3 →

← 6 + →

← 4 →

Lateral distance between vine and foreign species is more than six handbreadths, since ground level spacing from edge of hole must be a minimum of four handbreadths.

actual lateral distance between the vine and the foreign seed will be more than six handbreadths (see diagram B). Inasmuch as the mishnah speaks of planting at a distance of only six handbreadths (*we give it its work area and plant the remainder*), *Yerushalmi* assumes that the hole in question is not four handbreadths wide since this will require larger distancing. On the other hand, a hole which is narrower than three handbreadths wide is regarded as sealed. Accordingly, the distance on the floor of the hole cannot be added even to a four-handbreadth distance on the ground. The entire six handbreadths must

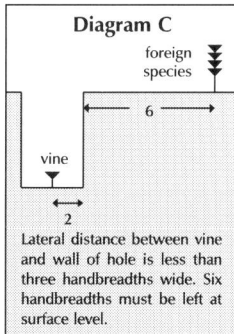

Diagram C

foreign species

vine

2

← 6 →

Lateral distance between vine and wall of hole is less than three handbreadths wide. Six handbreadths must be left at surface level.

be left on the ground from the edge of the hole, so that again, the actual distance between the vine and the foreign seed will be greater than six handbreadths (see diagram C). The only situation in which planting along

5
4

R' Yose says: If there are not four cubits, he may not bring [foreign] seed there.

the edge of the hole will be distanced laterally exactly six handbreadths from the vine is where the hole is between three and four handbreadths wide, as explained above. Accordingly, *Yerushalmi* gives this as the case of the mishnah (*R' Shlomo Sirilio; Meleches Shlomo*). [I am indebted to Rabbi David Strauss of Jerusalem for his assistance in deciphering this obscure passage.]

Chazon Ish 11:16, followed by *Derech Emunah* 7:142, has a different understanding of *Rash* and *Rosh* and consequently of *Yerushalmi* as well. In his view, when the hole is between three and four handbreadths wide, it is not necessary to distance foreign planting by six handbreadths. For some unexplained reason, in such a case, it is sufficient to distance the foreign planting by only four handbreadths. This four-handbreadth distancing is arrived at by combining the distance between the vine and the wall on the floor of the hole, with the distance from the edge of the hole at ground level. If the hole is less than three handbreadths wide, it is considered sealed and the full six handbreadths must be left at ground level. If the hole is wider than four handbreadths, it is permitted to plant right up to the edge of the hole at ground level. This is because a hole width of four handbreadths gives the sides of the hole the status of dividing walls and no distancing is required between foreign plants on one side of a divider and vines on the other (mishnah 4:3; *Chazon Ish* assumes that the hole is at least ten handbreadths deep so that its sides constitute dividing walls of the proper size). According to *Chazon Ish*, the mishnah here does not deal at all with planting outside the hole. The assertion of *Yerushalmi* that the mishnah's hole is between three and four handbreadths wide is based on a different consideration altogether. This is that if the hole is four handbreadths wide it is forbidden to plant on the floor of the hole even at a distance of six handbreadths from the vine, even according to the Sages (see *Rambam, Hil. Kilayim* 7:24). Since the Sages do permit planting inside the hole beyond six handbreadths from the vine, the hole of the mishnah is surely less than four handbreadths wide. Thus, according to *Chazon Ish*, the subsequent discussion in

Yerushalmi about planting outside the hole is unrelated to the mishnah. [Note that this is central to the differing approaches of *R' Shlomo Sirilio* and *Chazon Ish*. The former assumes that the mishnah itself deals not only with planting inside the hole, but with planting outside the hole also. Since the mishnah permits planting even outside at a distance of only six handbreadths, and this is precise only if the hole is between three and four handbreadths, the mishnah must be dealing with such a case. Accordingly, *Yerushalmi's* discussion is read as an interpretation of the mishnah. According to *Chazon Ish*, however, the mishnah does not discuss planting outside the hole at all. *Yerushalmi's* comments are thus unrelated to the mishnah. The one explicit statement of *Yerushalmi* that the mishnah's case involves a hole of between three and four handbreadths width is explained as based on the laws for planting *inside* the hole, and not on laws for combining distances on different levels to enable planting outside the hole.]

Rambam understood all these regulations of *Yerushalmi* as relating to *a house in a vineyard*, and not a vine inside a hole. Regardless of the width of the hole, planting *outside* it must be distanced six handbreadths from the vine.

On the other hand, the *depth* of the hole is significant according to *Rambam*. In *Hil. Kilayim* 7:24, *Rambam* writes that if a hole is ten handbreadths deep and four wide, and a single vine is growing inside it, then it is *not* permitted to plant within the hole a mere six handbreadths away from the vine. Rather, it is necessary in such a case to plant four cubits from the vine. *Rambam's* source for this is apparently *Tosefta* 4:1 (*Mahari Korkus; Beur HaGra; Yoreh Deah* 296:72; cf. *Kesef Mishneh*).

רַבִּי יוֹסֵי אוֹמֵר: אִם אֵין שָׁם אַרְבַּע אַמּוֹת, לֹא יָבִיא זֶרַע לְשָׁם. — *R' Yose says: If there are not four cubits, he may not bring [foreign] seed there.*

R' Yose argues that unless the hole is four cubits long, it may not be planted at all with foreign seed. If it is four cubits long, then foreign seed may be planted

וְהַבַּיִת שֶׁבְּכֶרֶם זוֹרְעִין בְּתוֹכוֹ.

[ה] **הַנוֹטֵעַ** יָרָק בַּכֶּרֶם אוֹ מְקַיֵּם, הֲרֵי זֶה מְקַדֵּשׁ אַרְבָּעִים וְחָמֵשׁ גְּפָנִים.

יד אברהם

six handbreadths away from the grape-vine (*Rash; Rosh; Rambam Comm.; Rav* as understood by *Tos. Anshei Shem*; cf. *Tos. Yom Tov*; see *Tif. Yis.*). R' Yose con-siders the law for a hole containing a vine to be similar in certain respects to the law of a vineyard perimeter (מחול הכרם) of mishnah 4:2. There it was taught: *If there are not twelve cubits there, he may not bring seed there. If there were twelve cu-bits there, we give it its work area, and he may plant the remainder.* That is, if the perimeter (a confined area of sorts) is not a certain minimum size, it may not be planted at all; if it is, then planting is per-mitted, as long as it is outside the work area. Likewise, a confined space such as a hole which contains a vine must be a cer-tain minimum size (four cubits) if it is to be permitted to plant foreign seed any-where inside the hole. If it is this large, then foreign planting need be distanced only by the vine's work area of six hand-breadths (*Rav; Rambam Comm.*).

וְהַבַּיִת שֶׁבְּכֶרֶם זוֹרְעִין בְּתוֹכוֹ. — *A house in a vineyard may be planted inside.*

Even though the house is in the middle of the vineyard and is surrounded on all four sides by vines, it is permitted to plant foreign seed inside it. It is thus unlike the winepress of the previous mishnah, which the Sages forbid to plant with foreign seed even though it is ten handbreadths deep and four handbreadths wide. As noted there, the winepress is enveloped by the airspace of the vineyard above it, and

hence planting inside it is considered like planting in the vineyard. The house in the vineyard, however, is separated from the vineyard by above-ground walls. The en-closed area is thus regarded as outside the vineyard, just like the top of the lookout, and therefore it may be planted (*Rav; Rash; Tos. Yom Tov*).

Rosh suggests that an area inside a vine-yard which is enclosed by walls may *not* be planted with foreign seed unless it also has a roof. Without a roof, the enclosed area is treated like a winepress in a vineyard which may not be planted. The presence of a roof converts the area from an open-air enclosure to a *house* which is considered to be outside the airspace of the vineyard. *Chazon Ish* (11:16), however, writes that *a house in a vine-yard* need not be roofed. In his opinion, enclo-sure by walls is sufficient to separate the area from the airspace of the vineyard and to per-mit planting.

Rambam (Hil. *Kilayim* 7:23)[1] based on *Yerushalmi* (see above) writes that the area within the *house in a vineyard* must be at least three square handbreadths. Otherwise, it is re-garded as sealed and planting inside it is for-bidden. [Clearly, the "house" referred to by the mishnah is not a dwelling (see *Succah* 3a). It is of interest that the term בָּתִּים, houses, oc-curs in an agricultural context in *Sheviis* 2:4 where it is explained by *Yerushalmi* to be a shelter which provides shade for the plant and protects it from excessive sun (see also ArtScroll *Yad Avraham Commentary* ibid.). In that case it might be a canopy supported on poles without any walls at all! (See "Com-ments on Mishnayoth in Tractate Kilayim" by Rabbi N. L. Rabinovitch, in *Collected Es-*

---

1. The printed versions of *Rambam* read: three handbreadths by three handbreadths *up to four*. The words *up to four* are not copied by *Shulchan Aruch Yoreh Deah* 296:53, which sug-gests that they are erroneous and should be deleted (*Chazon Ish* 11:18; see also *Derech Emunah* 7:131). [Recently published critical editions of *Rambam* corroborate this emendation (see *Mishneh Torah*, based on Yemenite manuscripts, edited by R' Yosef Kafich; and see *Rambam*, ed. Shabtai Frankel).]

5

5

A house in a vineyard may be planted inside.

5. **[I**f] someone plants greens in a vineyard or maintains [them], this condemns forty-five grapevines.

YAD AVRAHAM

says from HaDarom, p.151.) Reference might also be made to the commentary of Rabbeinu Chananel (*Avodah Zarah* 50b), from which it appears that he understood the houses mentioned in *Sheviis* as holes dug near the roots of trees in order to trap and collect water.]

5.

The consequences of planting foreign seed within four cubits of a vineyard (viz. the condemnation of two rows of the vineyard) were discussed in mishnah 4:5. Subsequently, the rules for planting inside a vineyard were discussed (4:8 through 5:4). The present mishnah discusses the consequences of illegally planting or maintaining foreign seed *inside* a vineyard. Unlike the case where foreign plants were growing within the four-cubit work zone outside the vineyard, plants inside a vineyard generate considerable condemnation of grapevines.

The coming mishnah is exceedingly obscure. Both *Rav* and *Tos. Yom Tov* composed extensive commentaries on this mishnah which appear in the Vilna mishnayos. After a thorough and lengthy analysis of the various interpretations advanced by *Rash*, *Rambam* and *Ravad*, *Tos. Yom Tov* found himself unable to accept any of their explanations. Instead, he proposed a novel interpretation which was subsequently accepted by *Gra* (*Yoreh Deah* 296:39).[1]

The mishnah considers four cases, and it is readily apparent that the second case (five-five) is the source of trouble. In the interests of simplicity, our treatment of the mishnah will adopt *Tos. Yom Tov's* explanation.

הַנּוֹטֵעַ יָרָק בַּכֶּרֶם אוֹ מְקַיֵּם, הֲרֵי זֶה מְקַדֵּשׁ אַרְבָּעִים וְחָמֵשׁ גְּפָנִים. — *[If] someone plants greens in a vineyard or maintains [them], this condemns forty-five grapevines.*

Illegally planting greens in a vineyard, or illegally maintaining greens which grew on their own, causes the condemnation of forty-five grapevines (in addition to the condemnation of the greens). As will be seen, this is the number of vines which are contained within a circle of radius sixteen cubits in an ordinary vineyard — i.e. one in which the vines are arranged so that they form horizontal and vertical rows which are separated from one another by *four* cubits (see diagram A). [If the center of the

circle does not coincide with a vine, as many as fifty-two vines fit inside the

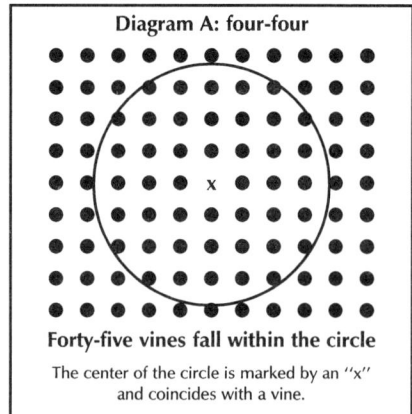

Diagram A: four-four

Forty-five vines fall within the circle

The center of the circle is marked by an "x" and coincides with a vine.

1. Remarkably, however, there is preserved a responsum written to *Rosh* in which the interpretation of *Rambam* is lauded as being "certainly the information which was handed to Moses at Sinai" (see *Kesef Mishneh* to Hil. *Kilayim* 6:2).

אֵימָתַי? בִּזְמַן שֶׁהָיוּ נְטוּעוֹת עַל אַרְבַּע אַרְבַּע אוֹ
עַל חָמֵשׁ חָמֵשׁ. הָיוּ נְטוּעוֹת עַל שֵׁשׁ שֵׁשׁ אוֹ עַל
שֶׁבַע שֶׁבַע, הֲרֵי זֶה מְקַדֵּשׁ שֵׁשׁ עֶשְׂרֵה אַמָּה לְכָל
רוּחַ, עֲגֻלוֹת וְלֹא מְרֻבָּעוֹת.

יד אברהם

Diagram B: four-four

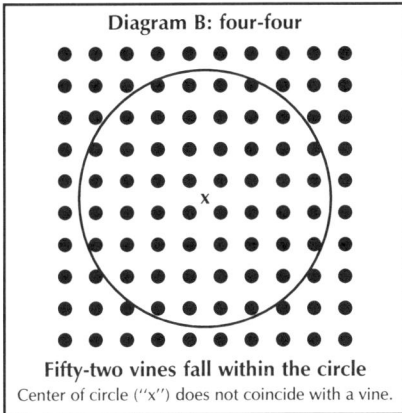

Fifty-two vines fall within the circle
Center of circle ("x") does not coincide with a vine.

Diagram C: five-five

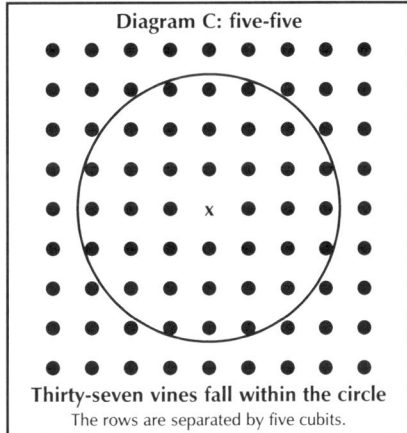

Thirty-seven vines fall within the circle
The rows are separated by five cubits.

---

circle (see diagram B).]

As a general rule, when greens are planted inside a vineyard only vines within sixteen cubits are condemned, as stated at the end of the mishnah. The reason the mishnah formulates the rule here in terms of the number of vines condemned, rather than simply stating the general rule that all vines within sixteen cubits are condemned, will be discussed below.

אֵימָתַי? בִּזְמַן שֶׁהָיוּ נְטוּעוֹת עַל אַרְבַּע אַרְבַּע אוֹ עַל חָמֵשׁ חָמֵשׁ. — *When? When they were planted four-four or five-five.*

The mishnah states that regardless of whether the vines are separated by four cubits (the four-four arrangement) or by five cubits (the five-five arrangement), the number of condemned vines is the same — forty-five. However, as diagram C (which depicts the five-five arrangement) reveals, a circle with a radius of sixteen cubits actually contains only thirty-seven vines!

To resolve this problem, *Tos. Yom Tov* proposes the following solution. Suppose

that only thirty-seven vines are in fact forbidden in the five-five case. To the naked eye, the difference between a four-four arrangement of vines and a five-five arrangement is not obvious. Consequently, if someone is faced with a *kilayim* problem in a five-five vineyard, an observer is not likely to realize that the vineyard in question is not an ordinary vineyard. He will thus assume that the elimination of vines which he witnesses takes place in an ordinary four-four vineyard. But in that case, if the observer is himself faced with a *kilayim* problem in an actual four-four vineyard, he is liable to implement the same eradication of condemned vines as that which he observed. Since he observed the removal of thirty-seven vines, he will remove the same number from his own ordinary vineyard. But this is not sufficient since in a four-four vineyard, forty-five vines are condemned. To prevent such a mistake, the Rabbis therefore enacted that even in a five-five vineyard, forty-five vines are to be condemned — thirty-seven which

When? When they were planted four-four or five-five.
[But if] they were planted six-six or seven-seven, this condemns sixteen cubits in each direction, round not square.

fall within the critical sixteen-cubit circle
plus another eight as a preventive measure to avoid the pitfall described above.
Since forty-five vines are condemned in
practice, even if an observer confuses a
five-five vineyard with a four-four vineyard, he will never err by eliminating too
few vines from an ordinary vineyard
containing *kilayim*.

It should be noted that the preventive measure which *Tos. Yom Tov* regards as embodied
in the legislation of the present mishnah is not
found anywhere explicitly. Moreover, the
farfetched assumption that a person will confuse a five-five arrangement with a four-four
one, as well as the notion that the Rabbis
would legislate for what one would imagine
to be a rarely occurring event, are problematic
(*Chazon Ish* 12:3; *Tos. Anshei Shem*, s.v. היו
נטועות).

הָיוּ נְטוּעוֹת עַל שֵׁשׁ שֵׁשׁ אוֹ עַל שֶׁבַע שֶׁבַע, הֲרֵי
זֶה מְקַדֵּשׁ שֵׁשׁ עֶשְׂרֵה אַמָּה לְכָל רוּחַ, עֲגֻלוֹת
וְלֹא מְרֻבָּעוֹת. — *[But if] they were planted
six-six or seven-seven, this condemns
sixteen cubits in each direction, round
not square.*

A vineyard in which the vines are
separated by six or more cubits is too
dispersed to be mistaken for an ordinary
four-four vineyard. Hence, there is no
need for precautionary legislation and the
basic rule can be followed. Therefore,
only vines occurring within a sixteen-cubit radius of the greens-encircled central
vine become condemned. As can be seen
in diagrams D and E, in both the six-six
case as well as the seven-seven case, the
number of vines thus condemned
amounts to twenty-one.

The reason the mishnah in the case of
four-four formulates its ruling in terms of
the number of vines condemned, rather
than simply stating (as it does with six-six
and seven-seven) that all vines within
sixteen cubits are condemned, can now be
understood. As explained above, the ex-

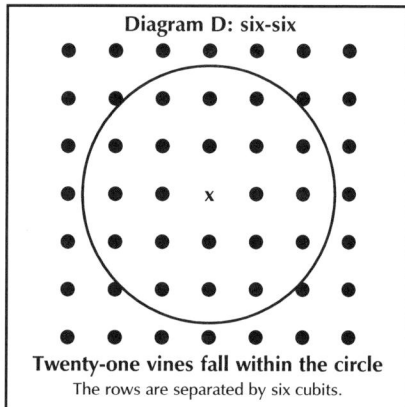

Diagram D: six-six

Twenty-one vines fall within the circle
The rows are separated by six cubits.

ception of the case of five-five from the
general sixteen-cubit rule was due to
possible confusion between a five-five
arrangement and one which is a four-
four. That the two might be interchanged
is alluded to by the fact of their being
grouped into one set. It is thus clear that
the condemnation of forty-five vines in
the five-five case is a consequence of the
like condemnation in the four-four case.
In the four-four case this number is the
result of applying the sixteen-cubit rule;

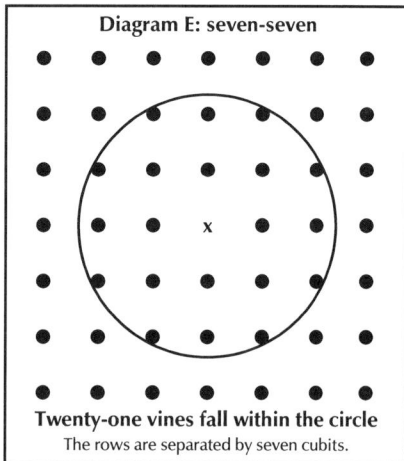

Diagram E: seven-seven

Twenty-one vines fall within the circle
The rows are separated by seven cubits.

כלאים
ה/ו

[ו] הָרוֹאֶה יָרָק בַּכֶּרֶם וְאָמַר: ,,כְּשֶׁאַגִּיעַ לוֹ אֲלַקְטֶנּוּ'' — מֻתָּר. ,,כְּשֶׁאֶחֱזוֹר אֲלַקְטֶנּוּ'' — אִם הוֹסִיף בְּמָאתַיִם, אָסוּר.

יד אברהם

in the five-five it is the result of increasing the number of condemned vines predicted by the rule to equate the number of vines condemned in the five-five case to the number condemned in the four-four case. Thus, the mishnah may be concisely summarized by stating that there is one generally applicable rule for calculating the number of vines condemned when foreign seed is planted inside a vineyard. This of course is the rule that condemnation extends *sixteen cubits in each direction, round not square*. In the case of five-five however,

precautionary legislation led to a larger number of condemned vines than that warranted on the basis of the sixteen-cubit rule alone.

The mishnah does not consider vineyards with rows eight or more cubits apart even though the Sages of mishnayos 4:8-9 are of the opinion that such spacing does not detract from the essential characterization of the arrangement as a vineyard. *Yerushalmi* explains this on the grounds that even though the Sages regard it as forbidden to plant foreign seed between the rows of such an arrangement, they nevertheless agree that no condemnation results.

6.

In addition to the prohibition on planting *kilayim*, there is a prohibition on maintaining *kilayim* in one's vineyard, even if it grew there on its own. Moreover, just as planting *kilayim* in the vineyard causes the plants to become forbidden for use, so too maintaining *kilayim* forbids the plants for use even though the *kilayim* came up on its own. However, this is so only if the presence of the *kilayim* is approved of by the owner. If he does not approve of it, then it is not *kilayim* and does not condemn anything for use (see *Tosafos* to *Bava Kamma* 100b, s.v. נתייאש and *Ramban* to *Bava Basra* 2a, s.v. אומר לו).

Clearly, as long as a person is unaware of the presence of *kilayim* in his vineyard — and hence has not approved of its presence — nothing becomes condemned. The present mishnah discusses the status of the plants following a person's discovery of *kilayim* in his vineyard. If his reaction indicates disapproval, everything will be permitted. If his reaction indicates approval, then the situation is more complicated. The type of reaction which indicates approval or disapproval is illustrated by the mishnah.

הָרוֹאֶה יָרָק בַּכֶּרֶם וְאָמַר: ,,כְּשֶׁאַגִּיעַ לוֹ אֲלַקְטֶנּוּ'' — מֻתָּר. — *[If] someone sees greens in the vineyard and says, "When I reach it I will pick it" — it is permitted.*

If a person's reaction on discovering *kilayim* growing in his vineyard is to remove it as soon as he reaches it, this is interpreted as disapproval of the presence of *kilayim*. He is not obligated to stop whatever he is doing and run immediately to remove the *kilayim*. As long as he intends to remove it as soon as he gets to it, and his delay is due to preoccupa-

tion with something else, the delay is not regarded as approval and acceptance of the *kilayim*. Consequently, no condemnation for use of the plants results (*Rav; Rosh; Rash;* see also *Kesef Mishneh* to *Hil. Kilayim* 5:9). Thus, if a grower is tending to his vines, and he notices greens growing among the vines a few rows ahead of him, he can continue tending to his vines in order, and when he reaches the greens, he removes them. As long as he intends to remove the greens as soon as he reaches them, no

5

6

6. **[I**f] someone sees greens in the vineyard and says, "When I reach it I will pick it" — it is permitted. "When I return I will pick it" — if it increased a two-hundredth, it is forbidden.

YAD AVRAHAM

condemnation results.

‏כְּשֶׁאֶחֱזוֹר אֲלַקְטֶנוּ״, — אִם הוֹסִיף בְּמָאתַיִם,‏ ‏אָסוּר. — *"When I return I will pick it"* — *if it increased a two-hundredth, it is forbidden.*

If the grower's reaction is to leave the *kilayim* in place even after reaching it, and to remove it only after he has finished attending to all his vines — *"When I return I will* [go back and] *pick it"* — this is taken as approval of the presence of the *kilayim*. Even though he intends to remove the *kilayim* eventually, since he does not intend to remove it as soon as he reaches it, his attitude implies short-term acceptance of the *kilayim*.

The mishnah states that in such a case, if during the time between the discovery of the *kilayim* until its eventual removal, the greens have grown by a two-hundredth, then a condemnation for use results. This may be explained as follows. The mishnah (*Orlah* 2:1) rules that if greens which were condemned as *kilayim* become mixed with something permissible, the mixture is permitted for use provided that the ratio of permissible matter to forbidden is at least two hundred to one. Thus, it may be said that *kilayim* of a vineyard is annulled when it constitutes less than a two-hundredth of a mixture. Now, in the case of our mishnah, only the growth which follows the discovery and approval of the *kilayim* is considered forbidden growth. Whatever preceded the owner's discovery and approval is not *kilayim* (see preface). Therefore, from the moment the owner expresses his approval the plant becomes a mixture of permissible with forbidden growth. As long as the grower succeeds in removing the greens before

they have grown an additional two-hundredth part, the greens will be permitted since the permissible growth annuls the forbidden growth. If, however, the greens increase by a two-hundredth between the time they are discovered and approved and until they are removed, then the forbidden growth is present in sufficient quantity to prevent annulment. Accordingly, the greens are forbidden (*Rashi* to *Pesachim* 25a and *Chullin* 116a; *Tos. Yom Tov*).

Alternatively, an additional growth which constitutes less than one two-hundredth of an existing plant is not regarded as a significant growth. Since the Torah (*Deut.* 22:9) refers to *the fullness of the seed* when discussing the prohibition for use generated by *kilayim* in a vineyard, it is understood that only a growth of significance activates the condemnation. Thus, if an addition of a two-hundredth takes place between the approval of the *kilayim* and its removal, the prohibition on use has been activated, and the entire plant is condemned as *kilayim*. If the additional growth is not this great, no condemnation results (*R' Shmuel Landau* in *Noda BiYehudah Tinyana Yoreh Deah* 55; see also *Toafos Re'em* to *Yereim HaShalem* §389 and *Mishnas Nechemiah* chapter 7). [According to the latter approach, the plant is not a mixture of permitted with forbidden growth. Rather, it is entirely forbidden.]

The need to determine an increase of half-a-percent poses a considerable practical problem. How can one know whether or not an increase beyond the critical level has transpired?

The matter is discussed by *Yerushalmi* but the procedure remains obscure. *Rav* and *Rosh* follow *Rambam* who expresses the growth as a function of time. A plant of the variety which was found in the vineyard is plucked from the ground, and a record is kept of the time it takes for it to dry out completely. If it takes one

[ז] הָיָה עוֹבֵר בַּכֶּרֶם וְנָפְלוּ מִמֶּנּוּ זְרָעִים, אוֹ
שֶׁיָּצְאוּ עִם הַזְּבָלִים אוֹ עִם הַמַּיִם, הַזּוֹרֵעַ
וְסִעֲרַתּוּ הָרוּחַ לְאַחֲרָיו – מֻתָּר. סִעֲרַתּוּ הָרוּחַ לְפָנָיו,

יד אברהם

hundred hours, for example, for the plucked plant to lose all its moisture, then it can be inferred that in a half-hour the plant lost a two-hundredth of its moisture. It is therefore concluded that similarly, a growing plant increases by a two-hundredth in a half-hour. A shorter method is suggested by *Ravad* (Hil. Kilayim 7:21). The plucked plant is weighed. Half an hour (or some other time period) is allowed to pass, and the plucked plant is weighed again. The weight loss recorded can easily be expressed as a percentage of the original weight, and divided into the time period, it will yield a rate of percentage of weight loss. Assuming that weight gain is directly proportional to weight loss, the time needed for a loss of half-a-percent is used as the time for an accretion of an additional two-hundredth.

A different system is mentioned by *Rosh*. A plant of the same variety and size of the *kilayim* plant is picked and then compared to a similar plant which is still growing. After waiting the amount of time which elapsed between the owner's approval of the *kilayim* and his removal of it (e.g. fifteen minutes), the plants are compared again. If the growing plant is now a two-hundredth larger than the picked one, then the *kilayim* greens are forbidden (see also *Tif. Yis., Boaz*). Unlike the systems outlined above, this system does not assume any correspondence between the loss of a detached plant and the gain of a growing one. The detached plant is merely used as a standard against which the increase of the growing plant can be measured. However, since *Yerushalmi* in fact states that the reduction experienced by the detached plant bears a direct correspondence to the increase experienced by the growing plant, *Rosh* rejects this system.

7.

This mishnah discusses the law for seeds which accidentally fell into a vineyard and grew.

הָיָה עוֹבֵר בַּכֶּרֶם וְנָפְלוּ מִמֶּנּוּ זְרָעִים, אוֹ שֶׁיָּצְאוּ עִם הַזְּבָלִים אוֹ עִם הַמַּיִם, — *[If] someone was passing through [his] vineyard and seeds fell from him, or [seeds] were released together with the dung or with the water,*

If someone was passing through his vineyard without any intention of planting foreign seed there (*Derech Emunah* 5:104), and without his knowledge he dropped some seeds there, this is not considered planting. Similarly, if he was spreading fertilizer in the vineyard, or watering it, unaware that some foreign seed had become mixed up with the fertilizer or water. Even though he actually casts the fertilizer or water to the ground, and with it the seed, since he is totally un-

aware of the presence of the seed this is not regarded as planting. The Torah (*Deut.* 22:9) forbids *planting* of *kilayim* in a vineyard with the words, *You shall not sow your vineyard with kilayim,* which implies that only a conscious act of planting is forbidden (*You shall not sow*). But seed which was planted inadvertently is not governed by this prohibition. Accordingly, as long as the owner is unaware of its presence in the vineyard, or as long as he indicates disapproval of its presence when he discovers it (see mishnah 6), no prohibitions have been contravened, and nothing becomes forbidden for use (*Rav; Rosh; Rash*).

Unlike *Rav* (et al.), *Rambam* (*Comm.* and Hil. Kilayim 5:17) locates the source of the

7. [I[f] someone was passing through [his] vineyard and seeds fell from him, or [seeds] were released together with the dung or with the water, [or if] someone was sowing and the wind blew [seed] behind him — it is permitted. [If] wind blew [seed] in front of him,

YAD AVRAHAM

rule of the mishnah that only intentional planting becomes forbidden to use, in the second half of the verse in *Deut.* (22:9): . . . *lest the fulness of the seed which "you" have sown be forbidden with the increase of the vineyard.* Only that which *you* have sown is condemned, not what was planted on its own.

Rav (et al.) seems to be of the view that the condemnation from use is a penalty for transgression of the prohibition on planting *kilayim* stated at the beginning of the verse. It is thus sufficient to prove that the prohibition, *You shall not plant your vineyard kilayim,* has not been violated, in order to prove that there is no prohibition on use.

Rambam, however, maintains that the Torah speaks of two distinct prohibitions on planting *kilayim,* only one of which is punishable by lashes. The punishment of lashes is only for planting two different grains or greens together with seeds of the grapevine, and it is that prohibition which is mentioned in the first part of the verse. But, in addition, according to *Rambam,* there is a prohibition (not punishable by lashes) on planting even a single seed of grain or greens in the vicinity of a grapevine. The product of both violations is prohibited for use according to *Rambam.* Thus, *Rambam* had to locate the exemption for unintentional planting in the second half of the verse, which speaks of the condemnation from use, not in the first half which speaks only of the prohibition punishable by lashes (*Mishnas Nechemiah,* p. 20, s.v. וֹהרי"ש; see below, 8:1).

הַזּוֹרֵעַ וְסִעֲרַתּוֹ הָרוּחַ לְאַחֲרָיו — מֻתָּר. — *[or if] someone was sowing and the wind blew [seed] behind him — it is permitted.*

The person was sowing his field and did not notice that the wind carried some of the seed into his vineyard. Since the vineyard was behind him, he is not held responsible for failing to see the seed being blown into the vineyard, and hence this too counts as a case of

unintentional planting in a vineyard (*Rav; Rosh; Rash*). As long as the person uproots the *kilayim* as soon as he discovers it (as explained in the previous mishnah), no ban on use is created (*Tos. Yom Tov* from *Rambam, Hil. Kilayim* 5:17).

סִעֲרַתּוֹ הָרוּחַ לְפָנָיו, — *[If] wind blew [seed] in front of him,*

If the vineyard was in front of him and he saw the seeds being blown ahead, he is considered to have consciously planted foreign seed in the vineyard and is obligated to remove it (*Rav; Rambam Comm.* and *Hil. Kilayim* 5:17; *Rosh*). However, it is nearly impossible to find seeds which have been scattered by the wind in a vineyard (see *Chazon Ish* 3:29), and some of the seeds will almost certainly grow in the vineyard. In what follows, R' Akiva addresses such an eventuality.

Ri ben Malki Tzedek and *Rash* describe the present case as involving a person who is deliberately using the wind to plant foreign seed in his vineyard. [This interpretation has support in a variant text found in many manuscripts (as well as in the manuscript edition of *Ri ben Malki Tzedek*), which has וְסִיַעַתּוֹ הָרוּחַ לְפָנָיו — i.e. the wind *assisted him* in front of him.] According to this interpretation, in the first case the person intended to plant in an empty field, but a strong wind blew some of the seed into a vineyard. Since the seed reached the vineyard unintentionally, no prohibition results. In the present case, however, the person deliberately uses the wind to introduce foreign seed into the vineyard.

Rav and *Kaftor VaFerach* (chap. 58) seem to have had the following slightly different text: סִעֲרַתּוֹ הָרוּחַ לְפָנָיו אָסוּר — [If] wind blew [seed] in front of him, *it is forbidden* (*Shinuyei Nuschaos;* see *Meleches Shlomo*).

רַבִּי עֲקִיבָא אוֹמֵר: אִם עֲשָׂבִים יוֹפַךְ; וְאִם אָבִיב,
יְנַפֵּץ; וְאִם הֵבִיאָה דָגָן, תִּדָּלֵק.

[ח] **הַמְקַיֵּם** קוֹצִים בַּכֶּרֶם, רַבִּי אֱלִיעֶזֶר
אוֹמֵר: קִדֵּשׁ. וַחֲכָמִים אוֹמְרִים:
לֹא קִדֵּשׁ אֶלָּא דָבָר שֶׁכָּמוֹהוּ מְקַיְּמִין.

יד אברהם

רַבִּי עֲקִיבָא אוֹמֵר: אִם עֲשָׂבִים יוֹפַךְ; וְאִם אָבִיב,
יְנַפֵּץ; וְאִם הֵבִיאָה דָגָן, תִּדָּלֵק. — *R' Akiva
says: If [it grows] grasses he must turn it;
if the grains have begun to ripen, he must
shake the grains out of the ears; if it has
produced completed grain, it must be
burned.*

If the foreign species is first spotted as
shoots resembling blades of grass, it can
be removed by plowing through it (see
above, mishnah 2:3). This turning prevents the foreign seed from further
growth so that no *kilayim* results (*Rav;
Rosh*).

The stage of growth intended by the
words, *if the grains have begun to ripen*,
is understood by *Rash* to be when the
kernels have begun to form, but have not
yet reached a third of their eventual size[1]
(*Tos. Yom Tov*). If the foreign seed is not
dealt with until ripening of the kernels of
grain has begun, this is considered negli-
gence and a prohibition on use takes effect. *Yerushalmi* records a dispute as to
whether the entire plant becomes condemned in this case, or merely the kernels
without the stalk. According to the first
view, the mishnah would be read to mean
that the kernels are beaten out of the ears
and then buried along with the stalks; according to the second view, the kernels
alone are buried. *Rav* following *Rambam
Comm.* adopts the latter view, while
Rambam in *Hil. Kilayim* 5:17 follows the
former view.

Although forbidden *kilayim* of the

vineyard is normally burnt (*Kiddushin*
56b, *Temurah* 33b), the moistness at this
stage of growth makes burning difficult,
and so they are buried instead. There is no
risk that burying them will enable the
kernels to generate new forbidden plants,
since at this early stage in their development, separation from the stalk kills them
(*Tif. Yis.*; see also *Boaz*). [As noted above,
Rash explains that the kernels in this case
have not yet reached a third of their size
at maturity. *Yerushalmi* (*Maasros* 1:2)
states that grain which is that immature
does not sprout.]

If the foreign seeds have produced
completed grains by the time they are discovered, then the entire plant including
the stalk must be burned (*Rav; Rosh;
Rash; Rambam Comm.*). *Completed
grain* is explained by *Rash* as grain which
has reached a third of its eventual size.
Rambam Comm. defines it as grain suitable for harvesting and threshing.

The mishnah limits its discussion to the
status of the foreign seed inside the vineyard,
even though *kilayim* of the vineyard results
in condemnation of both the foreign plant as
well as grapevines (see e.g. mishnah 5). *Radbaz* (to *Hil. Kilayim* 5:17) contends that in the
mishnah's case since the planting was done
by the wind, there is no condemnation of
the grapevines. Although the person is held responsible for the presence of foreign seed in
the vineyard, planting via the wind is not
equated to a person planting foreign seed
directly in a vineyard (see also *Tos. Yom Tov*
to mishnah 7:8). Others disagree and main-

1. The term used by *Rash* to denote a third of the growth is הֲבָאַת שְׁלִישׁ. There is some question
as to the definition of this term (lit. *bringing a third*), and we have assumed the definition used
by *Rash* in his commentary to *Sheviis* 4:9 (see ArtScroll *Sheviis* ibid.).

R' Akiva says: If [it grows] grasses he must turn it; if the grains have begun to ripen, he must shake the grains out of the ears; if it has produced completed grain, it must be burned.

8. [I f] someone maintains thistles in a vineyard, R' Eliezer says: This condemns. But the Sages say: Nothing condemns except something the likes of which is maintained.

YAD AVRAHAM

tain that despite the mishnah's silence, it is assumed that in those cases in which the foreign plant is condemned, there is a parallel condemnation of grapevines *(Tif. Yis.; Mishnah Rishonah* to mishnah 7:8; *Chazon Ish* 4:29).

8.

The present mishnah discusses the types of foreign seed which constitute *kilayim* if planted in a vineyard. The Torah *(Deut.* 22:9) refers to foreign seed which has become condemned as *kilayim* of the vineyard as *the seed which you have sown.* This suggests that the species referred to are those which a person normally sows, or maintains if they arise in his field. In both cases, the farmer is interested in the species' growth and they are therefore considered *kilayim* in a vineyard. But species which a person uproots if he finds them growing in his field are not *the seed which you have sown* and are therefore excluded *(Rav* and *Rambam Comm.* from *Sifri).* [The entire issue of which species constitute *kilayim* in a vineyard is much more complicated than would appear from the present mishnah. The matter will be taken up in greater detail in the treatment of mishnah 7:7.]

הַמְּקַיֵּם קוֹצִים בַּכֶּרֶם, רַבִּי אֱלִיעֶזֶר אוֹמֵר: קָדֵשׁ. וַחֲכָמִים אוֹמְרִים: לֹא קָדֵשׁ אֶלָּא דָבָר שֶׁכָּבְמוֹהוּ מְקַיְּמִין. — *[If] someone maintains thistles in a vineyard, R' Eliezer says: This condemns. But the Sages say: Nothing condemns except something the likes of which is maintained.*

Both R' Eliezer and the Sages agree that only cultivated species constitute *kilayim* in a vineyard. The issue between them is the status of species which are cultivated only in some other place. In Arabia, where thistles were used as camel fodder, it was common to maintain them in one's fields *(Shabbos* 144b, *Yerushalmi).* R' Eliezer maintains that the cultivation of thistles in Arabia is sufficient to make them *kilayim* in a vineyard anywhere in the world. Since there are places in which thistles were maintained, they are considered a cultivated species, subject to the

laws of *kilayim* of the vineyard, even in places in which they are not cultivated *(Rav; Rosh; Rash; Rambam Comm.).* The Sages, however, are of the opinion that a species which is cultivated in one country is not considered *kilayim* in places where it is not cultivated. In their view, thistles constituted *kilayim* of the vineyard only in Arabia where they were maintained. But in places where thistles were regarded as undesirable and were not maintained, they did not count as a cultivated species and did not constitute *kilayim.* The Sages thus state that *nothing condemns* in a given place unless it is *something the likes of which is maintained* in that place *(Rav; Rosh; Rash; Rambam Comm.* from *Yerushalmi).*

Under Biblical law the prohibition on *kilayim* of the vineyard is only in the Land of Israel. By Rabbinic enactment the laws of *ki-*

הָאֵרוּס, וְהַקִּיסוֹם, וְשׁוֹשַׁנַּת הַמֶּלֶךְ וְכָל מִינֵי
זְרָעִים אֵינָן כִּלְאַיִם בַּכֶּרֶם.
הַקִּנְבָּס — רַבִּי טַרְפוֹן אוֹמֵר: אֵינוֹ כִּלְאָיִם.
וַחֲכָמִים אוֹמְרִים: כִּלְאָיִם.
וְהַקִּינָרָס כִּלְאַיִם בַּכֶּרֶם.

יד אברהם

layim of the vineyard were extended even to the Diaspora (*Kiddushin* 39a). For this reason it is possible to speak of thistles as *kilayim* in Arabia. It should be noted, however, that there is disagreement as to the scope of the *kilayim* prohibition outside of Israel (see *Derech Emunah* 8:78 and *Tziyun HaHalachah* 8:11). According to *Rosh* (*Kiddushin* 1:9), for example, unless it is the product of planting the seeds of at least two foreign species simultaneously with grape seeds, the *kilayim* growing in a vineyard in the Diaspora is *not* subject to the prohibition on maintaining *kilayim* (see *Rama, Yoreh Deah* 296:69). Additionally, some authorities are of the opinion that outside of Israel *kilayim* of the vineyard does not generate a prohibition on use. Only planting *kilayim* was forbidden in the Diaspora; but even if someone planted illegally, the product would be permitted (*Sefer HaChinuch* precept 549).

הָאֵרוּס, וְהַקִּיסוֹם, וְשׁוֹשַׁנַּת הַמֶּלֶךְ וְכָל מִינֵי זְרָעִים אֵינָן כִּלְאַיִם בַּכֶּרֶם. — *The iris, and the kissom, and the shoshanas hamelech and all [similar] varieties of plants are not kilayim in the vineyard.*

The precise identity of some of the species mentioned here is not certain. The אֵרוּס is rendered by *Rambam Comm.* as the Arabic *sissin bar.* It can readily be seen that this corresponds to the definition of אֵרוּס as שׁוֹשָׁן בְּרָא (i.e. wild *shoshan*) found in *Sefer Asaf HaRofeh* (c. 600 c.e.). *Yerushalmi* defines it as iris and it is likely therefore that the iris is a variety of *shoshan* (see below). *Aruch* (s.v. אֵרוֹס) cited by *Ri ben Malki Tzedek* describes the plant as having use as a cooking spice (*Rav; Rosh; Rash*), or alter-

natively, as producing seeds which rattle in their case like the clapper in a bell (*Rosh; Rash*).

The קִיסוֹם (or according to many versions: קִיסוֹס) is apparently the *hedera helix*, i.e. ivy (*Plants and Animals of the Mishnah,* p. 142; see *Rav* and *Aruch HaShalem* [s.v. קסוס]). *Rav* describes it as a climbing vine which it was common to train over windows and awnings (*Rav;* see *Succah* 11a).

The שׁוֹשַׁנַּת הַמֶּלֶךְ is defined by *Rav* as the rose. This identification is rejected, however, by *Rash* (see *Meleches Shlomo*). *Yerushalmi* identifies שׁוֹשַׁנַּת הַמֶּלֶךְ as קְרִינְטוֹן (or according to some readings: קְרִינוֹן), which is explained by *Aruch* (s.v. קירינטון) as a Greek name for a certain white flower, presumably the white lily (see *Plants and Animals of the Mishnah,* p. 158; *Ibn Ezra* and *Rashi* to *Shir HaShirim* 2:1). *Rambam Comm.* appears to regard the שׁוֹשַׁנַּת הַמֶּלֶךְ as an anemone (see *Aruch HaShalem,* s.v. שׁשׁ).[1]

The mishnah states that the above species, as well as all other similar plants, are not *kilayim* in a vineyard. Apparently, this is because these plants were not cultivated (*Ravad* to Hil. Kilayim 5:19). *Rav* (following *Rosh* and *Rash*) maintains that although these are not *kilayim* under Biblical law, they are prohibited under Rabbinic law. However, *Rambam* (see *Kesef Mishneh* to Hil. Kilayim 5:6) appears to permit planting these species in a vineyard even under Rabbinic law.

Rambam (Hil. Kilayim 1:8-9) divides culti-

1. Recently, a case has been made for the identification of the שׁוֹשַׁנַּת הַמֶּלֶךְ as the iris. The iris mentioned at the beginning of the list would then be a wild variety (see *Teva VaAretz, Iyar* 5748, p. 17).

The iris, and the *kissom*, and the *shoshanas hamelech* and all [similar] varieties of plants are not *kilayim* in the vineyard.

Hemp — R' Tarfon says: It is not *kilayim*. But the Sages say: It is *kilayim*.

Globe artichoke is *kilayim* in the vineyard.

YAD AVRAHAM

vated plants into several groups. Plants which have edible parts but which do not produce edible seeds are known as *zeronei ginah*. These are divided into two types: *minei zeraim*, which are normally planted in large fields, and *minei yerakos*, which are normally grown in small patches.

In the context of *kilayim* of the vineyard, the following scheme emerges from *Rambam* (*Hil. Kilayim* 5:2-6,19 as understood by *Radbaz* to 5:3,6; cf. *Kesef Mishneh*). All five grains (i.e. wheat, barley, etc.), as well as certain members of the class of *minei yerakos*, are included in the Biblical prohibition of *kilayim* of the vineyard. The characteristic which determines whether there is a Biblical prohibition on a particular species of *minei yerakos* in a vineyard is the growth cycle of the plant. If it nears the completion of its growth cycle at the same time as the grapevine is producing fruit, then it is subject to the Biblical prohibition. Otherwise, it is forbidden only Rabbinically. Plants belonging to the class of *minei zeraim* are permitted even Rabbinically. Accordingly, the species listed here by the mishnah, which are referred to as *minei zeraim*, do not constitute *kilayim* in a vineyard even under Rabbinic law (*Radbaz* to *Hil. Kilayim* 5:6).

הַקַּנְבָּס — רַבִּי טַרְפוֹן אוֹמֵר: אֵינוֹ כִלְאָיִם. וַחֲכָמִים אוֹמְרִים: כִלְאָיִם. — *Hemp — R' Tarfon says: It is not kilayim. But the Sages say: It is kilayim.*

The species קַנְבָּס mentioned here (which we have vowelized as קָנְבָּס, following *Rambam Comm.*) should not be confused with קַנְבוֹס of mishnah 2:5. The latter is identified as caraway while the present species is identified as hemp.

The *Gemara* (*Menachos* 15b) mentions קַנְבוֹס and לוּף as two species whose inclusion

in the Biblical prohibition of *kilayim* of the vineyard is beyond doubt.[1] This would strengthen the assumption that the species referred to by our mishnah is not the same as the קַנְבוֹס of mishnah 2:5, which is grouped there together with לוּף. Nevertheless, *Rash* (as well as *Talmid HaRashba*) assume that קַנְבָּס of our mishnah *is* the species referred to by the *Gemara* and presumably also by mishnah 2:5.

The crux of the issue being debated by R' Tarfon and the Sages is not entirely clear. From *Rambam* (*Hil. Kilayim* 5:19) it seems that the dispute concerns a question of classification. If hemp is viewed as *minei zeraim*, it is not forbidden as *kilayim*. If it is viewed as *minei yerakos*, it will be. The Sages' assertion that hemp is *minei yerakos* is the accepted opinion, and therefore hemp is subject to all the laws of *kilayim* of the vineyard (*Rav; Rambam, Hil. Kilayim* 5:19).

וְהַקִּינְרָס כִּלְאַיִם בַּכֶּרֶם. — *Globe artichoke is kilayim in the vineyard.*

The דַּרְדַּר (*Genesis* 3:18), a weed which hinders the farmer, is identified by the Midrash *Bereishis Rabbah* as the קִינְרָס. It was called דַּרְדַּר because it consists of layer upon layer (in Aramaic: דְּרֵי דְרֵי, this being the presumed etymology of דרדר). This description fits well with the artichoke, an identification which is further confirmed from *Rambam Comm.* (*Uktzin* 1:6), where *Rambam* gives the popular Arabic name for artichoke (kharshuf) in definition of קִינְרָס.

The statement that the artichoke constitutes *kilayim* in the vineyard is presumably intended to prevent mis-classifi-

1. According to *Rambam*, this is because these two plants are members of the class of *minei yerakos* which satisfy the growth-cycle specifications mentioned above.

[א] **אֵיזֶהוּ** עָרִיס? הַנּוֹטֵעַ שׁוּרָה שֶׁל חָמֵשׁ גְּפָנִים בְּצַד הַגָּדֵר שֶׁהוּא גָּבֹהַּ עֲשָׂרָה טְפָחִים, אוֹ בְּצַד חָרִיץ שֶׁהוּא עָמֹק עֲשָׂרָה טְפָחִים וְרָחָב אַרְבָּעָה, נוֹתְנִין לוֹ עֲבוֹדָתוֹ אַרְבַּע אַמּוֹת.

בֵּית שַׁמַּאי אוֹמְרִים: מוֹדְדִין אַרְבַּע אַמּוֹת מֵעִקַּר הַגְּפָנִים לַשָּׂדֶה. וּבֵית הִלֵּל אוֹמְרִים: מִן הַגָּדֵר לַשָּׂדֶה.

יד אברהם

cation of the plant in a category not subject to *kilayim* law. [It has been suggested that since the artichoke is a perennial it might have been thought to belong to the family of trees and thus be exempt from the laws of *kilayim* of the vineyard (*Plants and Animals of the Mishnah*, p. 141).] *Rambam* (Hil. Kilayim 5:19) classes קִינָרַס as *minei yerakos*, and for this reason the mishnah rules that *globe artichoke is kilayim in the vineyard.*

Chapter 6

1.

The grapevine is a climbing shrub the branches of which straggle along the ground or climb by means of long tendrils. When the vine is left to grow on the ground, it spreads out much less than when it is trained on an arbor, for example. Until now the discussion of vineyards in the mishnah has involved vines growing on the ground, and it is with such vines that Beis Hillel maintain (mishnah 4:5) that only two rows count as a vineyard.

The present mishnah discusses vines which are trained on some support and may hence be called hanging vines. As will be seen, the requirements for hanging vines to qualify as a vineyard are different than for vines on the ground. In contrast with vines growing along the ground, which are called a כֶּרֶם when they constitute a legal vineyard, an arrangement of hanging vines which attains this status is known as an עָרִיס (*Rav; Rambam Comm.*)

אֵיזֶהוּ עָרִיס? — *What is an aris?*
I.e. what arrangement of hanging vines qualifies for a four-cubit work area within which foreign planting is forbidden, just like a legal vineyard.

The term עָרִיס derives from עֶרֶשׂ which means bed (see e.g. *Deut.* 3:11). Just as beds were constructed of a bedframe across which ropes were woven, so too the arbor is a frame upon which the vines climb and intertangle. The root has already been encountered in mishnah 4:7 above (*Rav, Rosh, Rash*; see also mishnah 5:3).

הַנּוֹטֵעַ שׁוּרָה שֶׁל חָמֵשׁ גְּפָנִים בְּצַד הַגָּדֵר שֶׁהוּא גָּבֹהַּ עֲשָׂרָה טְפָחִים, אוֹ בְּצַד חָרִיץ שֶׁהוּא עָמֹק עֲשָׂרָה טְפָחִים וְרָחָב אַרְבָּעָה, נוֹתְנִין לוֹ עֲבוֹדָתוֹ אַרְבַּע אַמּוֹת. — *[If] someone plants a row of five vines next to a wall which is ten handbreadths high, or next to a ditch which is ten handbreadths deep and four wide, we give this for its work area four cubits.*

Although a single row of five vines does not ordinarily constitute a vineyard according to Beis Hillel (mishnah 4:5), if the vines are trained upon a wall or the

6
1

1. **W**hat is an *aris?* [If] someone plants a row of five vines next to a wall which is ten handbreadths high, or next to a ditch which is ten handbreadths deep and four wide, we give this for its work area four cubits.

Beis Shammai say: We measure the four cubits from the base of the vines to the field. But Beis Hillel say: From the wall to the field.

YAD AVRAHAM

sides of a ditch of appropriate dimensions, the law is different. Even Beis Hillel agree that if a single row of five vines is designed as an *aris* of hanging vines, then it too qualifies as a vineyard with a four-cubit work area (*Rav* following R' Yochanan's opinion in *Yerushalmi*; see *Rosh, Rash*). The reason a hanging arrangement qualifies more readily as a legal vineyard than a level arrangement is not given. From *Rambam Comm.* it would seem that this is due to the fact that hanging vines grow more extensively than ground vines. Because of this, even a single row of hanging vines is significant enough to be deemed a legal vineyard and to be accompanied by a four-cubit work area in which foreign planting is forbidden.

Ravad (*Commentary* to *Eduyos* 2:4) writes that a single row of vines next to a wall is enhanced by virtue of being trained on the wall and has an appearance of a vineyard.

בֵּית שַׁמַּאי אוֹמְרִים: מוֹדְדִין אַרְבַּע אַמּוֹת מֵעִקַּר הַגְּפָנִים לַשָּׂדֶה. וּבֵית הִלֵּל אוֹמְרִים: מִן הַגָּדֵר לַשָּׂדֶה. — *Beis Shammai say: We measure the four cubits from the base of the vines to the field. But Beis Hillel say: From the wall to the field.*

If the vines which were trained on the wall were planted one cubit away from the wall on its eastern side, then according to Beis Shammai, planting on the western side of the wall must be distanced four cubits from the base of the vines on the other side of the wall. But according to Beis Hillel, the four cubits are measured from the wall, so that planting on the western side would be at least five cubits from the base of the vines (*Rav; Rambam, Hil. Kilayim*

8:3; see *Rosh, Rash* and *Rambam Comm.*).

Ravad (*Hil. Kilayim* 8:3,7) objects to this explanation on the grounds that the wall should serve as a separator between the foreign seed on the west and the vines on the east, and planting should therefore be allowed right up to the wall. *Kesef Mishneh* (loc. cit.) counters that because the vines here are trained on the wall, the wall itself is viewed as part of the vineyard, and hence does not separate.

This notion — that a wall which supports vines does not count as a separator between the vines on one side and the foreign seed on the other — would seem to be identical with the position of R' Yehudah in mishnah 4:7. There, it will be recalled, it was taught that a row of vines on one side of a ten-handbreadth-high wall cannot be combined with a row of vines on the opposite side of the wall to constitute a vineyard. R' Yehudah states, however, that אִם עֵרְסָן מִלְמַעֲלָה, *If he intertwined them above*, then the two rows are combined. It has already been pointed out that the term עָרִיס of our mishnah has the same root as עֵרְסָן of mishnah 4:7, and this would suggest that the intertwining referred to by R' Yehudah is none other than the arbor construction of this mishnah. Following *Kesef Mishneh*, then R' Yehudah's position is well understood: Since the wall functions as a support for the vines, it is itself viewed as part of the vineyard and hence does not separate. However, in view of the fact that the halachah rejects the opinion of R' Yehudah (see *Rambam Comm.* to mishnah 4:7 and *Hil. Kilayim* 7:6), it would seem that likewise the theory that a wall which supports vines does not separate is also rejected! In that case, *Ravad's* objection is revived.

To resolve this difficulty it would seem that despite the linguistic relationship, the term עֵרְסָן used by R' Yehudah does *not* in fact refer to an *aris* as defined here. Thus, al-

[143]   THE MISHNAH/KILAYIM — Chapter Six: *Eizehu Aris*

אָמַר רַבִּי יוֹחָנָן בֶּן נוּרִי: טוֹעִים, כָּל הָאוֹמְרִים כֵּן. אֶלָּא, אִם יֵשׁ שָׁם אַרְבַּע אַמּוֹת מֵעִקַּר גְּפָנִים וְלַגָּדֵר, נוֹתְנִין לוֹ אֶת עֲבוֹדָתוֹ וְזוֹרֵעַ אֶת הַמּוֹתָר. וְכַמָּה הִיא עֲבוֹדַת הַגֶּפֶן? שִׁשָּׁה טְפָחִים לְכָל רוּחַ. רַבִּי עֲקִיבָא אוֹמֵר: שְׁלֹשָׁה.

[ב] עָרִיס שֶׁהוּא יוֹצֵא מִן הַמַּדְרֵגָה —

יד אברהם

though his opinion is rejected there, it still remains possible that a wall which serves as the support of the *aris* arrangement of our mishnah does not separate, and this is why foreign seed must be distanced from the wall, as explained by *Kesef Mishneh* (see *Mishnah Rishonah* and *Tos. Anshei Shem* to mishnah 4:7).

Alternatively, the mishnah refers to planting on the same side of the wall as the vines. Assuming for example that the vines are one cubit from the wall, Beis Shammai will forbid planting within four cubits of the vines, i.e. five cubits from the wall. Beis Hillel, on the other hand, measure the four cubits from the wall, and they therefore will permit planting less than four cubits from the vines (*Rambam Comm.; Rosh; Rash*).

According to the latter approach that the planting is on the same side as the vines, it follows that Beis Hillel's opinion (that planting is permitted less than four cubits away from the vines) is more lenient than Beis Shammai's (that planting must be distanced four cubits from the vines). According to the former approach, that the planting is on the other side of the wall, it is Beis Shammai who permit planting closest to the vines, and hence it is Beis Shammai who is more lenient.

Disputes in which Beis Shammai are more lenient than Beis Hillel are ordinarily recorded in Tractate *Eduyos*. The omission of this dispute from Tractate *Eduyos* would therefore suggest that in fact it is Beis Hillel who are more lenient, i.e. that the correct interpretation of our mishnah is that the dispute concerns planting on the side of the wall occupied by the vines (*Rash; Rosh*).

On the other hand, this explanation too is not free from difficulty. In particular, the position of Beis Hillel that planting is distanced less than four cubits from the base of the vines is difficult to comprehend. Can it be that a greater distance is required between foreign seed and the wall which supports the branches of the vines than from the vines themselves? (*Kesef Mishneh* to *Hil. Kilayim* 8:3, quoted by *Tos. Yom Tov*).

Despite the difficulty noted above that the dispute between Beis Shammai and Beis Hillel is not recorded in *Eduyos*, *Rav* follows the view adopted by *Rambam* in his Code that the planting in question is on the opposite side of the wall to the vines. Indeed, *Rav* himself points out that according to this explanation Beis Shammai is more lenient than Beis Hillel. Evidently, our mishnah's dispute was not listed in *Eduyos* because of the opinion of R' Yochanan ben Nuri (below) who denies that any such dispute between Beis Shammai and Beis Hillel ever took place (*Kesef Mishneh* to *Hil. Kilayim* 8:3, quoted by *Tos. Yom Tov*).

אָמַר רַבִּי יוֹחָנָן בֶּן נוּרִי: טוֹעִים, כָּל הָאוֹמְרִים כֵּן. אֶלָּא, אִם יֵשׁ שָׁם אַרְבַּע אַמּוֹת מֵעִקַּר גְּפָנִים וְלַגָּדֵר, נוֹתְנִין לוֹ אֶת עֲבוֹדָתוֹ וְזוֹרֵעַ אֶת הַמּוֹתָר. — *Said R' Yochanan ben Nuri: They err, all those who say so. Rather, if there are four cubits from the base of the vines to the wall, we give it its work area and he may plant the remainder.*

R' Yochanan ben Nuri rejects the assertion that a single row of five hanging vines (an *aris*) has the legal status of a vineyard and is accompanied by a four-cubit work area. According to his teaching, the mention of four cubits in connec-

Said R' Yochanan ben Nuri: They err, all those who say so. Rather, if there are four cubits from the base of the vines to the wall, we give it its work area and he may plant the remainder.

And how much is the work area of a vine? Six handbreadths in every direction. R' Akiva says: Three.

2. [If] an *aris* protrudes from an embankment —

YAD AVRAHAM

tion with hanging vineyards occurred in an entirely different context. If there are less than four cubits between the hanging vines and their supporting wall, then the entire intervening space may not be planted. If the intervening space is four cubits, then after distancing the planting from the vines by the required six handbreadths, the remaining space may be planted. Thus, the row of hanging vines does not have a four-cubit work area, this being reserved only for two-rowed vineyards. It will readily be seen that this law is similar to the law of the vineyard perimeter in mishnah 4:2 and R' Yose's law in mishnah 5:4 (*Rav; Rosh; Rash; Rambam Comm.*).

וְכַמָּה הִיא עֲבוֹדַת הַגֶּפֶן? שִׁשָּׁה טְפָחִים לְכָל רוּחַ. רַבִּי עֲקִיבָא אוֹמֵר: שְׁלֹשָׁה. — *And how much is the work area of a vine? Six handbreadths in every direction. R'*

Akiva says: Three.

The six handbreadths in which planting is prohibited around a single vine were encountered already in mishnah 3:7. Although R' Akiva disputes this, and assumes it to be forbidden to plant only within a three-handbreadth radius of a single vine, the halachah accepts the former view, that it is forbidden to plant in the vicinity of a single vine *six handbreadths in every direction* (*Rav*). Since according to R' Yochanan ben Nuri a row of five hanging vines is not a vineyard, it is treated like a collection of single vines from which planting must be distanced six handbreadths. However, in the confined area between the vines and the supporting wall, R' Yochanan ben Nuri prohibited planting altogether unless the space was at least four cubits wide.

2.

Although the previous mishnah speaks of vines planted next to a wall or ditch, this was not the typical arrangement of a hanging vineyard or *aris*. Normally, vines were raised on a pergola-like arbor consisting of columns which supported an open roof of girders and crossbeams (*Rambam, Hil. Kilayim* 8:1; see mishnah 1, s.v. איזהו). The vines would grow along the roof-top lattice and would thus extend far beyond the spot in which they were planted. The present mishnah considers the law for a hanging vineyard planted on one level which extends by way of an arbor so that it overshadows a field on a lower level.

עָרִיס שֶׁהוּא יוֹצֵא מִן הַמַּדְרֵגָה — *[If] an aris protrudes from an embankment* —

I.e. a pergola upon which vines were trained protruded from an embankment and extended over the surrounding field

(*Rav; Rambam Comm.*). An embankment is referred to as a מַדְרֵגָה or *step*, since it appears like a step relative to the ground level below it (*Rav;* see *Rosh* and *Rash*).

רַבִּי אֱלִיעֶזֶר בֶּן יַעֲקֹב אוֹמֵר: אִם עוֹמֵד בָּאָרֶץ וּבוֹצֵר אֶת כֻּלּוֹ, הֲרֵי זֶה אוֹסֵר אַרְבַּע אַמּוֹת בַּשָּׂדֶה; וְאִם לָאו, אֵינוֹ אוֹסֵר אֶלָּא כְנֶגְדּוֹ. רַבִּי אֱלִיעֶזֶר אוֹמֵר: אַף הַנּוֹטֵעַ אַחַת בָּאָרֶץ וְאַחַת בַּמַּדְרֵגָה, אִם גְּבֹהָה מִן הָאָרֶץ עֲשָׂרָה טְפָחִים, אֵינָהּ מִצְטָרֶפֶת עִמָּהּ; וְאִם לָאו, הֲרֵי זוֹ מִצְטָרֶפֶת עִמָּהּ.

יד אברהם

רַבִּי אֱלִיעֶזֶר בֶּן יַעֲקֹב אוֹמֵר: אִם עוֹמֵד בָּאָרֶץ וּבוֹצֵר אֶת כֻּלּוֹ, הֲרֵי זֶה אוֹסֵר אַרְבַּע אַמּוֹת בַּשָּׂדֶה; — R' Eliezer ben Yaacov says: If while standing on the ground one can pick it completely, it prohibits four cubits in the field;

If a person can stand on the lower level and pick all the grapes hanging from the arbor, then although the vines were planted on the higher level, they are looked at as though they were planted on the lower level. The entire arbor — assuming it holds five vines and counts as an *aris* — is regarded as the site of the vineyard, and planting in the lower field within four cubits of any edge of the arbor is forbidden (*Rav; Rosh; Rash; Rambam Comm.*).

Although it is forbidden to plant foreign seed within four cubits of the arbor, foreign seed which is planted there will only be condemned for use if it is within six handbreadths of the arbor. This is explained below in mishnah 7:3 (*Rav; Rosh; Rash*).

וְאִם לָאו, אֵינוֹ אוֹסֵר אֶלָּא כְנֶגְדּוֹ. — if not, it prohibits only across from it.

If the grapes can only be reached from the lower level with the aid of a ladder, for example, then the area under the arbor on the lower level is not regarded as the site of the vines. While it remains forbidden to plant foreign seed *under the arbor* — i.e. *across from it* — it is permitted to plant within four cubits of the edge of the arbor. Moreover, since the actual site of the vines is on the surface of the embankment, planting on the lower level which is not under the arbor is allowed even within four lateral cubits of the base of the vines (*Rav; Rosh; Rash*).

Rambam Comm. seems to understand the phrase, *it prohibits across from it*, differently. In the first case, where a person could pick the hanging grapes while standing on the lower level, planting on the lower level must be distanced four cubits from each side of the arbor. In the present case, where the grapes cannot be picked while standing on the lower level,

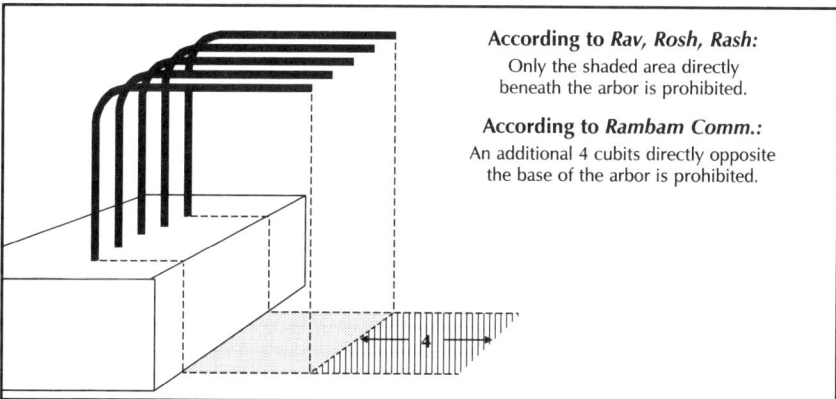

According to *Rav, Rosh, Rash*:
Only the shaded area directly beneath the arbor is prohibited.

According to *Rambam Comm.*:
An additional 4 cubits directly opposite the base of the arbor is prohibited.

6
2

R' Eliezer ben Yaacov says: If while standing on the ground one can pick it completely, it prohibits four cubits in the field; if not, it prohibits only across from it. R' Eliezer says: Even if someone plants one on the ground and one on the embankment, if it is higher than the ground by ten handbreadths, it is not combined with it; but if not, then it combines with it.

planting is not distanced from every side of the arbor, but only from the side which is across from the base of the vines (see diagram). In his Code, however, *Rambam* (*Hil. Kilayim* 8:8) adopts the conventional explanation given above that *across from it* means *under* the arbor.

רַבִּי אֱלִיעֶזֶר אוֹמֵר: אַף הַנּוֹטֵעַ אַחַת בָּאָרֶץ וְאַחַת בַּמַּדְרֵגָה, — *R' Eliezer says: Even if someone plants one on the ground and one on the embankment,*

Rav, following *Rambam Comm.* and *Rosh*, explains this case as dealing with the rules of a regular vineyard. Incidental to the mention of a split-level field above, the mishnah now considers whether two rows of vines can be combined to create the basic vineyard (as per mishnah 4:5-6) if they are on separate levels — one on an embankment and the other on the ground.

Rash mentions a different explanation according to which R' Eliezer is referring here to hanging vines. The question addressed is whether the five vines needed to constitute an *aris* can be planted on separate levels.

אִם גְּבֹהָה מִן הָאָרֶץ עֲשָׂרָה טְפָחִים, אֵינָה מִצְטָרֶפֶת עִמָּהּ; וְאִם לָאו, הֲרֵי זוֹ מִצְטָרֶפֶת עִמָּהּ. — *if it is higher than the ground*

by ten handbreadths, it is not combined with it; but if not, then it combines with it.

If the embankment is ten handbreadths high, so that the bases of the upper vines are ten handbreadths higher than the bases of the lower vines, the rows do not combine. Each is regarded as a collection of single vines from which foreign planting needs to be distanced only six handbreadths (*Rav; Rosh*). Alternatively, the base of the upper row must be ten handbreadths higher than the *top* of the lower row to prevent the rows from being combined into a single vineyard (*Rash*). [If the base of the upper row is within ten handbreadths of the top of the lower row, then even if the embankment itself is much higher than ten handbreadths, the rows will still combine.]

If the case in question involves an *aris*, the mishnah teaches that if, for instance, three of the requisite five vines are planted on the embankment, and two are on the ground below, they combine to form an *aris* only if the embankment is less than ten handbreadths high. Otherwise, planting must be distanced from those on the ground by only six handbreadths (*Rash*).

3.

Rambam (*Hil. Kilayim* 6:11) rules that foreign planting underneath the branches or leaves of a grapevine is forbidden and causes condemnation from use even if the planting is a considerable distance from the trunk of the vine (see below mishnah 7:4,7,8 and *Yerushalmi* end of chapter 6). Thus, aside from the prohibition to plant within a certain distance from a vine, there is a prohibition to plant where the planting is overshadowed by part of a vine.

The present mishnah focuses on the prohibition against planting *under* a hanging vine. Although a single vine does not necessitate distancing of foreign planting by

[147]   THE MISHNAH / KILAYIM — Chapter Six: *Eizehu Aris*

[ג] **הַמַּדְלֶה** אֶת הַגֶּפֶן עַל מִקְצָת אֲפִיפְיָרוֹת,
לֹא יָבִיא זֶרַע אֶל תַּחַת הַמּוֹתָר.
אִם הֵבִיא, לֹא קִדֵּשׁ. וְאִם הָלַךְ הֶחָדָשׁ, אָסוּר. וְכֵן
הַמַּדְלֶה עַל מִקְצָת אִילָן סְרָק.

[ד] **הַמַּדְלֶה** אֶת הַגֶּפֶן עַל מִקְצָת אִילָן
מַאֲכָל, מֻתָּר לְהָבִיא זֶרַע אֶל
תַּחַת הַמּוֹתָר. וְאִם הָלַךְ הֶחָדָשׁ, יַחֲזִירֶנּוּ. מַעֲשֶׂה

יד אברהם

four cubits, it is nevertheless forbidden to plant under it. Moreover, the supports used to elevate the vine are considered subordinate to the vine, and it becomes forbidden to plant under the supports just as if they themselves were vine.

הַמַּדְלֶה אֶת הַגֶּפֶן עַל מִקְצָת אֲפִיפְיָרוֹת, לֹא יָבִיא זֶרַע אֶל תַּחַת הַמּוֹתָר. אִם הֵבִיא, לֹא קִדֵּשׁ. — *[If] someone trains a grapevine along part of a lattice, he may not bring foreign seed under the rest. If he brought, it is not condemned.*

The crossbeams which make up the lattice roof of the pergola are known as אֲפִיפְיָרוֹת (*Tos. Yom Tov* from *Rambam, Hil. Kilayim* 8:1). Even if the branches of a grapevine are trained along only part of the lattice, it is nevertheless forbidden to bring foreign seed under the rest of the lattice which is not yet covered by vine. However, if a person illegally planted foreign seed under the part of the lattice not yet covered with vine, it does not become forbidden for use (*Rav; Rosh; Rash; Rambam Comm.*).

The law stated here, that if part of a lattice supports a grapevine it is forbidden to plant under the entire lattice, is not limited to a case of five hanging vines which form an *aris*. Even if a single vine is trained onto a supporting beam, it is forbidden to plant under the remainder of the beam (*Mishnah Rishonah; Chazon Ish* 13:1). Indeed, with an *aris* arrangement, planting is forbidden even beyond the *aris* (mishnah 2), and illegal planting under the lattice is condemned for use even if the planting is not directly under a vine (*Chazon Ish* 13:1).

וְאִם הָלַךְ הֶחָדָשׁ, אָסוּר. — *But if the new*

growth extended out, it becomes forbidden.

Although foreign seed illegally planted under the part of the lattice not yet covered by vine does not become forbidden, if the vine later proliferates and extends out to cover the part of the lattice over the foreign seed, the foreign seed becomes forbidden for use (*Rav; Rosh; Rash; Rambam Comm.*).

Rav writes that the foreign seed in this case becomes condemned only if after it is over-shadowed by the grapevine, the foreign seed increases by a two-hundredth (see mishnah 5:6). This is challenged by *Gra* (*Shenos Eliyahu*) and *Tif. Yis.*, who argue that if that is so, then there is no novelty in the mishnah's ruling here. In their opinion, the mishnah here teaches a novelty that the foreign seed becomes forbidden for use the moment it becomes overshadowed by the proliferating vine, even if the foreign seed has not grown at all. This is a penalty imposed for illegally planting under the lattice to begin with (cf. *Mishnah Rishonah*).

וְכֵן הַמַּדְלֶה עַל מִקְצָת אִילָן סְרָק. — *Similarly, if someone trains [a vine] on part of a barren tree.*

The term אִילָן סְרָק is defined more precisely in mishnah 5 below. For the moment, it suffices to recognize that a person is unlikely to allow a fruit-bearing tree to become overgrown with vine,

3. [I**f**] someone trains a grapevine along part of a lattice, he may not bring foreign seed under the rest. If he brought, it is not condemned. But if the new growth extended out, it becomes forbidden. Similarly, if someone trains [a vine] on part of a barren tree.

4. [I**f**] someone trains a grapevine onto part of a fruit-bearing tree, it is permitted to bring seed under the remainder. And if the new growth extended out, he must return it. It happened that

YAD AVRAHAM

whereas with a barren tree this is not the case. Accordingly, if a grapevine was trained onto part of a barren tree, it becomes forbidden to plant foreign seed anywhere under the tree. The barren tree is comparable to a beam which is partly covered by vine. Because both of these supports are subordinate to the vine, they are treated like vine, and planting foreign seed anywhere under them is forbidden.

However, as will be seen below, a fruit-bearing tree is not subordinate to a vine, and it is permitted to plant foreign seed under any part of the tree not covered by vine (*Rav; Rosh; Rash*).

Chazon Ish 13:2 writes that according to *Rash* it is forbidden to plant only under the remainder of a branch of a barren tree which is partially covered by vine. However, it is permitted to plant under branches which are not at all covered by vine (see mishnah 4).

4.

Since the purpose of a trellis is to support the expansion of a plant, a lattice which is at present only partially covered with vine is nonetheless treated as though it were already covered. Likewise, a barren tree upon which a vine is trained is regarded for all intents and purposes as a trellis. For this reason, the preceding mishnah taught that if a vine is trained on even part of a lattice or barren tree, it is forbidden to plant anywhere under them even though the vine has not yet reached that spot.

By way of contrast, if a vine has climbed onto part of a fruit-bearing tree, the owner is not likely to allow it to proliferate uncontrolled throughout the tree. Because he wants the tree to yield fruits, he will not abandon it as a trellis. For this reason, as will be seen in the coming mishnah, the law for a fruit-bearing tree partly occupied by a grapevine differs from that of a barren tree.

הַמַּדְלֶה אֶת הַגֶּפֶן עַל מִקְצָת אִילָן מַאֲכָל, מֻתָּר לְהָבִיא זֶרַע אֶל תַּחַת הַמּוֹתָר. וְאִם הִלֵּךְ הֶחָדָשׁ, יַחֲזִירֶנּוּ. — *[If] someone trains a grapevine onto part of a fruit-bearing tree, it is permitted to bring seed under the remainder. And if the new growth extended out, he must return it.*

If a grapevine occupied part of a fruit-bearing tree, it is permitted to plant foreign seed under the remainder of the tree. Moreover, even if the vine eventually spread to those parts of the tree

which overshadow the foreign seed, those parts do not become treated like trellises. Rather, once the new growth of vine has been removed, it is again permitted to plant foreign seed there (*Rav; Rosh; Rash;* see *Tos. Yom Tov* and *Mishnah Rishonah*).

If the vine occupies part of one branch of a fruit-bearing tree, it is clear from the mishnah that it is permitted to plant foreign seed under the other branches. However, it is not entirely clear whether it is permitted to plant

שֶׁהָלַךְ רַבִּי יְהוֹשֻׁעַ אֵצֶל רַבִּי יִשְׁמָעֵאל לִכְפַר עֲזִיז,
וְהֶרְאָהוּ גֶּפֶן מֻדְלָה עַל מִקְצָת תְּאֵנָה. אָמַר לוֹ: מָה
אֲנִי לְהָבִיא זֶרַע אֶל תַּחַת הַמּוֹתָר? אָמַר לוֹ: מֻתָּר.
וְהֶעֱלָהוּ מִשָּׁם לְבֵית הַמָּגַנְיָה וְהֶרְאָהוּ גֶּפֶן שֶׁהִיא
מֻדְלָה עַל מִקְצָת הַקּוֹרָה וְסַדָּן שֶׁל שִׁקְמָה וּבוֹ קוֹרוֹת
הַרְבֵּה. אָמַר לוֹ: תַּחַת הַקּוֹרָה זוֹ אָסוּר, וְהַשְּׁאָר מֻתָּר.

יד אברהם

even under the remainder of that very branch. *Chazon Ish* (13:2) understands the early commentators as disagreeing over this question. The matter will be discussed more fully below.

מַעֲשֶׂה שֶׁהָלַךְ רַבִּי יְהוֹשֻׁעַ אֵצֶל רַבִּי יִשְׁמָעֵאל לִכְפַר עֲזִיז, וְהֶרְאָהוּ גֶּפֶן מֻדְלָה עַל מִקְצָת תְּאֵנָה. אָמַר לוֹ: מָה אֲנִי לְהָבִיא זֶרַע אֶל תַּחַת הַמּוֹתָר? אָמַר לוֹ: מֻתָּר. — *It happened that R' Yehoshua went to R' Yishmael in Kfar Aziz, and he showed him a grapevine trained onto part of a fig tree. He said to him: May I bring seed under the remainder? He said to him: It is permitted.*

This incident serves to illustrate the rule stated above that a fruit tree is not regarded as a trellis for a grapevine even if a vine is trained onto part of it. R' Yishmael, who resided at the time in Kfar Aziz, showed his guest R' Yehoshua a fig tree which was partially occupied by a grapevine and inquired into the law for planting foreign seed under the remainder of the tree. R' Yehoshua responded that planting there is permitted, since as explained above, a fruit tree is not subordinate to the vine, and hence is not viewed as a trellis under which planting would be forbidden (*R' Shlomo Sirilio*).

וְהֶעֱלָהוּ מִשָּׁם לְבֵית הַמָּגַנְיָה וְהֶרְאָהוּ גֶּפֶן שֶׁהִיא מֻדְלָה עַל מִקְצָת הַקּוֹרָה וְסַדָּן שֶׁל שִׁקְמָה וּבוֹ קוֹרוֹת הַרְבֵּה. אָמַר לוֹ: תַּחַת הַקּוֹרָה זוֹ אָסוּר, וְהַשְּׁאָר מֻתָּר. — *And he took him from there up to the house of Hamganyeh and*

showed him a grapevine trained on part of a beam and the stump of a sycamore with many beams. He said to him: Under this beam it is forbidden, but [under the] rest it is permitted.

R' Yishmael then took his distinguished guest to the fields of the Hamganyeh family (residents of Kfar Aziz) and showed him another case of halachic interest (*R' Shlomo Sirilio*; cf. *Rav*). This was a grapevine trained onto part of one of the branches (beams) growing from a sycamore stump. Although the sycamore produced edible fruit (*Demai* 1:1), it was generally cultivated for its wood rather than its fruit (*Rav*). It was the practice to cut the trunk off at a certain height to stimulate the growth of straight branches ideal as building beams (see ArtScroll *Sheviis* 4:6).

The wording of the mishnah, גֶּפֶן שֶׁהִיא מֻדְלָה עַל מִקְצָת הַקּוֹרָה וְסַדָּן שֶׁל שִׁקְמָה וּבוֹ קוֹרוֹת הַרְבֵּה, *a grapevine trained on part of a beam and the stump of a sycamore with many beams*, is very awkward, but is universally understood to mean that the beam which was partially occupied by vine was itself growing from the *stump of a sycamore with many beams*. The conjunction *and* would thus seem to be out-of-place. *R' Shlomo Sirilio* has a different and somewhat clearer text which reads: גֶּפֶן שֶׁהִיא מֻדְלֵית בְּסַדָּן שֶׁל שִׁקְמָה עַל מִקְצָת הַקּוֹרָה וּבוֹ קוֹרוֹת הַרְבֵּה, *a vine which was trained on a stump of sycamore on part of a beam and [the stump] had many beams. Gra* (*Notes on Seder Zeraim*)[1] emends the text of the mishnah by replacing *and* with *of*. The

---

1. These are found in the Vilna ed. of the Talmud, in the volume containing Tractate *Berachos*, immediately following Tractate *Bikkurim*.

R' Yehoshua went to R' Yishmael in Kfar Aziz, and he showed him a grapevine trained onto part of a fig tree. He said to him: May I bring seed under the remainder? He said to him: It is permitted. And he took him from there up to the house of Hamganyeh and showed him a grapevine trained on part of a beam and the stump of a sycamore with many beams. He said to him: Under this beam it is forbidden, but [under the] rest it is permitted.

YAD AVRAHAM

resultant text is: מִקְצָת הַקּוֹרָה שֶׁל סָדָן שֶׁל שִׁקְמָה, part of a beam "of" the stump of a sycamore etc.

Shinuyei Nuschaos notes that sometimes ו, which generally means and, is used instead of ב, which generally means in. Accordingly, the standard text may be interpreted to mean: part of a beam in the stump of a sycamore with many beams. [See, for example, Rosh Hashanah 30a, where the Gemara suggests that the expression אִישׁ וּבֵיתוֹ, a man "and" his household, should be understood as אִישׁ בְּבֵיתוֹ, a man "in" his home.]

As a tree which is not cultivated for its fruit (a barren tree), one would have expected the sycamore to fall under the law of the previous mishnah and that the entire tree be viewed as a trellis for the grapevine. R' Yehoshua, however, ruled that only the particular beam (i.e. branch) on which the grapevine was growing was regarded as a trellis. Thus, planting anywhere under that branch even away from the vine is prohibited. But the other branches of the sycamore are each regarded as distinct trees, and so the fact that a vine converts one of the branches into a trellis does not affect the other branches. Accordingly, it is permitted to plant under the other branches (Rav; Rosh; Rash).

Rambam Comm. explains R' Yehoshua's ruling differently. In his view, the sycamore is treated as a fruit-bearing tree. This explains why planting under the other branches not inhabited by a vine is permitted. However, even with fruit-bearing trees, it is only the other branches under which one may plant. But under the branch which is partly

covered by a vine, it is forbidden to plant even under the remainder of the part which is not yet covered by a vine. Accordingly, R' Yehoshua ruled: Under this beam it is forbidden, but [under the] rest of the beams it is permitted (see Tos. Yom Tov from Rambam, Hil. Kilayim 6:12).

Chazon Ish 13:2 writes that according to Rash, if part of a branch of a fruit tree is occupied by a vine, it is permitted to plant not only under the remaining branches but even under the remainder of that branch itself. If part of a branch of a non-fruit-bearing tree is occupied by a vine, then it is forbidden to plant under the remainder of that particular branch, but it is permitted to plant under the remaining branches. [This follows from the case of the sycamore stump which according to Rash is a barren tree.] On the other hand, Rambam views the entire barren tree as a trellis and forbids planting under all the branches of a partially inhabited barren tree as explained in the previous mishnah.

Assuming Chazon Ish's explanation of Rash, it is clear why the mishnah records two incidents. The episode of the fig tree comes to teach that planting even under the remainder of a branch of a fruit tree on which a vine is growing is permitted, while the episode of the sycamore teaches that planting is prohibited only under those branches of a non-fruit-bearing tree on which a vine is growing.

According to Rambam, however, both incidents deal with fruit trees. Why then does the mishnah have to bring both? Chazon Ish (ibid.) suggests that according to Rambam the episode of the sycamore is brought in order to teach that the sycamore is considered a fruit-bearing species. Thus, the first episode illustrates the general law of fruit-bearing trees, but does not teach that a sycamore is

[ה] **אֵיזֶהוּ** אִילָן סְרָק? כָּל שֶׁאֵינוֹ עוֹשֶׂה פֵּרוֹת.
רַבִּי מֵאִיר אוֹמֵר: הַכֹּל אִילַן סְרָק,
חוּץ מִן הַזַּיִת וְהַתְּאֵנָה. רַבִּי יוֹסֵי אוֹמֵר: כָּל שֶׁאֵין
כָּמוֹהוּ נוֹטְעִין שָׂדוֹת שְׁלֵמוֹת – הֲרֵי זֶה אִילַן סְרָק.

[ו] **פִּסְקֵי** עָרִיס – שְׁמוֹנֶה אַמּוֹת וָעוֹד. וְכָל
מִדּוֹת שֶׁאָמְרוּ חֲכָמִים בַּכֶּרֶם אֵין
בָּהֶם ,,וְעוֹד'' חוּץ מִפִּסְקֵי עָרִיס.

יד אברהם

fruit-bearing. On the other hand, the sycamore episode is insufficient on its own, since one might have explained that the sycamore is non-fruit-bearing (as *Rash* indeed does). Therefore, the first episode which uses fig trees to illustrate the law for fruit-bearing trees is needed. Since the sycamore is also a variety of fig, the mishnah's inclusion of both incidents teaches that like other fig trees, the sycamore too is considered a fruit-bearing tree for the purposes of this law.

5.

This mishnah defines the barren tree, referred to by mishnah 3 above.

אֵיזֶהוּ אִילַן סְרָק? כָּל שֶׁאֵינוֹ עוֹשֶׂה פֵּרוֹת. — *Which [tree] is a barren tree? Any [tree] that does not produce fruit.*

According to this *Tanna*, a tree which bears fruit will not be relegated to the role of a trellis, regardless of how insignificant its fruit is relative to grapes. Therefore, only trees which are non-fruit-bearing can be considered subordinate to the vine growing on them. Accordingly, the *Tanna* states that the barren tree, which mishnah 3 treated as identical to a trellis, is any non-fruit-bearing tree.

רַבִּי מֵאִיר אוֹמֵר: הַכֹּל אִילַן סְרָק, חוּץ מִן הַזַּיִת וְהַתְּאֵנָה. — *Rabbi Meir says: All are barren trees, except for the olive and the fig.*

R' Meir argues that in the present context, the term אִילַן סְרָק is used with reference to all trees aside from the olive and fig. Because of the importance of their fruit, these species will not be made subordinate to a grapevine. Accordingly, even if part of the fig or olive tree is occupied by a vine, it will not be treated as a trellis. However, other species of tree, even if they are fruit bearing, might be considered secondary to the vine, and hence if they are partially used to support a vine, they are regarded as trellises.

In other contexts — e.g. the laws of grafting (see *Rav* to mishnah 1:7) — there is no uncertainty as to the meaning of the term אִילַן סְרָק, and all agree that it refers to non-fruit-bearing trees only. In the present discussion, where the key issue is whether or not a tree is viewed by the farmer as subordinate to the vine, the term is applied to any tree which is comparable in this respect to a non-fruit-bearing tree. Since, in R' Meir's opinion, the law of mishnah 3 applies equally to a genuinely barren tree as to an apple tree, for example, he explains that the term אִילַן סְרָק used there encompasses much more than merely non-fruit-bearing trees (*Mishnah Rishonah*).

רַבִּי יוֹסֵי אוֹמֵר: כָּל שֶׁאֵין כָּמוֹהוּ נוֹטְעִין שָׂדוֹת שְׁלֵמוֹת – הֲרֵי זֶה אִילַן סְרָק. — *Rabbi Yose says: Any tree the likes of which is not planted in whole fields — this is a barren tree.*

The exact species referred to by R' Yose are not identified. Nevertheless, his criterion is clear enough. Any species which is

5. **W**hich [tree] is a barren tree? Any [tree] that does not produce fruit. Rabbi Meir says: All are barren trees, except for the olive and the fig. Rabbi Yose says: Any tree the likes of which is not planted in whole fields — this is a barren tree.

6. **D**isruptions of an *aris* — eight cubits plus [a bit] more. And none of the measures which the Sages said concerning a vineyard have "plus [a bit] more" other than disruptions of an *aris*.

YAD AVRAHAM

important enough that it is normally planted in full orchards is not one which will be subordinated to the vine. A species which is not planted this extensively is not significant vis-a-vis the vine, and hence, for the present discussion, is considered a barren tree (*Rav; Rosh; Rash*).

6.

In mishnah 4:1, the law of a vineyard clearing — i.e. a regular vineyard *which has been destroyed in the middle* — is discussed. The present mishnah considers the law for an *aris*, a hanging vineyard, which has been destroyed in the middle.

פִּסְקֵי עָרִיס – שְׁמוֹנֶה אַמּוֹת וָעוֹד. — *Disruptions of an aris — eight cubits plus [a bit] more.*

The mishnah explains the meaning and consequences of *disruptions of an aris* below.

The exact size of the additional bit is explained by *Yerushalmi* and *Tosefta* (4:5) to be one-sixth of a cubit, i.e. a handbreadth (*Rav; Rosh; Rash*). *Rambam* apparently had a variant text of these sources (*Meleches Shlomo*), and in his *Commentary* he defines the additional bit as a sixtieth of a cubit, i.e. a tenth of a handbreadth. This view is reflected in *Hil. Kilayim* 8:5 and adopted also by *Shulchan Aruch* (*Yoreh Deah* 296:60).[1]

Before defining *disruptions of an aris*, the mishnah proceeds to make a parenthetical comment on the measure specified by the mishnah, viz. *eight cubits plus [a bit] more*.

וְכָל מִדּוֹת שֶׁאָמְרוּ חֲכָמִים בַּכֶּרֶם אֵין בָּהֶם ,,וְעוֹד" חוּץ מִפִּסְקֵי עָרִיס. — *And none of the measures which the Sages said concerning a vineyard have "plus [a bit] more" other than disruptions of an aris.*

[The mishnah remarks that in general the measures given in connection with vineyards are whole-number measurements. The only exception is the present case of *disruptions of an aris*, for which the measurement is *eight cubits plus [a bit] more*.]

According to some, the correct text of our mishnah is without the word בַּכֶּרֶם, so that the mishnah reads: וְכָל מִדּוֹת שֶׁאָמְרוּ חֲכָמִים אֵין בָּהֶם וְעוֹד חוּץ מִפִּסְקֵי עָרִיס — *And none of the measures which the Sages said have "plus [a bit] more" other than disruptions of an aris.* That is, the occurrence here of a measure of length which is not a whole number is unique, not just in the context of the laws of vineyards, but in the entire literature (*Shenos Eliyahu* and *Tif. Yis.* from *Yerushalmi*). However, *R' Shlomo Sirilio* interprets the

---

1. Basing himself on the *Gemara* (*Menachos* 41b), *Rambam Comm.* adds that a handbreadth is equal to four thumbwidths or, equivalently, the width of five index fingers.

אֵלּוּ הֵן פִּסְקֵי עָרִיס: עָרִיס שֶׁחָרַב מֵאֶמְצָעוֹ,
וְנִשְׁתַּיְּרוּ בוֹ חָמֵשׁ גְּפָנִים מִכָּאן וְחָמֵשׁ גְּפָנִים מִכָּאן
— אִם יֵשׁ שָׁם שְׁמוֹנֶה אַמּוֹת, לֹא יָבִיא זֶרַע לְשָׁם;
שְׁמוֹנֶה אַמּוֹת וְעוֹד, נוֹתְנִין לוֹ כְּדֵי עֲבוֹדָתוֹ וְזוֹרֵעַ
אֶת הַמּוֹתָר.

יד אברהם

conclusion of *Yerushalmi* as accepting the standard text. There is a case of a length measure which is not a whole number and is unrelated to vineyards in the mishnah *Eruvin* 2:5. Accordingly, the comment of our mishnah (*and none of the measures*) means only in the context of vineyards (see *Meleches Shlomo*).

אֵלּוּ הֵן פִּסְקֵי עָרִיס: עָרִיס שֶׁחָרַב מֵאֶמְצָעוֹ, וְנִשְׁתַּיְּרוּ בוֹ חָמֵשׁ גְּפָנִים מִכָּאן וְחָמֵשׁ גְּפָנִים — מִכָּאן — *These are disruptions of an aris: [If] an aris was destroyed in its middle, and there remained five vines on one side and five vines on the other —*

The mishnah now explains the *disruptions of an aris* referred to above. A row of eleven vines was trained on a wall, thus constituting an *aris* (mishnah 1). The middle vine was subsequently removed, leaving five vines on each side of the gap. This gap is termed a *disruption of an aris*. The remaining five-vine segments of the original row are themselves each an *aris*, so that following the removal of the middle vine, the resulting gap is flanked on each side by an *aris* (*Rav; Rosh; Rash*). The law for planting foreign seed in this gap follows.

אִם יֵשׁ שָׁם שְׁמוֹנֶה אַמּוֹת, לֹא יָבִיא זֶרַע לְשָׁם; שְׁמוֹנֶה אַמּוֹת וְעוֹד, נוֹתְנִין לוֹ כְּדֵי עֲבוֹדָתוֹ וְזוֹרֵעַ אֶת הַמּוֹתָר. — *if there are eight cubits, he may not bring seed there; eight cubits plus [a bit] more, we give it its work area and he may plant the remainder.*

If the resultant five-vine segments are separated by no more than eight cubits, then it is forbidden to plant any foreign seed in the gap. Since each segment is itself an *aris*, foreign planting must be distanced from each by four cubits. Thus, if the gap is eight cubits or less, it may not

be planted. If it is eight cubits plus the requisite additional bit, then it is permitted to plant the middle part of the gap which is four cubits from the segments on the sides of the gap (see diagram).

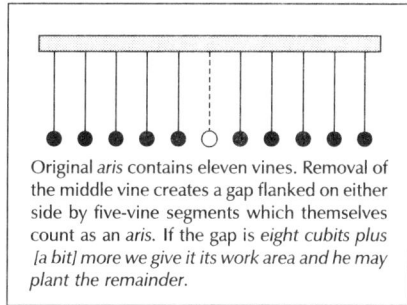

Original *aris* contains eleven vines. Removal of the middle vine creates a gap flanked on either side by five-vine segments which themselves count as an *aris*. If the gap is *eight cubits plus [a bit] more* we give it its work area and he may plant the remainder.

In the case of a regular vineyard it was taught that a *vineyard clearing* remains forbidden for foreign planting unless it is sixteen cubits across (mishnah 4:1). [This is so even according to those *Tannaim* who permit planting between rows which were initially separated by only eight cubits (mishnah 4:9).] It is therefore necessary for the mishnah here to stress that with respect to an *aris* the rule is different. A clearing created within an *aris* which remains bounded by an *aris* on each side may be planted, as long as it is *eight cubits plus a bit* (*Rav; Rosh; Rash*). [Note, however, that only that part of the gap which is four cubits away from the vines bounding the gap may be planted.]

According to R' Yochanan ben Nuri of mishnah 1, a five-vine *aris* does not qualify as a vineyard from which planting must be distanced four cubits. Nevertheless, even he agrees that planting *between* vines, at a distance of six handbreadths from a vine, is permitted only if the gap between the vines is eight cubits and a bit more (*Rav; Rash*). [It is

These are disruptions of an *aris:* [If] an *aris* was destroyed in its middle, and there remained five vines on one side and five vines on the other — if there are eight cubits, he may not bring seed there; eight cubits plus [a bit] more, we give it its work area and he may plant the remainder.

YAD AVRAHAM

not entirely clear whether this large a gap is needed only for planting in a gap created by removal of a vine, or even for planting in the spacing initially left between vines. Whatever the case, it is difficult to understand why according to R' Yochanan ben Nuri the right to plant in this gap is dependent on the size of the gap. Since he regards the single-row hanging-vine arrangement as a collection of single vines from which planting needs to be distanced only six handbreadths, one would expect that planting at this distance should be allowed even between vines separated by less than eight cubits. The matter therefore requires further study.]

Gra (Shenos Eliyahu) maintains that even according to the accepted opinion that a single row of five hanging vines constitutes a vineyard, distancing of four cubits is needed only when the planting faces the row (see diagram). Planting to the side of the row,

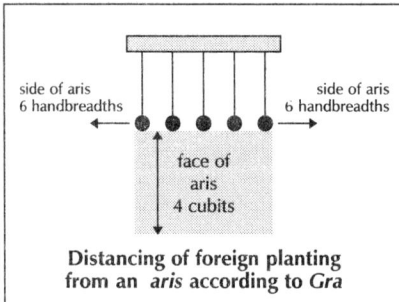

side of aris
6 handbreadths

side of aris
6 handbreadths

face of
aris
4 cubits

**Distancing of foreign planting
from an *aris* according to *Gra***

however, need only be distanced by six handbreadths. Accordingly, if removing a vine creates a gap bounded on both sides by five hanging vines (as in the mishnah's case), planting in the gap will be equivalent to planting at the side of an *aris* which is permitted at a distance of only six handbreadths. However, unless the gap is eight cubits and a bit more, the two five-vine arrangements which bound the gap are considered a single ten-vine *aris* and planting within the gap is considered planting *within*

an *aris* itself, which is forbidden. But when the gap is eight cubits and a bit more, planting within it is regarded as planting at the side of two independent *aris* arrangements and it is permitted at a distance of only six handbreadths from each. It follows, then, that of a gap of eight cubits and a bit more, all but two cubits — twelve handbreadths — may be planted, even according to the view that an *aris* is regarded like a vineyard (see also *Chazon Ish* 12:11).

Rambam (Comm. and *Hil. Kilayim* 8:5) has a markedly different interpretation of the *disruptions of an aris.* To understand his approach, it would seem that a peculiarity which exists according to *Rambam* with regard to planting within a regular vineyard must be borne in mind. According to *Rambam (Hil. Kilayim* 7:4), if the rows of a regular vineyard are initially separated by eight cubits or more, then although it is forbidden to plant outside the vineyard within four cubits of the edge of the vineyard, nevertheless it is permitted to plant between the rows at a distance of only six handbreadths from a row (see above 4:9, s.v. רי׳ מאיר). Thus, according to *Rambam* there is a difference between planting outside a vineyard and planting inside a vineyard: Planting outside remains forbidden within four cubits; planting inside is permitted at a separation of only six handbreadths (see *Hasagos HaRavad* and *Kesef Mishneh* to *Hil. Kilayim* 7:4).

Now, in the case of a hanging vineyard consisting of parallel rows of at least five vines each, planting outside the vineyard must be distanced by four cubits, as explained in mishnah 1. Within the vineyard, planting is completely forbidden by virtue of the fact that the entire area un-

[ז] עָרִיס שֶׁהוּא יוֹצֵא מִן הַכֹּתֶל מִתּוֹךְ הַקֶּרֶן
וְכָלָה – נוֹתְנִין לוֹ עֲבוֹדָתוֹ
וְזוֹרֵעַ אֶת הַמּוֹתָר. רַבִּי יוֹסֵי אוֹמֵר: אִם אֵין שָׁם

יד אברהם

der the pergola is viewed as the site of the vines (see mishnah 2). In contrast with the case of a regular vineyard, even the area between the rows of a hanging vineyard is forbidden for planting, possibly because the common lattice unites the rows and thus causes the entire area beneath it to be viewed as a single continuity. However, if the hanging vineyard or *aris* is disrupted, the situation changes. It is such a case that the mishnah here addresses.

Consider a pergola which is supported at either end by walls. Along each wall is a five-vine row of hanging vines, and there is a third row of vines between these two (see diagram). As it stands, this constitutes an *aris* from which outside planting must be distanced by four cubits and under which no planting is permitted. If, however, the middle row is removed, then the law with respect to planting between the remaining rows changes. If there are eight cubits plus a bit more between these rows, then it is permitted to plant at a distance of only six handbreadths from the rows, provided that care is taken not to plant under the crossbeams of the pergola (the אַפִּיפָּיָרוֹת — see mishnah 3). When an *aris* is destroyed in this manner, the entire area covered by

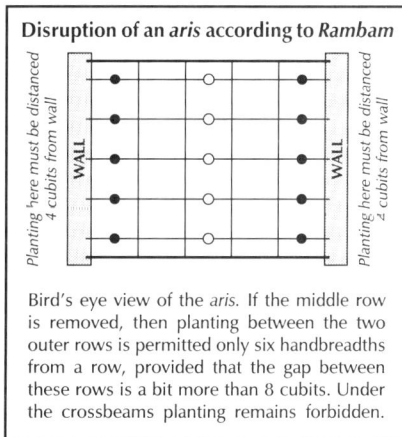

Disruption of an *aris* according to *Rambam*

Bird's eye view of the *aris*. If the middle row is removed, then planting between the two outer rows is permitted only six handbreadths from a row, provided that the gap between these rows is a bit more than 8 cubits. Under the crossbeams planting remains forbidden.

the pergola is no longer characterized as the site of the vines. Although planting *outside* the pergola must still be distanced by four cubits, planting between the two outside rows of the original *aris* is permitted at a distance of only six handbreadths, provided that the two outer rows are separated by a bit more than eight cubits.[1] But if these two rows are separated by exactly eight cubits (or less), then no planting is permitted between them (cf. *Chazon Ish* 12:12, *Derech Emunah* 8:28 and *Beur HaHalachah* 8:5, s.v. עריס).

7.

The following mishnah is exceedingly obscure and has spawned numerous interpretations. *Rav* copies *Rash*, who would appear to be following the first interpretation of *Ri ben Malki Tzedek*. In addition to the latter commentators' second approach to this mishnah, each of the remaining major commentators (*Rambam, Rosh, R' Shlomo Sirilio, Gra*) has his own unique interpretation. The sampling of explanations presented below is illustrative alone, and by no means exhaustive.

---

1. It might be added that these two rows are viewed as associated with the walls to which they are respectively adjacent, rather than with each other. For this reason, the area between them is no longer regarded as part of a single large *aris* and consequently planting there is permitted even though the pergola is still in place. Planting directly under the crossbeams, however, remains forbidden.

7. **A**n *aris* which emerges from a wall from within a corner and ends — we give it its work area and he may plant the remainder. R' Yose says: If there are not

YAD AVRAHAM

עָרִיס שֶׁהוּא יוֹצֵא מִן הַכֹּתֶל מִתּוֹךְ הַקֶּרֶן וְכָלָה — נוֹתְנִין לוֹ עֲבוֹדָתוֹ וְזוֹרֵעַ אֶת הַמּוֹתָר. — *An aris which emerges from a wall from within a corner and ends — we give it its work area and he may plant the remainder.*

Above (mishnah 3) it was taught that planting is forbidden under a pole upon which a grapevine is trained. It likewise might have been thought that to support foreign plants on a wall used for supporting grapevines is forbidden.

The case described involves five vines which are trained onto a wall and arranged in an L-shape such that they envelop a corner of the wall (see diagram).

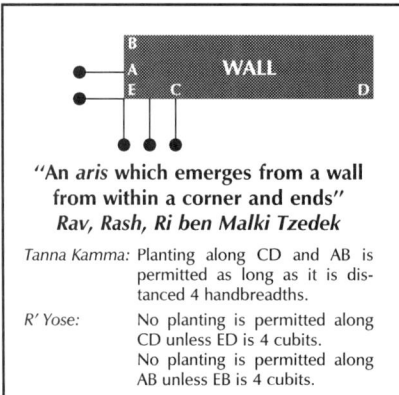

"An *aris* which emerges from a wall from within a corner and ends"
Rav, Rash, Ri ben Malki Tzedek

Tanna Kamma:	Planting along CD and AB is permitted as long as it is distanced 4 handbreadths.
R' Yose:	No planting is permitted along CD unless ED is 4 cubits. No planting is permitted along AB unless EB is 4 cubits.

Now, because the vines are not arranged in a straight row, they do not constitute a legal *aris* from which foreign planting must be distanced by four cubits (see *Yerushalmi* 6:1). Nevertheless, it might have been thought that in such a situation the wall should be regarded as subordinate to the vines, much as the poles (אַפִּיפְיָרוֹת) of mishnah 3. If that were so, then the entire wall would be viewed as a

grape trellis, and foreign planting alongside it would be disallowed even at a distance from the vines. The *Tanna Kamma* therefore teaches that this is not so. As long as planting is distanced from the vines by six handbreadths — *we give it its work area* — it is permitted to plant foreign seed along the remainder of the wall. Even if the wall is less than four cubits long, it does not become subordinate to the vines, and the remainder may be planted (*Rav*[1]; *Rash; Ri ben Malki Tzedek* in his first explanation).

Rosh understands the case referred to here as involving five vines which are sandwiched between two parallel walls (see diagram). Three vines are along one

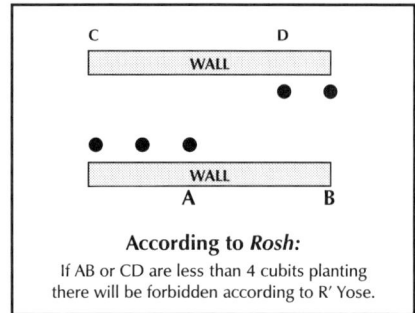

According to *Rosh*:
If AB or CD are less than 4 cubits planting there will be forbidden according to R' Yose.

of the walls forming a line which begins at the corner (edge) of that wall while the remaining two vines are along the other wall forming a line that begins at the opposite end of that wall. Neither wall has vines planted along it from one end to the other and this is what the mishnah means by *an aris which emerges from a wall . . . and ends:* It starts at one end of the wall but stops in the middle and does not reach until the other end. Since it begins at the

1. The later commentators understand *Rav* and *Rash* differently and raise many serious problems with their explanation (see e.g. *Mishnah Rishonah*). However, a careful consideration of *Rav's* and *Rash's* wording and a comparison with *Ri ben Malki Tzedek* convinces me that it is *Ri ben Malki Tzedek's* first explanation which *Rav* and *Rash* intend.

אַרְבַּע אַמּוֹת, לֹא יָבִיא זֶרַע לְשָׁם.

[ח] **הַקָּנִים** הַיּוֹצְאִים מִן הֶעָרִיס וְחָס עֲלֵיהֶם
לְפָסְקָן, כְּנֶגְדָּן מֻתָּר.
עֲשָׂאָן כְּדֵי שֶׁיְּהַלֵּךְ עֲלֵיהֶן הֶחָדָשׁ, אָסוּר.

[ט] **הַפֶּרַח** הַיּוֹצֵא מִן הֶעָרִיס, רוֹאִין אוֹתוֹ

<hr>

יד אברהם

end or corner of the wall, it is described as emerging *from a wall from within a corner*. The mishnah teaches that since the five vines are divided between two walls, they do not count as an *aris* from which foreign planting must be distanced by four cubits. Rather, after leaving a work area of six handbreadths, *he may plant along the remainder of each wall*.

רַבִּי יוֹסֵי אוֹמֵר: אִם אֵין שָׁם אַרְבַּע אַמּוֹת, לֹא יָבִיא זֶרַע לְשָׁם. — *R' Yose says: If there are not four cubits there, he may not bring foreign seed there.*

R' Yose maintains that if the wall is not four cubits long, then it is considered subordinate to the vines and no foreign planting at all is permitted along it, even if the planting is six handbreadths from the vines. This is similar to R' Yose's position in the case of *a grapevine planted inside a winepress or a hole* of mishnah 5:4. There too, R' Yose argues that unless the hole or press is four cubits across, no foreign planting is permitted inside it, even if it is distanced by six handbreadths from the vine. In both these cases R' Yose applies a similar idea: A defined place occupied by vine is considered to be the domain of the vine and cannot be planted by foreign species. However, each ruling

contains a novelty not evident from the other, and it is therefore necessary for R' Yose to clearly spell out his position in both cases. In the present case of trellised vines, in contrast with the case of a vine inside a hole, the site of the vines is not confined by walls. It is thus necessary for R' Yose to stress that the wall upon which they are growing is nevertheless considered the domain of the vines. On the other hand, from the present ruling, which applies only to a minimum of five vines, it would not be possible to infer that even a single vine can be said to have its own private domain in which all planting is forbidden. Accordingly, it is necessary for R' Yose to explicitly state (above 5:4) that a single vine inside a hole renders the hole the private domain of the vine, unless it is four cubits across (*Rav; Rash; Ri ben Malki Tzedek* from *Yerushalmi*).

According to *Rosh*, it will be recalled that the vines of the mishnah are sandwiched between two walls. R' Yose's ruling apparently means that even though the five vines do not qualify as an *aris*, nevertheless the two walls upon which they are trained are subordinate to the vines, unless there are four cubits from the last vine on a wall until the end of that wall (see 2nd diagram on previous page).

8.

In mishnah 3, it was taught that it is forbidden to plant anywhere under a pole which supports a grapevine, even if the vine currently occupies only part of the pole. Accordingly, if a vine is trained upon a trellis, it is forbidden to plant anywhere under the trellis. The present mishnah discusses the status of a pole of a trellis which extends beyond the edge of the trellis.

four cubits there, he may not bring foreign seed there.

8. **[** I **f]** poles protrude from the trellis and he values them [as is] and does not want to cut them, opposite them it is permitted [to plant].

[If] he made them in order for new growth to go on them, it is forbidden.

9. **[** I **f]** a shoot protrudes beyond the trellis, we view it

YAD AVRAHAM

הַקָּנִים הַיּוֹצְאִים מִן הֶעָרִיס וְחָס עֲלֵיהֶם לְפָסְקָן, כְּנֶגְדָּן מֻתָּר. — *[If] poles protrude from the trellis and he values them [as is] and does not want to cut them, opposite them it is permitted [to plant].*

Poles which jut out beyond the edge of the trellis are not necessarily regarded as parts of grapevine supports (אַפִּיפְיָרוֹת) under which planting is forbidden. It might have been argued that by not cutting off the protruding parts of the poles, the owner demonstrates that he views them as an integral part of the trellis — i.e. as grapevine supports. However, it may be that the excess pole is left in place for other reasons and not because the owner wants the vine to grow there. Accordingly, the mishnah states that if the owner is reluctant to shorten these poles because *he values them as is,* for example, and he has no intention to train vines on the excess which protrudes beyond the edge of the trellis, then it is permitted to plant underneath these extensions (*Rav; Rosh; Ri ben Malki Tzedek*).

Rambam Comm. (and see also *Hil. Kilayim* 6:13 and 8:1) seems to explain that the poles in question are part of the structural support of the trellis. The vines are not trained along these poles even within the frame of the trellis, but without these structural poles the entire trellis could collapse. Thus, if the owner does not cut these poles because he is afraid that it could cause the collapse of his trellis, it is permitted to plant under these poles. This is because he has not designated these poles as vine supports, but merely as trellis supports, and these are not subordinate to the vine.

עֲשָׂאָן כְּדֵי שֶׁיְּהַלֵּךְ עֲלֵיהֶן הֶחָדָשׁ, אָסוּר. — *[If] he made them in order for new growth to go on them, it is forbidden.*

If, however, the farmer intended these extensions also as supports for the future growth of the vine, then they are regarded as vine supports and planting beneath them is forbidden (*Rav; Rosh; Ri ben Malki Tzedek*).

9.

In addition to the prohibition on planting within six handbreadths of a vine or four cubits of a vineyard, it is prohibited to plant directly under a branch of a vine, even outside the work area (see mishnah 7:3-4). This is illustrated in the following mishnah.

הַפֶּרַח הַיּוֹצֵא מִן הֶעָרִיס, — *[If] a shoot protrudes beyond the trellis,*

If a branch[1] of a trellised grapevine extends beyond the four-cubit work

1. The tip of a growing branch of a grapevine is called פֶּרַח (*Rambam Comm.*). *Rav* (following *Rosh* and *Rash*) cites *Shir HaShirim* 6:11 where the root פרח is used in connection with the growth of the grapevine.

כְּאִלּוּ מִטְטֶלֶת תְּלוּיָה בּוֹ, כְּנֶגְדּוֹ אָסוּר. וְכֵן בַּדָּלִית.
הַמּוֹתֵחַ זְמוֹרָה מֵאִילָן לְאִילָן, תַּחְתֶּיהָ אָסוּר.
סִפְּקָהּ בְּחֶבֶל אוֹ בְּגָמִי, תַּחַת הַסִּפּוּק מֻתָּר. עֲשָׂאוֹ
כְּדֵי שֶׁיְּהַלֵּךְ עָלָיו הֶחָדָשׁ, אָסוּר.

[א] הַמַּבְרִיךְ אֶת הַגֶּפֶן בָּאָרֶץ, אִם אֵין עָפָר
עַל גַּבָּהּ שְׁלֹשָׁה טְפָחִים, לֹא

יד אברהם

area of the *aris*,

רוֹאִין אוֹתוֹ כְּאִלּוּ מִטְטֶלֶת תְּלוּיָה בּוֹ, כְּנֶגְדּוֹ
אָסוּר. — *we view it as though a plumbline were hanging from it, and it is forbidden [to plant] opposite it.*

It is prohibited to plant foreign seed directly under the branch (*Rav; Rosh; Rash*). Within the four-cubit work area, planting is forbidden even if the planted spot is not overshadowed by vine. Beyond this area, only a location which is directly under a branch is forbidden for planting. Such planting generates a condemnation of both the vine which overshadows and the foreign seed beneath it (*Rambam, Hil. Kilayim* 6:11).

To determine the precise areas on the ground which are overshadowed by the vine, the mishnah states that *we view it* (i.e. the vine branch) *as though a plumbline were hanging from it.* That is, only the area directly beneath the branch may not be planted. Outside this area, planting is permitted and no distancing is required (see *Shenos Eliyahu*).

Both the six-handbreadth work area of single vines and the four-cubit work area of a vineyard are measured from the base of the vines, i.e. from the point at which the trunk of the vine emerges from the ground (*Ri ben Malki Tzedek*). This is why no distancing is required from the branch which protrudes beyond the four-cubit work area, and only the area directly overshadowed by the vine is forbidden for planting.

Above (mishnah 6:2; see *Mishnah Rishonah* loc. cit.), *Rav* stated that although

planting within the four-cubit work area of an *aris* is forbidden even if it is not under a branch, such planting does not cause any condemnation for use unless it is within six handbreadths of a vine. However, planting under a branch causes condemnation even if it is far from the base of the vine. Consequently, it is not entirely clear why *Rav* explains the mishnah's case in terms of a branch which protrudes beyond the four-cubit work area of an *aris*. The mishnah here could have easily been explained as involving planting under a branch *within* the work area, inside the four-cubit work area but beyond the six-handbreadth limit. It teaches that even though planting at this point in the work area is anyhow forbidden, it causes condemnation only if it is under a branch (*Rashash*).

וְכֵן בַּדָּלִית. — *And likewise for a raised vine.*

Planting under a branch of a single-raised vine is forbidden even if the planting is more than six handbreadths away from the base of the vine. As in the previous case of the trellised vineyard (i.e. *aris*), only the area directly overshadowed by the branch is forbidden, and no distancing from this area is required. Thus, the area which would be delineated if a plumbline were dropped from the branch to the ground is forbidden for planting, but all around this area planting is permitted (*Rav*).

הַמּוֹתֵחַ זְמוֹרָה מֵאִילָן לְאִילָן, תַּחְתֶּיהָ אָסוּר.
— *[If] someone stretches a vine branch from one tree to another, it is forbidden [to plant] beneath it.*

as though a plumbline were hanging from it, and it is forbidden [to plant] opposite it. And likewise for a raised vine.

[If] someone stretches a vine branch from one tree to another, it is forbidden [to plant] beneath it. [If] he extended it by means of a hemp rope or a reed rope, under the extension it is permitted [to plant]. [If] he made it in order for new growth to go on it, it is forbidden.

1. [I]f] someone propagates a grapevine in the ground, if there are not three handbreadths of soil on top

YAD AVRAHAM

[A branch is stretched from one tree to another where it is secured to the second tree, making it unnaturally straight.] Here, again, the prohibition applies only to what is directly beneath the branch (*Rav; Rosh; Rash*). Planting there is prohibited even though it might not have been overshadowed by the branch if it had been left to grow freely. [By the same token, it would seem that only the area currently overshadowed by the branch in its stretched state is prohibited; those areas which the branch overshadowed before it was stretched, but no longer does, are permitted (see *Shenos Eliyahu* and *Mishnah Rishonah*).]

סְפָקָה בְּחֶבֶל אוֹ בְגֶמִי, תַּחַת הַסְּפוּק מֻתָּר. עֲשָׂאוֹ כְּדֵי שֶׁיְּהַלֵּךְ עָלָיו הֶחָדָשׁ, אָסוּר. — *[If] he extended it by means of a hemp rope or a reed rope, under the extension it is permitted [to plant]. [If] he made it in order for new growth to go on it, it is forbidden.*

If the branch did not reach all the way to the second tree, and the person tied it to the tree with a rope, it is permitted to plant under the rope. This is provided of course that the rope is not intended to support future growth of the vine. If it was intended to support the vine's growth, then planting even under the extension rope is forbidden, as in the case of vine supports in mishnah 3 (*Rav; Rosh; Rash*).

Chapter 7

1.

A new grapevine can be generated from an existing one by burying a branch of the parent vine underground in such a way that its tip protrudes where one wants a new vine to grow. This process, known as propagation, stimulates the growth of a new set of roots from the buried branch. These roots sustain a new vine that develops from the tip of the propagation branch (*Rosh*). Eventually, the new vine can be severed from the parent vine to become an entirely independent vine (*Meiri* to *Bava Basra* 83a).

The mishnah considers the law for planting foreign seed in the vicinity of a propagation branch.

הַמַּבְרִיךְ אֶת הַגֶּפֶן בָּאָרֶץ, — *[If] someone propagates a grapevine in the ground,*

In contrast with the propagation procedure described in the prefatory remarks, *Rambam Comm.* appears to understand the procedure referred to here as

involving burial of the *entire* parent vine, not just a branch of it.

The different explanations of propagation have practical consequences with regard to the prohibition on planting within six handbreadths of the parent vine. If, as *Rosh*

יָבִיא זֶרַע עָלֶיהָ, אֲפִילוּ הִבְרִיכָה בִּדְלַעַת אוֹ בְּסִילוֹן.

הַבְרִיכָה בְּסֶלַע, אַף עַל פִּי שֶׁאֵין עָפָר עַל גַּבָּהּ אֶלָּא שָׁלֹשׁ אֶצְבָּעוֹת, מֻתָּר לְהָבִיא זֶרַע עָלֶיהָ.

יד אברהם

explains, the parent vine is left standing and only a branch is buried for propagation, the prohibition on planting within six handbreadths of the parent vine remains in effect. If the parent vine is completely buried, as *Rambam* explains, it no longer retains a six-handbreadth work area (see *Mareh HaPanim*, s.v. המבריך; *Mishnah Rishonah*).

אִם אֵין עָפָר עַל גַּבָּהּ שְׁלֹשָׁה טְפָחִים, לֹא יָבִיא זֶרַע עָלֶיהָ, — *if there are not three handbreadths of soil on top of it, he may not bring seed above it,*

If the propagation branch is within three handbreadths of the surface, it is forbidden to plant foreign seed directly above it. To the side of the buried branch, however, planting is permitted (*Rav; Rosh; Rash*).

The reason that it is forbidden to plant above the branch is that the roots of the foreign plant will penetrate the branch, resulting in a forbidden graft. But if the foreign seed is planted to the side of the propagation branch, this does not occur, since the roots grow straight, not to the side. If the branch is buried at least three handbreadths below the surface, planting above it will not lead to grafting, since the roots of foreign seed planted on the surface will not penetrate a branch at that distance. Accordingly, the mishnah prohibits foreign planting only if there are less than three handbreadths between the surface and the buried branch, and only directly above the branch (*Rav; Rosh; Rash*).

The mishnah is discussing planting outside the six-handbreadth work area of the parent vine. Within the work area of the parent vine, planting is forbidden regardless of whether it is directly above a propagation branch or not. Thus, the case of the mishnah involves a propagation branch which ex-

tended beyond the work area of the parent vine, and the mishnah teaches that even beyond the six-handbreadth work area of the parent vine, planting above a propagation branch which is within three handbreadths of the surface is forbidden (*Rav; Rosh; Rush*).

The prohibition on planting above the propagation branch is intended to prevent a forbidden grafting of the roots of the foreign seed to the propagation branch. Now, the prohibition on grafting plants to trees applies not only to grapevines, but also to other trees (mishnah 1:7-8). In that case, one would expect that if someone propagated some other variety of fruit tree, he should be forbidden from planting grain above the propagation branch lest the roots of the grain become grafted to the branch. Yet *Yerushalmi*, pointing to the mishnah's specification here of grapevine, states explicitly that only in the case of propagated grapevines is there a prohibition on planting above the propagated branch!

To explain why planting is forbidden only above the propagation branch of a grapevine, even though it is also forbidden to graft to other trees, *Rav* (following *Rosh* and *Rash*) writes that the branch of a grapevine is much softer than branches of other trees. Because of this, the propagation branch of a grapevine can be penetrated by roots of a foreign plant, resulting in a forbidden graft. However, other trees are not so soft, and even if their propagation branch is within three handbreadths of the surface, it will not be penetrated by roots of foreign seed above it. Accordingly, no general prohibition on planting above propagation branches is warranted.

אֲפִילוּ הִבְרִיכָה בִּדְלַעַת אוֹ בְּסִילוֹן. — *even if he propagates it in gourd [pipe] or [earthenware] pipe.*

Dried gourd shells were used to construct piping through which a propa-

of it, he may not bring seed above it, even if he propagates it in gourd [pipe] or [earthenware] pipe.

[If] he propagated it in rock, even though there are only three fingerbreadths of soil above it, he is permitted to bring seed above it.

gated branch could be directed. The mishnah teaches that even if the vine is propagated through a pipe, it is still forbidden to plant above it if the branch is less than three handbreadths from the surface. This is because the roots of the foreign seed are strong enough to penetrate gourd or earthenware pipe, and hence despite the pipe, there remains the risk of a forbidden graft between the roots of the foreign seed and the propagation branch. Yerushalmi states, however, that lead piping is impenetrable to roots of foreign seed. Therefore, if the propagation branch is drawn through a lead pipe, it is permitted to plant above it even though the branch is close to the surface (Rav; Rosh; Rash).

Rav, following Rash, points out that the penetration of the gourd piping by the roots of the foreign seed does not constitute a forbidden graft between greens and greens (see mishnah 1:7) because the gourd used for piping is dried out and no longer growing. Thus, the mishnah's only concern is preventing a graft between the roots of the foreign seed and the propagation branch of the vine.

In fact, the insertion of a vine branch into a growing gourd would also constitute a forbidden graft (see mishnah 1:8). Since the mishnah permits propagating a vine through a gourd, it is evident that the gourd pipe used in the propagation is constructed of dead, dried-out gourds which are not subject to the grafting prohibition. Tos. Yom Tov therefore questions why Rav et al. infer that the gourds here are dried out only from the mishnah's lack of concern with a graft between greens and greens created by the penetration of the gourd by the roots of the foreign seed. They should have inferred this directly from the fact that the mishnah permits the propagation of a vine through a gourd pipe!

הַבְרִיכָהּ בְּסֶלַע, אַף עַל פִּי שֶׁאֵין עָפָר עַל גַּבָּהּ אֶלָּא שָׁלֹשׁ אֶצְבָּעוֹת, מֻתָּר לְהָבִיא זֶרַע עָלֶיהָ.

— [If] he propagated it in rock, even though there are only three fingerbreadths of soil above it, he is permitted to bring seed above it.

If the propagation branch was drawn through hard rock, which cannot be penetrated by the roots of foreign seed, then it is permitted to plant above the propagation branch. In such a case it is not necessary for there to be three handbreadths of soil between the foreign seed and the propagation branch. If there are merely three fingerbreadths of soil above the branch, planting above it is permitted (Rav; Rosh; Rash).

Actually, it is permitted to plant above a branch propagated through impenetrable rock even if there are less than three fingerbreadths of soil above it. Inasmuch as there is no risk whatsoever of a forbidden graft between the roots of the foreign seed and the vine, there is no reason for planting to be forbidden (Mishnah Rishonah). The mishnah mentions three fingerbreadths simply because less than this depth of soil is not suitable for planting (Rosh; R' Shlomo Sirilio).

Alternatively, the three-fingerbreadth depth is essential in order to permit planting above the branch. If there is not at least this much soil, then planting above the branch is forbidden, even though the branch is encased in solid rock (Derech Emunah 6:45 from Tosefta Kilayim 4:9; see Tziyun HaHalachah 6:79). The reason for such a prohibition is not clear.

הָאַרְכּוּבָה שֶׁבַּגֶּפֶן, אֵין מוֹדְדִין לָהּ אֶלָּא מִן הָעִקָּר הַשֵּׁנִי.

[ב] הַמַּבְרִיךְ שָׁלֹשׁ גְּפָנִים וְעִקְרֵיהֶם נִרְאִים, רַבִּי אֱלִיעֶזֶר בַּר צָדוֹק אוֹמֵר:

יד אברהם

הָאַרְכּוּבָה שֶׁבַּגֶּפֶן, אֵין מוֹדְדִין לָהּ אֶלָּא מִן הָעִקָּר הַשֵּׁנִי. — *[If there is] a knee in a grapevine, we do not measure other than from the second trunk.*

There is considerable controversy as to the meaning of the term אַרְכּוּבָה. *Rav* follows *Rambam Comm.* who explains the term as referring to a knee-shaped growth pattern. When a vine emerges from the ground, and briefly grows vertically before bending and continuing horizontally along the ground, until it turns again and rises vertically, it is said to have formed a knee. If the point at which the vine emerges from the ground is not discernible,[1] the six handbreadths by which foreign planting must be distanced from a vine are measured from the point at which the vine again tends upward. This point is referred to as the עִקָּר הַשֵּׁנִי, *the second trunk*.

Rash understands the term אַרְכּוּבָה as related to הַרְכָּבָה, i.e. grafting (see *Rashbam* to *Bava Basra* 83a, s.v. הרכובה). The mishnah thus translates as: *if there is a graft in a grapevine, we do not measure other than from the second trunk.* The case involves the graft of a narrow grape branch onto a wider grape trunk (see diagram). This results in a single vine which

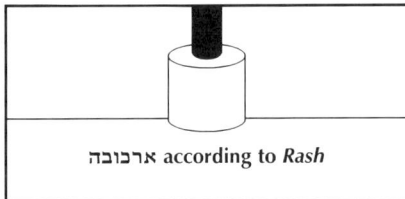

ארכובה according to *Rash*

is wider at the bottom than at the top, and the question under discussion is how to measure the six handbreadths by which planting must be distanced from the vine: Are these measured from the wider base or from the narrower graft? As long as the wider base is covered by soil and hence not discernible, the six handbreadths are measured from the narrower graft, i.e. the second trunk. If, for example, the wider base exceeds the graft by two handbreadths on each side, foreign planting may be located as near as four handbreadths to the base. This is because the distancing is measured from the graft.

According to both preceding interpretations, the case of the אַרְכּוּבָה has nothing to do with propagation of vines underground, the subject of the first part of our mishnah. However, *Tosafos* (*Bava Basra* 83a, s.v. הרכובה) has yet a third interpretation of אַרְכּוּבָה which assumes it to be a specific form of propagation: When a grapevine was very old, it was buried somewhere along its middle to stimulate growth of new roots. This second growth center or trunk becomes the point from which distancing of foreign planting must be measured.

Yerushalmi remarks that the law of our mishnah applies only when the first trunk is not discernible; but if the first trunk is discernible, then planting must be distanced six handbreadths from both the first trunk *and* the second trunk. *Rambam Comm.* apparently had a somewhat different text or interpretation of *Yerushalmi*, since he writes in his *Commentary* that if the first trunk (i.e.

1. This qualification is based on a statement of *Yerushalmi* (see below). According to *Rav*, if the point of emergence from the ground — i.e. the *first* trunk — is discernible, then planting must only be distanced six handbreadths from the first trunk, not from the second.

7
2

[If there is] a knee in a grapevine, we do not measure other than from the second trunk.

2. [If] someone propagates three vines and their trunks are visible, R' Eliezer bar Tzadok says:

the point of emergence of the vine from the ground) is discernible, then the six hand-breadths are measured from it. His wording indicates that in such a case the measure-ments are *only* from the first trunk and not from the second (i.e. the point at which the vine resumes an upward course). While this is not unreasonable, since the roots are indeed located at the first trunk, it is difficult to un-derstand why, when the first trunk is not discernible, the measurements are made only from the second trunk. After all, the second trunk only *appears* to be the main trunk, but in reality the roots of the vine extend from the first trunk (see *Rashash*). Moreover, in

Hil. Kilayim 8:10, *Rambam* seems to main-tain that even when the first trunk is dis-cernible, the measurements are made only from the second trunk![1] It would seem there-fore that the entire vine until the point where it assumes a definite upward course is re-garded by *Rambam* as merely a root, and not the central trunk of the vine. It is similar to propagating a vine by burying it entirely and bringing up its tip elsewhere. In such a case, the buried part is no longer treated like the trunk of the vine, which is considered in-stead to be located where the propagation emerges (see *Ramban* to *Bava Basra* 83a; see also *R' Shlomo Sirilio*).

2.

הַמַּבְרִיךְ שָׁלֹשׁ גְּפָנִים וְעִקָּרֵיהֶם נִרְאִים, — *[If] someone propagates three vines and their trunks are visible,*

The case involves three parent vines aligned in a row which are propagated so as to produce a parallel row of three new vines (see diagram). The propagation is

Propagation by burying a branch
(Rav, Rosh, Rash)

accomplished by burying a branch from each of the parent vines and bringing up its tip at the desired point. The parent vines remain exposed — i.e. *their trunks are visible* — so that the net result is two parallel rows of three

vines each (*Rav; Rosh; Rash*).

Rambam (*Comm. Kafich* ed. and *Hil. Kilayim* 6:9) appears to have understood that following the propagation there are only three vines. Evidently, then, the propagation was performed by burying the three parent vines entirely. However, the original location of the vines was still discernible since the trunk or roots of these vines protruded there (see diagram). Additionally, it would seem

Circled vines are buried and emerge where marked (o).

The original location of the buried vines is still dis-cernible as "protruding trunks" or roots.

The status of the propo-gated vines (◉) as single vines (requiring 6 hand-breadth distancing) or vine-yard vines (requiring 4 cubit distancing) depends on spacing of original vines.

from *Rambam* that although the original vines were aligned in a row, the vines resulting from the propagation were not (see also *Ri Migash* to *Bava Basra* 83a).

1. The distinction of *Yerushalmi* between where the first trunk is discernible and where it is not is recorded by *Rambam* in his Code in connection with the law of the first part of our mishnah concerning propagation (see *Hil. Kilayim* 6:8).

כלאים ז/ב

אִם יֵשׁ בֵּינֵיהֶם מֵאַרְבַּע אַמּוֹת וְעַד שְׁמוֹנֶה, הֲרֵי
אֵלּוּ מִצְטָרְפוֹת; וְאִם לָאו, אֵינָן מִצְטָרְפוֹת.
גֶּפֶן שֶׁיָּבְשָׁה אֲסוּרָה וְאֵינָהּ מְקַדֶּשֶׁת.

יד אברהם

רַבִּי אֱלִיעֶזֶר בַּר צָדוֹק אוֹמֵר: אִם יֵשׁ בֵּינֵיהֶם
מֵאַרְבַּע אַמּוֹת וְעַד שְׁמוֹנֶה, הֲרֵי אֵלּוּ מִצְטָרְפוֹת;
— Rabbi Eliezer bar Tzadok says: If
there are from four cubits up to eight
between them, then they combine;

It was taught above (mishnayos 4:8-9
and 5:2) that two rows of vines combine
to form a vineyard, from which planting
must be distanced by four cubits, as long
as the rows are separated by a gap of no
less than four cubits and no more than
eight. Accordingly, R' Eliezer bar Tzadok
teaches that the two rows of vines which
result from the propagation of the original row will constitute a vineyard as long
as they are properly spaced. Thus, even
though the propagated vines are still
connected with the parent vines, the two
rows are considered separate and can be
combined to form a vineyard (Rav;
Rosh; Rash).

Actually, to constitute a vineyard it is
not necessary to propagate three vines. It
will be recalled from mishnah 4:6 that
five vines arranged in a protruding-tail
formation also constitute a vineyard.
Thus, if one starts with a row of three
vines and propagates two adjacent vines,
the third of the original vines will count
as the protruding tail of the resulting
formation and the five-vine resulting set
will count as a vineyard[1] (Rav; Rosh;
Rash). The mishnah speaks of propagating three vines to simplify the presentation and obviate the need to specify that
in addition to the two propagated vines,
there must be a third vine which serves
as a protruding tail (Rosh).

וְאִם לָאו, אֵינָן מִצְטָרְפוֹת. — if not, they do
not combine.

If the parent vines are spaced by less

than four cubits or by more than eight cubits from the new vines, the parent row
cannot be combined with the row of new
vines to constitute a vineyard. Each row is
treated as single vines from which foreign
planting must be distanced by only six
handbreadths (Rash).

Rosh (quoted by Tos. R' Akiva) questions
why it is necessary for the mishnah to reiter-
ate the law in the event that the vines are not
properly spaced. The same spacing laws apply when planting a vineyard from scratch,
not just when generating a vineyard formation through propagation. Once the mishnah
has taught us that the new row is independent of the parent row and combines to form
a vineyard, it follows that if the new row is
not properly spaced, then no vineyard results!

Rambam (Comm. and Hil. Kilayim 6:9-10)
has a completely different understanding of
the issue being discussed by the mishnah. According to Rambam, there is no multiplica-
tion of vines here, since the propagation entails burying the entire parent vine. Thus, the
issue is not whether the propagated vines are
viewed as independent of the parent vines.
Rather, since the original trunks still jut out a
bit and are visible, the question arises as to
whether these original trunks retain the
status of vines, and whether such vines, if
they previously were part of a vineyard, retain their status as vineyard vines even on being buried. R' Eliezer bar Tzadok rules that if
the three original trunks are spaced by four to
eight cubits one from another, then they combine. [Apparently the spacing of the vines
where they eventually emerge is immaterial
— see Ri Migash to Bava Basra 83a.] That is,
they are combined with the rest of the standing vineyard just as if they had not been
buried, and they retain their status as members of the vineyard. Thus, planting must be
distanced from them by four cubits. If, however, the protruding trunks are not spaced between four and eight cubits apart from one

---

1. This, of course, assumes that a protruding-tail formation consists of two parallel rows, one
of three vines and the other of two — see commentary to mishnah 4:6 at length.

If there are from four cubits up to eight between them, then they combine; if not, they do not combine.

A vine which has dried is forbidden but does not condemn.

another, then they are no longer viewed as part of the standing vineyard and are regarded instead as single vines from which planting must be distanced by six handbreadths (see *Tos. Anshei Shem* from *Mareh HaPanim*). Likewise, if there are less than three buried vines, and hence less than three protruding trunks, they do not retain their status as members of a larger standing vineyard and are treated like single vines (*Rambam, Hil. Kilayim* 6:10).

גֶּפֶן שֶׁיָּבְשָׁה אֲסוּרָה וְאֵינָהּ מְקַדֶּשֶׁת. — *A vine which has dried is forbidden but does not condemn.*

There is a difference of opinion among the commentators as to whether *a vine which has dried* refers to a vine which is still alive but which has lost its leaves as in the fall, or whether this refers to a dead vine. All agree that under Biblical law there is no prohibition on planting in the vicinity of a dead vine. However, it is possible that by Rabbinic enactment even planting next to a dead vine is forbidden.

Rav, following *Rash*, explains that planting next to a dead vine is forbidden Rabbinically lest an observer mistakenly conclude that it is permitted to plant next to live vines which have lost their leaves. Since it is difficult to distinguish between a vine which is actually dead, and a vine which is merely going through a phase in its life cycle (as in the fall), it was feared that if planting next to dead vines were permitted, then people might confuse a dead vine with a live one which lost its leaves. Consequently, they will mistakenly think that planting next to a live vine which has lost its leaves is permitted and they will come to plant next to live vines which are temporarily dried out. But planting next to live vines which are temporarily dried out is Biblically forbidden. Accordingly, the Rabbis prohibited planting even next to dead vines. Since

however such planting is only Rabbinically forbidden, no condemnation of the vine or the foreign seed results, and this is what the mishnah means here when it rules: *A vine which has dried is forbidden but does not condemn.*

While it is true that in the winter — when even live vines lose their leaves — it is difficult to distinguish between live vines and dead ones, in the summertime — when live vines are flourishing — the contrast between them and dead vines is readily apparent. Accordingly, *Yerushalmi* questions why planting next to dead vines was forbidden even during the summer when there is no risk of confusing dead vines with live vines. *Yerushalmi* answers that in some places vines lose their leaves in the summer and therefore even in the summertime it is possible to mistake a dead vine for a live one. Therefore, planting next to dead vines is forbidden even in the summer (*Rav; Rosh; Rash*).

Rambam Comm. seems to have understood the phrase *a vine which has dried* as referring to a live vine which has temporarily lost its leaves, as in the autumn. As will be explained below in mishnah 7, *Rambam* is of the opinion that *kilayim* of the vineyard is condemned for use under Biblical law only if the vine is carrying clusters of grapes which have reached a certain minimum size (*Hil. Kilayim* 5:14). Moreover, according to *Rambam*, to plant next to a vine which is not in the state in which it can cause condemnation is Biblically permitted (see *Tziyun HaHalachah* 5:138). Now, a vine which has lost its foliage is not carrying any fruit and hence planting next to it does not result in any condemnation. Consequently, planting next to it is Biblically permitted (*Derech Emunah* 5:97). Nevertheless, the mishnah teaches that it is Rabbinically prohibited to plant next to it. Thus, it is Rabbinically prohibited to plant next to a vine which has dried out, as in the fall;

רַבִּי מֵאִיר אוֹמֵר: אַף צֶמֶר גֶּפֶן אָסוּר וְאֵינוֹ מְקַדֵּשׁ.

רַבִּי אֶלְעָזָר בַּר צָדוֹק אוֹמֵר מִשְּׁמוֹ: אַף עַל גַּבֵּי הַגֶּפֶן אָסוּר וְאֵינוֹ מְקַדֵּשׁ.

[ג] **אֵלּוּ** אוֹסְרִין וְלֹא מְקַדְּשִׁין: מוֹתַר חָרְבָּן

יד אברהם

but no condemnation results.

[Apparently, the Rabbis prohibited planting near such a live vine which is not bearing any fruit, because it will eventually reach a stage during which foreign planting *will* result in Biblically mandated condemnation and will be Biblically forbidden. To insure that no planting will take place when the vine is carrying the requisite grapes, planting was forbidden next to the vine throughout the year. It follows, then, that it should be permitted according to *Rambam* to plant next to a *dead* vine, since it will never reach a stage at which it causes condemnation. It might be argued that planting next to a dead vine should also be forbidden lest people come to plant next to a live one which has merely lost its leaves. However, since as explained according to *Rambam*, planting next to a live vine which has lost its leaves is itself only Rabbinically forbidden, it is unlikely that the Rabbis promulgated a prohibition concerning dead vines merely to prevent violation of a different Rabbinic prohibition regarding vines which have lost their leaves [אֵין גּוֹזְרִין גְּזֵרָה לִגְזֵרָה].

רַבִּי מֵאִיר אוֹמֵר: אַף צֶמֶר גֶּפֶן אָסוּר וְאֵינוֹ מְקַדֵּשׁ. — *R' Meir says: Even cotton is forbidden but does not condemn.*

Above (mishnah 5:8) it was taught that the class of plants known as *minei zeraim* does not constitute *kilayim* in a vineyard, and may be planted there even under Rabbinic law. According to R' Meir, although cotton belongs to this class of plants, it is forbidden Rabbinically to plant it next to a vine. However, if cotton

was illegally planted near a vine, no condemnation results (*Rambam Comm.*, Kafich ed.; *Rav* apparently followed an erroneous version of *Rambam Comm.* — see *Tos. Yom Tov* and *Meleches Shlomo*; see also *Chiddushei R' Eliyahu Guttmacher*). [The reason for the special stringency regarding cotton as compared with other plants belonging to the class of *minei zeraim* is not given. However, it is evident from the accepted classification of cotton as *minei yerakos* (see below) that it must be a borderline case of *minei zeraim*. Perhaps this accounts for the stringency. See also *Beur HaHalachah* 5:19, s.v. וצמר גפן.]

The halachah does not follow R' Meir's opinion, and cotton is in fact classified as *minei yerakos*. Accordingly, if planted near a vine, condemnation results (*Rambam, Hil. Kilayim* 5:19).

Alternatively, R' Meir is not discussing the planting of cotton next to a vine, but rather the planting of foreign seed next to cotton. In Hebrew, cotton is known as צֶמֶר גֶּפֶן, literally *wool of the vine*, which reflects the fact that the cotton plant bears a strong resemblance to the grapevine (*Rav; Rosh; Rash*). Accordingly, R' Meir prohibits planting foreign seed next to a cotton plant lest people mistake it for a grapevine. But since the prohibition is entirely Rabbinical, such planting causes no condemnation (*Meleches Shlomo* from R' Yehosef Ashkenazi; Shenos Eliyahu; Tif. Yis.).

רַבִּי אֶלְעָזָר בַּר צָדוֹק אוֹמֵר מִשְּׁמוֹ: אַף עַל גַּבֵּי הַגֶּפֶן אָסוּר וְאֵינוֹ מְקַדֵּשׁ. — *R' Elazar bar Tzadok says in his name: Even above the*

R' Meir says: Even cotton is forbidden but does not condemn.

R' Elazar bar Tzadok says in his name: Even above the vine [planting] is forbidden but does not condemn.

3. The following prohibit but do not condemn: the

vine [planting] is forbidden but does not condemn.

This refers back to the law stated in mishnah 1 that it is forbidden to plant foreign seed above a propagated vine branch which is less than three handbreadths from the surface (*Rav, Rosh, Rash* following Rabbi Shmuel in the *Yerushalmi*). It will be recalled that planting above the propagation branch is forbidden lest it result in a graft of the roots of the foreign seed to the vine branch. Grafting is forbidden under the general prohibition of *kilayim* of plants (*Rambam, Hil. Kilayim* 1:5), not under the special prohibition of *kilayim* of the vineyard. Since *kilayim* of plants does not cause any condemnation (*Rambam, Hil. Kilayim* 1:7), a graft between the roots of foreign seed and the propagation branch will also not result in any condemnation (see *Tos. Anshei Shem*, s.v. אף from *Shoshanim LeDavid; Chazon Ish* 2:5; *Tif. Yis., Boaz* §1; cf. *Mishnah Rishonah*).

Rav following *Rambam Comm.* writes that the halachah does not follow R' Elazar bar

Tzadok. This can mean only one of two things: either planting above the vine is permitted, or else planting above the vine is not only forbidden but it also condemns. Now, the first possibility does not seem admissible since the law forbidding such planting is stated anonymously in mishnah 1 and is recorded by *Rambam (Hil. Kilayim* 6:7). Accordingly, the second possibility must be correct — namely, that planting above the vine causes condemnation. But that too is difficult, since the *kilayim* in question is the *kilayim* of grafting which does not carry any condemnation from use (*Shoshanim LeDavid* quoted by *Tos. Anshei Shem; Tif. Yis., Boaz* §1; see *Shenos Eliyahu* to mishnah 1).

According to Rabbi Bun in *Yerushalmi*, the meaning of *above the vine* is something else altogether. In his opinion, this refers to the airspace above a vine. It is forbidden to plant within the ten handbreadths above a vineyard or above a single vine (*Rambam, Hil. Kilayim* 6:5) by planting, for example, in a flowerpot suspended over the vine (*Shenos Eliyahu, Peirush HaAroch*). If someone did so, he has committed a transgression, but no condemnation results.

3.

The following mishnah lists situations (other than those cases already given in the previous mishnah) in which planting is prohibited but does not result in condemnation from use. This list provides a helpful summary of some of the laws encountered over the last two chapters. The mishnah concludes with a list of those situations in which planting does result in condemnation.

אֵלּוּ אוֹסְרִין וְלֹא מְקַדְּשִׁין: — *The following prohibit but do not condemn:*

In the following four cases, planting of foreign seed is prohibited, but ille-

gal planting does not lead to any condemnation from use and there is no need to burn the plant (*Rav*; see mishnah 5:7).

הַכֶּרֶם, מוֹתַר מְחוֹל הַכֶּרֶם, מוֹתַר פְּסְקֵי עָרִיס,
מוֹתַר אַפִּיפִירוֹת. אֲבָל תַּחַת הַגֶּפֶן, וַעֲבוֹדַת הַגֶּפֶן,
וְאַרְבַּע אַמּוֹת שֶׁבַּכֶּרֶם, הֲרֵי אֵלּוּ מִתְקַדְּשׁוֹת.

יד אברהם

מוֹתַר חָרְבָּן הַכֶּרֶם, מוֹתַר מְחוֹל הַכֶּרֶם, מוֹתַר
פְּסְקֵי עָרִיס, מוֹתַר אַפִּיפִירוֹת. — *the extra
[part] of a destroyed vineyard, the extra
[part] of a vineyard perimeter, the extra
[part] of disruptions of a hanging vineyard, and the extra [part] of vine supports.*

The *destroyed vineyard* mentioned
here refers to the vineyard clearing encountered above in mishnah 4:1. It will be
recalled from there that if a vineyard
clearing measures sixteen cubits across,
then it is permitted to plant inside it. If it
is less than sixteen cubits, however, *he
may not bring seed there* (mishnah 4:1).
Nevertheless, illegal planting in such a
clearing does not necessarily result in a
condemnation from use. Only if the
planting is located within four cubits of
the vineyards bordering on the clearing
does a condemnation result. But if the
planting is located in *the extra [part] of a
destroyed vineyard* — i.e. in the central
area of the clearing which is more than
four cubits away from the vineyards
which flank the clearing, then no condemnation results. Thus, in a fifteen-cu-
bit clearing, for example, if the person
illegally plants the central seven cubits of
the clearing, no condemnation will result,
since the planting is four cubits away
from the vineyards at the sides of the
clearing (*Rav; Rosh; Rash*).

Similarly, *the extra [part] of a vineyard perimeter* refers to the part of a
vineyard perimeter which is four cubits
away from the vineyard. It will be
recalled from mishnah 4:2 that a vineyard perimeter is the area between the
edge of a vineyard and the surrounding
wall. If there are not twelve cubits
between the edge of the vineyard and the
surrounding wall, then planting inside
this area is forbidden. However, such

illegal planting will result in condemnation only if it is within four cubits of the
vineyard. If it is outside the four cubits,
then no condemnation results. This is
what is meant by the mishnah's statement that *the extra [part] of a vineyard
perimeter* is prohibited for planting, but
does not result in condemnation (*Rav;
Rosh; Rash*).

The *disruptions of a hanging vineyard* refers to the law of mishnah 6:6 that
a gap in an *aris* may not be planted if it is
eight cubits wide or less (see there).
Nevertheless, illegal planting in the part
of the gap which is six handbreadths
away from the vines at either side does
not cause any condemnation. The part of
the disruption which is six handbreadths
away from the hanging vines on either
side is referred to here as *the extra [part]
of disruptions of a hanging vineyard*,
and although planting here is illegal, it
does not cause any condemnation (*Rav;
Rosh; Rash*).

Rav (following *Rosh* and *Rash*) notes that
planting at the side of a hanging vineyard (i.e.
an *aris*) *never* causes condemnation if it is six
handbreadths away (see *Rav* to mishnah 6:2
and *Mishnah Rishonah* there). The mishnah
gives this law in the context of a disruption of
a hanging vineyard to stress that even when
it is flanked on both sides by hanging vineyards, no condemnation results.

Mareh HaPanim (6:2, s.v. הרי זה אוסר) chal-
lenges the view that planting six handbreadths away from an *aris* does not condemn, on the grounds that this is the opinion
of Reish Lakish but is disputed by R'
Yochanan whose opinion normally prevails
(*Yerushalmi* 6:4; see *Mareh HaPanim* there,
s.v. עריס עצמו).

The final case listed here in which it is
prohibited to plant, but in which illegal
planting does not cause condemnation, is
the case of *the extra [part] of vine
supports.* In mishnah 6:3 it was taught

extra [part] of a destroyed vineyard, the extra [part] of a vineyard perimeter, the extra [part] of disruptions of a hanging vineyard, and the extra [part] of vine supports. But under the vine, the work area of a vine, and the four cubits of the vineyard, these become condemned.

YAD AVRAHAM

that it is forbidden to plant under a beam upon which a vine is trained. Even if the vine occupies only part of the supporting beam, *he may not bring foreign seed under the rest* (mishnah 6:3). The rest of the beam — i.e. the part of a vine support which is not yet occupied by vine — is known as *the extra [part]* of the vine support (see mishnah 6:3). Although planting under this extra part is forbidden, it does not result in condemnation (*Rav; Rosh*).

Rash, based on *Yerushalmi* (7:2 and 6:3), indicates that the prohibition on planting under the part of a vine support not yet occupied by vine does not apply to the entire extent of the support. Rather, according to one view, it is forbidden to plant under the support only up to six handbreadths[1] beyond the tip of the vine. According to a second view, it is forbidden to plant under the support for four cubits beyond the tip of the vine. According to both views, planting within these limits does not condemn, and planting beyond these limits is permitted.

R' Shlomo Sirilio (see also *Ri ben Malki Tzedek*) understands *the extra [part] of vine supports* to mean the section of the vine support which is six handbreadths away from the tip of the vine. With ground vines, the six-handbreadth work area is measured from the trunk of the vine, and not from the tips of the branches; with a hanging vine, the branches are regarded as the trunk (see mishnah 6:2), and the six handbreadths are measured from the tip of the vine along the vine support. Accordingly, planting under a section of a vine support which is not yet occupied by vine but which is within six handbreadths of the tip of the vine will result in condemnation (cf. *Rash*).

אֲבָל תַּחַת הַגֶּפֶן, וַעֲבוֹדַת הַגֶּפֶן, וְאַרְבַּע אַמּוֹת שֶׁבַּכֶּרֶם, הֲרֵי אֵלּוּ מִתְקַדְּשׁוֹת. — *But under*

the vine, the work area of a vine, and the four cubits of the vineyard, these become condemned.

[Many versions read: מְקַדְּשׁוֹת, i.e. these condemn. See *Shinuyei Nuschaos.*]

In the following situations, illegal planting causes condemnation: planting directly under a vine even when the planting is outside the work area of the vine (see mishnah 6:9); planting within the six-handbreadth work area of a vine (see mishnah 6:1); and planting within the four-cubit work area of a vineyard (see mishnah 4:5) (*Rav; Rosh; Rash*).

The mishnah specifies the work area of a vineyard as four cubits but fails to specify the work area of a single vine. Instead, the mishnah refers to *the work area of a vine* without elaboration. This would seem to be due to the fact that there is no disagreement with respect to the extent of the work area of a vineyard, whereas the size of the work area of a vine is the subject of a dispute between R' Akiva and the Sages. To avoid controversy, the mishnah simply refers to *the work area of a vine.*

It might not be remiss at this point to note that although we have generally assumed — following *Rambam* (Comm. to 6:1 and *Hil. Kilayim* 7:1), *Rav* (to mishnah 6:1), and *Shulchan Aruch Yoreh Deah* (296:31) — that the accepted work area of a vine is in fact six handbreadths, there is not unanimous agreement on this point. *Tosafos* (Bava Basra 82b, s.v. זורע), for example, adopt R' Akiva's position that the work area of a vine is three handbreadths (see *Rash* to mishnah 1:8). [Moreover, from *Rashi* (Bava Basra 19b, s.v. המבריך) it appears that the prevailing view is that of R' Yishmael found in *Yerushalmi* (2:8, 4:6; see *R' Shlomo Sirilio* to *Yerushalmi* 3:6) that a single vine has no work area at all. For an extensive summary of the different opinions, see *Beur HaHalachah* 6:3, s.v. אלא ששה טפחים.]

---

1. Some versions of *Yerushalmi* (6:3) read six *cubits* rather than six handbreadths. See *Ri ben Malki Tzedek* and *R' Shlomo Sirilio.*

[ד] הַמְסַכֵּךְ אֶת גַּפְנוֹ עַל גַּבֵּי תְבוּאָתוֹ שֶׁל חֲבֵירוֹ, הֲרֵי זֶה קָדַשׁ, וְחַיָּב בְּאַחֲרָיוּתוֹ. רַבִּי יוֹסֵי וְרַבִּי שִׁמְעוֹן אוֹמְרִים: אֵין אָדָם מְקַדֵּשׁ דָּבָר שֶׁאֵינוֹ שֶׁלּוֹ.

יד אברהם

4.

הַמְסַכֵּךְ אֶת גַּפְנוֹ עַל גַּבֵּי תְבוּאָתוֹ שֶׁל חֲבֵירוֹ, הֲרֵי זֶה קָדַשׁ, — [If] someone positions his vine so that it overshadows the grain of his fellow, this condemns,

In the previous mishnah it was taught that foreign planting which is overshadowed by vine constitutes *kilayim* and causes condemnation from use. The present *Tanna* (who is identified in *Yevamos* 83a as R' Meir; see also *Tos.* to *Bava Kamma* 100a) states that even if the vine belongs to Reuven and the grain belongs to Shimon, the result of Reuven's placing his vine over Shimon's grain is that Reuven's vine as well as Shimon's grain become forbidden for use.

The condemnation of Shimon's grain would seem to be in conflict with the principle that a person cannot condemn that which is not his[1] (see *Avodah Zarah* 54b). Evidently, R' Meir had a Biblical inference indicating that *kilayim* is an exception (*Rav* from *Rash*; see *Tos. Yom Tov* and *Mareh HaPanim*, s.v. כתיב; for an alternative approach, see *Tos. Rid* [*Mahadura Telisaah*] to *Avodah Zarah* 54a).

וְחַיָּב בְּאַחֲרָיוּתוֹ. — and he is responsible for it.

Reuven is obligated to compensate Shimon for the grain which has been rendered forbidden for use.

The condemnation of the grain does not take effect immediately upon the overshadowing of the grain. Only if the vine remains over the grain and the state of *kilayim* persists long enough for a growth of more than one part in two hundred to occur is

there condemnation (*Yerushalmi; Mishnah Rishonah; Lechem Shamayim* quoted in *Tos. Anshei Shem*; see above, mishnah 5:6). Moreover, the damage is perpetrated here without Reuven directly touching Shimon's grain. Accordingly, it might have been argued that for such an indirect sort of damage, compensation cannot be extracted from Reuven. The mishnah therefore teaches that Reuven *is* responsible for it and must compensate Shimon for having effectively destroyed his grain. The *Gemara* (*Bava Kamma* 100a) explains that even those who ordinarily exempt the perpetrator of indirect damage from payment concede that in the present case he is liable. This is because the damage was caused by Reuven's positive action of moving the vine over Shimon's grain. As such, it is not regarded as indirect damage at all (*Rav; Rosh; Rash*).

Yerushalmi seems to maintain that those who ordinarily exempt the perpetrator of indirect damage from payment do so in this case also, and they would not hold Reuven liable. The mishnah which rules that payment is due in the present case reflects the opinion of those who normally obligate payment for indirect damage (see *Ridbaz*, s.v. רשב"ל and see also *Tos. Chadashim*, s.v. וחייב).

רַבִּי יוֹסֵי וְרַבִּי שִׁמְעוֹן אוֹמְרִים: אֵין אָדָם מְקַדֵּשׁ דָּבָר שֶׁאֵינוֹ שֶׁלּוֹ. — R' Yose and R' Shimon say: A person cannot condemn something which is not his.

This is derived from the words *your vineyard* (*Deut.* 22:9), which indicate that the laws of *kilayim* of the vineyard apply only to planting one's own vine-

---

1. Actually, from *Yerushalmi* it appears that R' Meir disputes this principle entirely and maintains in general that a person *is* capable of condemning someone else's property. However, the *Rishonim* seem to assume that in general R' Meir accepts this rule, but considers the case of *kilayim* to be an exception.

4. [I]f] someone positions his vine so that it over-shadows the grain of his fellow, this condemns, and he is responsible for it. R' Yose and R' Shimon say: A person cannot condemn something which is not his.

YAD AVRAHAM

yard. Thus, a person cannot condemn as *kilayim* someone else's grain, or someone else's vineyard (*Rav; Rosh; Rash*).

If a person cooks meat in someone else's milk, R' Yose and R' Shimon agree that both the meat and the milk become forbidden for use, even though the milk did not belong to the person who owned and cooked the meat. Thus, in general they maintain that it *is* possible to condemn someone else's property from use[1]; an exception is made in the mishnah's case only because of the Biblical exclusion noted above (see *Rash*, second explanation).

Alternatively, a distinction may be made between two classes of prohibitions: those in which a physical condition causes the condemnation, and those in which the person's intent causes the condemnation. Where the physical state generates the condemnation, it is possible for one person to condemn the property of another; where it is not the physical state which generates the condemnation, it is not possible to condemn another person's property.

In the case of milk and meat, it is the intermixing of the milk with the meat via cooking which causes the condemnation. This condition exists regardless of who owns or cooks the milk and meat. Accordingly, it will become condemned even if the milk does not belong to the person who cooks it with meat. In the case of idolatry, on the other hand, the person's intent is critical. For example, if he bows to something without intending the object of his bowing as an idol, it does not become prohibited. Since the condemnation of an idol is generated by the person's intent, a person cannot condemn as an idol the property of someone else. Such property is outside of his sphere of influence, and is not intrinsically

affected by his thoughts. It is thus beyond his ability to render it condemned in this fashion.

According to this approach, *kilayim* is categorized as a prohibition belonging to the class of prohibitions for which a person's intent is critical to the creation of a condemned state. This can be demonstrated by considering the law stated in mishnah 5:6 that if a person approves of the presence of *kilayim* in his vineyard, then a condemnation will result, whereas if he opposes its presence, no condemnation results. The physical proximity of vine to grain does not cause condemnation without the vineyard owner's approval of such a condition. Since a person's approval is critical, it follows that the condemnation of *kilayim* cannot be effected by one person in the property of another (*Tosafos Yevamos* 83b; see *Rash* and *Hagahos R' Akiva Eiger* [complete edition] to *Shulchan Aruch Orach Chaim* 253:2).

Although R' Yose and R' Shimon clearly state that Shimon's grain is not condemned, they do not discuss the status of Reuven's vine. The matter is disputed in *Yerushalmi* by R' Yochanan who assumes Reuven's vine to be condemned, and R' Elazar who assumes that Reuven's vine is treated no differently than Shimon's grain and is not condemned. Evidently, R' Yochanan assumes that the combination of Reuven's vine with Shimon's grain does constitute *kilayim*; however, Shimon's grain is excluded from condemnation. R' Elazar assumes that the vine of one person with the grain of another is not *kilayim* at all, and there is no condemnation whatsoever.

1. This follows *Yerushalmi* which maintains that if Reuven bows down to Shimon's animal, the animal becomes disqualified for sacrifice since it is an object of idol worship.
Bavli (*Avodah Zarah* 54b, *Chullin* 40a-b) assumes it to be universally agreed that Reuven's bowing has no effect whatsoever on Shimon's animal.

[ה] **אָמַר** רַבִּי יוֹסֵי: מַעֲשֶׂה בְּאֶחָד שֶׁזָּרַע אֶת כַּרְמוֹ בַּשְּׁבִיעִית. וּבָא מַעֲשֶׂה לִפְנֵי רַבִּי עֲקִיבָא, וְאָמַר: אֵין אָדָם מְקַדֵּשׁ דָּבָר שֶׁאֵינוֹ שֶׁלּוֹ.

[ו] **הָאַנָס** שֶׁזָּרַע אֶת הַכֶּרֶם וְיָצָא מִלְּפָנָיו,

יד אברהם

It should be noted that if R' Yose and R' Shimon imply their position from the words *your vineyard* in the verse which prohibits planting *kilayim* — *you shall not plant your vineyard kilayim* (Deut. 22:9) — then it would seem that a combination of one person's vine with another's grain should not constitute *kilayim* at all (*Mishnah Rishonah*). However, if their reason is that condemnations generated by a mental attitude cannot be effected in someone else's property (see above), then this relates exclusively to the condemnation. The combination of Reuven's vine with Shimon's grain may indeed constitute *kilayim*, which it is forbidden to create, but such *kilayim* will not result in condemnation of Shimon's grain.

Tosafos (*Yevamos* 83a, s.v. רבי יוסי) write that according to R' Yose and R' Shimon the combination of one person's vine with another's grain does not at all constitute *kilayim* and neither the grain nor the vine becomes condemned. This is consistent with the opinion of R' Elazar in *Yerushalmi*. However, *Rambam* (*Hil. Kilayim* 5:8) rules that if Reuven places his vine over Shimon's grain, then Reuven's vine is condemned even though Shimon's grain is not. This accords with R' Yochanan's opinion (see also *Rash* from *Menachos* 15b).

5.

The mishnah continues to investigate whether or not a person can condemn something which is not his. R' Yose, who in mishnah 4 takes the position that a person cannot condemn something which is not his, reports a ruling of R' Akiva which supports this viewpoint.

אָמַר רַבִּי יוֹסֵי: מַעֲשֶׂה בְּאֶחָד שֶׁזָּרַע אֶת כַּרְמוֹ בַּשְּׁבִיעִית. — *R' Yose said: It happened once that someone planted his vineyard during sheviis.*

Sheviis, the seventh year, is the Sabbatical year during which planting is forbidden, and any produce which grows is rendered ownerless and available for all to take (*Rav*; see General Introduction to ArtScroll *Sheviis*). Grapes, for example, which grow during *sheviis* do not belong to the owner of the vineyard but are ownerless property which anyone is entitled to take for himself. If someone violates both the prohibition on planting during *sheviis*, as well as the prohibition on planting in vineyards, by planting wheat in his vineyard during *sheviis*, the status of the grapes as well as the wheat depends on the question of whether a person can cause that which does not belong to him to become condemned.

וּבָא מַעֲשֶׂה לִפְנֵי רַבִּי עֲקִיבָא, וְאָמַר: אֵין אָדָם מְקַדֵּשׁ דָּבָר שֶׁאֵינוֹ שֶׁלּוֹ. — *The incident came before R' Akiva, and he said: A person cannot condemn something which is not his.*

R' Akiva ruled that nothing is condemned in this case since neither the grapes nor the wheat belong to the planter, and a person cannot condemn that which is not his (*Rash* from *Yerushalmi*).

The mishnah does not seem to distinguish

5. R' Yose said: It happened once that someone planted his vineyard during *sheviis*. The incident came before R' Akiva, and he said: A person cannot condemn something which is not his.

6. [If] a robber plants a vineyard and then it leaves his

YAD AVRAHAM

between a case in which the wheat and vine which constitute *kilayim* are owned by people and the case in which they are ownerless. In both instances, one or both of the components are not owned by the one who causes *kilayim* and hence both are subject to the law that a person cannot condemn that which is not his. Therefore, it is clear that Reuven's inability to cause Shimon's grain to be forbidden to use is not because of Shimon's ownership of the grain, but rather because Reuven can only affect that which is within his domain. Something outside of his domain, even if it is ownerless, can therefore not be condemned by him (*Oneg Yom Tov* §83).

6.

הָאַנָּס שֶׁזָּרַע אֶת הַכֶּרֶם וְיָצָא מִלְּפָנָיו, — *[If] a robber plants a vineyard and then it leaves his [control]*,

A violent non-Jewish robber (*Ri ben Malki Tzedek*) took control of a Jewish person's vineyard by force and planted it with grain. Later, the vineyard returned to the control of the original Jewish owner,[1] who now has a vineyard with grain growing in it (*Rav; Rosh*). The mishnah now discusses the procedure which the owner must follow to eliminate the *kilayim* from his vineyard.

קוֹצְרוֹ אֲפִילוּ בַּמּוֹעֵד. — *[the owner] harvests even during the festival.*

The owner[2] must immediately remove the grain from the vineyard, even if he regained control of the vineyard during *Chol Hamoed* (the intermediate days of a festival), when harvesting is normally forbidden. The Rabbis were concerned lest the owner appear to be illegally maintaining *kilayim* in his vineyard, and they therefore permitted harvesting of the grain even during *Chol Hamoed* (*Rav; Rosh*).

Ordinarily, it is permitted during *Chol Hamoed* to engage in otherwise forbidden activities whose neglect would result in financial loss. The present case seems to involve financial loss, since delaying the removal of the *kilayim* from the vineyard long enough for an additional 200th part to grow causes the vineyard to become condemned from use (see mishnah 5:6).[3] Nevertheless, *Rav* following *Rosh* states that the right to harvest the grain during *Chol Hamoed* is not due to the consideration that delaying its removal will cause a loss, but rather to the fact that the Rabbis were

1. The phrase וְיָצָא מִלְּפָנָיו has been translated following *Rav* and *Rosh* as *it leaves his [control]*, i.e. the vineyard leaves the robber's control and returns to the control of the original owner. However, *Rambam* (Hil. Kilayim 5:12) seems to have understood this phrase as referring to the robber; i.e. *he [the robber] leaves it [the vineyard]*.

2. Had the robber been a Jew, it is possible that it would be the robber's responsibility to remove the *kilayim*, rather than the owner's responsibility (see *Chazon Ish* 3:16, s.v. ויש).

3. When the vineyard was retrieved by the owner, the grapes were still permitted despite the presence of *kilayim*. The thief's planting of grain in the vineyard did not affect the permitted status of the vineyard since a person cannot condemn another person's property (*Rosh* from mishnah 4; see *Tos. Yom Tov* and *Rishon LeTzion*).

קוֹצְרוֹ אֲפִילוּ בַמּוֹעֵד. עַד כַּמָּה הוּא נוֹתֵן לְפוֹעֲלִים? עַד שְׁלִישׁ. יָתֵר מִכָּאן, קוֹצֵר כְּדַרְכּוֹ וְהוֹלֵךְ אֲפִילוּ לְאַחַר הַמּוֹעֵד. מֵאֵימָתַי הוּא נִקְרָא אַנָס? מִשֶּׁיִּשְׁקַע.

יד אברהם

concerned lest it appear as though the vineyard owner was maintaining kilayim illegally. Evidently, it must be assumed that in the present case it is certain that an additional growth of a 200th part will not occur as a result of delaying the removal of the kilayim until after the festival. Thus, postponement of the removal of the grain would not cause the owner any financial loss. Nonetheless, the mishnah mandates its removal even on Chol Hamoed, by reason of a special Rabbinic allowance (Rosh).

Alternatively, the harvesting of the grain here even during Chol Hamoed is not a special exception in order to prevent the impression that the owner is illegally maintaining kilayim. Rather, it is a reflection of the general rule that activities whose neglect will result in financial loss are permitted during Chol Hamoed. Delaying the removal of kilayim long enough for a growth of an additional 200th part to occur causes condemnation of the vineyard. If such growth might occur if the removal of kilayim is postponed until after the festival, then removal is deemed an activity whose neglect involves financial loss. Accordingly, it is permitted to remove the grain even on Chol Hamoed (Rav second explanation; Rosh).

A delay in removal of kilayim causes a condemnation only when such neglect can be interpreted as acceptance, however temporary, of the presence of the kilayim. Thus, if a person says that as soon as he gets to the kilayim he will remove it, no condemnation results even if in the interim there has been an increase of a 200th part (mishnah 5:6). Accordingly, R' Akiva Eiger questions why postponement of the removal of the kilayim until after the festival should generate condemnation. Since the owner delays the removal only because it is forbidden to harvest on Chol Hamoed, not because he wants the

kilayim, such delay should not generate any condemnation. And since the delay will not cause any condemnation, it will not involve any financial loss. Therefore, unless we follow the first interpretation and posit a specific Rabbinic enactment to permit this case, it is difficult to understand why the possibility of a 200th increase should allow the owner to engage in an activity (harvesting) which is normally forbidden during Chol Hamoed.

עַד כַּמָּה הוּא נוֹתֵן לְפוֹעֲלִים? עַד שְׁלִישׁ. יָתֵר מִכָּאן, קוֹצֵר כְּדַרְכּוֹ וְהוֹלֵךְ אֲפִילוּ לְאַחַר הַמּוֹעֵד. — How much must he give to workers? Up to a third. More than this, he harvests his usual way and continues even after the festival.

Even if it is only possible to hire workers for a third more than the normal wage, the owner of the vineyard is required to do so in order to expedite the removal of the kilayim. Alternatively, the owner must spend up to one-third the value of the grapes and the grain to hire workers. He is not required to pay more than this, however, even if this will delay the complete removal of the kilayim until after the festival (Rav, Rosh, Rash from Yerushalmi).

A person is required to spend all his money even to avoid a passive transgression of a Rabbinic prohibition (Shulchan Aruch Yoreh Deah 157; Hagahos R' Akiva Eiger and Hagahos HaGra ibid.). Nevertheless, the mishnah sets a spending limit here because when neglecting to remove kilayim is not willful, such neglect is not regarded as maintaining kilayim and does not constitute a transgression. When removing kilayim becomes unbearably expensive, it is assumed that a person's failure to remove it does not derive from acceptance of the kilayim, but rather from financial strain. Under such circumstances, leaving the kilayim in place does not constitute a transgression (Chazon Ish 4:14).

7　　[control], [the owner] harvests even during the festival.

6　　How much must he give to workers? Up to a third.
More than this, he harvests his usual way and continues
even after the festival. From when is he called a robber?
From when [the name of the original owner] sinks.

מֵאֵימָתַי הוּא נִקְרָא אַנָּס? מִשֶּׁיִּשְׁקַע. — *From
when is he called a robber? From when
[the name of the original owner] sinks.*

When does the vineyard become the
property of the robber? From the time
that the original owner's name is no
longer associated with the vineyard — i.e.
his name sinks from the public conscious-
ness. At that point, if the thief plants or
maintains *kilayim* in the vineyard, even
the vineyard will be condemned, since
the vineyard now belongs to him (*Rav;
Rosh; Rash*). *Rambam Comm.* explains
מִשֶּׁיִּשְׁקַע to mean when the owner goes
into hiding. If the owner sinks from view
out of fear of the violent thief, then he has
forfeited the vineyard.

The mishnah thus deals with two cases.
In the first case, the owner's name has not
been forgotten, and hence the planting
by the thief does not cause condemnation
of the vineyard, since a person cannot
condemn that which is not his. In the second case, the vineyard actually becomes
the property of the thief, and accordingly
his planting it generates condemnation.
[If the thief abandons the vineyard after
it has become his, then whoever acquires
it acquires a vineyard forbidden for use,
since it has become condemned by the
thief's planting of *kilayim*.]

Gra (*Shenos Eliyahu*) explains the mishnah's question here with reference to the first
case. Unlike the other major commentators,
he assumes that in the mishnah's first case
the vineyard was in fact condemned by the
time it returned to the control of the original
owner. He posits further that the urgency in
removing the *kilayim*, which is evidenced by
the requirement to spend extra money to
remove it even on *Chol Hamoed*, is due
precisely to this fact — that the *kilayim* has
already been condemned. Accordingly, the
mishnah proceeds to investigate at what

point in fact the vineyard becomes the thief's
so that his planting will generate condemnation. It answers that this occurs when the
name of the original owner is no longer
associated with the vineyard. It is such a case
which was discussed in the first part of the
mishnah, and only in such a case must a
person spend additional money to remove
the *kilayim* even on *Chol Hamoed*. But if the
vineyard did not become the thief's, so that
his planting did not condemn it, then when it
returns to the original owner, he need not
pressure himself to remove the *kilayim* before the end of the festival. Since nothing has
been condemned, there is no urgency in
removing it during *Chol Hamoed* when
harvesting is generally forbidden. The delay
in removing it until after the festival does not
constitute maintenance of *kilayim* and hence
it is permissible.

The notion that once the name of the
original owner is no longer associated
with the vineyard, the vineyard is forfeited and becomes the property of the
thief, would seem to conflict with the
principle that *land cannot be stolen*
(*Succah* 30b; see *Bava Kamma* 117b).
Rash explains that although giving up
hope on stolen land does not normally
make it the property of the thief,
when the owner's name is no longer
associated with the property there is no
chance of retrieval at all. Under such
circumstances, even land can be stolen
(see also *Tosafos* to *Succah* 30b, *Rosh*
here and *Tosafos HaRosh* to *Succah*
30b; see also *Marcheshes-Kunteres
HaYiush*). [*Tosafos* to *Bava Basra* 44a
take the position that even the normal
loss of hope, not accompanied by dissoci-
ation of the original owner's name from
the property, is also sufficient to give a
thief proprietary rights to the stolen land.
See *Shach, Choshen Mishpat* 371:2.]

[ז] **הָרוּחַ** שֶׁעִלְעֲלָה אֶת הַגְּפָנִים עַל גַּבֵּי תְבוּאָה, יִגְדֹּר מִיָּד; אִם אֵרְעוֹ אֹנֶס, מֻתָּר.

תְּבוּאָתוֹ שֶׁהִיא נוֹטָה תַּחַת הַגֶּפֶן, וְכֵן בְּיָרָק, מַחֲזִיר וְאֵינוֹ מְקַדֵּשׁ.

יד אברהם

7.

The first part of the following mishnah deals with overshadowing of grain by vine, and the second part addresses the question of when the grain and the vine become condemned. This mishnah is one of the most important sources for determining the rules of condemnation of *kilayim*.

הָרוּחַ שֶׁעִלְעֲלָה אֶת הַגְּפָנִים עַל גַּבֵּי תְבוּאָה, יִגְדֹּר מִיָּד; — *[If] the wind blew vines over grain, he must cut [them] at once;*

Grain was planted at the requisite distance away from the vines, but a strong gust of wind blew[1] some branches of the vines over the grain. As soon as the farmer discovers this overshadowing, he must correct the situation by removing the vines.

The term יִגְדֹּר is used by the mishnah to describe what must be done to the overshadowing vine branches. *Rav* relates this verb to that for harvesting dates (גּוֹדֵר), which means cutting and collecting. That is, he must cut off these overshadowing branches from the vine and remove them. Others explain that this term is derived from the word גֶּדֶר, *fence*, and means that a fence must be erected to prevent recurrence of this event. According to this understanding, the person would not be required to sever the branches from the vine, but must remove them from over the grain and fence them in so that they cannot return to overshadow the grain again (*Ri ben Malki Tzedek; Rash; Rosh*). Some texts

read: יִגְרֹר, which means to drag away or remove (*R' Shlomo Sirilio*), while others have: יִגְרֹד, which is explained as meaning to lift and remove (*Rambam Comm.* Kafich ed.; see *Hil. Kilayim* 5:11; *Kesef Mishneh* and *Mahari Korkus* ad loc.).

Since the farmer's objective is to remove the vines from over the grain, it is not clear why the mishnah specifies (according to *Rav's* explanation) that the branches must be cut. *Tos. Yom Tov* suggests that the branches have broken in the wind and become partly severed from the vine, so that pulling them away from the grain will not help. Only cutting them off completely will prevent them from returning to overshadow the grain.

אִם אֵרְעוֹ אֹנֶס, מֻתָּר. — *if some accident befalls him, it is permitted.*

If something occurred which made it impossible for the person to remove the vines right away, no condemnation results as long as he removes them as soon as possible. For example, if he suffered a bereavement necessitating a period of mourning during which it is forbidden to do work, or if he hired workers to remove the vines and they failed to appear, the farmer is not viewed as

1. Our translation of עִלְעֲלָה as blowing follows *Rav, Rosh, Rash,* and *Ri ben Malki Tzedek* and derives from *Aruch,* s.v. עלעל. This definition is based on the Targum of the term *storm wind* as רוּחַ עַלְעוֹלָא in *Psalms* 148:8 and *Ezekiel* 1:4. *Rambam Comm.,* however, relates this verb to the Aramaic term for rib, עלעא, and explains עִלְעֲלָה as the movement of a branch (rib) of the vine. That is, the wind caused a branch to overshadow the grain (see also *Tosafos* to *Chullin* 22b, s.v. יעלעו דם).

7. **[I** f] the wind blew vines over grain, he must cut [them] at once; if some accident befalls him, it is permitted.

[If] his grain leans under a vine, and likewise with greens, he returns it and it does not condemn.

negligent with respect to removal of the kilayim (Ri ben Malki Tzedek; see Moed Katan 12b). However, as soon as he can, he must attend to its removal since any willful delay in removal will cause a condemnation (see mishnah 5:6).

תְּבוּאָתוֹ שֶׁהִיא נוֹטָה תַּחַת הַגֶּפֶן, וְכֵן בְּיָרָק, מַחֲזִיר וְאֵינוֹ מְקַדֵּשׁ. — *[If] his grain leans under a vine, and likewise with greens, he returns it and it does not condemn.*

Here again the grain or greens was planted in a permissible location. However, in the course of its growth it bent over so that its tip came under a vine. Since the grain or greens is overshadowed by the vine, the situation must be corrected. The mishnah therefore states that the farmer must remove the grain or greens from under the vine and return it to its proper place.

Tosefta 4:7 records a dispute between R' Akiva and Ben Azai with respect to greens which lean under a vine. R' Akiva rules that it suffices to return the greens to their proper place, while Ben Azai maintains that the leaves which reached under the vine must be trimmed. Regarding grain, however, all agree that it is sufficient to restore the grain to its proper place away from the vine, and no trimming is required. The additional precautions insisted upon by Ben Azai in the case of greens may be due to the greater tendency of greens in general to grow horizontally. Moving the leaves out from under the vine might not prevent them from growing back there, and for this reason Ben Azai requires them to be cut off. On the other hand, grain normally grows vertically, so that in the rare case in which it leans over until its tip is under a vine, it is sufficient to return it to its proper spot. It may also be that trimming grain inhibits the production of seed and is therefore not re-

quired. Whatever the reason, it seems likely that the mishnah's specification — *likewise with greens* — is intended to exclude Ben Azai's view. The mishnah stresses that even with greens it is sufficient to move the plant out from under the vine and no trimming is necessary.

The mishnah states that the owner must return the grain or greens and *it does not condemn.* Rav, following Rosh, explains this to mean that even if the owner did not return the grain or greens to its proper place, but rather left it under the vine, no condemnation results. Although above (mishnah 3) it was clearly stated that overshadowing causes condemnation, this is only when the point at which the stem of the grain or greens emerges from the ground is overshadowed. Thus, if a vine overshadows an entire plant, condemnation will result. But in the present case, the grain or greens was not planted under the vine. Only the tip of the grain or a leaf of the green protrudes into the area overshadowed by the vine, but the site at which the stem of the grain or greens emerges from the ground is not overshadowed at all. In such a case, no condemnation results even if the tip of the plant is left under the vine. Nevertheless, it is incumbent upon the owner to move the tip out of the way so that it does not remain under the vine; however, if he failed to do so, *it does not condemn.*[1]

Ravad (quoted by *Ritva* to *Eruvin* 92b, s.v. גפנים) understands the mishnah as teaching that in a situation in which the grain or greens are planted legally, but are subsequently overshadowed by vine, the usual rules for condemnation do not apply. When the planting

---

1. *Rambam* makes no explicit distinction between overshadowing of the main stem and overshadowing of the tip of the plant (*Chazon Ish* 13:4; *Derech Emunah* 6:58).

יד אברהם

itself is illegal, the grain or greens become condemned as soon as they take root. In the present case, however, in which the planting was legal, the plants will only become condemned when their produce attains a third of its growth. According to *Ravad's* text of the mishnah, this critical detail — that once the one-third stage is reached condemnation occurs — is in fact spelled out in the course of the mishnah (see below).

◈§ Condemnation of Kilayim of the Vineyard

Concerning *kilayim* of the vineyard, the Torah writes: לֹא־תִזְרַע כַּרְמְךָ כִּלְאָיִם פֶּן־תִּקְדַּשׁ הַמְלֵאָה הַזֶּרַע אֲשֶׁר תִּזְרָע וּתְבוּאַת הַכָּרֶם, *You shall not sow your vineyard with a mixture, lest the fullness of the seed which you have sown be forfeit along with the product of the vineyard* (*Deut.* 22:9). Evidently it is at the stage known as the *fullness of the seed* for grain and greens, and *product of the vineyard* for grapevines, that condemnation of the *kilayim* takes effect.

The phrase used by the Torah to refer to the stage at which the grain or greens are condemned is הַמְלֵאָה הַזֶּרַע. This obscure and seemingly repetitious phrase is expounded by the *Gemara* (*Pesachim* 25a) as referring to two distinct situations. In one situation, the condemnation takes effect on the seed as soon as it starts to grow; while in the other, condemnation affects only a later stage in growth known as *kilayim*.

In the first situation, *kilayim* is created by planting seeds of grape and grain together, so that both the vine and the grain have been planted illegally from the start. Since the *kilayim* is created in the seed state, as soon as *kilayim* growth begins, i.e. as soon as the seeds take root, condemnation sets in. It is this case which

the Torah refers to with הַזֶּרַע, *the seed*. Thus, if someone plants grape and grain seeds together illegally, both the vine and the grain plants will become condemned as soon as they take root.

In the second case, the vine and the grain have been planted legally in separate areas. However, the grain, for example, was planted in a perforated flowerpot[1] and subsequently moved to the vineyard and set down next to a vine. In this second case, both the vine and the grain began their growth legally, and only later on were they brought together into a *kilayim* situation. As will be explained below, in this case condemnation takes effect only once the plants have reached a stage known as *fullness*. In the case of grain, this corresponds to the one-third state — i.e. the point at which the produce reaches one-third of its eventual size. In the case of the grapevine, this is when the grapes reach the size of a hyacinth bean (see below, s.v. וענבים).

Yerushalmi (5:6 and 7:5) records a dispute between R' Hoshaya and R' Yochanan in cases where one of the two components of the *kilayim* was planted legally. According to R' Hoshaya, if grain was planted near an existing vine, or if a grape seed was planted near standing grain, both components would become condemned only at the stage of fullness. R' Yochanan, on the other hand, judges each component independently, condemning the legally planted component as of "fullness," but condemning the illegally planted one from the moment it takes root. Thus, in his opinion, if a seed of grain was planted near a growing vine, the grain seed will be condemned from the moment it takes

---

1. The flowerpot must be perforated so that the grain will be considered to be growing from the ground, and is thus an eligible component of *kilayim* — see next mishnah. The law would be the same if the grain was initially planted in the ground in a legal spot, and later transplanted. The case of the flowerpot is borrowed from the next mishnah.

From when is grain condemned? From when it takes
root.

root, but the vine (which had been legally planted) will only be condemned on reaching fullness. Similarly, if a grape seed was planted next to standing grain, he rules that the grape seed would be condemned from the moment it takes root, while the grain (which had been legally planted) would only be condemned when it reaches fullness (*Rash*).

מֵאֵימָתַי תְּבוּאָה מִתְקַדֶּשֶׁת? מִשֶּׁתַּשְׁרִישׁ.
From when is grain condemned? From when it takes root.

Some versions read: מִשֶּׁתַּשְׁלִישׁ, *From when it reaches the one-third stage* (*Rav; Rash; Ri ben Malki Tzedek*), this being the point at which the produce has attained one-third of its eventual size[1] (see *Maasros* 1:3 and ArtScroll *Sheviis* 4:9).

Yerushalmi attributes the reading מִשֶּׁתַּשְׁרִישׁ, *from when it takes root*, to R' Yochanan, and the reading מִשֶּׁתַּשְׁלִישׁ, *from when it reaches the one-third stage*, to R' Hoshaya.[2]

Yerushalmi assumes that the mishnah's case is where grain was illegally planted near an already growing legally planted vine. In such a case, the law according to R' Hoshaya is that the grain will be condemned only upon reaching the one-third stage. Consequently, the text must read: מִשֶּׁתַּשְׁלִישׁ, *from when it reaches the one-third stage*. According to R' Yochanan, the grain is condemned

as of taking root, even though the vine is condemned at *fullness*. Accordingly, the mishnah must give root-taking (מִשֶּׁתַּשְׁרִישׁ) as the condemnation stage of the grain (*Tos. R' Akiva*).

Aside from rooting and fullness, we have already encountered a third measure of growth at which condemnation takes effect: an increase of a two-hundredth (see mishnah 5:6 and 7:8). *Rash* contends that this law applies where the vine and the grain have already passed the fullness stage by the time they become *kilayim* — i.e. the grapes are the size of hyacinth beans, and the grain has reached one-third its eventual size. In such a case, if they increase by a two-hundredth while growing together as *kilayim*, then condemnation takes effect. Thus, the case in mishnah 5:6, for instance, must be that the farmer first discovered the *kilayim* after the grain was already beyond the one-third stage. If he tarries in removing it long enough for it to increase by a two-hundredth part it will become condemned.

Rash also discusses the status of the wood of a condemned vine and the stalks of condemned grain. He appears to conclude that where the condemnation takes effect with rooting, then the entire plant is condemned. Not only are the grapes of the vine forbidden for use, but the vine itself is also forbidden for benefit. Likewise, if grain is condemned from the time it takes root, then the stalk as well as the ear is condemned. But if condemnation takes effect at the one-third stage for grain, or the hyacinth-bean stage for grapes, the condemnation affects only the ear of the grain and the grapes, but not the

1. *Rav* writes that the source for the condemnation of the grain only when it reaches the one-third stage is the wording of the Torah (*Deut.* 22:9): וּתְבוּאַת הַכָּרֶם, *and the product of the vineyard*, a description which is only apt for a somewhat developed grain. This derivation, however, seems odd since the quoted phrase refers to the product of the vine and not to the grain. Indeed, for this reason, it is tempting to consider an emendation of *Rav* according to which the intended reference is to the words הַמְלֵאָה הַזֶּרַע, *the fullness of the seed*, which in fact refers to the grain (*Mishnah Rishonah*). It must be noted, however, that both from *Rosh* and R' *Shlomo Sirilio*, it also appears that the inference concerning grain is from the words וּתְבוּאַת הַכָּרֶם.

2. Actually, the standard printed versions have the reverse, but it is clear from the context that this is the correct reading (see *Pnei Moshe*).

וַעֲנָבִים? מִשֶּׁיֵּעָשׂוּ כְּפוֹל הַלָּבָן. תְּבוּאָה שֶׁיָּבְשָׁה כָּל צָרְכָּהּ, וַעֲנָבִים שֶׁבָּשְׁלוּ כָּל צָרְכָּן, אֵין מִתְקַדְּשׁוֹת.

יד אברהם

stalk or vine. However, *Rash* entertains the possibility that even in the latter case the wood and stalks will be condemned if they increase by a two-hundredth part (see *Chazon Ish* 3:17-18, 27; for a summary of the different opinions on this question see *Beur HaHalachah* 5:7, s.v. הקש; see also *Tziyun HaHalachah* 5:160).

⋙ **Condemnation of One Component Without the Other**

According to *Rash's* explanation of R' Yochanan, the condemnation of *kilayim* operates independently for each component. If grain seeds are planted in a growing vineyard, for example, the grain will become condemned upon taking root, even if the grapes on the vine have not yet reached the critical size of a hyacinth bean. If the condemned grain is uprooted before the grapes reach this stage, so that at the time that they attain the size of hyacinth beans, there is no longer *kilayim* in the vineyard, the grapes will not become condemned. Similarly, if a person plants grape seeds in a growing grain field in which the grain has not yet reached the one-third stage, the vine is condemned from the moment it takes root, but the grain remains permitted until it reaches the one-third stage. If in the meantime the vine has been removed, then the grain is not forbidden for use.

⋙ **Condemnation of Kilayim of the Vineyard According to Rambam**

Rambam (*Hil. Kilayim* 5:13-16) disputes the approach of *Rash* and views the condemnation of one component as dependent on the condemnation of the other. In his opinion, there can never be condemnation of either component unless they have both reached their critical stages. *Rambam* rules that the critical stage for grain or greens is when they take root, while the critical stage for vines is when the grapes reach the size of a hyacinth bean. Thus, if someone plants grain in a vineyard whose grapes are not yet the size of a hyacinth bean, no condemnation results even when the grain takes root. Similarly, if someone plants grain in a vineyard whose grapes have reached the critical size, but he removes the grain before it takes root, no condemnation of the grapes or grain occurs. Only when the grapes are the size of hyacinth beans, and the grain or greens take root, will there be condemnation, and it will include both the vines and the grain. *Rambam* learns this from the verse (*Deut.* 22:9): *lest the fullness of the seed which you have sown be forfeit along with the product of the vineyard.* He understands that the condition for condemnation is that the grain or greens be at the fullness stage (which he takes to mean rooting), and at the same time the vine is at the product stage (which is once the grapes are the size of hyacinth beans).[1] Since *Rav* adopts *Rambam's* approach in his explanation of the rest of the mishnah, this approach will be given priority.

If a person brought an already growing plant of grain or greens into a vineyard, *Rambam* (*Hil. Kilayim* 5:23) maintains that it will become condemned upon growing an additional two-hundredth part. This will be discussed further in the next mishnah.

וַעֲנָבִים? מִשֶּׁיֵּעָשׂוּ כְּפוֹל הַלָּבָן. — *And grapes? From when they reach the size of*

1. Note that according to *Rambam*, the rooting of a grapevine is not relevant to its condemnation, and there is no significance, with respect to condemnation, in grain reaching the one-third stage.

7
7
And grapes? From when they reach the size of a hyacinth bean.

Grain which has dried to its full extent, and grapes which have ripened to their fullest, do not become condemned.

a hyacinth bean.

According to *Rambam*, if someone plants grain or greens in a vineyard whose grapes have not yet reached the size of hyacinth beans, and then uproots the grain or greens before the grapes reach this size, no condemnation will result. Although the grain or greens were planted and took root illegally in the vineyard, no condemnation takes effect until the grapes reach the size of a hyacinth bean. If by the time the grapes reach this size, there is no longer *kilayim* in the vineyard, no condemnation is effected at all (*Rav; Rambam, Hil. Kilayim* 5:14). [*Rambam* (ibid.) maintains that although no Biblical condemnation occurs, nevertheless if someone planted grain or greens in a vineyard in which the grapes were not yet the size of hyacinth beans, the Rabbis penalized him by declaring the grain or greens forbidden for use as soon as they take root. His source for this is *Menachos* 15b (*Radbaz* ad loc.).]

If the grapes of the vineyard are already the size of hyacinth beans when the owner plants grain or greens in his vineyard, everything will become condemned as soon as the grain or greens take root.[1] If the owner removes the grain or greens before they take root, then no condemnation results and even the grapes remain permitted (*Rav; Rambam, Hil. Kilayim* 5:15).

In both preceding cases (assuming that R' Yochanan's position prevails), *Rash* would presumably rule that one of the components is condemned. In the first case in which the grapes have not yet reached the critical size, *Rash* would permit the grapes, but would

regard the grain or greens which took root illegally in the vineyard as Biblically condemned from that point. In the second case, planting seeds in a vineyard whose grapes have already reached the critical size would cause immediate condemnation of the grapes, even before the grain or greens have taken root. Possibly, the grapes will be condemned only after an increase of a two-hundredth part (see *Rash*); but if this occurs before the grain or greens have taken root, the grapes will be condemned. [It is arguable, however, that in this last case, *Rash* would agree that until the grain or greens take root, no condemnation at all will occur. This is because until they have rooted in the vineyard, the grain or greens might not constitute *kilayim*.]

תְּבוּאָה שֶׁיָּבְשָׁה כָּל צָרְכָּהּ, וַעֲנָבִים שֶׁבָּשְׁלוּ כָּל צָרְכָּן, אֵין מִתְקַדְּשׁוֹת. — *Grain which has dried to its full extent, and grapes which have ripened to their fullest, do not become condemned.*

If a farmer plants a grapevine next to grain whose kernels have fully dried, or if he plants grain next to a vine bearing fully ripened grapes, no condemnation results. This emerges from the verse (*Deut.* 22:9): *Lest the fullness of the seed which you have sown be forfeit along with the product of the vineyard.* The phrase *the fullness of the seed* (הַמְלֵאָה הַזֶּרַע) for grain describes the growing period from rooting to fully drying. Prior to taking root, and after fully drying, this description is not appropriate. Likewise, for grapes, *product of the vineyard* (תְּבוּאַת הַכֶּרֶם) means grapes which have reached the size of a hyacinth bean but have not yet fully ripened. Before a grape has reached the size of a hyacinth bean, and after it is fully ripe, it is not referred

---

1. If the reading מִשֶּׁתַּשְׁלִישׁ is adopted above, then condemnation will occur once the grain or greens reaches the one-third stage (*Rav*).

עָצִיץ נָקוּב מְקַדֵּשׁ בַּכֶּרֶם, וְשֶׁאֵינוֹ נָקוּב [ח]
אֵינוֹ מְקַדֵּשׁ. וְרַבִּי שִׁמְעוֹן אוֹמֵר: זֶה
וְזֶה אוֹסְרִין, וְלֹא מְקַדְּשִׁין.

יד אברהם

to by this term. When grapes are fully ripe and grain is fully dried, they are called עֲנָבִים, *grapes*, and חִטִּים, *wheat*, respectively: grapes, rather than *product of the vineyard*; and wheat, rather than *fullness of the seed*. The verse therefore teaches that only when both components are in their formative stages of development are they subject to condemnation (*Rav; Rambam Comm.*).

Rash and *Rosh* (based on *Yerushalmi*) interpret the words אֵין מִתְקַדְּשׁוֹת to mean that the component of *kilayim* which has reached the end of its growth cycle cannot itself become condemned; it can, however, cause the condemnation of the other component which has not yet completed its growth. For example, if someone plants grain next to a vine with fully ripened grapes, the grapes will not be condemned. As noted above,

grapes which are already the size of hyacinth beans are condemned according to *Rash* only by an increase in growth of a two-hundredth part. Since a grape which is fully ripe does not grow any more, its condemnation is no longer possible. But this does not mean that the full-grown grape cannot cause condemnation. The grain which is planted next to such a vine will indeed be condemned when it takes root. And if a vine bearing fully grown grapes is placed over grain which has not yet fully dried, the grain will become condemned as a result of the overshadowing as soon as it increases by a two-hundredth part. Similarly, if someone plants grapes next to fully dried grain, the grapes can become condemned, but not the grain since it cannot grow any more. [According to *Rambam* and *Rav*, there is no condemnation of either component unless both are eligible for condemnation.]

8.

עָצִיץ נָקוּב מְקַדֵּשׁ בַּכֶּרֶם, — *A perforated pot condemns in a vineyard,*

Planting in an earthenware[1] flowerpot which has a hole large enough to permit passage of a small root is equivalent to planting in the ground (*Demai* 5:10; *Shabbos* 95b). Accordingly, if such a pot was located inside a vineyard or within the four-cubit work area of a vineyard, planting in it is not only forbidden but generates condemnation as well, just as if the person had illegally planted directly in the ground (*Rav; Rosh; Rash*). [The extent of the condemnation of the vineyard is as stated above, mishnah 4:5 and 5:5 (*Ri ben Malki Tzedek*).]

וְשֶׁאֵינוֹ נָקוּב אֵינוֹ מְקַדֵּשׁ. — *but an unperforated pot does not condemn.*

Planting in an earthenware pot which is not perforated at all (or, even if it has a hole, the hole is not large enough to allow passage of a small root) is not equivalent to planting in the ground. If such a pot was located in a vineyard, planting in it would not generate any condemnation, as stated here by the mishnah (*Rav; Rosh; Rash*). Nevertheless, it is forbidden Rabbinically to do so (*Menachos* 70a; *Rambam, Hil. Kilayim* 5:16). [*R' Shlomo Sirilio* (apparently based on his text of *Yerushalmi* at the end of chapter 7) writes that *kilayim* created by planting in

1. We have followed *R' Shlomo Sirilio* in specifying that the perforated pot is earthenware. This accords with the view of *Tosafos* (*Gittin* 7b) that planting in wooden pots is like planting in the ground even if the wooden flowerpot is not perforated. Only earthenware pots need perforation for planting in them to be considered like planting in the ground. (For a survey of the different opinions with regard to the composition of the flowerpot, see *Mishneh LaMelech* to *Hil. Bikurim* 2:9 at length.)

8. **A** perforated pot condemns in a vineyard, but an unperforated pot does not condemn. R' Shimon says: This and that forbid, but do not condemn.

an unperforated pot is forbidden Rabbinically for consumption, even though it is not forbidden for other uses.]

וְרַבִּי שִׁמְעוֹן אוֹמֵר: זֶה וְזֶה אוֹסְרִין, וְלֹא מְקַדְּשִׁין.
— *R' Shimon says: This and that forbid, but do not condemn.*

[Some texts, including *Rav's*, have: זֶה וְזֶה אֲסוּרִין, *this and that are forbidden,* rather than: זֶה וְזֶה אוֹסְרִין, *this and that forbid.*]

R' Shimon disputes the contention that planting in a perforated pot is like planting in the ground. In his view, there is no difference between a perforated pot and an unperforated one, and therefore even planting in a perforated pot is not considered equivalent to planting in the ground.[1] According to R' Shimon, neither planting in a perforated pot nor planting in an unperforated pot in a vineyard causes condemnation. Planting in both of these cases is forbidden, however, and this is what is meant by: *this and that forbid*. I.e. it is forbidden to plant in *any* pot in a vineyard, but such planting, although forbidden Rabbinically, does not cause any condemnation (*Rav; Rosh; Rash*).

It is generally assumed that the distinction between perforated and unperforated pots is clearcut: i.e., planting in perforated pots is definitely equivalent to planting in the ground, while planting in unperforated pots is definitely not equivalent to planting in the ground. It is perhaps therefore of interest that *Yerushalmi* (*Demai* 5:8) regards the status of planting in unperforated pots as questionable: It might be like planting in the ground, and it might not be. Planting in unperforated pots does not generate condemnation because there is a doubt as to whether it creates

kilayim under Biblical law, and doubtful *kilayim* does not condemn (see *Pnei Moshe* ad loc.). Thus, according to this approach, the dispute between the *Tanna Kamma* and R' Shimon is even more pronounced: The *Tanna Kamma* considers even planting in unperforated pots as possibly equivalent to planting in the ground; R' Shimon maintains that even planting in perforated pots is not like planting in the ground.

Gra (as explained by *Ridbaz* ad loc., s.v. רבב"ח) maintains that the *Tanna Kamma's* ruling that planting in an unperforated flower pot does not condemn refers only to the Diaspora, where the laws of *kilayim* of the vineyard apply only Rabbinically. Since the law applies only Rabbinically, and since the status of unperforated pots is questionable, the rule that doubtful cases of Rabbinic law are decided leniently (סְפֵק דְּרַבָּנָן לְקוּלָא) is applied. Therefore, the *Tanna Kamma* rules that an unperforated pot does not condemn. In the Land of Israel, however, where *kilayim* is Biblically prohibited, doubtful cases are decided stringently (סְפֵק דְּאוֹרַיְיתָא לְחוּמְרָא), and therefore, questionable *kilayim* such as that resulting from illegal planting in an unperforated pot *does* cause condemnation (see also *Tziyun HaHalachah* 5:176).

[From *Tosefta Kilayim* 4:11 (as interpreted by *Beur HaGra*, *Yoreh Deah* 296:37) it appears that R' Shimon's ruling — אוֹסְרִין, וְלֹא מְקַדְּשִׁין, *forbid, but do not condemn* — may be understood as distinguishing between a condemnation from general use and a prohibition on eating alone. That is, R' Shimon maintains that planting in any type of pot in a vineyard is forbidden only Rabbinically. Accordingly, such planting does *not condemn* anything from general use. It does however *forbid* the product of such *kilayim* for consumption.]

1. This is R' Shimon's position in general although he makes an exception concerning the laws for rendering food susceptible to *tumah* (see *Shabbos* 95b and *Tosefta Kilayim* 4:11).

הַמַּעֲבִיר עָצִיץ נָקוּב בַּכֶּרֶם, אִם הוֹסִיף בְּמָאתַיִם, אָסוּר.

[א] כִּלְאֵי הַכֶּרֶם אֲסוּרִין מִלִּזְרוֹעַ וּמִלְקַיֵּם, וַאֲסוּרִין בַּהֲנָאָה.

יד אברהם

הַמַּעֲבִיר עָצִיץ נָקוּב בַּכֶּרֶם, אִם הוֹסִיף בְּמָאתַיִם, אָסוּר. — [If] someone transports a perforated pot through a vineyard, if it increases by a two-hundredth part, it is forbidden.

In this case, grain which has already reached the one-third stage is growing in a perforated pot which is carried through a vineyard under the vines without being placed on the ground of the vineyard. The mishnah states that if the grain in the pot increases by a two-hundredth part[1] as it passes through the vineyard under the branches, then the grain is forbidden. The vines, however, are not forbidden, since the pot was never set down on the ground (Rav; Rosh). The distinction between the status of the grain and the status of the vines is suggested by the mishnah's wording — אָסוּר, it is forbidden — rather than קִידֵשׁ, it condemns. That is, the grain in the pot which is carried through the vineyard is forbidden, but does not condemn the vines (Tos. Yom Tov; see Tosefta Kilayim 4:11).

It was explained in the commentary to mishnah 7 that when grain which is already growing is brought into a kilayim situation, according to Rash it becomes condemned on reaching the one-third stage. An increase in growth of a two-hundredth part is relevant only for grain which becomes kilayim after reaching the one-third stage. Since the condemnation of the grain here is the result of an increase of a two-hundredth part, the case under discussion must involve grain which has already reached the one-third stage and only then was brought into a kilayim situation (see Rosh here, and Rosh and Rash to mishnah 7).

According to Rambam, there is no signifi-

cance to the one-third stage as far as condemnation of grain is concerned, and the previous mishnah teaches that grain becomes condemned as of taking root. Where grain is introduced into a kilayim situation only after it has taken root legally outside of the vineyard, it will become condemned on achieving an increase of a two-hundredth part while in the kilayim situation. Accordingly, the case under discussion here involves even grain which has not yet reached the one-third stage, as long as it has already taken root (see Tos. Yom Tov).

As far as the vines are concerned, the significance of setting the pot down on the ground of the vineyard is not entirely clear. Since the grain in the pot is condemned, it is evident that the grain is viewed as deriving nourishment from the ground even as it is being carried through the vineyard (Mishnah Rishonah). In that case, why should the vines become condemned only if the pot is set down on the ground?

Tos. Yom Tov suggests that the condemnation of the grain here is only a Rabbinic penalty for having brought the pot into the vineyard. That is, the pot while being transported is not considered attached to the ground, and does not create true kilayim. Nevertheless, the Rabbis forbade carrying grain in a perforated pot through a vineyard, and to enforce this enactment they decreed further that doing so condemns the grain in the pot. If the pot is set down in the vineyard, however, the grain is regarded as growing from the ground. Accordingly, the resulting kilayim is Biblical and both the grain and the vine become condemned. [Ac-

---

1. The method for measuring such an increase is discussed above in the commentary to mishnah 5:6.

[If] someone transports a perforated pot through a vineyard, if it increases by a two-hundredth part, it is forbidden.

1. **K**ilayim of the vineyard is forbidden to plant and to maintain, and it is forbidden for use.

YAD AVRAHAM

cording to this approach, the reason the Rabbis outlawed carrying a perforated pot through a vineyard, even though this itself does not constitute *kilayim*, may have been in order to prevent people from creating Biblical *kilayim* by setting such pots down in the vineyard (see *Dvar Avraham*, Vol. 1, chapter 25:6-7).]

Mishnah Rishonah assumes that the condemnation of the grain is Biblical even when the pot was not set down in the vineyard. To explain how it is that only the grain in the pot is subject to condemnation, but not the grapes of the vineyard, he adapts an idea advanced by *Tosafos* (to *Eruvin* 92b). According to this idea, the condemnation of the grain is a consequence of the grain being in a vineyard; but the condemnation of the vine is due to the fact that the grain and vines are sharing a common spot. For grain to be condemned it is not essential that it grow near vines — it suffices if somehow the site of the grain is called a vineyard. For vines to be condemned, however, the grain must actually be growing in the same place as the vines (see also *Radbaz* to *Hil. Kilayim* 5:17 and *Toras Zeraim* to mishnah 5:7). *Mishnah Rishonah* proposes that the flowerpot is regarded as part of the vineyard

as it is moved through it, and for this reason the grain which is growing in a vineyard becomes condemned. However, the grain itself is growing in the pot and not together with the vines. Therefore, the vines remain permitted. If the pot is set down, however, then the grain is said to be growing together with vines, and these too are forbidden.

Rambam (*Comm.* and *Hil. Kilayim* 5:23) maintains that it is forbidden Rabbinically to transport a perforated pot through a vineyard, even if it is not put on the ground. However, unless the pot is put down in the vineyard, even the grain is not condemned. *Rambam* apparently does not attach significance to the mishnah's use of the term אָסוּר, *it is forbidden*, instead of קִידַשׁ, *it condemns*, and he explains that the case involves a pot which was put down in the vineyard. The mishnah must be understood as follows: *[If] someone transports a perforated pot through a vineyard*, and puts it down in the vineyard under a vine, then *if it increases by a two-hundredth part, it is forbidden*, i.e. it causes condemnation.

Chapter 8

1.

The following mishnah compares and contrasts the four different types of *kilayim* mentioned in the Torah. These are: *kilayim* of the vineyard (*Deut.* 22:9), *kilayim* of plants (*Lev.* 19:19), *kilayim* of clothes (*Lev.* 19:19; *Deut.* 22:11), and *kilayim* of animals (*Lev.* 19:19; *Deut.* 22:10).

כְּלְאֵי הַכֶּרֶם אֲסוּרִין מִלִּזְרוֹעַ — *Kilayim of the vineyard is forbidden to plant*

The source for the prohibition on planting foreign seed in a vineyard is the verse (*Deut.* 22:9): *You shall not sow your vineyard with kilayim, lest the fullness of the seed which you have sown be for-*

feit along with the product of the vineyard. *Yerushalmi* records a Tannaitic dispute over the interpretation of this verse. According to R' Yonasan, planting a single variety of foreign seed in a vineyard is a transgression punishable by lashes; according to R' Yoshiyah, only the planting

of two varieties of foreign seed in a vineyard is a punishable transgression.

R' Yonasan reads the verse to mean: *Do not sow your vineyard and thus create kilayim.* In other words, sowing even a single foreign species together with the vineyard is a forbidden *kilayim* mixture. R' Yoshiyah, on the other hand, regards the term *kilayim* used in the verse as superfluous. He therefore interprets it as a reference to *kilayim* of plants encountered elsewhere in the Torah (Lev. 19:19). The verse thus reads: *Do not sow your vineyard with kilayim of plants.* That is, the Torah issues a special prohibition on sowing a *kilayim* mixture of two foreign species in a vineyard. Although planting such a mixture is anyhow forbidden as *kilayim* of plants, the Torah imposed an additional prohibition on planting such a mixture in a vineyard. According to R' Yoshiyah, then, planting *kilayim* of the vineyard incurs a double penalty: one for the prohibited planting of a mixture of foreign species, and the other for the prohibited planting of such a mixture in a vineyard. Violation of the prohibition of *kilayim* of the vineyard involves three distinct species: the grapevine along with two foreign species (*Rav; Rosh; Rash*).

Talmud *Bavli* makes no mention of the opinion of R' Yonasan. R' Yoshiyah's opinion is related (see *Berachos* 22a et al.), but an important difference exists between the version of his position found in Talmud *Bavli* and that in *Yerushalmi.* According to Talmud *Bavli*, only simultaneously planting a *seed* of the grape together with the *seeds* of two foreign species incurs the penalty of lashes for *kilayim* of the vineyard. The verse is read to mean: *When planting a vineyard, do not plant the grape "seeds" together with a kilayim mixture of foreign "seeds"* (*Rashi* to *Kiddushin* 39a). Planting two foreign species in an *existing* vineyard is not the activity outlawed by the Torah as *kilayim* of the vineyard (*Tos. Yom Tov*). [Such planting is of course a

violation of the prohibition on *kilayim* of plants and is punishable under that heading; an additional punishment for *kilayim* of the vineyard, however, is not warranted unless the seed of the vine is simultaneously planted together with the other seeds (*Tosafos* to *Shabbos* 84b, *Kiddushin* 39a, *Chullin* 82b, *Bechoros* 54a; cf. *Rashi* to *Shabbos* 84b and *Bechoros* 54a; *Tosafos* to *Chullin* 60a).]

The halachah follows the opinion of R' Yoshiyah as recorded in Talmud *Bavli* (*Rambam*, Hil. *Kilayim* 5:1; *Shulchan Aruch Yoreh Deah* 296:1). This, however, raises a serious problem: If *kilayim* of the vineyard is Biblically forbidden only in the case in which a person planted the seed of the grape together with the seeds of two foreign species, then how is one to account for all those mishnayos above (e.g. mishnah 7:5 and 7:8; see also *Pesachim* 25a) which deal with cases that do not satisfy these criteria, yet apparently speak of Biblical condemnation of the *kilayim*?

Numerous solutions to this problem have been suggested.[1] *Tosafos* (*Kiddushin* 39a, *Menachos* 15b) maintain that all those sources which conflict with R' Yoshiyah's ruling reflect the opinion of the disputants of R' Yoshiyah who assume that Scripture forbids planting even a single foreign species in an existing vineyard. But according to the accepted view of R' Yoshiyah, all those cases are permitted. [*Rosh* (Hil. *Kilayim* §4) writes that according to *Tosafos*, planting a single foreign species in an existing vineyard, for example, is permitted even Rabbinically according to R' Yoshiyah. He cites *Rama*, however, to the effect that R' Yoshiyah agrees that such planting is Rabbinically forbidden.]

Rambam (Hil. *Kilayim* 5:1,7) distinguishes between Biblical prohibitions which are punishable by lashes and those which are not punishable. A prohibition is only punishable by lashes when it is formulated by the Torah as a negative command; but even prohibitions which are not formulated in this way are still Biblically forbidden. The prohibition on planting *kilayim* of the vineyard is formulated by the Torah as a negative precept, "Do not sow your vineyard with *kilayim*," and its violation is hence punishable by lashes. According to R' Yoshiyah, this refers specifically to simultaneously planting the seed of two foreign species together with the seed of the

---

1. An exhaustive survey may be found in *Derech Emunah* 5:27. See also *Chazon Ish, Dinei Kilayim* §31.

grape, and only such planting is a punishable Biblical transgression. In addition to the negative precept, the Torah states: *lest the fullness of the seed which you have sown be forfeit along with the product of the vineyard* (*Deut.* 22:9). The Torah's condemnation includes not only *kilayim* created by violating the punishable negative precept; rather, even if someone plants a single foreign species in an existing vineyard, this is also condemned for use by the Torah. From the fact that such *kilayim* is Biblically condemned, it follows that it must also be Biblically prohibited to plant. However, because the prohibition is not formulated as an explicit negative command, it is not punishable by lashes. Thus, according to R' Yoshiyah there are two forms of *kilayim* of the vineyard prohibited by the Torah: planting seeds of two foreign species together with a grapeseed (which is punishable by lashes), and planting even a single foreign species in an existing vineyard (which is not punishable). Both forms of *kilayim* of the vineyard are included in the Biblical condemnation and hence, all those sources which deal with the second form of *kilayim* are consistent with R' Yoshiyah[1] (see *Chazon Ish* 1:6 and 3:12; see also above 5:7, s.v. עובר היה).

According to *Tosafos'* understanding of R' Yoshiyah, the Torah's command against planting *kilayim* and the condemnation of *kilayim* both refer to one and the same case; according to *Rambam*, the scope of the condemnation is much wider than that of the negative command. An intermediate position between that of *Tosafos* and that of *Rambam* is adopted by many *Rishonim*. This is that the Torah's condemnation of *kilayim* of the vineyard is of greater scope than the negative command, but not as wide ranging as *Rambam* would have. The punishable planting prohibition is limited to planting seeds of two foreign species simultaneously with grapeseed; the Biblical condemnation applies even if the planting was not simultaneous, as long

as it involves two foreign species. Thus, if someone planted two foreign species in an existing vineyard, the planting will not be punishable, but the *kilayim* thereby created will be subject to Biblical condemnation from use. However, if someone planted a single foreign species in a vineyard, nothing is condemned, not even under Rabbinic law. [According to this approach, in order to harmonize mishnah 7:8 for example with the view of R' Yoshiyah, it must be posited that the flowerpot in the vineyard contained two foreign species — see *Ran* to *Kiddushin* 39a.]

וּמְלַקְיֵם, — *and to maintain,*

If someone sees *kilayim* growing in his vineyard and is negligent about removing it, he is guilty of maintaining *kilayim* (see mishnah 5:6). Where the maintenance of *kilayim* involves nothing more than neglecting to uproot it, it is not punishable with lashes. Such corporal punishment is warranted only for actively maintaining *kilayim*, such as by erecting a fence around it in order to protect it (*Rav; Rosh; Tosafos* to *Avodah Zarah* 64a).

The Biblical source which prohibits the maintaining of *kilayim* is not entirely clear.[2] Rabbeinu Chananel (to *Moed Katan* ibid.) derives the prohibition in the following manner. In the verse, *Do not sow your vineyard kilayim*, the word *kilayim* is superfluous. This is because the term sowing in the Torah is generally reserved for plants other than trees, in particular grain. Thus, if the Torah were to write simply, *do not sow your vineyard*, we would know that it is forbidden to plant grain in a vineyard. The word *kilayim* comes to teach that maintaining *kilayim* is also forbidden, and the verse is thus understood to mean: *do not sow your vineyard*, and do not keep *kilayim*. The words *do not* refer both to sowing *kilayim* as well as to maintaining *kilayim*.[3]

1. *Raavan* (responsum 53) independently advances a similar solution. He concludes his epistle with the remarks: "Blessed is He Who teaches wisdom, Who has led me on the path of truth in explaining this passage. When I die, my lips will talk, and R' Yoshiyah will greet me, since I have resolved the mishnayos with his view."

2. The *Gemara* (*Moed Katan* 2b, *Makkos* 21b, *Avodah Zarah* 64a) gives a cryptic derivation which is explained by *Rashi* (and in *Makkos* by *Rivan*) differently in each place (see also *Yerushalmi* and *Rash*). In addition to its obscurity, the derivation appears to be based on a verse which deals with *kilayim* of plants, rather than *kilayim* of the vineyard (see *Eretz Chemdah* 2:5:1, p. 215).

3. This derivation would not seem to work according to R' Yoshiyah, who limits the planting prohibition to the case in which the seed of two foreign species is planted together with grape

כְּלְאֵי זְרָעִים אֲסוּרִים מִלִּזְרוֹעַ וּמִלְּקַיֵּם, וּמֻתָּרִין
בַּאֲכִילָה וְכָל שֶׁכֵּן בַּהֲנָאָה.
כִּלְאֵי בְגָדִים מֻתָּרִין בְּכָל דָּבָר, וְאֵינָן אֲסוּרִין
אֶלָּא מִלְּלְבּוֹשׁ.

יד אברהם

The opinion that maintaining *kilayim* of the vineyard is outlawed Biblically by a negative prohibition is attributed by *Tosefta* (*Kilayim* 1:10) to R' Akiva. Both Talmuds reflect uncertainty as to the opinion of the Sages (see *Yerushalmi* here and *Bavli Moed Katan* 2b and *Makkos* 21b). It is possible that they do not consider maintaining *kilayim* to be Biblically forbidden at all (and they entirely reject R' Akiva's derivation), or perhaps they agree that it is Biblically forbidden but dispute the assertion that maintaining *kilayim* is punishable by lashes. *Rambam's* position on this question (and likewise the position of *Shulchan Aruch Yoreh Deah* 296:4 who follows him) is the subject of controversy, but the trend amongst recent authorities is to assume that *Rambam* follows the Sages and considers maintaining *kilayim* to be forbidden only Rabbinically (see *Chazon Ish* 2:8 and 4:13; *Eretz Chemdah* 2:5:9, p. 221; *Derech Emunah* 5:54).

וַאֲסוּרִין בַּהֲנָאָה. — *and it is forbidden for use.*

The Torah (*Deut.* 22:9) concludes the prohibition on planting *kilayim* in the vineyard with the words: פֶּן־תִּקְדַּשׁ הַמְלֵאָה הַזֶּרַע אֲשֶׁר תִּזְרָע וּתְבוּאַת הַכָּרֶם, which has been translated as: *lest the fullness of the seed which you have sown be forfeit along with the product of the vineyard.* The meaning of the phrase פֶּן תִּקְדַּשׁ is actually not so clear. Normally, the root קדשׁ refers to sanctity. But this would not seem relevant in the present context, unless perhaps it means that just as sacred items are set aside from general use, so also is *kilayim* set aside, i.e. it is forbidden for use (see *Rambam, Hil. Maachalos Asuros* 10:6). The

Gemara (*Kiddushin* 56b), as well as *Yerushalmi*, interpret תִּקְדַּשׁ as a contraction of two words תּוּקַד אֵשׁ meaning: *it will be burnt by fire.* That is, the verse states that *kilayim* of the vineyard must be burnt. It follows therefore, that it is forbidden for general use, and this is the source of the mishnah's statement here (*Rav; Rosh; Rash; Rambam Comm.*; see *Rambam Comm.* 5:7).

Aruch HaShulchan (*Yoreh Deah* 294:3, 296:2) writes that although the method of disposal of *kilayim* is by burning, a person is not obligated to destroy detached *kilayim* in his possession. He must uproot it, of course, and he is forbidden to benefit from it, but he is not required to destroy it. If, however, he does wish to destroy it (e.g. to prevent himself from accidentally using it in some way), then he should do so by burning. But, he is not obligated per se to destroy it. This ruling is based on a responsum of *Chasam Sofer* (*Yoreh Deah* §286) concerning eradication of *orlah*. From the fact that the law that *orlah* must be burnt is recorded by *Rambam* only incidentally in *Hil. Pesulei HaMukdashin* 19:10, *Chasam Sofer* concludes that there is no *obligation* to burn *orlah*. Amazingly, *Chasam Sofer* appears to have overlooked *Rambam's* statement of this law in *Hil. Maachalos Asuros* 16:27, which can hardly be viewed as incidental! *Derech Emunah* 5:37 (based on *Tosafos* to *Temurah* 33b, s.v. הנשרפין) indicates that burning *kilayim* of the vineyard is obligatory. [Interestingly, in *Yoreh Deah* 296:15, *Aruch HaShulchan* appears to reconsider this question.]

כִּלְאֵי זְרָעִים אֲסוּרִים מִלִּזְרוֹעַ וּמִלְּקַיֵּם, וּמֻתָּרִין בַּאֲכִילָה וְכָל שֶׁכֵּן בַּהֲנָאָה. — *Kilayim of plants is forbidden to plant and to maintain, but it is permitted for eating*

seed. If the Torah had written simply, *Do not sow your vineyard*, we would not have known that the reference is to two species of foreign seed (see *Tosafos* to *Kiddushin* 39a; cf. however *Rashi* ad loc.).

8
1

Kilayim of plants is forbidden to plant and to maintain, but it is permitted for eating and certainly for use.

Kilayim of clothes is permitted in every way, and is forbidden only for wearing.

and certainly for use.

The Torah (*Lev.* 19:19) writes, *Do not plant kilayim in your field,* which teaches that it is prohibited to plant together two[1] species of grain, legumes, or greens[2] in a manner which constitutes *kilayim.* [The laws of *kilayim* of plants are treated in the first four chapters of the tractate.]

The source for the prohibition on maintaining *kilayim* of plants is in dispute. R' Akiva considers it Biblically forbidden and punishable, while according to the Sages maintaining *kilayim* of plants might be only a Rabbinic prohibition. Many authorities maintain that *Rambam* (whose formulation is followed by *Shulchan Aruch Yoreh Deah* 297:2) considers maintaining *kilayim* to be only a Rabbinic prohibition (see esp. the responsum of R' Chaim of Volozhyn in *Chut HaMeshulash* §24). *Ritva* (to *Kiddushin* 39) suggests that according to the Sages, maintaining *kilayim* of plants is only Rabbinically forbidden, whereas maintaining *kilayim* of the vineyard is prohibited by Scripture (see *Eretz Chemdah* 2:5:1, p. 216; cf. *Chazon Ish* 2:9).

Unlike the product of *kilayim* of the vineyard which is forbidden for use and cannot be eaten, the product of *kilayim* of plants is permitted for consumption and for general use. This is derived from Scripture by the *Gemara Chullin* 115a (*Meleches Shlomo*).

Rashbam (*Bava Basra* 94a, s.v. כל סאה) speaks of *kilayim* of plants becoming forbidden for use once the seeds take root. This would seem to be in open contradiction of our mishnah as noted already by *Tosafos*

(ibid., s.v. סאה). See also *Ri ben Malki Tzedek* to mishnah 2:11 and *R' Shlomo Sirilio* there.

כִּלְאֵי בְגָדִים מֻתָּרִין בְּכָל דָּבָר, וְאֵינָן אֲסוּרִין אֶלָּא מִלְּבוּש. — *Kilayim of clothes is permitted in every way, and is forbidden only for wearing.*

Kilayim of clothes refers to a garment containing a forbidden combination of linen and wool (*Deut.* 22:11). [This type of *kilayim* is discussed in detail in the next chapter of the tractate.]

The mishnah states that it is permitted to make and to keep *kilayim* of clothes (*Tif. Yis.*). Likewise, it is permitted to derive benefit from such clothes, such as by selling them (*Rambam, Hil. Kilayim* 10:12). Only wearing or covering oneself with a garment containing *kilayim* is forbidden. Covering oneself with a *kilayim* fabric is forbidden only when the fabric warms the body in a manner similar to clothing. Thus, for example, it is permitted to sit under a tent of *kilayim* fabric. Although one is covered by the tent, there is no contact with the *kilayim* material and such covering is hence not comparable to clothing. However, sleeping under a blanket containing *kilayim* is forbidden since this type of covering resembles clothing in directly warming the body (*Rambam* ibid.). Both wearing and covering are alluded to by the mishnah's statement that *kilayim* of clothes *is only forbidden for wearing* (*Tos. Anshei Shem*). That these two forms of "wearing" are prohibited emerges from a comparison between the Torah's wording in *Lev.* 19:19 and *Deut.* 22:11. In the former it is stated: *a garment*

1. Cf. R' Yehudah's opinion in mishnah 1:9 and see *Rash* ad loc.

2. See *Rambam* (*Hil. Kilayim* 1:4).

כִּלְאֵי בְּהֵמָה מֻתָּרִים לְגַדֵּל וּלְקַיֵּם, וְאֵינָם אֲסוּרִים אֶלָּא מִלְהַרְבִּיעַ. כִּלְאֵי בְּהֵמָה אֲסוּרִים זֶה בָזֶה.

[ב] **בְּהֵמָה** עִם בְּהֵמָה וְחַיָּה עִם חַיָּה, בְּהֵמָה עִם חַיָּה וְחַיָּה עִם בְּהֵמָה, טְמֵאָה

יד אברהם

of kilayim . . . shall not come upon you, which prohibits merely having such a fabric upon you. This includes even being covered, and not merely wearing. In the latter verse we read: do not wear . . . wool and linen combined, which outlaws wearing. The Gemara (Yevamos 4b) explains that both covering and wearing are forbidden, but only covering which resembles wearing is included in the prohibition (Rav; Rosh; Rash).

כִּלְאֵי בְּהֵמָה מֻתָּרִים לְגַדֵּל וּלְקַיֵּם, — Kilayim of animals is permitted to raise and maintain,

The phrase kilayim of animals used here refers to animals of different kinds. The Torah (Lev. 19:19) forbids coupling animals of different kinds, and the Gemara (Bava Metzia 91a) explains that this prohibition applies only to manually joining in sexual union the male of one kind to the female of another. It is permitted, however, to place the male of one kind of animal together with the female of a different kind in the same pen, even though they may copulate together (Rav; Rosh; Rash). This is what is meant here by the mishnah's assertion that it is permitted to raise and maintain together animals of different kinds.

The phrase to raise and to maintain is unclear. Tos. Yom Tov suggests that to maintain means to keep for personal benefit. If the mishnah had only stated that it is permitted to raise animals of different kinds, we would not have known that it is also permitted to benefit from them. Likewise, had it only stated that it is permitted to maintain different kinds of animals, we might have thought that raising them to-

gether is forbidden, and that a mixed herd could be acquired by a Jew for his personal use only if it was raised by a non-Jew.

Mishnah Rishonah understands to raise as referring to feeding the animals together, and to maintain as referring to enclosing the animals together. The mishnah thus teaches that not only may animals of different kinds be fed together from the same trough, but they may even be maintained and kept together in the same pen. As explained above, only manually joining them is forbidden (see also Tos. Anshei Shem from Lechem Shamayim).

וְאֵינָם אֲסוּרִים אֶלָּא מִלְהַרְבִּיעַ. — and only mating is forbidden.

Only direct manual coupling of animals of different kinds is forbidden, not raising them or keeping them together. The mishnah's wording "only" mating is forbidden does not mean to suggest that this is the only prohibition involving two kinds of animals. After all, the Torah (Deut. 22:10) also forbids employing a team of animals of different kinds to do work (see mishnah 2 below and ff.). Rather, within the context of the prohibition on coupling animals of different kinds, the mishnah teaches that even though raising or keeping them together might cause them to copulate, this is permitted, since only manually mating animals of different kinds is forbidden by the verse in Lev. 19:19 (Mishnah Rishonah).

כִּלְאֵי בְּהֵמָה אֲסוּרִים זֶה בָזֶה. — Animals of kilayim are forbidden one with another.

The phrase animals of kilayim is used differently here than above. Here it means the offspring of illegal crossbreed-

Kilayim of animals is permitted to raise and maintain, and only mating is forbidden.

Animals of *kilayim* are forbidden one with another.

2. A domestic animal with a domestic animal or a wild animal with a wild animal, a domestic animal with a wild animal or a wild animal with a domestic animal,

YAD AVRAHAM

ing. A mule, for example, is a hybrid between a horse and an ass. A mule can be bred either by crossing a male ass with a mare (type-1), or by crossing a stallion with a female ass (type-2). Both types of mule are *animals of kilayim* referred to here. The mishnah teaches that manually mating a type-1 mule with a type-2 mule is forbidden. Although both are part horse and part ass, the mother of the type-1 mule is a horse, while the mother of the type-2 mule is an ass. Because of this, the mishnah considers the type-1 mule to be a member of the horse family, and the type-2 mule to be a member of the ass family. Just as it is forbidden to mate asses with horses, so too it is forbidden to mate two mules whose

mothers are of different kinds. [Note that such mating is forbidden even though mules are sterile.] Thus, hybrids which are crosses between the same two species are not necessarily classified as animals of one kind. Two hybrids are regarded as the same kind of animal only if both of their mothers were of the same species (*Rav; Rosh; Rash; Tif. Yis.*).

The *Gemara* (*Chullin* 79a) notes that according to Chananya not only the maternal factor of a hybrid determines the animal's kind, but also the paternal factor. In his opinion, since all mules are part horse-part ass, they are all considered the same kind of animal. Thus, mating a type-1 mule with a type-2 would be permitted according to Chananya. Our mishnah does not conform with his opinion (*Rav; Rosh; Rash*).

2.

The rest of the present chapter is devoted to the laws of *kilayim* of animals. The previous mishnah ended with a discussion of the prohibition on crossbreeding animals founded on *Lev.* 19:19. The present mishnah continues with that subject and introduces the prohibition on working with a team consisting of animals of different kinds. This prohibition is based on *Deut.* 22:10: *Do not plow with an ox and a donkey together.*

בְּהֵמָה עִם בְּהֵמָה וְחַיָּה עִם חַיָּה, בְּהֵמָה עִם חַיָּה וְחַיָּה עִם בְּהֵמָה, — *A domestic animal with a domestic animal or a wild animal with a wild animal, a domestic animal with a wild animal or a wild animal with a domestic animal,*

The mishnah lists combinations of different types of animals which it is forbidden to crossbreed or to work with in teams. Thus, it is forbidden to couple a male domestic animal of one kind with a female one of another kind, and likewise it is forbidden to couple a male wild

animal of one kind with a female wild animal of a different kind. Similarly, it is prohibited to couple a male domestic animal of one kind with a female wild animal of another kind, or a male wild animal of one kind with a female wild animal of another. In the same way, it is forbidden to work with a team of different kinds of animals, regardless of whether both are wild, both are domestic, or one is wild and the other domestic.

In its prohibition of crossbreeding the Torah (*Lev.* 19:19) refers to בְּהֶמְתְּךָ, which

עם טְמֵאָה וּטְהוֹרָה עִם טְהוֹרָה, טְמֵאָה עִם טְהוֹרָה
וּטְהוֹרָה עִם טְמֵאָה — אֲסוּרִין לַחֲרשׁ, וְלִמְשׁוֹךְ,
וּלְהַנְהִיג.

could be understood to mean *your do-mestic animal*. However, in connection with the resting of animals on the Sabbath (*Exodus* 20:10), this term is also used, even though that law applies equally to domestic animals, wild animals, and birds (see *Bava Kamma* 54b). The *Gemara* (ibid.) draws a parallel between the usage here concerning cross-breeding and the usage concerning Sabbath, and concludes that the prohibition on crossbreeding animals of different kinds applies to all animals, whether mammal or fowl, domestic or wild (*Rav; Rosh; Rash*). Accordingly, the mishnah lists all possible combinations, as included in the prohibition.

With regard to working with a team including animals of different kinds, the Torah (*Deut.* 22:10) writes: *Do not plow with an ox and a donkey together.* Here, too, the specification of a team consisting of an ox with an ass might have been misconstrued as limiting the prohibition to this specific combination alone. However, the *Gemara* (*Bava Kamma* 54b) notes that the same combination occurs in *Deut.* 5:14 where the law concerning resting of animals on the Sabbath is repeated. Just as there the law applies to all animals, and the mention of an ox and an ass is merely by way of an example, so also with the prohibition on working with a team of different kinds of animals. The law applies to any combination of animals of different kinds, and the specific mention of ox and ass is merely by way of example (*Rav; Rosh; Rash*).

טְמֵאָה עִם טְמֵאָה וּטְהוֹרָה עִם טְהוֹרָה, טְמֵאָה
עִם טְהוֹרָה וּטְהוֹרָה עִם טְמֵאָה — *a non-kosher animal with a non-kosher animal or a kosher animal with a kosher animal, a non-kosher animal with a*

kosher animal or a kosher animal with a non-kosher animal —

Just as there is no difference whether the two kinds of animals involved in the crossbreeding or work team are wild or domestic, so too there is no difference whether they are kosher or non-kosher. The mishnah finds it necessary to emphasize this (see *Rash* and *Mishnah Rishonah*), presumably to dispel the notion that the mention by the Torah (*Deut.* 22:10) of *an ox and an ass* limits the prohibition on working with a mixed team exclusively to a mix of kosher and non-kosher animals. Likewise, the Torah's example might have been misconstrued as limiting this prohibition exclusively to domestic animals, such as the ox and the ass. For this reason, the mishnah stresses that all animals are included, whether wild or domestic, kosher or non-kosher, and any team consisting of two kinds of animals is forbidden for work. The combinations mentioned here are of course also forbidden for crossbreeding, but the mishnah emphasizes the work prohibition, since the Torah's example of it might have been misconstrued (*Mishnah Rishonah*; see also *Rosh, Hil. Kilayim* sec. 5 [p. 137a in Vilna ed.] and *Responsa* 2:16).

Rambam (*Comm.* here and to *Bava Kamma* 5:7; see also *Sefer HaMitzvos* negative precept §218 and *Hil. Kilayim* 9:8; cf. *Guide for the Perplexed* III:49) writes that the Torah's example of a team consisting of an ox with an ass is not merely illustrative, but serves to fundamentally qualify the scope of the Biblical prohibition. Inasmuch as an ox is a kosher animal, while an ass is a non-kosher one, *Rambam* maintains that only working with a team consisting of a kosher animal and a non-kosher one is outlawed by the Torah. The distinction between domestic and wild animals is irrelevant to the Biblical prohibition on

8
2

a non-kosher animal with a non-kosher animal or a kosher animal with a kosher animal, a non-kosher animal with a kosher animal or a kosher animal with a non-kosher animal — [these teams] are forbidden for plowing, for pulling, and for leading.

working with a team of different kinds of animals. If one animal is wild and the other domestic, but they are both kosher, for example, there is no Biblical prohibition on working with such a team. It is only by Rabbinic enactment that a team with only kosher animals (e.g. cow and goat) or a team with only non-kosher animals (e.g. horse and elephant) is included in the prohibition on working with different kinds of animals. [According to Rambam, there is a basic difference in scope between the Biblical prohibition on cross-breeding and the Biblical prohibition on working with a mixed team. The prohibition on crossbreeding which is formulated by the Torah (Lev. 19:19) in terms of your animal applies to all crosses, regardless of whether or not both are kosher. The prohibition on working with a mixed team, where an ox and an ass is specified by the Torah, applies Biblically only when the team consists of kosher together with non-kosher animals.] Rambam assumes our mishnah to be discussing the Biblical prohibition, and he explains that the mishnah consists of two statements. First the mishnah refers back to the prohibition on crossbreeding with which the previous mishnah closed. [In Rambam's version (see Kafich ed.), our mishnah opens with the words: בַּמֶּה דְבָרִים אֲמוּרִים, When are these things said, a clear reference to the preceding discussion (see also Meleches Shlomo).] The opening sentence of the mishnah is a list of combinations which are Biblically forbidden to crossbreed but are not forbidden as work teams. These are: A domestic animal with a domestic animal or a wild animal with a wild animal, a domestic animal with a wild animal or a wild animal with a domestic animal, a non-kosher animal with a non-kosher animal or a kosher animal with a kosher animal. The mishnah then makes another statement: A non-kosher animal with a kosher animal or a kosher animal with a non-kosher animal — [these teams] are forbidden for plowing, for pulling, and for leading. That is, these last two combinations are forbidden not only for cross-

breeding, but also for work teams as well (see also Radbaz to Hil. Kilayim 9:8).

אֲסוּרִין לַחֲרוֹשׁ, וְלִמְשׁוֹךְ, וּלְהַנְהִיג. — [these teams] are forbidden for plowing, for pulling, and for leading.

When the Torah (Deut. 22:10) writes: Do not plow with an ox and an ass together, it is not only plowing with a mixed team which is prohibited, but any type of work (see Sifrei ad loc.). Accordingly, the mishnah adds that the activities prohibited with a team of animals of different kinds include such things as pulling and leading as well.

From Bava Metzia (8b-9a) it seems that pulling refers to tugging an animal by a leash, while leading refers to prodding an animal into motion by hitting or kicking. The Gemara indicates that a camel is normally pulled, while a donkey is normally led. Nevertheless, a forbidden team such as a donkey with an ox may neither be led nor pulled. Similarly, a team consisting of a camel with a horse may neither be pulled nor led. Even though one of the animals is normally moved in a different fashion from the other animal, the prohibition still applies (Rav; Rosh; Rash).

Rambam Comm. understands pulling as referring to the action of the animals, e.g. the pulling of a wagon, but the person is not necessarily holding onto a leash and tugging. Leading is explained by Rambam as tying the animals together and leading them.

From the above definitions it is difficult to ascertain whether or not the animals must be performing some work together in order to violate the prohibition. Although Rambam's definition of leading, and Rav's definitions for both leading and pulling, make no mention of any work, it is nonetheless possible

[ג] **הַמַּנְהִיג** סוֹפֵג אֶת הָאַרְבָּעִים, וְהַיּוֹשֵׁב
בַּקָּרוֹן סוֹפֵג אֶת הָאַרְבָּעִים. רַבִּי
מֵאִיר פּוֹטֵר. וְהַשְּׁלִישִׁית שֶׁהִיא קְשׁוּרָה לָרְצוּעוֹת
אֲסוּרָה.

יד אברהם

that they refer to animals hitched to a wagon or the like which are therefore working (viz. pulling the wagon) as they are being lead or pulled.

Rosh (*Hil. Kilayim* p. 137 a-b) follows *Ravya* §193 (Vol. 1, p. 223) who maintains that unless the animals are both tied to each other and jointly performing some labor, no prohibition applies. On this basis, *Ravya* permits riding a horse while a dog runs alongside, even when the dog's leash is tied to the saddle horn. Although the animals are connected, they are not jointly performing any labor, and hence there is no prohibition involved (see also *Tosafos* to *Shabbos* 54a, *Makkos* 22a and *Beur HaGra, Yoreh Deah* 297:27). However, *Rabbeinu Ephraim of Regensburg* maintains that the prohibition on leading the animals together applies even if they are not performing any

labor (*Ravya* loc. cit.; see also *Ohr Zarua, Hil. Kilayim* 291, and *Sefer Yereim HaShalem* §388).

There is also disagreement as to whether or not the animals must be somehow tied or otherwise joined to each other in order for the prohibition to apply. As noted above, *Rosh* maintains that the animals must be tied together. Thus, if someone put a board across the backs of a horse and a donkey without tying it to them, *Rosh* permits riding on the board (*Rosh* to mishnah 1 and *Hil. Kilayim* sec. 5, p. 137a). However, *Radbaz* (*Hil. Kilayim* 9:7) suggests that *Rambam* follows the view of *Rabbeinu Ephraim* (*Ravya* ibid. p. 221f.) that as long as the animals move in unison, it is forbidden to lead them even if they are not connected. Both of these views are recorded by *Rama* (*Yoreh Deah* 297:11; see *Shach* and *Taz*).

3.

The following mishnah elaborates on the prohibition of leading a mixed team of animals.

הַמַּנְהִיג סוֹפֵג אֶת הָאַרְבָּעִים, — *The driver receives forty [lashes],*

[The literal meaning of the expression סוֹפֵג אֶת הָאַרְבָּעִים would seem to be: *absorbs forty* (lashes). *Rav* to *Zevachim* 6:5 suggests a relationship to the root ספק, meaning to clap, as in *Numbers* 24:10 (*Tos. Yom Tov*).]

Someone who drives or leads a mixed team of animals is punishable even if he is not sitting in the wagon they are pulling (*Tif. Yis.*). Moreover, he need not have any physical contact with the team of animals. Even if he prompts them to move by shouting at them, he is liable (*Ri ben Malki Tzedek* from *Yerushalmi*; see also *Bava Metzia* 90b).

The statement here that הַמַּנְהִיג, *the driver,*

is punishable by lashes would seem to be superfluous, since it was already taught at the end of mishnah 2 that the prohibition on working with a mixed team of animals refers not only to plowing, but to pulling and leading (i.e. driving) as well. From *Ri ben Malki Tzedek* it appears that the restatement of the liability of a driver comes to teach that driving a mixed team of animals is forbidden and punishable even when achieved by shouting without any physical contact with the animals. [It might also be suggested that the previous mishnah alone could have been understood to mean that pulling and leading are only Rabbinically forbidden, as a precautionary measure to prevent plowing with a mixed team. The present mishnah therefore stresses that driving (i.e. leading) is Biblically prohibited and therefore punishable by lashes.]

וְהַיּוֹשֵׁב בַּקָּרוֹן סוֹפֵג אֶת הָאַרְבָּעִים. — *and someone sitting in the coach receives forty [lashes].*

Yerushalmi explains that a person's

3. **T**he driver receives forty [lashes], and someone sitting in the coach receives forty [lashes]. R' Meir exempts him. And the third which is tied to straps is forbidden.

weight makes the animals aware of his presence and prompts them to move. Thus, a person sitting in a wagon being drawn by a mixed team is like a driver of the team, since the animals pull the wagon because of the passenger. Accordingly, he is punishable by lashes (*Rav; Rosh; Rash;* see *Mishnah Rishonah*).

Rambam (Comm. and *Hil. Kilayim* 9:9) appears to have understood the mishnah to mean that the driver of a coach being pulled by a mixed team, as well as the passenger in that coach, both receive lashes. The mishnah does not mean that a person who sits in a wagon being pulled by a mixed team is punishable by lashes only if there is no driver. Rather, even if there is a driver who prods and directs the team, both the driver and the passenger are punishable. Indeed, *Rambam* (ibid.) rules that even if one hundred people jointly lead a mixed team, they all incur lashes.

The ruling that every person who participates in driving the mixed team is punishable would seem to conflict with a well-known principle found in connection with the Sabbath laws. Concerning the forbidden labors of the Sabbath, it is taught that if two people *jointly* perform a forbidden labor, which each could have performed on his own, then neither party is liable (*Shabbos* 92b; *Rambam, Hil. Shabbos* 1:15). The verse (*Lev.* 4:27) from which this is derived relates to the obligation of bringing a sin offering for inadvertent transgressions *in general.* This would suggest an exemption from liability for any Torah prohibition which is violated by two people jointly, when each is capable of committing the transgression on his own. But in that case, how can it be that even one hundred people who jointly lead the team are all punishable?

To resolve this difficulty, R' Akiva Eiger (*Hagahos* to *Rambam Hil. Shabbos* 1:16) notes that the verse (*Lev.* 4:27) from which the exemption is learned relates specifically to the obligation of bringing sin offerings for inadvertent transgressions. He therefore argues that the exemption from liability for a jointly

committed transgression affects only the liability to bring a sin offering; and a jointly performed willful transgression is punishable by lashes. Thus, even if many people participate in leading a mixed team of animals, they are all punishable by lashes (see also *Yeshuos Malko* to *Hil. Kilayim* 9:9 and *Mekor Chaim,* *Hagahos* to *Orach Chaim* 266).

רַבִּי מֵאִיר פּוֹטֵר. — *R' Meir exempts him.*

In R' Meir's opinion, since the passenger does not do anything to prod the animals, he is not liable (*Rav; Rambam Comm.*). Although physical contact with the animals is not necessary, and even activating the team by shouting is also a punishable offense (*Bava Metzia* 90b), it is still necessary that the person do something to cause the animals to move. According to R' Meir, sitting in the passenger's seat does not constitute such an act, and hence he rules that the passenger sitting in the coach is exempt.

The *Gemara (Bava Metzia* 8b) reports that the *Amora* Shmuel, who ruled that the passenger is not liable, attributed this view to the Sages of our mishnah rather than to R' Meir (*Rash; Rosh*). It is not entirely clear whether Shmuel's version is accepted, and *Rambam,* for example, follows the Sages of our text of the mishnah (i.e. the *Tanna Kamma*) who consider the passenger liable (*Rambam Comm.* and *Hil. Kilayim* 9:9; see *Rosh, Hil. Kilayim* sec. 6 and *Divrei Chamudos* ad loc. §24).

וְהַשְּׁלִישִׁית שֶׁהִיא קְשׁוּרָה לָרְצוּעוֹת אֲסוּרָה. — *And the third which is tied to straps is forbidden.*

This is a new case, unrelated to the preceding segment of the mishnah. If two horses are hitched to a wagon, it is forbidden to move the wagon with a *third* animal — e.g. a donkey — tied to the straps of the horses. Although the pair of horses are sufficient to pull the wagon on their own without the donkey,

[ד] אֵין קוֹשְׁרִין אֶת הַסּוּס לֹא לְצִדְדֵי הַקָּרוֹן
וְלֹא לְאַחַר הַקָּרוֹן, וְלֹא אֶת הַלְּבְדָקִים
לַגְמַלִים. רַבִּי יְהוּדָה אוֹמֵר: כָּל הַנּוֹלָדִים מִן הַסּוּס,
אַף עַל פִּי שֶׁאֲבִיהֶן חֲמוֹר, מְתָרִין זֶה עִם זֶה; וְכֵן
הַנּוֹלָדִים מִן הַחֲמוֹר, אַף עַל פִּי שֶׁאֲבִיהֶם סוּס,

יד אברהם

and although the donkey is tied to the straps rather than directly to the wagon, the donkey cannot be ignored. Driving this wagon is considered to be driving a mixed team and is hence forbidden (*Rav; Rosh; Rash; Tif. Yis.*).

Normally, if two people (Mr. A and Mr. B) perform an act together, and one of them (Mr. A) is capable of performing the act entirely on his own, while the other (Mr. B) is not, then Mr. B's participation is considered to be insignificant (*Shabbos* 93 a-b). Accordingly, it is not clear why the donkey in the present case is considered part of the team. Since its contribution is entirely unnecessary, its participation should be considered insignificant and its presence ignored (*Tos. Anshei Shem*; see *Maadanei Yom Tov, Hil. Kilayim* 6:40).

Rambam Comm. has a different interpretation of *the third*, which relates it to the first part of the mishnah. In his opinion, the קָרוֹן, *coach*, referred to by the mishnah above, consists of two wagons connected together side by side, and a third one tied behind them by the straps of the other two. The third wagon

is what is referred to here by the mishnah as the third, and the subject under discussion is the liability of a passenger who sits in this third wagon. The *Tanna Kamma* and *R' Meir* argued above about the liability of a passenger seated in one of the two front wagons. According to the *Tanna Kamma*, the presence of a person seated there is sensed by the animals and prompts them to move, and therefore the passenger is liable. However, even the *Tanna Kamma* agrees that a person seated in the trailing third wagon is not viewed as prompting the animals to move. Nevertheless, it is forbidden Rabbinically to sit there when a mixed team is hitched to the wagon, and this is what is meant by *And the third . . . is forbidden* (*Tos. Anshei Shem*; cf. *Mishnah Rishonah* and *Tif. Yis.*). [Although R' Meir exempts a front-wagon passenger from punishment, he might still agree that it is Rabbinically forbidden to sit there lest he come to shout at the animals or otherwise actively prod them on. Accordingly, he might agree also to the assertion here that it is forbidden for a person to ride in the third wagon.]

4.

אֵין קוֹשְׁרִין אֶת הַסּוּס לֹא לְצִדְדֵי הַקָּרוֹן וְלֹא לְאַחַר הַקָּרוֹן, — *It is forbidden to tie a horse to the sides of a wagon or to the back of a wagon,*

When oxen are pulling a wagon, it is forbidden to tie to the side or back of the wagon a horse which is being trained to pull. Although the horse is attached only in order to become accustomed to running while tied to a wagon, this is forbidden because the horse occasionally pushes the wagon with its body, thus helping to move it forward (*Rash; Ravad to Tamid* 27b [printed on 33a]). Accordingly, the horse is also viewed as a member of the team moving the wagon, and since that

team consists of oxen together with a horse, it is forbidden (*Rav; Rosh*).

Sifrei (Deut. 22:10) infers from the word יַחְדָּו, *together*, in the verse *Do not plow with an ox and a donkey together*, that heterogeneous animals constitute a forbidden team with which it is forbidden to work, only when they are working together in unison. However, a horse tied to the side or back of a wagon pulled by oxen is not working in unison with the oxen, and therefore does not come under the prohibition. *Sifrei* can be reconciled with our mishnah which forbids a horse tied to the back or side of an oxen-drawn wagon if it is assumed that the prohibition in our mishnah is only Rabbinic; but under Biblical law — which *Sifrei* is discussing — the case of our

4. **I**t is forbidden to tie a horse to the sides of a wagon or to the back of a wagon, or [to tie] a libdicum to camels. Rabbi Yehudah says: All those born of a mare, even though their father is an ass, are permitted one with another; and so also those born of an ass, even though their father is a horse, are permitted one with

YAD AVRAHAM

mishnah would be permitted (see *Ravad* to *Tamid* 27b [printed on 33a], *Tziyun HaHalachah* 9:95). [See, however, *Tur Yoreh Deah* 297 who understands the prohibition of our mishnah to be Biblical.]

Tosefta (*Kilayim* 5:3) records a dissenting opinion of R' Meir who rules that the case of our mishnah is permitted. [According to the version of *Yerushalmi*: *R' Meir exempts*.] He concedes, however, that a horse tied to the side or back of an oxen-drawn wagon does constitute a forbidden team when the wagon is traveling on a slope. This is because on a slope, the horse and oxen together stabilize the wagon and enable it to be safely driven up or down the slope. Rabbeinu Hillel (*Comm.* to *Sifrei* ibid.) writes that *Sifrei's* inference from יַהְדָּו, *together*, that the animals must be working in unison for the prohibition to apply, reflects the view of R' Meir of the *Tosefta*. Our mishnah, on the other hand, which rules that *it is forbidden to tie a horse to the sides of a wagon etc.*, reflects the opinion of the Sages of the *Tosefta*, who do not require the team to work in unison. It would seem according to this approach that the prohibition on tying a horse to the side or back of an oxen-drawn wagon is indeed Biblical and is based on the assumption that it is not necessary for the animals to work in unison for the prohibition to be relevant.

Rambam Comm. explains that it is prohibited to have a horse tied to the side or back of the wagon because the wagon connects the horse to the oxen. Evidently, the point of the mishnah is that it is not necessary for the animals to be joined under one yoke or harness in order to constitute a mixed team. [In *Hil. Kilayim*, however, *Rambam* omits mention of this law.]

וְלֹא אֶת הַלִּבְדְּקִים לַגְּמַלִים. — *or [to tie] a libdicum to camels.*

Rav (following the standard edition of *Rambam Comm.*) writes that the libdicum (or, according to some versions,

libdicus) is a Lydian ass. *Yerushalmi* identifies it as a Lybian ass (so also in Kafich ed. of *Rambam Comm.*). This variety of ass is more powerful than other varieties and bears a resemblance to camels. The mishnah teaches that despite this resemblance, the two are distinct species, and therefore it is forbidden to tie a libdicum to a camel and work with them (see *Maseches Kilayim im Beurim*).

From *Sifrei* (*Deut.* 22:10) it is clear that the law that a libdicum may not be joined to camels is related to the previous law concerning the tying of a horse to the side or back of a wagon (see *Tif. Yis.* and *Mishnah Rishonah*). *Sifrei* states that the term *together* used in *Deut.* 22:10 teaches that it is permitted to tie a horse to the side or back of a wagon and to tie a libdicum to camels. As explained above, *Sifrei* assumes that the prohibition on working with a mixed team applies only when the animals work in unison. Apparently, the libdicum did not co-operate when tied to camels, and hence a team of camels and a libdicum did not satisfy the criterion of working together, and the prohibition did not apply (*Teshuvos Baalei HaTosafos* ed. Aegus, p. 100). However, our mishnah does not accept the qualification that the team must work in unison in order for the prohibition on working with a mixed team to be relevant. Accordingly, the mishnah forbids tying a horse to the side or back of an oxen-drawn wagon, and likewise forbids tying a libdicum to camels. Even though they may not move in unison, since they are tied and driven together, it is forbidden (*Tosefta K'Peshutah*).

רַבִּי יְהוּדָה אוֹמֵר: כָּל הַנּוֹלָדִים מִן הַסּוּס, אַף עַל פִּי שֶׁאֲבִיהֶן חֲמוֹר, מֻתָּרִין זֶה עִם זֶה; וְכֵן הַנּוֹלָדִים מִן הַחֲמוֹר, אַף עַל פִּי שֶׁאֲבִיהֶם סוּס, מֻתָּרִין זֶה עִם זֶה. — *Rabbi Yehudah says: All those born of a mare, even though their father is an ass, are permitted one with another;*

מֻתָּרִין זֶה עִם זֶה. אֲבָל הַנּוֹלָדִים מִן הַסּוּס עִם
הַנּוֹלָדִים מֵחֲמוֹר אֲסוּרִים זֶה עִם זֶה.

[ה] **הַפְּרוֹטִיּוֹת** אֲסוּרוֹת, וְהָרַמָּךְ מֻתָּר.

יד אברהם

*and so also those born of an ass, even
though their father is a horse, are permitted one with another.*

R' Yehudah is discussing only mules. It
might have been thought that even two
mules of identical lineage — e.g. where
both had a mare for a mother, or where
both had an ass for a mother — should be
forbidden with each other as different
kinds of animals, on the grounds that the
horse part of one crosses with the ass part
of the other. R' Yehudah therefore states
that this is not so. As long as both mules
have the same type of mother, they are
viewed as an identical blend, and there is
no question of a forbidden crossing of a
horse and an ass (*Rav; Tos. Yom Tov*).

According to Chananya (*Chullin 79a*), all
mules are permitted to one another. He considers both parents as contributing equally to
the determination of the kind of the offspring. Thus, for him, a mule with a horse for
a mother and a donkey for a father is identical
in kind to a mule with a donkey for a mother
and a horse for a father.

R' Yehudah, however, was uncertain
whether the paternal component should be
taken into consideration when determining
the kind of an animal. If only the maternal
component is relevant, then a mule with a
horse for a mother should be permitted to
mate with a purebred horse, even though the
mule is a hybrid and the horse is not. Similarly, a mule with a donkey for a mother
should be permitted with a purebred donkey.

However, because of his uncertainty as to
the significance of the paternal component, R'
Yehudah did not permit a mule with a horse
for a mother to mate with a purebred horse, or
a mule with a donkey for a mother with a
purebred donkey. He only permitted similar
hybrids to one another, i.e. hybrids whose
mothers are of the same kind and whose fa-
thers are of the same kind, which would be
permitted regardless of whether or not the pa-

ternal component is included (*Rosh*; see also
Rosh, Hil. Kilayim sec. 5).

Rambam (*Hil. Kilayim* 9:6) appears to take
the position that the paternal component is
ignored. This is evident also from *Rambam
Comm.* and followed by *Rav* (see *Tos. Yom
Tov*). It should follow from this that a hybrid
is permitted with its purebred mother. For example, a mule whose mother was a horse and
father a donkey should be permitted with its
mother even though both of the mother's parents were horses. Yet, *Rambam* (*Hil. Kilayim*
9:6) rules that it is forbidden to couple the hybrid with its mother! (*Rosh, Hil. Kilayim* sec.
5). [The same difficulty appears to be present
with *Rav* who follows *Rambam* (*Tos. Yom
Tov*).]

Evidently, *Rambam* understood that R' Yehudah does not ignore the paternal factor
completely; he takes it into account but does
not give it the same weight as the maternal
factor. Thus, similar hybrids (same type of father, same type of mother) are permitted to
each other. But dissimilar hybrids (the father
of one is the same type as the mother of the
other and vice versa) are not of the same kind
since their mothers are different and the primary determinant is the mother. [Note that
such mating is forbidden even though mules
are sterile.] Likewise, a hybrid will definitely
be forbidden to its purebred mother since the
paternal element makes them different kinds
(see *Merkeves HaMishneh* to *Hil. Shechitah*
12:8 and *Aruch HaShulchan Yoreh Deah*
16:25-28 for a resolution of the relevant Talmudic passages).

אֲבָל הַנּוֹלָדִים מִן הַסּוּס עִם הַנּוֹלָדִים מֵחֲמוֹר
אֲסוּרִים זֶה עִם זֶה. — *However, those born
of a horse with those born of an ass are
forbidden with one another.*

Dissimilar mules, which is to say, one
mule which has a horse mother and an ass
father, and another mule which has an
ass mother and a horse father, *are forbidden one with another.* The kind of the

8
5
another. However, those born of a horse with those born of an ass are forbidden with one another.

5. **P**rutiyos are forbidden, and the *ramach* is permitted.

YAD AVRAHAM

mother is the primary factor in determining the kind of the offspring, and since the two mules in question have mothers of different kinds, the mules are also considered to be of different kinds (*Rav; Rambam Comm.*).

5.

The mishnah continues with the classification of different species. This is important not only for the laws of *kilayim* but also in other contexts, as will be seen.

הַפְּרוּטִיוֹת אֲסוּרוֹת, — *Prutiyos are forbidden,*

This is a variety of mule in which those with horses for mothers are physiologically indistinguishable from those with asses for mothers. Ordinarily, a mule born of a horse has three features which distinguish it from a mule born of an ass: its ears, its tail, and its voice. A mule whose mother was a horse has short ears, a short tail, and a soft voice. A mule whose mother was an ass has long ears, a long tail, and a deep voice. Thus, with the common variety of mule, it is possible to know whether two specimens are born of like mothers and hence of the same kind (*Chullin* 79a). The *prutiyos*, however, do not display these differences between animals born of asses and animals born of horses. Thus, any given pair of these mules may include one whose mother was a horse and another whose mother was an ass. But as explained in the previous mishnah, such hybrids are regarded as different kinds of animals which may not be coupled together or used as a work team. Accordingly, the mishnah teaches that out of doubt, *prutiyos are forbidden* one to another (*Rav; Rosh; Rash*).

Gra (*Shenos Eliyahu*) understands *prutiyos* as young mules in which the differences between the two types are not yet discernible. It is not a different variety of mule under discussion; merely, the regular mule when it is too young to be classified conclusively. [*Rambam Comm.* defines

פְּרוּטִיוֹת as a term for all crosses between horses and asses (i.e. for all mules) regardless of whether the mother was a horse or an ass.]

וְהָרַמָּךְ מֻתָּר. — *and the ramach is permitted.*

The exact identity of the *ramach* is not known (see *Megillah* 18a). What is known is that all *ramachs* have horses for mothers, as is reflected in the word *ramach*, which in Arabic means mare (*Rav; Ibn Ezra* to *Esther* 8:10). Accordingly, all *ramachs* are of the same kind, and are permitted one to another (*Rav; Rosh; Rash*).

Rambam Comm. writes that the *ramach* is a variety of wild horse. The point of the mishnah is not to permit *ramachs* one to another, but to permit a *ramach* with a horse (*Rambam, Hil. Kilayim* 9:5; see *Tos. Anshei Shem*). Although wild, a *ramach* is still considered the same kind of animal as a domestic horse.

The word יַחְדָּו, *together,* used by the Torah (*Deut.* 22:10) in the prohibition on working with a mixed team is understood by *Sifrei* as excluding the *ramach* from the purview of this prohibition altogether. Evidently, as an animal so wild that it cannot be harnessed (*Yerushalmi*), a *ramach* could not be teamed up with any animal for work in unison. Following this approach, the mishnah here could be interpreted to mean that the *ramach* is permitted to be teamed with all other animals, since it is not compatible with any, and can therefore never work in unison (*Emunas Yosef* to *Yerushalmi*, s.v. ר׳ אמי). [It is possible, however, that *Sifrei's* exclusion is only according to the opinion of R' Meir and

וְאַדְנֵי הַשָּׂדֶה חַיָּה. רַבִּי יוֹסֵי אוֹמֵר: מְטַמְּאוֹת
בָּאֹהֶל כְּאָדָם. הַקֻּפָּד וְחֻלְדַּת הַסְּנָיִים חַיָּה. חֻלְדַּת
הַסְּנָיִים — רַבִּי יוֹסֵי אוֹמֵר בֵּית שַׁמַּאי אוֹמְרִים:
מְטַמֵּא כַּזַּיִת בְּמַשָּׂא וְכָעֲדָשָׁה בְּמַגָּע.

יד אברהם

is disputed by the mishnah (see *Rabbeinu Hillel* ad loc. and *Teshuvos Baalei Tosafos*, ed. Aegus p. 100 cited above, mishnah 4, s.v. ולא את הלובדקים לגמלים).]

וְאַדְנֵי הַשָּׂדֶה חַיָּה. — The *adnei hasadeh is a wild animal.*

Rav defines *adnei hasadeh*[1] as a creature which lived in the fields (or jungles) and was attached by its navel to a cord which emerged from the ground. Its face, hands, and legs resembled a human's, and the creature was very dangerous. Although its movement was limited to the radius of the cord, it was unapproachable, and killed anything which entered its domain. Its life depended on the cord remaining intact, and severing this lifeline was the only way to kill it. Hunters would stand outside the creature's domain, and shoot arrows at the cord. If they severed it, the creature would let out a horrendous groan and immediately drop dead. The creature was also known as *yidoa* and one of its bones was used by sorcerers called *yidonim*. *Rav's* description more or less matches the description given by *Rash* in the name of Rabbi Meir ben R' Klonimus of Speyer (see also *Semag* negative precepts §39 and *Sefer HaChinuch* §514).

Yerushalmi translates *adnei hasadeh* as *mountain man* and mentions that it

lives from its navel. *Aruch* (s.v. אדני השדה) offers two explanations of the term: (1) humans who grew up in the jungle; (2) a creature which resembles a human. *Rambam Comm.* identifies the *adnei hasadeh* with *al-nasnas*, a creature which was reputed to speak incessantly without interruption and whose speech was like that of a human. [In modern Egyptian Arabic, *al-nasnas* means a monkey; in medieval Arabic it connoted a mythical one-armed and one-legged creature.]

Tif. Yis. identifies the mountain man as an orangutan which was trained to eat and dress like a human (see also *Boaz*).

The classification of the *adnei hasadeh* as a wild animal is significant in contract law. If someone sells all the wild animals in his possession, the *adnei hasadeh* is also included. If he sells all his domestic animals, this is not included (*Rambam Comm.* to mishnah 6; see *Tosefta* 5:5).

רַבִּי יוֹסֵי אוֹמֵר: מְטַמְּאוֹת בָּאֹהֶל כְּאָדָם. — *R' Yose says: It conveys tumah through overshadowing just like a human.*

The corpse of a human being conveys tumah through overshadowing.[2] This means that things or people which are under the same roof as the corpse, or

---

1. Literally, *adnei hasadeh* would seem to mean lords or masters of the field or jungle. If so, however, it ought to be read: *adonei hasadeh*. Some texts have אבני השדה (see *Job* 5:23). The term אבני can be understood as equivalent to בני which would translate as: children or people of the field or jungle. (See *Talmudic Encyclopedia*, s.v. אדני השדה.)

2. There is a dispute as to whether this is true for corpses of all human beings, or only of Jews (*Yevamos* 61a and *Tosafos* ad loc. s.v. וממגע). The *Tanna* here who assigns this *tumah* even to *adnei hasadeh* certainly follows the view that the corpses of all human beings convey such *tumah*, since obviously *adnei hasadeh* are not Jews (*Meleches Shlomo* to mishnah 6; see also R' Yosef Engel, *Beis HaOtzar* Vol. 1, *Klal* 8). As to whether *tumah* contracted through being over the corpse is considered overshadowing or contact, see *Rashash* to *Niddah* 57a.

The *adnei hasadeh* is a wild animal. R' Yose says: It conveys *tumah* through overshadowing just like a human. The porcupine and the stone marten are wild animal(s). The stone marten — R' Yose says that Beis Shammai say: It conveys *tumah* through carrying as the size of an olive's bulk, and [*tumah*] through contact as the size of a lentil.

YAD AVRAHAM

which are over the corpse, contract tumah (see *Numbers* 19:14). R' Yose maintains that the corpse of an *adnei hasadeh* also conveys *tumah* in this way. His source for this is the verse (*Numbers* 19:16): *Whoever touches* [a corpse] *in the open field ... becomes tamei*, which he renders as: Whoever touches the corpse of a creature which grows in the open field [i.e. an *adnei hasadeh*] ... becomes *tamei*. The halachah does not follow R' Yose (*Rav; Rambam Comm.*).

It is possible to understand R' Yose to mean merely that *adnei hasadeh* conveys tumah like a human being, but not that it is in fact considered a human. However, *Rash* and *Rav* both suggest that according to R' Yose, *adnei hasadeh* is a type of human (see *Aruch* quoted above).

הַקֻּפָּד וְחֻלְדַּת הַסְּנָיִים חַיָּה. — *The porcupine and the stone marten are wild animals.*

[The identification of חֻלְדַּת הַסְּנָיִים (lit. *chuldah* of the bushes) follows Y. Feliks, *Plants and Animals of the Mishnah*, p. 227.]

These animals might have been thought to be among the eight crawling creatures listed in *Lev.* 11:29-30 whose corpses convey *tumah*. The mishnah therefore stresses that the porcupine and stone marten are not crawling creatures, but wild animals. [Corpses of wild animals also convey *tumah*, but in different ways than the eight crawling creatures — see below.] The classification of these creatures as wild animals has additional ramifications: If someone sells the wild animals in his possession, these creatures are included (*Mishnah Rishonah*).

חֻלְדַּת הַסְּנָיִים — רַבִּי יוֹסֵי אוֹמֵר בֵּית שַׁמַּאי אוֹמְרִים: מְטַמֵּא כַּזַּיִת בְּמַשָּׂא וְכָעֲדָשָׁה בְּמַגָּע. — *The stone marten — R' Yose says that Beis Shammai say: It conveys tumah through carrying as the size of an olive's bulk, and [tumah] through contact, as the size of a lentil.*

According to R' Yose, Beis Shammai were uncertain whether the חֻלְדַּת הַסְּנָיִים is a type of חֹלֶד, one of the eight crawling creatures listed in *Lev.* 11:29-31, or whether it is a land mammal. There is a difference between crawling creatures and land mammals with respect to the laws of *tumah*. With regard to the types of *tumah* which they convey, the law for land mammals is more severe: The carcasses of land mammals (whether of non-kosher animals, or of kosher animals which were not ritually slaughtered) convey *tumah* via contact, as well as by being carried (*Lev.* 11:24-28); the carcass of one of the eight crawling creatures conveys *tumah* only through contact, but not through being carried (*Lev.* 11:32; *Keilim* 1:1). On the other hand, with respect to the minimum quantity which conveys *tumah*, the law for crawling creatures is more severe: The carcass of a crawling creature conveys *tumah* with pieces as small as a lentil (*Chagigah* 11a); but the carcass of a land mammal conveys *tumah* only with pieces at least as large as an olive (*Niddah* 42b).

Because of their uncertainty as to how to classify the חֻלְדַּת הַסְּנָיִים, Beis Shammai ruled that its carcass must be given the stringencies of both crawling creatures and land mammals. That is, it conveys *tumah* through carrying as the

שׁוֹר [ו] בָּר מִין בְּהֵמָה. וְרַבִּי יוֹסֵי אוֹמֵר: מִין חַיָּה.

כֶּלֶב מִין חַיָּה. רַבִּי מֵאִיר אוֹמֵר: מִין בְּהֵמָה.

יד אברהם

size of an olive's bulk, just like the carcass of a land mammal; at the same time it conveys *tumah* through contact as the size of a lentil, just like the carcass of one of the eight crawling creatures (*Rav; Rosh; Rash; Rambam Comm.*).

6.

The mishnah continues its classification of various animals as either wild or domestic. It closes its treatment of the laws of *kilayim* of animals with the rule for a team consisting of an animal together with a person.

שׁוֹר בָּר מִין בְּהֵמָה. וְרַבִּי יוֹסֵי אוֹמֵר: מִין חַיָּה. — *The wild ox is a variety of domestic animal. R' Yose says: A variety of wild animal.*

The Torah (*Deut.* 14:4-5) names ten species of kosher animals which it separates into two groups, one of three species (ibid. verse 4) and the other of seven (ibid. verse 5). The first group apparently corresponds to domestic animals and the second to wild animals. The Sages (the *Tanna Kamma*) and R' Yose dispute the identity of the תְּאוֹ, one of the animals listed in the group of seven wild animals (v. 5). R' Yose maintains that the תְּאוֹ is the wild ox. Since the domestic ox (i.e. the שׁוֹר) is listed as a distinct species among the three domestic species which are kosher (ibid. v. 4), it follows according to R' Yose that the wild ox is a different kind of animal from the domestic ox, and the two may not be mated or teamed together (*Tosefta* 1:6; *Yerushalmi*).

The Sages, however, do not identify the תְּאוֹ as the wild ox. In their opinion, the wild ox is the same kind of animal as the domestic ox, and both animals are included in the kosher domestic species שׁוֹר. According to the Sages, the wild ox was at one time domestic prior to fleeing to the wilds. Thus, the wild ox and the domestic ox are not *kilayim* with one another, and

they may be mated or teamed together (*Tosefta* 1:6; *Yerushalmi*).

The question of whether the wild ox is just another variety of ox, or a different kind of animal altogether, has indications in other areas besides *kilayim*. For example, the Torah (*Lev.* 7:23) forbids consumption of the fat of kosher *domestic* animals, but not of kosher *wild* animals (Mishnah *Chullin* 8:6). If the wild ox is one of the kosher wild animals, as R' Yose maintains, its fat will be permitted. But according to the *Tanna Kamma*, the wild ox is a variety of the domestic ox and its fat is forbidden (*Rav; Rambam Comm.* from *Tosefta* 1:6).

This is suggested by the mishnah's wording: *The wild ox is a variety of domestic animal*, rather than simply: *The wild ox is an ox*. If all the mishnah wanted to teach is that these two animals are the same kind with respect to *kilayim*, the latter formulation would have sufficed. The assertion by the *Tanna Kamma* that the wild ox is a *domestic animal* teaches that all the laws applicable to domestic animals apply to the wild ox. Accordingly, its fat is forbidden for consumption (*Shach Yoreh Deah* 297:6).

Rav Huna bar Chiya (*Chullin* 80a) asserts that even the *Tanna Kamma* accepts the identification of תְּאוֹ listed in *Deut.* 14:5 as the wild ox.[1] Nevertheless, they consider it a

---

1. The *Gemara* (*Chullin* 80a) translates wild ox as תּוֹרְבַּלָא in Aramaic. This is the same as the translation given by *Yerushalmi*, תּוֹר בַּר, it being common for the letters ר and ל to be

6. The wild ox is a variety of domestic animal. R' Yose says: A variety of wild animal.

The dog is a variety of wild animal. R' Meir says: A variety of domestic animal.

YAD AVRAHAM

domestic animal rather than a wild one (see *Maggid Mishneh* and *Kesef Mishneh* to *Rambam, Hil. Maachalos Asuros* 1:8). This conflicts with *Yerushalmi* which states that the *Tanna Kamma*, who considers the wild ox to be a kind of domestic ox, identifies תְּאוֹ differently. However, *Beur HaGra* (*Yoreh Deah* 28:6) elegantly demonstrates that the conclusion of the *Gemara* (*Chullin* ibid.) agrees with *Yerushalmi*.

כֶּלֶב מִין חַיָּה. רַבִּי מֵאִיר אוֹמֵר: מִין בְּהֵמָה. — *The dog is a variety of wild animal. R' Meir says: A variety of domestic animal.*

The classification of a dog as a wild animal or a domestic one has consequences in contract law, as for example when a person sells or donates all the wild animals in his possession (*Rav; Rosh; Rash; Rambam Comm.* from *Tosefta* 5:5). [As explained below, this dispute has consequences for *kilayim* as well.]

In mishnah 1:6, it was taught that wolves and dogs are *kilayim* with one another, as are country dogs and foxes. *Yerushalmi* 1:6 infers from the mishnah's structure that dogs are not *kilayim* with country dogs. That is, country dogs and dogs are all the same kind of animal.

Yerushalmi adds that this view conflicts with that of R' Meir in our mishnah, since all agree that the country dog is a wild animal. It follows that the country dog cannot be the same kind of animal as the dog, and they are therefore *kilayim* with one another according to R' Meir.

From the foregoing, it emerges that the classification of the dog as a wild or domestic animal has implications not only for contract law, but for the laws of *kilayim* as well (*R' Shlomo Sirilio*). It is odd therefore that *Tosefta* 5:5 seems to maintain that the *only*

consequence of the dispute between R' Meir and the *Tanna Kamma* is with regard to the laws of contracts! *Tzofnas Pane'ach* (*Hil. Kilayim* 9:5) notes an additional difficulty with *Tosefta* 1:5, which asserts, without hint of any dissenting opinion, that the wild ox and ox are *kilayim* one with the other. Yet, in the mishnah this seems to be disputed by the Sages and R' Yose (above). In fact, *Rambam* (*Hil. Kilayim* 9:5), presumably following the Sages of our mishnah, extrapolates from the case of a wild ox and an ox, and the case of a *ramach* and a horse (see *Rambam's* interpretation to previous mishnah), that in general for a kind of animal which has a domestic variety (יִשׁוּבִי) as well as a wild variety (מִדְבָּרִי), the two varieties are considered the same kind. This is clearly at odds with *Tosefta* 1:5 which lists several examples of animals with domestic and wild varieties and states that the wild varieties *are kilayim* with the domestic ones.

Evidently, at issue here is the basis for classification. *Yerushalmi* maintains that the wild variety of a particular kind of animal is *not* a different kind of animal from the domestic variety. [Perhaps this is because the wild variety itself began as a domestic one (see above, s.v. שׁוֹר, concerning the wild ox).] Accordingly, both the wild and the domestic variants will be characterized identically. Since R' Meir here considers the dog to be a domestic animal, it must be a different kind of animal from the country dog which is a wild animal. And since mishnah 1:6 holds that a dog and a country dog are not *kilayim* (according to *Yerushalmi*), that mishnah must disagree with R' Meir.

Tosefta, on the other hand, has different criteria for classification, according to which the domestic and wild varieties of a particular kind of animal are *kilayim* with one another. Thus, both R' Meir and the Sages

interchanged (*Sefer Haltur* ed. R' Meir Yonah, *Hil. Shechitah Shaar II* p. 43).

According to Rav Huna bar Chiya, the second grouping of kosher animals (*Deut.* 14:5) includes six which are wild along with the תְּאוֹ, the *wild ox*, which is domestic. It is therefore not at all clear why the Torah separated the ten kosher animals into two groups.

חֲזִיר מִין בְּהֵמָה. עָרוֹד מִין חַיָּה. הַפִּיל וְהַקּוֹף מִין חַיָּה.
וְאָדָם מֻתָּר עִם כֻּלָּם — לִמְשׁוֹךְ, וְלַחֲרוֹשׁ, וּלְהַנְהִיג.

[א] אֵין אָסוּר מִשּׁוּם כִּלְאַיִם אֶלָּא צֶמֶר וּפִשְׁתִּים. וְאֵינוֹ מְטַמֵּא בַּנְּגָעִים אֶלָּא צֶמֶר וּפִשְׁתִּים. אֵין הַכֹּהֲנִים לוֹבְשִׁין לְשַׁמֵּשׁ בְּבֵית הַמִּקְדָּשׁ אֶלָּא צֶמֶר וּפִשְׁתִּים.

יד אברהם

can agree that a dog and a country dog are *kilayim* regardless of whether a dog is classified as domestic or wild. Although the Sages classify a common dog as a wild animal just like the country dog, they view the two as different kinds of animals which are *kilayim* with one another. Since both R' Meir and the Sages agree that a dog and a country dog are *kilayim*, it follows that the dispute between R' Meir and the Sages has nothing to do with *kilayim*, as *Tosefta* explains. [See *Shach Yoreh Deah* 297:6. *Tos. Yom Tov's* opinion would seem to accord with that of *Tosefta*. The law as formulated by *Rambam* (*Hil. Kilayim* 9:5) and *Shulchan Aruch* (*Yoreh Deah* 297:7) follows *Yerushalmi*.]

חֲזִיר מִין בְּהֵמָה. עָרוֹד מִין חַיָּה. הַפִּיל וְהַקּוֹף מִין חַיָּה. —*The pig is a variety of domestic animal. The arod is a variety of wild animal. The elephant and the monkey are varieties of wild animals.*

[As explained above, the classification of a species as חַיָּה or בְּהֵמָה affects the interpretation of a contract which mentions one of these groupings (cf. *Tif. Yis.*).]

The *arod* is a wild donkey (*Rav; Rambam Comm.*). Above (mishnah 1:6) it was

taught that an *arod* is *kilayim* with a donkey despite their resemblance. [Although in general a wild variety of an animal is *not* considered to be *kilayim* with the domestic variety, the *arod* is nonetheless *kilayim* with the donkey (*Rambam, Hil. Kilayim* 9:4-5). Evidently, the *arod* did not originate in a domestic environment.]

וְאָדָם מֻתָּר עִם כֻּלָּם — לִמְשׁוֹךְ, וְלַחֲרוֹשׁ, וּלְהַנְהִיג. — *And man is permitted with them all — to pull, to plow, and to lead.*

That is, it is permitted, for example, for a human to harness himself together with an animal and pull something. Likewise, if a person is teamed up with some animal, it is permitted for another person to lead such a team (see *Meleches Shlomo*). This is because the Torah (*Deut.* 22:10) specifies that it is prohibited to plow *with an ox and a donkey together*, implying that only a mixed team of animals is forbidden. But a mixed team consisting of an animal with a person is permitted (*Rav; Rosh; Rash; Rambam Comm.* from *Sifrei*).

Chapter 9

1.

The final chapter of the tractate is devoted to the laws of *kilayim* of garments. The Torah (*Lev.* 19:19) states: *A garment containing a shaatnez mixture shall not come upon you.* In *Deut.* 22:11 this prohibition recurs in a slightly different form, as follows: *Do not wear shaatnez, wool and linen together.* The term *shaatnez* is defined later in

The pig is a variety of domestic animal. This is body content.

9
1

The pig is a variety of domestic animal. The *arod* is a variety of wild animal. The elephant and the monkey are varieties of wild animals.

And man is permitted with them all — to pull, to plow, and to lead.

1. **N**o [fabrics are prohibited because of *kilayim* other than wool or flax. No [fabrics] contract *tzaraas* other than wool or flax. The *Kohanim* do not wear for service in the Temple any [fabrics] other than wool and flax.

YAD AVRAHAM

the chapter, and is generally used as a synonym for *kilayim* of garments. It will be recalled from mishnah 8:1 that there is no prohibition on making *shaatnez*. The only prohibition is to wear it (or to have it upon you, a concept which will be discussed below). The following mishnah discusses the materials which constitute *kilayim* together and thus are governed by the above prohibitions.

אֵין אָסוּר מִשּׁוּם כִּלְאַיִם אֶלָּא צֶמֶר וּפִשְׁתִּים. — *No [fabrics] are prohibited because of kilayim other than wool or flax.*

The Torah's specification of wool and flax (*Deut.* 22:11) teaches that only these materials are included in the *kilayim* prohibition (*Rav; see Mishnah Rishonah*). The Scriptural term *wool* refers exclusively to sheep's wool, and does not include fabrics made of hairs of any other animals (*Rav, Rosh, Rash* from *Yerushalmi*). The term *flax* refers to both the flax plant as well as the linen fabric derived from it. However, only the authentic flax plant is referred to. Plants which resemble it, and produce fibers which can be spun and woven, are not included (*Rosh*). Thus, only a combination of sheep's wool and linen is forbidden to wear as *shaatnez*. [Exactly what type of combination is forbidden to wear will be discussed below.]

וְאֵינוֹ מִטַּמֵּא בַּנְּגָעִים אֶלָּא צֶמֶר וּפִשְׁתִּים. — *No [fabrics] contract tzaraas other than wool or flax.*

Green or red discolorations of white wool or linen garments can be indications of *tzaraas*, a type of *tumah* which affects people, garments and houses (see

Lev. 13:1-14:57). That only garments of wool or of linen are susceptible to *tzaraas* is stated explicitly in the Torah (*Lev.* 13:47): *When a garment is afflicted with tzaraas, a garment of wool or a garment of linen.* The repeated specification of wool or linen (see *Lev.* 13:52,59) teaches that the reference is to white garments only. This is because linen did not hold dye well and was hence generally white (see *Rashi* to *Niddah* 61b). The repeated mention of wool and linen teaches that likewise, the wool garment referred to is a white one. Neither a dyed wool nor a naturally colored wool (such as from a black sheep) is susceptible to this *tumah* (*Rosh, Rash* from *Yerushalmi*). [With *kilayim*, however, color is not a factor and a mixture of dyed wool with linen is also prohibited (ibid.).]

אֵין הַכֹּהֲנִים לוֹבְשִׁין לְשַׁמֵּשׁ בְּבֵית הַמִּקְדָּשׁ אֶלָּא צֶמֶר וּפִשְׁתִּים. — *The Kohanim do not wear for service in the Temple any [fabrics] other than wool and flax.*

The uniform worn by the regular *Kohen* (as opposed to the *Kohen Gadol*, high priest) for service in the Temple consisted of four garments: a tunic, a turban, pants, and a belt. Of these, all but

צֶמֶר גְּמַלִּים וְצֶמֶר רְחֵלִים שֶׁטְּרָפָן זֶה בָּזֶה —
אִם רֹב מִן הַגְּמַלִּים מֻתָּר; וְאִם רֹב מִן הָרְחֵלִים
אָסוּר; מֶחֱצָה לְמֶחֱצָה, אָסוּר. וְכֵן הַפִּשְׁתָּן
וְהַקַּנְבּוֹס שֶׁטְּרָפָן זֶה בָּזֶה.

יד אברהם

the belt were pure linen. The belt consisted of a mixture of linen and wool, and was an exception to the laws of *kilayim* which normally forbid wearing such a garment (*Arachin* 3b).

The production of the *Kohen's* uniform is discussed by the Torah in *Exodus* chapter 28 and again in chapter 39. The materials mentioned are: *sheish, bud, techeiles, argaman,* and *tolaas shani. Sheish* and *bud* are synonyms for linen. The flax plant was called *bud* which means single (as in לבד) and refers to the single stem which emerges from the flax seed (*Rav, Rosh, Rash* from *Yerushalmi* and *Zevachim* 18b). The term *sheish,* which apparently refers to six-ply thread, is shown by *Yerushalmi* to refer to linen (see also *Yevamos* 4b). *Techeiles, argaman* and *tolaas shani* are all dyed wools. *Techeiles* is bluish wool, *argaman* is reddish, and *tolaas shani* is crimson (*Rav; Rambam Comm.*).

צֶמֶר גְּמַלִּים וְצֶמֶר רְחֵלִים שֶׁטְּרָפָן זֶה בָּזֶה — אִם רֹב מִן הַגְּמַלִּים מֻתָּר; וְאִם רֹב מִן הָרְחֵלִים אָסוּר; מֶחֱצָה לְמֶחֱצָה, אָסוּר. — *Camel's hair and sheep's wool which he mixed together — if the majority is from camels it is permitted; if the majority is from sheep it is forbidden; half and half, it is forbidden.*

If a person mixed camel's hair together with sheep's wool, and the majority of the mixture was camel's hair, then it is permitted to add flax to this mixture. This is because the sheep's wool is nullified by the majority of camel's hair, and the mixture of camel's hair and sheep's wool is thus viewed as containing camel's hair alone. Since it is permitted to mix flax with camel's hair, it is permitted to mix flax with this mixture which is

treated as if it consists of camel's hair alone (*Rav; Rosh; Rash;* cf. *Noda BiYehudah Tinyana* §186). If, however, the original mixture was primarily wool, or even if it was only half wool, the wool is not ignored, and it is forbidden to mix this with flax.

[A mixture of flax and wool as such is not subject to any prohibitions. Only garments containing flax and wool are forbidden to wear, but raw flax and raw wool do not constitute *shaatnez*. When the mishnah here states that it is permitted to add flax to the mixture, the point is that it is permitted to spin threads from the resulting mixture and weave them into a garment. Although the mixture contains flax and wool, the garment will not be *shaatnez* since the wool was nullified by the camel's hair. The resulting garment is considered to be composed of camel's hair and flax, a combination which it is permitted to wear.]

Yerushalmi states further that if raw wool became mixed up with flax, it can be salvaged by adding camel's hair in sufficient quantity to annul the wool. That is, by adding to the mixture of flax and wool a quantity of camel's hair greater than that of the wool, the wool is nullified and the mixture is viewed as containing camel's hair and flax only. A garment spun from this mixture is permitted for wearing (*Rosh, Hil. Kilei Begadim* par. 5; *Tur, Yoreh Deah* 299).

It is evident from *Yerushalmi* that although sheep's wool is nullified by a majority of camel's hair, it is not nullified by a majority of flax. If a small amount of wool was mixed together with a large quantity of flax, the thread spun from this mixture would be *shaatnez*. Although a minority component of a mixture is normally disre-

9
1
Camel's hair and sheep's wool which he mixed together — if the majority is from camels it is permitted; if the majority is from sheep it is forbidden; half and half, it is forbidden. And so too with flax and hemp which he mixed together.

garded (בִּיטוּל בְּרוֹב), that is only when the minority component is something prohibited which has become mixed with a greater quantity of something permitted. The prohibited item loses its significance and is ignored. In the case of kilayim, however, the two components, wool and linen, are independently both permitted, and it is only the combination of the two which creates a prohibited item. It is therefore not possible to speak of the one component being annulled by the other; on the contrary, on being mixed one with the other, both components contribute to the creation of a prohibited item, and neither can therefore be ignored (Tosafos to Niddah 61b, Avodah Zarah 65b; see Beur HaGra, Yoreh Deah 299:5). [Rambam apparently disputes this premise and maintains that wool thread is not nullified by flax thread; but raw wool is nullified by raw flax. See Hasagos HaRavad and Kesef Mishneh to Hil. Kilayim 10:7, and Malbim, Artzos HaChaim, Eretz Yehudah 9:1, p. 43b.]

וְכֵן הַפִּשְׁתָּן וְהַקַּנְבּוֹס שֶׁטְּרָפָן זֶה בָּזֶה. — And so too with flax and hemp which he mixed together.

As above, if flax was mixed with hemp, and hemp formed the majority of the mixture, it is permitted to mix in wool (Rav; Rosh; Rash).

The law of this mishnah that sheep's wool is nullified by camel's hair, and that likewise flax is nullified by hemp, is at the forefront of a major halachic controversy concerning nullification of prohibited items. There is a general rule that if a prohibited item becomes mixed up with a sufficient quantity of some permitted item, then it is nullified and the prohibition is effectively abrogated. The question therefore arises as to the possibility of nullification when a permitted item becomes mixed with another permitted item:

Perhaps nullification is a function of the contrast between the prohibited state of the one item and the permitted state of the other, but if both are permitted, the process of nullification does not operate[1] (see Ran, Nedarim 52a).

The question assumed significance in the context of the laws of Passover. During Passover, the law is that even minute amounts of leaven are not nullified in a mixture. If a crumb of bread falls into a stew on Passover, the entire stew becomes forbidden. The question raised, however, is whether leaven (chametz) which was mixed up in some unleavened product before Passover is nullified. Since at that time the leaven is a permissible item, it may be argued that even permissible items can be nullified by a majority. The proof marshaled for this is the law of our mishnah that sheep's wool is annulled by camel's hair (Ran, responsa 54 & 59; cf. Noda BiYehudah Tinyana §186). Others take the view that the sheep's wool must not be viewed as a permitted item at all. Since at all times it is forbidden in combination with flax, it is characterized as a forbidden item, which can be nullified by something such as camel's hair which is permitted. However, this cannot be compared to leaven, which is not at all prohibited before Passover, and cannot be characterized then as a prohibited item (Rabbeinu Chaim Or Zarua §17 and independently, R' Akiva Eiger, Responsa §38). Another position is that neither sheep's wool, nor leaven before Passover, should be viewed as permitted items. The sheep's wool must be viewed as prohibited since it is always forbidden with flax, and the leaven must be viewed as prohibited, since it will be prohibited on Passover (Temim Deim §36; see Malbim, Artzos HaChaim, Eretz Yehudah 9:1).

1. R' Akiva Eiger (Responsa §207) suggests that this question may be the subject of a dispute between the Amoraim Abaye and Rava. See also R' Baruch Frankel, Baruch Taam, Shaar 1 at length.

[ב] **הַשִּׁירָיִים** וְהַכָּלָךְ אֵין בָּהֶם מִשּׁוּם
כִּלְאַיִם, אֲבָל אֲסוּרִים מִפְּנֵי
מַרְאִית הָעַיִן.
הַכָּרִים וְהַכְּסָתוֹת אֵין בָּהֶם מִשּׁוּם כִּלְאַיִם,
וּבִלְבַד שֶׁלֹּא יִהְיֶה בְשָׂרוֹ נוֹגֵעַ בָּהֶן.

יד אברהם

2.

הַשִּׁירָיִים וְהַכָּלָךְ אֵין בָּהֶם מִשּׁוּם כִּלְאַיִם, אֲבָל
אֲסוּרִים מִפְּנֵי מַרְאִית הָעַיִן. — *Shirayim and kalach are not kilayim, but they are forbidden because of their appearance.*

The term *shirayim* means silk (*Rav; Rambam Comm.*). [Apparently it is related to the word Seres, the name of the Chinese people who discovered silk. The term still in use today for the cultivation of the silkworm is sericulture.] *Kalach* is explained by some to be a different grade or weave of silk (see *Aruch*, s.v. כלך (1), *Rashi, Shabbos* 20b). *Rambam* (*Hil. Kilayim* 10:1), possibly based on *Yerushalmi* (see *Dictionary of the Targumim*, etc. M. Jastrow, s.v. אגבין), describes *kalach* as a woolly substance with a golden hue which grows on the rocks of the ocean and is very soft.[1]

It was taught in the previous mishnah that the prohibition of *kilayim* of garments applies exclusively to a combination of linen and wool. Obviously, then, silks are not at all prohibited. However, because *shirayim* is soft, just like flax, and *kalach* is coarse, just like wool, these fabrics could be mistaken for flax and wool respectively (*Rambam Comm.* and

Hil. Kilayim 10:1; see *Tosefta Shabbos* 10:2 where *kalach* is listed as a woolly substance). Accordingly, it was forbidden to wear a garment containing a combination of *kalach* and *shirayim* since this would appear like a forbidden combination of wool and linen. Likewise, a combination of *shirayim* and wool, or a combination of *kalach* and linen, appears like a forbidden combination of flax and wool. Although all these combinations are permissible under Biblical law, they were forbidden Rabbinically *because of their appearance* (*Rambam, Hil. Kilayim* 10:1; see *Kesef Mishneh* ad loc. and *Bach, Yoreh Deah* 298, s.v. ואע"פ).

Ri ben Malki Tzedek explains *shirayim* as a blend of linen with silk, and *kalach* as a blend of wool with silk. He explains that *because of their appearance*, it is forbidden to wear either of these fabrics. Thus, it is forbidden to wear *shirayim* since the blend of silk with linen might be mistaken for forbidden *shaatnez*. Likewise, it is forbidden to wear a blend of wool and silk (*kalach*), since this blend might be mistaken for *shaatnez*. However, according to *Ri ben Malki Tzedek*, a blend of silks would apparently be permitted.[2]

1. *Rav* appears to combine the two definitions of *kalach* and describes it as a type of משי (a term which normally is understood to mean silk) which is woolly and golden, and grows in seaside towns. *Rambam Comm.* also refers to *kalach* as משי even though in his Code he explains it as a substance which grows on ocean rocks. Possibly, the term משי is being used loosely for any silk-like fabric (see *Ezekiel* 16:10,13).

2. *Rav*, following *Rosh*, writes that today since silk is more familiar, there is no risk of confusing it with wool or linen, and blends of *shirayim* — silk and wool — or *kalach* — silk and linen — are permitted (see also *Rash*). [This view is recorded also by *Shulchan Aruch* (*Yoreh Deah* 298:1).] For a discussion of how the Rabbinic prohibition of our mishnah was suspended — see *Rosh* (Responsa 2:8) and *Tif. Yis.*; see also *Malbim, Artzos HaChaim, HaMeir LaAretz* 9:41 at length.

2. **S**hirayim and kalach are not kilayim, but they are forbidden because of their appearance.

Mats and cushions do not [pose a problem of] kilayim, provided that his skin does not touch them.

YAD AVRAHAM

הַכָּרִים וְהַכְּסָתוֹת אֵין בָּהֶם מִשׁוּם כִּלְאַיִם, וּבִלְבָד שֶׁלֹא יִהְיֶה בְשָׂרוֹ נוֹגֵעַ בָּהֶן. — *Mats and cushions do not [pose a problem of] kilayim, provided that his skin does not touch them.*

[Although it is more or less unanimously agreed that the phrase הַכָּרִים וְהַכְּסָתוֹת refers to sleeping mats and pillows, it is not entirely clear which is which — see *Tos. Yom Tov* to *Mikvaos* 10:2. Our translation *mats and cushions* follows *Tif. Yis.*]

Under Biblical law, to lie or sit on sleeping mats or cushions which contain *shaatnez* should be permitted. This is because the Torah prohibits a person from wearing *shaatnez* (*Deut.* 22:11) and from having *shaatnez* upon him (*Lev.* 19:19); it does not prohibit him from lying upon it (*Beitzah* 14b et al.). Nevertheless, the Rabbis were concerned about a violation of the *shaatnez* prohibition which would occur if, while sitting or reclining on such *kilayim* mats, a thread frayed and became wrapped on the person's flesh. They therefore forbade even lying on *kilayim* mats or cushions.

However, if the mat is very hard, or if the cushion is empty (e.g. a cushion cover or pillow case) and located on a hard surface, the Rabbis permitted sitting or lying upon it, provided that *his skin does not touch them.* This is because hard mats or cushions were not likely to fray. Thus, as long as something separates between the person's skin and the hard *kilayim* mat or cushion, sleeping on them is not a problem. However, soft mats and cushions containing *kilayim* may not be used at all. Soft mats exhibited a greater tendency to fray and in addition a person sinks into soft mats and cushions, causing the sides to bend upwards. Consequently, the risk of having *kilayim* upon oneself

with a soft mat or cushion was greater than with a hard mat. Accordingly, even though it was permitted to lie on hard mats using a separator to prevent skin contact, with soft *kilayim* mats even this was forbidden. Even if the soft *kilayim* mat is at the bottom of a pile of ten non-*kilayim* (e.g. cotton) mats, it is forbidden to lie down on the top of the pile. Although the person's body is separated from the *kilayim* by the ten cotton mats, since the *shaatnez* mat is soft, it is forbidden to sit or lie down on it even with multiple separators (*Rav* here and to mishnah 4; see *Rash* and *Rosh*).

The *Gemara* (*Beitzah* 14b) mentions two Rabbinic enactments regarding the use of *shaatnez* as a sleeping or sitting mat. The first states that although it is permitted Biblically to sit on *shaatnez*, this was Rabbinically prohibited *lest a thread become wrapped on his skin.* This would suggest that the Rabbinic prohibition applies only where direct contact is possible, but not where there is some separation between the person and the *shaatnez*. The second enactment states that it is forbidden to sleep upon a pile of ten non-*shaatnez* mats if at the bottom of the pile there is *shaatnez*. Evidently, no manner of separation between the person and the *shaatnez* is sufficient to permit sitting or lying upon it. Yet, the mishnah here teaches that there is no problem with sitting on mats or cushions, *provided that his skin does not touch them,* an apparent contradiction to the second enactment above! (*Ritva* to *Beitzah* 14b).

Some authorities resolve this conflict by assuming that indeed under the second Rabbinic enactment above, it is forbidden to use mats and cushions which contain *shaatnez*, even if there is no physical contact. The mishnah here which states otherwise does not reflect the Rabbinic legislation and in practice is not valid (see *Chiddushei HaMeiri* and *Beis HaBechirah* to *Beitzah* 14b). Most authorities, however, resolve this difficulty differently. *Ritva* (loc cit.), for example, distinguishes

אֵין עֲרַאי לְכִלְאַיִם, וְלֹא יִלְבַּשׁ כִּלְאַיִם אֲפִילוּ
עַל גַּבֵּי עֲשָׂרָה, אֲפִילוּ לִגְנוֹב אֶת הַמֶּכֶס.

יד אברהם

between hard mats and soft ones. The mishnah here which permits use of mats with a
separation is referring to hard mats alone. The
Rabbinic enactment which forbids using
shaatnez mats even with a separation is referring to soft ones. The difference between
hard and soft mats is that the latter exhibit a
greater tendency to fray or to wrap themselves around the person sitting on them. Although both enactments were designed to
prevent the possibility of such wrapping
from occurring (see Rambam, Hil. Kilayim
10:12), the second enactment was an extension intended as a reinforcement of the first.
That is, in order to enforce the first enactment, which permitted sleeping on a kilayim
mat covered by a separator but forbade sleeping in direct contact with the mat, the Rabbis
found it necessary to forbid using these mats
altogether, even with separators. This extension was needed only for soft shaatnez mats
and so only these were prohibited even with
separators. Hard mats, such as those of the
mishnah, remained permitted with a separator. The basis for the distinction between
hard and soft mats and between hard and soft
surfaces can be found in Yerushalmi, which
appears to limit the permissive ruling of the
mishnah to cases in which the mats and cushions are empty and located on hard surfaces
(cf. however interpretation of R' Aharon
HaLevi quoted by Shitah Mekubetzes and
Ritva to Beitzah ibid., and see Hasagos
HaRavad to Hil. Kilayim 10:13). [Rav, who
explains our mishnah as referring to hard
mats or cushion covers on hard surfaces, also
follows this approach.]

Ran (on Rif to Beitzah 14b) makes a different distinction. In his view, the second enactment — forbidding sleeping on a pile of ten
mats when there is shaatnez underneath —
refers specifically to shaatnez which might
normally be worn. Thus, if a shirt containing
shaatnez was located under a pile of ten non-
shaatnez mats, it would be forbidden to sleep
on the pile. The basis for this enactment was
a fear that if shaatnez which can be worn is
used as padding for sleeping — a Biblically
permitted use — then a person might come to
violate a Biblical prohibition by wearing it (cf.
Rambam, Hil. Kilayim 10:12). However,

shaatnez which is not wearable, such as a
sleeping mat, was not prohibited out of fear
that it might come to be worn. Such shaatnez
is governed only by the first enactment that
prohibits direct bodily contact with shaatnez
sleeping or sitting mats. Thus, shaatnez
which is not normally worn may be used as
padding for sitting or sleeping as long as
there is no direct contact. Since the mishnah
here is discussing mats and cushions, items
which are not normally worn, there is no need
for concern that their use as padding for
sleeping will lead to illegal wearing. There is
still, however, concern that sleeping on these
directly may lead to a thread becoming
wrapped on the person's body. Accordingly,
the mishnah states that these items do not entail a kilayim problem provided that his skin
does not touch them. Items not ordinarily
worn are subject only to the first enactment
but not to the second. Accordingly, a separator which alleviates the risk of a thread becoming wrapped on the person is enough to
permit lying upon them (see Rash; Shenos
Eliyahu).

אֵין עֲרַאי לְכִלְאַיִם, — There is no casual
kilayim,

It might have been thought that the
prohibition on wearing garments containing shaatnez is restricted to garments
in which a person is not embarrassed to
appear in public. Perhaps only such
garments count as clothes which are
governed by the laws of kilayim; but
something which a person would not
wear in public even occasionally might
not count as such and might be excluded
from the shaatnez prohibition. The mishnah therefore teaches that with respect to
kilayim there is no such distinction
operative, and there is no such thing as a
casual garment which may be worn even
though it contains shaatnez. Something
which a person would not wear outside
his house is still subject to the laws of
shaatnez just like his most elegant clothing (see Taz, Yoreh Deah 301:5). Additionally, there is no minimum time which

There is no casual *kilayim*, and a person may not wear *kilayim* even on top of ten [garments], and even in order to evade the tax.

YAD AVRAHAM

a garment must be worn in order for the wearing to constitute a transgression. If a person wears a garment which contains *shaatnez*, even for a moment, he has violated the prohibition. Even though a moment's wearing might seem casual, there is no exemption from the prohibition on *kilayim* because of casual wear (*Rav; Rosh; Rash; Rambam Comm.*).

וְלֹא יִלְבַּשׁ כִּלְאַיִם אֲפִילוּ עַל גַּבֵּי עֲשָׂרָה, — *and a person may not wear kilayim even on top of ten [garments],*

Even though the wearer does not derive any physical enjoyment from a garment worn on top of ten others, such wearing is forbidden (*Rav; Rosh; Rash*). [*Rambam* (*Hil. Kilayim* 10:18) considers wearing *kilayim* on top of ten other garments to be an illustration of the preceding rule that *there is no casual kilayim*. It is hardly something a person would normally do for any duration of time, but it is nevertheless forbidden.]

From the *Gemara* (*Yevamos* 4b) it seems that the prohibition on wearing *shaatnez* is limited to wearing which provides some direct physical benefit. However, it is possible that such benefit is not a condition for transgression, but merely a characteristic used to define prohibited forms of wearing. Thus, protecting oneself with an umbrella which contains *shaatnez* does not count as forbidden wearing even though it provides the body with protection. This is because this protection does not resemble in form the wearing of a garment on one's body. However, wearing a garment over another resembles in form wearing which provides benefit.

Thus, even though wearing a garment on top of ten others does not provide any benefit, it is forbidden (see *Beis HaLevi* I:1-3 and *Kesef Mishneh* to *Hil. Kilayim* 10:18; see also *Taz, Yoreh Deah* 301:7).

אֲפִילוּ לִגְנוֹב אֶת הַמֶּכֶס. — *and even in order to evade the tax.*

[The tax referred to is an illegal tax such as one collected by an unauthorized official, or one which has no defined rate. To evade legally imposed taxes is forbidden irrespective of the laws of *kilayim* (*Tos. Yom Tov*; see *Rav* to *Bava Kamma* 10:1 and to *Nedarim* 3:4).]

If a person was transporting merchandise and encountered a customs official, he would be taxed on his merchandise but not on his clothing. Knowing this, a person who was distributing *shaatnez*-containing garments (for the gentile market) might be tempted to evade the tax by wearing as many of these as possible in the hope that they will be mistaken for personal clothes rather than merchandise.[1] Now, the person's intention in wearing these garments is solely in order to evade the tax, and not in order to derive any physical benefit from the garments. It might therefore be argued that this does not count as a forbidden form of wearing. The mishnah therefore teaches that the person's intentions are disregarded and wearing *kilayim* in order to avoid taxation is also forbidden (*Rav; Rosh; Rash*).

According to *Rambam* (*Hil. Kilayim* 10:18), wearing *kilayim* on top of ten

---

1. Although *Rav* opts for the approach whereby the tax evasion is based on the representation of merchandise as clothing, he mentions a different explanation which he attributes to some of his teachers, according to which the wearing of *shaatnez* is intended to disguise the Jewish merchant as a gentile. The tax in question was levied only on Jews, and therefore if the Jewish merchant could succeed in disguising himself like a gentile, he would avoid being taxed. This approach assumes that it is permitted for a Jew to represent himself as a gentile for reasons such as tax avoidance, even though this is not life threatening. However, most authorities dispute this position — see *Rosh, Bava Kamma* 10:11, and *Rama, Yoreh Deah* 297:3.

[ג] מִטְפְּחוֹת הַיָּדַיִם, מִטְפְּחוֹת הַסְּפָרִים, מִטְפְּחוֹת הַסְּפָג אֵין בָּהֶם מִשּׁוּם כִּלְאַיִם. רַבִּי אֶלְעָזָר אוֹסֵר. וּמִטְפְּחוֹת הַסַּפָּרִים אֲסוּרוֹת מִשּׁוּם כִּלְאַיִם.

יד אברהם

other garments in order to evade the tax is Biblically prohibited and is punishable by lashes. However, *R' Yehudah Sir Leon* (*Tosafos Rabbeinu Yehudah to Berachos* 18a) writes that the prohibition here is by Rabbinic enactment only. Under Scriptural law, wearing *kilayim* in a way which provides no physical enjoyment is not forbidden (see below, mishnah 5).

From mishnah 5 below it appears that a person's intentions do indeed determine whether or not a given instance of wearing shaatnez is permitted or forbidden. *Rav*, among others, maintains that our mishnah and mishnah 5 are in conflict, and that according to the system of mishnah 5 — which is accepted by the halachah — it is *permitted* to wear *shaatnez* in order to evade the tax. *Rambam*, however, harmonizes the two mishnayos and records both the ruling of the mishnah below as well as the ruling here that it is forbidden to wear *kilayim* even to evade the tax. The matter will be discussed below in the commentary to mishnah 5.

3.

מִטְפְּחוֹת הַיָּדַיִם, מִטְפְּחוֹת הַסְּפָרִים, מִטְפְּחוֹת הַסְּפָג אֵין בָּהֶם מִשּׁוּם כִּלְאַיִם. — *Hand towels, handkerchiefs for [Torah] scrolls, and bath towels do not involve kilayim restrictions.*

The translation of מִטְפְּחוֹת הַיָּדַיִם is based on *Rav. Rash* and *Rosh* seem to understand this as napkins used to serve and hold food (such as meat and bread), and used also as place mats. *Handkerchiefs for [Torah] scrolls* are cloths which a person holds when reading from the Torah [which prevent him from directly touching the Torah] (*Rambam Comm.*; see *Zavim* 5:12). *Rosh* explains these to be cloths upon which the Torah is rested, while from *Rav* it appears that the reference here might be to the jackets of the Torah scrolls. *Bath towels* differ from hand towels in being much larger and used for drying the whole body, not just the hands. *Rambam* (*Hil. Kilayim* 10:22) seems to have rendered מִטְפְּחוֹת הַסְּפָג (which translates approximately as *absorbent cloths*) as dish towels used for drying or cleaning dishes and mopping floors (cf. *Rambam Comm.*).

Since these various towels and cloths are not garments, and are not intended for use in the manner of garments (i.e. to provide warmth or to protect from the sun — see mishnah 5), the *Tanna Kamma* considers them to be outside the domain of *kilayim* law (see *Mishnah Rishonah*).

רַבִּי אֶלְעָזָר אוֹסֵר. — *R' Elazar forbids.*

Rabbi Elazar argues that each of the items listed is sometimes used in the manner of a garment: A person sometimes wraps his hands and warms them in hand towels, the Torah cloths are sometimes placed on the lap and provide warmth, and bath towels are sometimes wrapped like a skirt such as when a person is embarrassed to be seen naked by his teacher (*Rav; Rosh; Rash;* cf. *Rambam, Hil. Kilayim* 10:22).

Although none of these cloths are intended as garments, Rabbi Elazar maintains that they are subject to *kilayim* law when used as such. The *Tanna Kamma*, however, maintains that only something intended for use as a garment is subject to *kilayim* law. But the items

3. **H**and towels, handkerchiefs for [Torah] scrolls, and bath towels do not involve *kilayim* restrictions. R' Elazar forbids.

Barbers' aprons are forbidden due to *kilayim*.

YAD AVRAHAM

here are not intended as garments which provide warmth. Accordingly, even if used as such, they are not subject to the restrictions of the laws of *shaatnez* (*Mishnah Rishonah*; see *Rambam, Hil. Kilayim* 10:19).

Mishnah Rishonah assumes that according to the *Tanna Kamma* the listed items are never subject to *kilayim* restrictions, while according to R' Elazar they are subject to restrictions when used as garments. However, even according to R' Elazar, when a hand towel containing *shaatnez* is used as a towel and not to provide warmth, it is permitted. The dispute then concerns the use of these cloths as garments; when they are not being used as garments, even though they contain *shaatnez*, they are permitted by all.

[It would seem possible, however, to explain that even the *Tanna Kamma* agrees that using these cloths as garments is forbidden. The dispute concerns the use of these cloths in their intended normal way. In R' Elazar's view, since these cloths are sometimes used like garments, it is forbidden to use them in any fashion lest they be used as garments (see *Beur HaGra, Yoreh Deah* 301:15). The *Tanna Kamma*, however, maintains that although as garments they are forbidden since they contain *shaatnez*, nevertheless if used in their intended way (i.e. as towels etc., not as garments) they are permitted.]

וּמִטְפְּחוֹת הַסְּפָרִים אֲסוּרוֹת מִשּׁוּם כִּלְאָיִם. — *Barbers' aprons are forbidden due to kilayim.*

Barbers' aprons are the smocks which are worn by a person having his hair cut to prevent the hair from falling on his clothes (*Rav; Rosh;* cf. *Ri ben Malki Tzedek*). If these contain *shaatnez* and are worn like a garment, they are forbidden. Even though their main purpose is to protect the *clothes* from hair, and not to protect the *body* from the cold or the sun, they are governed by the laws of *shaatnez*. This assumes that the smock

in question is in fact cut like a garment and worn like one. Thus, a sheet-like cloth which has no opening for the head, and must be attached to the clothes, would not qualify as a garment-like apron. However, a poncho-like smock with an opening which fits over the head is considered a garment. Even the *Tanna Kamma*, who excludes non-garments such as hand or bath towels from the laws of *kilayim*, agrees that a poncho-like smock is considered a garment and is subject to the laws of *shaatnez* (*Rav; Rosh* from *Yerushalmi*; see *Meleches Shlomo* and *Tos. R' Akiva*).

R' Yehosef Ashkenazi (quoted by *Meleches Shlomo*) and independently R' Akiva Eiger (in *Tos. R' Akiva*) raise a difficulty with the qualification mentioned by *Rav* and *Rosh* that the smock in question is forbidden because of *shaatnez* only if it is poncho-like and is worn like a garment. The Torah forbids two uses of *shaatnez* — wearing (*Lev.* 19:19) and having it on oneself (*Deut.* 22:10). Although if the smock does not have an opening for the head it might not be worn like a garment, nevertheless its manner of use should certainly qualify as being upon oneself. Moreover, even though the *Gemara* (*Yevamos* 4b) indicates that the prohibition on having *shaatnez* upon oneself applies only when the *shaatnez* provides benefit similar to wearing clothes, protection from falling hair should be such a benefit. This follows from the next mishnah where protection from dirt is considered a benefit which resembles wearing. Accordingly, it must be explained why a barbers' smock which does not have a head-hole is permitted.

Tif. Yis. (*Boaz* §3) suggests that there is a difference between something which protects the *clothes*, and something which protects the *body* (see also *Rashash* from *Yerushalmi* 9:2, *R' Shlomo Sirilio* to mishnah 4, s.v. אפילו, and *Beur HaGra, Yoreh Deah* 301:15; cf. *Shach, Yoreh Deah* 301:8 and *Taz, Yoreh Deah* 301:8). If *kilayim* are worn, this is forbidden even

[ד] תַּכְרִיכֵי הַמֵּת וּמַרְדַּעַת שֶׁל חֲמוֹר אֵין בָּהֶם מִשּׁוּם כִּלְאַיִם. לֹא יִתֵּן הַמַּרְדַּעַת עַל כְּתֵפוֹ, אֲפִלּוּ לְהוֹצִיא עָלֶיהָ זֶבֶל.

יד אברהם

though the wearing is in order to protect the clothes and not to benefit the body. But, if the *kilayim* are not worn like a garment, but are merely upon the person, they must be used for the body in order to be included in the *kilayim* prohibition. In the case of mishnah 4 (below), the blanket prevents the *body* from becoming soiled. Protection of the body is indeed a benefit similar to wearing clothes, and hence having *kilayim* upon oneself for the purpose of protecting the body from garbage is an offense. However, protection of the clothes is not considered a benefit resembling that

derived from garments, and hence to have *kilayim* upon oneself in order to protect one's clothes is not a violation.

A barbers' apron which has a head opening and is worn like a garment is forbidden even though its purpose is to protect the clothes and not the body. But an apron without such a slit is not forbidden, since it is used only to protect the clothes and not to protect the body. Protection of the clothes does not count as a garment-like use and is not forbidden under the prohibition of having *kilayim* upon oneself.

4.

תַּכְרִיכֵי הַמֵּת — *Shrouds for the dead*

Dead people are not subject to the commandments of the Torah and hence it is permitted to bury a person in shrouds which contain *shaatnez* (*Rav; Rosh; Rash*).

Although a dead person is not obligated in any commandments, the *Gemara* (*Menachos* 41a) indicates that *tzitzis* fringes should be attached to a four-cornered burial garment. A live person is forbidden from wearing a four-cornered garment without such fringes, and failure to attach them to a four-cornered burial garment is tantamount to mocking the dead person. It is as if we are saying to him, "We the living are still able to accumulate *mitzvos* (righteous deeds), while you are not." Now, mocking someone who is incapacitated is reprehensible behavior and even borders on blasphemy (see *Proverbs* 17:5), and for this reason the dead man is not buried in a four-cornered garment without *tzitzis*.[1]

From the above, it follows that it is forbidden to place a dead person in a situation which for a living person would amount to a transgression. But in that case, why is it permitted to bury someone in shrouds containing *shaatnez*? Even though the dead person

does not violate any prohibitions, nevertheless for us to dress him in *shaatnez* would seem to be equivalent to mocking him by reminding him that he is no longer subject to the Torah. Why is it forbidden to bury a dead person in a four-cornered garment lacking *tzitzis*, yet permitted to bury him in a garment containing *shaatnez*?

Rashbam answers that the prohibition of *shaatnez* applies only to garments which are worn in such a way as to provide the wearer with some physical benefit. Since the dead person does not derive any physical benefit from the shrouds, his wearing them does not constitute wearing which would be prohibited to a live person under *kilayim* law. Since even a live person is permitted to wear *shaatnez* if he derives no benefit from it (see below, mishnah 5; cf. mishnah 2), clothing a dead person in *shaatnez* does not emphasize the inability of the dead to do *mitzvos* and is not mocking (*Tosafos* to *Niddah* 61b).

Rabbeinu Tam has a different explanation. The *Gemara's* concern, that burying a dead person in clothes which are forbidden to a live person is reprehensible mockery, refers only to *tzitzis*. Since this particular commandment is reminiscent of all the 613 commandments of the Torah (see *Menachos* 43b), to remind

---

1. There are contradictory sources with regard to this — see *Tosafos* to *Berachos* 18a, s.v. למחר et al. For the modern custom, see *Rama, Yoreh Deah* 391:2.

4. **S**hrouds for the dead and the saddle blanket of a donkey are not subject to [the prohibitions of] *kilayim*. A person may not place a saddle blanket on his shoulder, even in order to take out the garbage.

YAD AVRAHAM

the dead person that he is exempt from this precious commandment is particularly offensive. This consideration does not apply to other commandments, such as *shaatnez*. Since the dead person is exempt from the commandments, there is nothing wrong with burying him in *shaatnez* (ibid.; *Rosh; Rash; Tos. R' Akiva;* cf. *Tif. Yis.*).

וּמַרְדַּעַת שֶׁל חֲמוֹר אֵין בָּהֶם מִשּׁוּם כִּלְאָיִם. — *and the saddle blanket of a donkey are not subject to [the prohibitions of] kilayim.*

Under Biblical law, sitting on *shaatnez* is always permitted, and the Rabbis outlawed it only because of a fear that a thread would become unraveled and wrap on the person's skin (see mishnah 2). Now, the saddle blanket of a donkey is very stiff, and even if a person sits directly upon it, there is no risk that threads might come loose and wrap themselves upon the person's skin. It is therefore permitted to use such a saddle blanket for a donkey, even though the blanket contains *shaatnez* and even though there is direct contact with the blanket. In contrast with the *mats and cushions* of mishnah 2 (above) upon which a person is permitted to sit only if *his skin does not touch them,* the *saddle blanket of a donkey* may be sat upon directly, even if there is skin contact (*Rav; Rosh*).

Alternatively, the law for the saddle blanket is identical to that of the mats and cushions above. That is, it is permitted to sit on the *shaatnez*-containing saddle blanket only if something separates between the skin and the saddle (*Rash* to mishnah 2, *Rambam, Hil. Kilayim* 10:25). The reason the mishnah specified this in mishnah 2 and did not find it necessary to do so here is that mats and cushions are often used for sleeping,

a situation in which contact with the skin is common. However, a person riding a donkey is usually dressed, so that normally his clothes separate between his skin and the saddle. Thus, in the case of mishnah 2 where normally no separation is present, the mishnah specifies that use of the mats and cushions is limited to the case in which a separator is present; in the present case of the saddle where a separator is normally present, this was not deemed necessary to stipulate. In fact, however, the law is the same, and use of the *shaatnez*-containing saddle is permitted only if there is a separator present (such as clothes) which prevents contact between the *shaatnez* and the person's skin (*Tif. Yis.; Shenos Eliyahu* to mishnah 2).

Although the mishnah permits sitting on a saddle containing *shaatnez*, this is only if the *shaatnez* is easily discernible. If the *shaatnez* in the saddle blanket is not easily discernible, there is a risk that the person might cut some of it out for use as a patch for his garment, which is Biblically forbidden. Where the *shaatnez* in a saddle is not easily visible, the Rabbis forbade its use even for sitting, lest the person cut part of it out to use as a patch in his garment (*Rav, Rosh, Rash* from *Niddah* 61b).

לֹא יִתֵּן הַמַּרְדַּעַת עַל כְּתֵפוֹ, אֲפִילוּ לְהוֹצִיא עָלֶיהָ זֶבֶל. — *A person may not place a saddle blanket on his shoulder, even in order to take out the garbage.*

Although it is permitted under Biblical law to sit upon *kilayim*, it is forbidden to have *kilayim upon oneself* (*Lev.* 19:19). However, the *Gemara* (*Yevamos* 4b) explains that the Scriptural prohibition of having *kilayim* upon oneself refers only to a situation in which the *kilayim* provides the person with a benefit similar to that derived from wearing clothes. For example, if *kilayim* which a person

[ה] מוֹכְרֵי כְסוּת מוֹכְרִין כְּדַרְכָּן, וּבִלְבַד שֶׁלֹּא יִתְכַּוְּנוּ בַּחַמָּה מִפְּנֵי הַחַמָּה, וּבַגְּשָׁמִים מִפְּנֵי הַגְּשָׁמִים. וְהַצְּנוּעִים מַפְשִׁילִין בְּמַקֵּל.

hangs on his shoulder provides him with warmth, this is considered a benefit resembling wearing and is Biblically forbidden. If the *kilayim* upon him does not provide any benefit resembling the benefit derived from wearing a garment, then no Biblical prohibition has been violated.

R' Shlomo Sirilio suggests that the padding provided by the blanket protects his shoulder from the pressure of the weight he is carrying, and therefore this counts as a benefit resembling that derived from clothing. Accordingly, the mishnah states that even though slinging the blanket over his shoulder is done in order to assist in the transporting of the garbage, nevertheless, this too counts as a benefit resembling wearing and is forbidden. [A similar approach is adopted by *Shach* (*Yoreh Deah* 301:8), who argues that protection of clothes is also a forbidden benefit, and that this is the mishnah's point here. I.e. the blanket may not be placed on his shoulder even to protect his clothes from the garbage, since protection of clothes is also a forbidden benefit (*Tos. R' Akiva*; see commentary to mishnah 3, s.v. ומטפחות הספרים).]

There is a considerable controversy as to whether stiff fabrics are included in the Biblical prohibitions of *kilayim*. Some of the *Baalei HaTosafos* (see *Tosafos* to *Shabbos* 57b

and *Beitzah* 15a) as well as *Baal HaMaor* (end of first chapter of *Beitzah*) maintain that under Biblical law, stiff fabrics are not subject to *shaatnez* prohibitions on the grounds that they do not provide warmth (see also *Rashi* to *Yoma* 69a). According to this school, the prohibition on placing the stiff saddle blanket on one's shoulder is a Rabbinic prohibition.

Rabbeinu Tam, however, takes the position that stiff fabrics are Biblically forbidden (ibid.). Although the Rabbis were lenient with regard to sitting on such fabrics (as e.g. in the preceding case of sitting on the saddle blanket), this was because *sitting on kilayim* itself is only a Rabbinical prohibition, and was instituted where there was a risk of threads becoming frayed; with stiff fabrics for which this risk is non-existent, the Rabbis were therefore lenient. However, having *kilayim* upon oneself is a Biblical prohibition, and therefore even having stiff *kilayim* upon oneself is forbidden (*Tos. Yom Tov* from *Kesef Mishneh*). Assuming that in the mishnah's case the benefit derived from the blanket over the shoulder is a benefit resembling wearing, it would follow that the prohibition here in the mishnah is Biblical. However, *Gra* (*Beur HaGra*, *Yoreh Deah* 301:15) suggests that the benefit when using the saddle blanket to assist in garbage removal is *not* a benefit resembling wearing. Nevertheless, because the blanket is *sometimes* used in a way which resembles wearing, it was Rabbinically forbidden to have it upon oneself in all cases (*Derech Emunah* 301:15).

5.

The mishnah discusses the law of garment sellers who have *shaatnez*-containing garments for sale to non-Jews (*Meiri* to *Yevamos* 4b [ed. Dikman p. 36]). As will be seen, in certain cases it is permitted for the salesman to have *shaatnez* upon him.

מוֹכְרֵי כְסוּת מוֹכְרִין כְּדַרְכָּן, — *Garment sellers may sell in their usual manner,*

Garment sellers were allowed to wear their *shaatnez*-containing merchandise in order to model it for customers (*Rav*, *Rosh*, *Rash*; see also *Tosafos* to *Bava*

Kamma 113a and *Rashi* to *Shabbos* 29b and *Pesachim* 26b). When the mishnah states that *garment sellers may sell in their usual manner*, this means that garment sellers may sell by *wearing* their merchandise *in the usual manner* (see

5. Garment sellers may sell in their usual manner, as long as they do not intend in the sun [to protect themselves] from the sun, and in the rains [to protect themselves] from the rains. The discreet ones hang [them] on a stick.

YAD AVRAHAM

Mishnah Rishonah to mishnah 2).

Alternatively, the mishnah states that they may *sell in their usual manner* with reference to their normal manner of marketing, not the normal manner of wearing (*Piskei HaRid* to *Shabbos* 29b, *Ritva* [ed. Reichman] *Shabbos* ibid.). This refers to carrying the garments on their shoulders when taking them to be sold (*Rabbeinu Chananel* to *Pesachim* 26b and *Tur, Yoreh Deah* 301; *Rabbeinu Avraham ben HaRambam, Bircas Avraham* §19 [also printed in Pardes ed. of *Rambam Sefer Zemanim*]; *Mahari Korkus* to *Hil. Kilayim* 10:16 and *Kesef Mishneh* to *Hil. Kilayim* 10:18; see also *Ri ben Malki Tzedek, Rambam Comm.* and *Hil. Kilayim* 10:16).

וּבִלְבַד שֶׁלֹּא יִתְכַּוְּנוּ בַּחַמָּה מִפְּנֵי הַחַמָּה, וּבַגְּשָׁמִים מִפְּנֵי הַגְּשָׁמִים. — *as long as they do not intend in the sun [to protect themselves] from the sun, and in the rains [to protect themselves] from the rains.*

[The term *rains* used by the mishnah can refer either to precipitation or to cold, since the rainy season in Israel occurs in the winter (see *Taanis* 1:1-2). Accordingly, *Perishah* (*Yoreh Deah* 301:10), based on *Rambam Comm.*, suggests that the mishnah should be translated: *as long as they do not intend in the "summer" [to protect themselves] from the sun and in the winter [to protect themselves] from the "cold"* (see also *Tosafos* to *Shabbos* 29b).]

Trying on *shaatnez* garments to model them is permitted only if the salesman wearing the garment does not intend to derive any physical benefit from it. For example, he does not have in mind that the *shaatnez* garment he is

modeling should protect him from the sun or the rain. If, however, his intention is to benefit in these ways from the garment, then it is Biblically forbidden for him to put it on (*Rav; Rosh; Rash*).

As understood by *Rav* et al., the mishnah here is of the opinion that as long as the person does not *intend* to benefit from the *shaatnez*-containing garment in the manner one benefits from clothes, then he is permitted to wear it. This would seem to conflict with the position of mishnah 2 above that it is forbidden to wear a *shaatnez*-containing garment on top of ten other garments in order to evade the tax. There is no intent there to derive physical protection or enjoyment from the garment and nevertheless it is forbidden (see *Bava Kamma* 113a). The conflict between mishnah 2 and the present mishnah reflects a Tannaitic dispute concerning a forbidden act performed without intention: R' Yehudah maintains that such an act is forbidden, and R' Shimon maintains that it is permitted (see *Beitzah* 23b, *Shabbos* 29b et al.). Accordingly, the present mishnah represents the view of the permissive school of R' Shimon, while mishnah 2 above represents the view of the stringent school of R' Yehudah (*Rav; Rosh; Rash;* see *Shabbos* 29b and *Bava Kamma* 113a). Since the law follows R' Shimon (*Shabbos* 95a), the present mishnah prevails and accordingly, contrary to what is stated in mishnah 2, it is *permitted* to wear *kilayim* on top of ten other garments in order to evade the tax. [Of course, this is provided that the person does not intend to protect himself from the sun or the rain.]

Even when the wearer does not consciously intend to benefit from the garment, wearing *shaatnez* is not always permitted. If benefit from the garment is inescapable and automatic (פְּסִיק רֵישָׁא), then even though the person does not want the benefit, he is viewed as intending it and hence such wearing is forbidden (see *Shabbos* 75a). For example, if the seller's own clothes do not suffice to protect him from the sun, and the addition of the

shaatnez garment does provide him with such protection, then wearing the shaatnez is forbidden even though the seller's intention is to model the garment. Accordingly, the case of our mishnah must be where the seller's other clothes already provide him with adequate protection (Tosafos Shabbos 29b, s.v. ובלבד, Tos. Rid Bava Kamma 113a).

Alternatively, some benefit from the wearing is inescapable regardless of how many garments the person has underneath the shaatnez one. Nevertheless, R' Shimon permits such wearing as long as the wearer's intention is for some purpose other than the derivation of physical benefit from the wearing (e.g. he wears it to model it for customers or to evade the tax). Even though some benefit is inescapable, we do not view the wearer as intending this benefit. This is because pleasure or benefit which a person enjoys automatically without intending it is not considered pleasure. Thus, the usual rule of פְּסִיק רֵישָׁא, that an action which automatically involves a violation is forbidden even if the person did not intend the prohibition, is not applicable. Although the Torah prohibits wearing shaatnez in a manner which provides physical benefit, and although all wearing provides some such benefit, nevertheless, if the person does not wear the shaatnez in order to derive physical benefit from the wearing, the benefit is not considered a benefit, and hence no violation has occurred (Ran to Rif, Chullin 32a [Vilna ed.]; Tos. R' Akiva).

Aruch (s.v. פסק) advances a theory that unintended but automatic violations are only prohibited when the perpetrator is pleased about the forbidden act, even though this was not his primary objective. If however, the perpetrator has no interest in the forbidden act, then even though it is an inescapable consequence of his action, the action is permitted since his intention was for a permitted objective and not for a violation. Accordingly, when the salesman tries on the clothes, there is an inescapable violation since the clothes certainly provide some protection and benefit. However, the salesman put the clothes on not in order to gain this benefit from the clothes, but in order to test them for size. Since this is a permissible objective, and since furthermore the salesman is indifferent to any protection or benefit automatically derived from the wearing, the wearing is permitted (Ramban to Shabbos 111a; see Drush VeChidush Maarachah §10).

According to the alternative approach (above), that the mishnah here is discussing carrying shaatnez garments on one's shoulder, and not wearing them, the mishnah teaches that doing so is permitted if the person does not intend to derive benefit from the garments on his shoulder. Carrying garments on one's shoulder is an example of having shaatnez upon oneself, and this is forbidden only when the shaatnez provides some physical benefit comparable to that derived from wearing clothes (Yevamos 4b). Unlike clothes which are worn, clothes carried on the shoulder do not automatically provide protection or warmth. The mishnah therefore teaches that as long as the person does not intend for the shaatnez garments carried on his shoulders to provide him with such benefit, the carrying is permitted (Rabbeinu Avraham ben HaRambam, Bircas Avraham §19 [also printed in Pardes ed. of Rambam, Sefer Zemanim]; see also Taz, Yoreh Deah 301:7 and Merkeves HaMishneh to Hil. Shabbos Chapter 1 [quoted by Tos. Anshei Shem to mishnah 2, s.v. את המכס, and Pischei Teshuvah, Yoreh Deah 301:5]).

According to this latter system that our mishnah is discussing carrying shaatnez, not wearing it, there is no need to assume that the law stated in mishnah 2 (about wearing shaatnez on top of ten garments in order to evade the tax) is in conflict with the law of our mishnah. In mishnah 2 the case involves wearing shaatnez, as evidenced by the wording of that mishnah: a person may not wear kilayim even on top of ten [garments] etc. Wearing a shaatnez garment is forbidden even though the person does so to evade the tax. Although his intention is not for any benefit provided by the wearing, it is forbidden nonetheless, either because such benefit is automatic (Rabbeinu Avraham ben HaRambam loc. cit.) or because wearing is forbidden even if no benefit is derived (Mahari Korkus to Hil. Kilayim 10:16 and Kesef Mishneh to Hil. Kilayim 10:18; Shenos Eliyahu). However, having shaatnez upon oneself, as in our mishnah, is forbidden only if it provides benefit. Since such benefit is not automatic when shaatnez is carried on the shoulder, if he carries shaatnez on his shoulder and does not in-

tend thereby to protect himself *in the sun from the sun* or *in the rains from the rains*, then it is permitted.

[The assertion that wearing *shaatnez* is forbidden because it automatically provides benefit would seem to be disputed by *Rambam* (*Hil. Kilayim* 10:18), who writes that *wearing* a *shaatnez* garment on top of ten others to avoid the tax is forbidden and punishable by lashes, even though it provides him with *no benefit at all* (see however *Mahari Korkus* ibid. who tries to reinterpret this statement). Likewise, it is difficult to understand the contention that wearing *shaatnez* is forbidden even where it provides no benefit, whereas having *shaatnez* upon oneself is forbidden only if it provides benefit. The rule limiting the prohibition of having *shaatnez* on oneself to a case when one derives benefit from it is learned by the *Gemara* from a comparison to the prohibition of wearing *shaatnez* (see *Yevamos* 4b). If wearing itself need not provide any benefit, what source is there for requiring such benefit as a definitive part of having *shaatnez* upon oneself? (See *Mahari Korkus* loc. cit. and *Beis HaLevi* I:1:6.) Perhaps, a *shaatnez* garment worn on top of ten others is considered having *shaatnez* upon oneself and not wearing it (see *Tos. R' Akiva* to *Shabbos* 16:4, §142 and §144). When the Torah forbids *wearing shaatnez*, the reference is only to normal wearing which provides benefit (see *Ramban* to *Shabbos* 111a). The prohibition on having *shaatnez* upon oneself refers to having *shaatnez* upon oneself in a way which resembles wearing (*Yevamos* 4b and see *Rambam, Hil. Kilayim* 10:12). If the *shaatnez* is carried on the shoulder, the similarity to wearing is in the provision of benefits such as warmth and protection from the sun. If the *shaatnez* is worn on top of ten garments, even though it provides *no* benefit, it nevertheless resembles wearing in form. Such wearing is not outlawed by the verse which prohibits wearing *shaatnez*, since that verse refers exclusively to normal wearing which provides benefit; but it is outlawed by the verse which forbids having *shaatnez* upon oneself in a manner resembling wearing. Moreover, since the resemblance in this case is not based on benefit, this type of wearing (which is categorized as *carrying* rather than *wearing*) is forbidden even though it provides no benefit at all, as stated by *Rambam*. The entire matter, however, requires further study.]

[The harmonization of the two mishnayos presented above assumes, as is evident from *Rambam* (*Hil. Kilayim* 10:18), that the mishnah's prohibition to wear *shaatnez* on top of ten other garments to evade the tax (mishnah 2) is a Biblical prohibition. Additionally, the harmonization is based on the assumption that the present mishnah does not involve wearing *shaatnez*, but rather carrying it on the shoulder. According to *R' Yehudah Sir Leon* (*Berachos* 18a), however, the prohibition in mishnah 2 on wearing *shaatnez* to evade the tax is Rabbinic. If follows that the apparent contradiction between the mishnayos can be resolved even if the present mishnah is understood to permit wearing *shaatnez* in order to model it. Even though wearing *shaatnez* is permitted as long as the person does not intend to protect himself from the sun etc. as stated here, nevertheless wearing *shaatnez* to avoid the tax, as in mishnah 2, was forbidden Rabbinically.]

וְהַצְּנוּעִים מַפְשִׁילִין בְּמַקֵּל. — *The discreet ones hang [them] on a stick.*

The term צְנוּעִים, which translates literally as *modest* or *discreet people*, is used by the mishnah to refer to scrupulous people (see *Demai* 6:6 and *Yerushalmi* ad loc.). Although strictly speaking it was permitted for garment sellers to *sell in their usual manner* as explained above, the more scrupulous amongst them did not in fact do so (*Rav; Rosh; Rash*). Instead, they would hang their *shaatnez*-containing merchandise on a stick, either in order to display it (assuming that the first part of the mishnah refers to modeling), or when carrying it.[1] In this way there would be no contact with the *shaatnez*, and hence no risk of using it for warmth and protection.

---

1. Some texts read: מַפְשִׁילִין בְּמַקֵּל לַאֲחוֹרֵיהֶן, *hang them on a stick behind them*. This version would seem to support the approach that the activity discussed by the mishnah is carrying *shaatnez* garments. Someone carrying garments could very easily be envisioned as hanging them from a stick over his shoulder. It is more difficult to see why a salesman would display a garment by hanging it over his back.

[ו] **תּוֹפְרֵי** כְסוּת תּוֹפְרִין כְּדַרְכָּן, וּבִלְבַד שֶׁלֹּא יִתְכַּוְּנוּ בַּחַמָּה מִפְּנֵי הַחַמָּה וּבַגְּשָׁמִים מִפְּנֵי הַגְּשָׁמִים. וְהַצְּנוּעִים תּוֹפְרִים בָּאָרֶץ.

[ז] **הַבִּרְסִין** וְהַבַּרְדְּסִין, וְהַדַּלְמַטְקִיּוֹן, וּמִנְעָלוֹת הַפִּנּוֹן — לֹא יִלְבַּשׁ בָּהֶן עַד שֶׁיִּבְדֹּק. רַבִּי יוֹסֵי אוֹמֵר: הַבָּאִים מֵחוֹף הַיָּם וּמִמְּדִינַת הַיָּם אֵינָן צְרִיכִין בְּדִיקָה, מִפְּנֵי שֶׁחֶזְקָתָן בְּקַנְבּוֹס.

יד אברהם

6.

תּוֹפְרֵי כְסוּת תּוֹפְרִין כְּדַרְכָּן, וּבִלְבַד שֶׁלֹּא יִתְכַּוְּנוּ בַּחַמָּה מִפְּנֵי הַחַמָּה וּבַגְּשָׁמִים מִפְּנֵי הַגְּשָׁמִים. — *Garment makers may sew in their usual manner, provided that they do not intend in the sun [to protect themselves] from the sun and in the rains [to protect themselves] from the rains.*

Tailors who sew garments containing *shaatnez* may support the fabric on their knees or lap while they sew it. This is the usual manner of sewing, and it is permitted provided that the tailor does not intend to use the fabric for protection or warmth (*Rav; Rosh; Rash*).

[Since the fabric here is not being worn, but is merely being supported on the tailor's lap or knees, the relevant prohibition of *kilayim* is the prohibition on having *shaatnez* upon oneself, i.e. the one stated in *Leviticus* 19:19. But, as explained by the *Gemara* (*Yevamos* 4b; see the commentary to the previous mishnah at length), this prohibition outlaws having *shaatnez* upon oneself only when the *shaatnez* provides benefit similar to that derived from clothes (e.g. protection, warmth). Where it does not do so, there is nothing wrong with having the *shaatnez* upon oneself. Since the fabric supported on the tailor's lap or knees does not necessarily provide him with warmth or comfort, and since his intention in resting the fabric on his lap is not in order to derive such benefit, it is permitted for him to do so and to sew in his usual manner.]

וְהַצְּנוּעִים תּוֹפְרִים בָּאָרֶץ. — *The discreet ones sew on the ground.*

The more scrupulous tailors (see previous mishnah for the meaning of צְנוּעִין), rather than supporting the *shaatnez*-containing fabric on their laps or knees, rested it on the ground while sewing it. [The reference is of course to tailors who were sitting on the ground. Those who worked at tables rested the fabric on the table (*Tif. Yis.*).] As explained in the previous mishnah, these people wanted to avoid all possible risk of a violation and hence took special care to minimize as much as possible any contact with the *kilayim* article.

Basically, the present mishnah reiterates the principles expounded in the previous mishnah (*Rash*). Nevertheless, the present mishnah contains a novel element. In mishnah 3 it was seen that towels and the like, which a person is wont to wrap around his hands, can be forbidden for use. Accordingly, it might have been thought that since the activity of sewing involves constant contact between the hands and the fabric, it should be forbidden with *shaatnez*-containing fabric. The mishnah therefore teaches that it is permitted (*Tif. Yis.*; see also *Meleches Shlomo*).

6. **G**arment makers may sew in their usual manner, provided that they do not intend in the sun [to protect themselves] from the sun and in the rains [to protect themselves] from the rains. The discreet ones sew on the ground.

7. **B**irrusins and brundisians, dalmatics, and pinon shoes — he may not wear them until he checks [them]. R' Yose says: Those which come from the coast and from overseas do not need checking, because they are presumably made with hemp. A

YAD AVRAHAM

7.

The following mishnah discusses *shaatnez*-testing for a variety of garments in use in mishnaic times. The precise identity of these garments is not known for certain.

הַבְּרְסִין וְהַבַּרְדְּסִין, וְהַדַלְמַטְקְיוֹן, וּמִנְעָלוֹת הַפְּנוֹן לֹא יִלְבַּשׁ בָּהֶן עַד שֶׁיִּבְדֹּק. — *Birrusins and brundisians, dalmatics, and pinon shoes — he may not wear them until he checks [them].*

Rav, Rosh, and *Rash* follow *Aruch,* who explains הַבְּרְסִין וְהַבַּרְדְּסִין, *birrusins and brundisians,* as woolen bedspreads differing in thickness, one being lighter than the other. [However, this definition does not seem to fit well with the implication of the mishnah that these items were worn.] *R' Shlomo Sirilio* identifies *birrusins* as a type of trousers (*Meleches Shlomo*). A similar identification is evident from *Rambam Comm.* who writes that although the exact meaning of the terms occurring here is not known, it is clear that they refer to various woolen garments worn on the feet or legs. דַלְמַטְקְיוֹן, *dalmatics,* are explained by *Rav* to be long woolen underwear. Alternatively, this was some type of hooded cloak (*Rosh; Meleches Shlomo*). *Pinon shoes* were footware made from poor quality wool (*Rav; Rosh; Rash*). The term derives from a town of this name (*Meleches Shlomo* from *Aruch*).

The mishnah teaches that all these woolen items must be checked for shaat-

nez, i.e. for possible linen content, before they are worn.

רַבִּי יוֹסֵי אוֹמֵר: הַבָּאִים מֵחוֹף הַיָּם וּמִמְדִינַת הַיָּם — אֵינָן צְרִיכִין בְּדִיקָה, מִפְּנֵי שֶׁחֶזְקָתָן בְּקַנְבּוֹס. *R' Yose says: Those which come from the coast and from overseas do not need checking, because they are presumably made with hemp.*

The term מְדִינַת הַיָּם, *overseas,* refers to places outside Israel (*Rashi* to *Gittin* 2a). *Yerushalmi* explains R' Yose as referring only to garments acquired in places such as Tyre and Caesarea which are on the coast of Israel, but outside the area sanctified by the returnees from Babylon (see *Yad Avraham* to *Sheviis* 6:1). He is not referring to garments acquired in places far from Israel, regardless of whether these places are coastal or inland. Thus, the exemption from *shaatnez*-checking supported by R' Yose refers only to garments from places which are *both* on the coast of Israel, i.e. *from the coast,* as well as outside the sanctified area, i.e. *from overseas* (*Rav; Rosh; Rash*). Garments acquired in distant places must be checked even according to R' Yose (*R' Shlomo Sirilio*).

Yerushalmi explains further that R'

וּמִנְעָל שֶׁל זֶרֶד אֵין בּוֹ מִשּׁוּם כִּלְאָיִם.

[ח] **אֵין** אָסוּר מִשּׁוּם כִּלְאַיִם אֶלָּא טָווּי וְאָרוּג, שֶׁנֶּאֱמַר: "לֹא תִלְבַּשׁ שַׁעַטְנֵז" — דָּבָר שֶׁהוּא שׁוּעַ, טָווּי, וְנוּז. רַבִּי

יד אברהם

Yose's position reflects the limited use of linen thread in his day (see *Tif. Yis.*). In times when the use of linen is widespread, R' Yose also requires woolen garments to be checked for possible *shaatnez* (*Rav; Rosh; Rash*).

Mishnah Rishonah suggests that the *Tanna Kamma* and R' Yose are debating a fundamental question. The *Tanna Kamma*, despite the limited use of linen thread, does not permit reliance on the presumed absence of linen to permit wearing the garment. In their view, since it is possible to ascertain the contents of the garment with certainty via checking, it is forbidden to rely on a presumption. R' Yose, however, maintains that a presumption may be relied on even where it is possible to test it.

וּמִנְעָל שֶׁל זֶרֶד אֵין בּוֹ מִשּׁוּם כִּלְאָיִם. — *A cloth-lined boot does not have any problems of kilayim.*

[Many versions read זֶרֶב (with a ב rather than a ד). The root זרב occurs in *Job* 6:17 where it is explained to mean warming. Accordingly, the item referred to by the mishnah is a winter boot which has a special lining to provide warmth (*Rabbeinu Nosson Av HaYeshivah; Rav; Rosh; Rash; Ravad* to *Hil. Kilayim* 10:15).]

Rav following *Rash* and *Rosh* understands the mishnah's point here to be that the boot in question was known to contain wool only, without any admixture of linen, and hence it was free of any risk of *shaatnez*. [However, previously the phrase אֵין בּוֹ מִשּׁוּם כִּלְאָיִם was used by the mishnah for situations in which the item in question did in fact contain both wool and linen, but nevertheless did not pose a *shaatnez* problem (see mishnayos 2, 3, 4). If the statement here was intended merely to convey that these boots do not contain

any linen, the mishnah, consistent with the wording above in the first part of this mishnah, ought to have said that these do not need checking for *shaatnez* (see *Mahari Korkus* to *Hil. Kilayim* 10:15).]

A different approach to this statement emerges from *Shenos Eliyahu* (see *Ridbaz* to *Yerushalmi* 9:4, s.v. מנעל). *Tosafos* (to *Shabbos* 57b, *Beitzah* 15a) maintain that a linen garment which is stuffed with wool in such a way that the wool is contained within the linen, but is not attached to it, is not *shaatnez*. For example, consider a coat in which the inside and outside is linen, and in between is a woolen filling. The linen is sewed, of course, but not in a way which traps any wool. Thus, if the linen is slit at some point, it is possible to remove all the wool inside. Since the wool is not attached to the linen by the stitching, the garment does not constitute *shaatnez*, even though it consists of wool and linen. In a similar vein, the boot under discussion by the mishnah here may be explained as a linen slipper with a woolen filling which is not held fast by the stitches which close the linen exterior. Accordingly, the boot here in fact contains both linen and wool, but nevertheless does not constitute a *shaatnez* problem.

Rambam (*Hil. Kilayim* 10:15) discusses a *shaatnez*-containing shoe or slipper which lacks a posterior and is permitted to be worn since the skin of the foot is tough and does not experience sensations of pleasure or warmth like the rest of the skin. *Ravad* (loc. cit.) assumes that *Rambam* is referring to the shoe in our mishnah, and if so, the mishnah is discussing a shoe which is made up of both linen and wool and is nevertheless permitted to wear. [The legal basis for this permit is not entirely clear, and appears to be due to the

cloth-lined boot does not have any problems of *kilayim*.

8. **N**othing is prohibited because of *kilayim* unless it is spun and woven, as it says: *You may not wear shaatnez* — something which is *shua, tavui,* and *noz.*

YAD AVRAHAM

style of shoe (i.e. its lack of a posterior) which makes it less of a garment, as well as the reduced sensation of the feet (see *Radbaz* to *Hil. Kilayim* 10:15).] In any event, it is likely that *Rambam* (ibid.) is not discussing the shoe of our mishnah, but is describing instead an item mentioned in the *Gemara* (*Beitzah* 15a) — see the Geonic Responsum quoted by *Tur, Yoreh Deah* 300 and cf. *Rashi* to *Beitzah* 15a, s.v. ערדילין; see also *Mahari Korkus* and

Merkeves HaMishneh to *Hil. Kilayim* 10:15. [*Rambam Comm.* defines the מִנְעָל שֶׁל זֶרֶד as a kind of shoe with which one walks upon mats or rugs. Since he does not explain that the mishnah's ruling is based on a novel principle, it appears that he concurs with the standard approach that the mishnah is referring to an item which was known to contain wool but not linen, and was hence known to be *shaatnez* free.]

8.

The coming mishnah analyzes the Scriptural word שַׁעַטְנֵז, shaatnez (*Lev.* 19:19; *Deut.* 22:11) to determine what combinations of wool with linen are Biblically forbidden to wear. [There are a number of different interpretations of this mishnah. *Rav* presents those of *Rabbeinu Tam* and *Rash* anonymously and favors the latter's explanation.]

אֵין אָסוּר מִשּׁוּם כִּלְאַיִם אֶלָּא טָווּי וְאָרוּג, — *Nothing is prohibited because of kilayim unless it is spun and woven,*

Rashi (to *Niddah* 61b) understands this to mean that wool and flax were spun together, producing a thread containing a mixture of linen and wool. [It is assumed, as will be seen below, that the wool and flax fibers were first mixed and combed together before spinning.] If this linen-wool thread is then woven, the resulting cloth is *shaatnez*. However, weaving a pure linen thread together with a pure woolen thread is not Biblical *shaatnez*.

Rash, on the other hand, maintains that even a weave of pure linen thread with pure woolen thread is considered by Scripture to be *shaatnez*. Thus, the mixing of linen with wool does not occur during combing or spinning, but only during weaving. The statement here that Biblical *shaatnez* must be *spun and woven* does not mean that a mixture of linen and wool was spun. Rather, the mishnah means that only threads pro-

duced by spinning can be combined (by weaving) to give *shaatnez*. The weaving of pure linen thread with pure woolen thread is *shaatnez* only if the threads were manufactured by spinning. [Additionally, as will be seen below, the spinning was preceded by combing.] Thus, if the threads are combed and *spun* independently *and* then *woven* together, the resulting fabric is *shaatnez*.

As will be seen below, both *Rashi* and *Rash* assume that the three processes of combing, spinning, and weaving are all implied by the term *shaatnez*. *Rabbeinu Tam*, however, maintains that weaving is not alluded to by this term. [For *Rabbeinu Tam*'s explanation of the mishnah, see below.]

שֶׁנֶּאֱמַר: ,,לֹא תִלְבַּשׁ שַׁעַטְנֵז" — דָּבָר שֶׁהוּא שׁוּעַ, טָווּי, וְנוּז. — *as it says: "You may not wear shaatnez"* — *something which is shua, tavui, and noz.*

The term *shaatnez* used by the Torah (*Lev.* 19:19; *Deut.* 22:11) is understood by the mishnah to be a contraction of three

terms: *shua, tavui,* and *noz. Shua* derives from a root meaning smooth (see *Targum Onkelos* to *Genesis* 27:11) and refers to the process of hackling or combing the fibers prior to spinning (*Rav; Rashi* to *Niddah* 61b; cf. *Rambam Comm.*). As for the other two terms, *tavui* refers to spinning, as is evident from *Exodus* 35:25,26. The meaning of *noz,* however, is not so clear. *Rashi* (loc. cit.) and *Rash* understand *noz* to be synonymous with אָרוג and hence it refers to weaving (cf. *Rabbeinu Tam* below). The mishnah's opening remark that *kilayim* must be *spun and woven* is thus based on the current analysis of the term *shaatnez* as meaning *combed, spun, and woven.* For a fabric to count as *shaatnez* according to Scripture, its manufacture must include these three stages. As mentioned earlier, however, there is disagreement between *Rashi* and *Rash* as to which of these processes must be performed on a *mixture* of linen with wool. *Rashi* maintains that Biblical *shaatnez* is a fabric produced by combing a mixture of linen and wool, spinning the mixture of fibers, and then weaving the resulting linen-woolen thread.[1] *Rash,* however, assumes that the mixing of linen and wool occurs only at the weaving. The linen threads which are woven together with the woolen threads must each have been produced by combing and spinning if their weave is to be considered Biblical *shaatnez.*

Rabbeinu Tam defines *noz* as twisted or twined (*Tosafos* to *Yevamos* 5b; *Rosh*). For a thread to be a component of Biblical *shaatnez,* the thread must be combed, spun, and twined. Thus, if two single woolen yarns which were produced by combing and spinning are twisted together, the resulting two-ply woolen yarn is one which has undergone the three processes of *shua, tavui,* and

noz alluded to by the term *shaatnez.* In *Rabbeinu Tam's* opinion, the woolen component as well as the linen component must each independently undergo these three processes. If a two-ply woolen yarn as described above is woven together with a two-ply linen thread also produced as above, the resulting weave is what Scripture designates as *kilayim.* The term *shaatnez* according to this interpretation alludes to the three processes involved in producing the components of *kilayim.* When these components are then combined, e.g. by weaving, the result is *kilayim.* Thus, the mishnah's statement above that *kilayim is spun and woven* means that the components of Biblical *kilayim* are independently spun, and are then combined by weaving. Actually, the components of *kilayim* are independently *combed, spun,* and *twisted* as taught in the course of the mishnah. However, the roots for combing, שע, and twisting, נז, are more or less apparent in the term שעטנז and these processes need not be emphasized. That the letter ט in the word שעטנז corresponds to *tavui,* i.e. spinning, is much less obvious and therefore the mishnah stresses this procedure (*Tos. Yom Tov*). Combination via weaving is not derived from the word *shaatnez* at all, according to this explanation, and its source is the term יַחְדָּו, *together,* in the verse (*Deut.* 22:11): *Do not wear shaatnez, wool and linen together.* According to *Rabbeinu Tam,* this teaches that if woolen yarn produced via the processes of combing, spinning, and twisting is woven *together* with linen thread also produced in this way, the resulting weave is forbidden to wear.

The various approaches outlined thus far assume that all three processes alluded to by the term *shaatnez* are necessary in order to produce Biblical *shaatnez.* There is disagreement as to which processes are

---

1. Serious difficulties are raised by *Tosafos* (to *Yevamos* 5b, *Niddah* 61b) with *Rashi's* approach. A resolution of these difficulties may be found in *Maharach Ohr Zarua* §54, R' *Eliyahu Mizrachi* to *Rashi, Leviticus* 19:19, and *Chiddushei HaGrach* (stencil) §74. See also commentary to mishnah 9 below, s.v. רבי יוסי.

performed on a mixture (according to *Rashi*, all three; according to *Rash*, only *noz* which he defines as weaving), and disagreement as to the meaning of *noz* (*Rashi* and *Rash* understand this to be weaving; *Rabbeinu Tam* understands it to be twining). All concur, however, that it is *shua* plus *tavui* plus *noz* which leads to Biblical *shaatnez*.

However, *Rambam* (*Hil. Kilayim* 10:2, *Hil. Eidus* 10:3; see also *Rambam Comm.*, Kafich ed.) disputes this premise.[1] In his view, each of these processes *by itself* produces Biblically forbidden *kilayim*. Thus *shua*, which literally means smoothing, refers to the felting process, and a mixture of flax and wool fibers which is felted together is Biblically forbidden as *shaatnez* according to *Rambam*. A thread spun out of a mixture of wool and linen fibers is *shaatnez*, and so also a weave of linen thread with wool thread. According to this approach, the term *noz* apparently refers to combining of threads or fabrics by sewing or weaving or tying (see *Taz* and *Beur HaGra* to *Yoreh Deah* 300:1 and see *Aruch*, s.v. עש). If a linen cloth, the threads for which were spun without combing, was sewn to a woolen felt (which, of course, was neither spun nor woven), the result would be *noz* and would be Biblical *kilayim*. It follows from this approach that each of the three processes alluded to by the term *shaatnez* refers to combining linen and wool which had previously been separate. *Shua* means felting together linen with wool; *tavui* means spinning together linen with wool; and *noz* means connecting a linen fabric to a woolen one. When the mishnah says above that *kilayim* must be *spun and woven*, this involves only *tavui* and the requirement of *woven* has nothing to do with *noz*. Clearly, to weave a cloth from thread which is a blend of linen and wool does not increase the connection of the linen to the wool. (That connection resulted from the spinning of linen fibers together with wool ones to produce a blended thread.) Such weaving is not *noz*, which refers to combining linen and wool which were pre-viously separate. However, although a thread consisting of a blend of linen and wool is indeed *shaatnez*, a thread on its own is not a garment and even having it upon oneself will not be a violation of the prohibition on wearing *kilayim* (see *Rambam, Hil. Kilayim* 10:19). Thus, if a person has only a blended thread and he wishes to produce Biblical *shaatnez* which it will be forbidden to wear or to have upon himself, he must make it into a garment. The simplest way to do so is to weave it, and this is what the weaving mentioned by the mishnah is all about (see *Taz* and *Beur HaGra* to *Yoreh Deah* 300:1; see also *Yeshuos Malko* to *Hil. Kilayim* 10:4, s.v. עוד נחלקו). [Of course, if he takes such thread and sews it onto an existing garment, that garment will be forbidden to wear as *shaatnez*. But, then he has to have another garment, and the mishnah assumes that by starting with *only* raw wool and linen, it is possible to produce Biblical forbidden *shaatnez* which is forbidden because it was combined via *tavui*, spinning.] Thus, when the mishnah states that *kilayim* must be *spun and woven*, this comes to explain how the spinning process alluded to by the letter ט of שעטנז can produce a *shaatnez*-containing garment. That the processes of עש, felting, and נז, combining, e.g. by weaving, can do so is obvious, and that these processes are also alluded to by the word שעטנז is also obvious.

Actually, whether the Torah requires *shua* plus *tavui* plus *noz* (as per *Rashi* et al.) or merely *shua* or *tavui* or *noz* (like *Rambam*) is disputed by *Amoraim* in the *Gemara* (*Niddah* 61b). Although the *Gemara* seems to conclude that the former view prevails (namely, *shua* plus *tavui* plus *noz*), *Rambam Comm.* writes that this conclusion is not part of the Talmudic text, and was part of a commentator's gloss which was inadvertently incorporated into the *Gemara* (see *R' Shlomo Sirilio* quoted by *Meleches Shlomo* and *Mareh HaPanim* 9:6, s.v. ניתני). [Additionally, *Rambam's* position has support in *Toras Kohanim* to *Lev.* 19:19 and *Yerushalmi* (see *Artzos HaChaim, Eretz Yehudah* 11:6).]

---

1. Initially *Rambam Comm.* followed a different approach to our mishnah, similar to the standard approach in that it assumed that all three processes are essential, but different in its understanding of *shua*. Later on, *Rambam* corrected his commentary to conform with the position he incorporates in his Code. Both the original as well as the corrected versions of the commentary were known to *Kesef Mishneh* and *Radbaz* (*Hil. Kilayim* 10:2) and are preserved in the Kafich ed. of *Rambam Comm.*

שִׁמְעוֹן בֶּן אֶלְעָזָר אוֹמֵר: נָלוֹז וּמֵלִיז הוּא אֶת אָבִיו שֶׁבַּשָּׁמַיִם עָלָיו.

[ט] **לְבָדִים** אֲסוּרִים מִפְּנֵי שֶׁהֵם שׁוּעִים. פִּיו שֶׁל צֶמֶר בְּשֶׁל פִּשְׁתָּן אָסוּר מִפְּנֵי שֶׁהֵם חוֹזְרִין כָּאָרִיג. רַבִּי יוֹסֵי אוֹמֵר: מְשִׁיחוֹת שֶׁל אַרְגָּמָן אֲסוּרוֹת מִפְּנֵי שֶׁהוּא מוֹלֵל עַד שֶׁלֹּא קוֹשֵׁר.

יד אברהם

רַבִּי שִׁמְעוֹן בֶּן אֶלְעָזָר אוֹמֵר: נָלוֹז וּמֵלִיז הוּא אֶת אָבִיו שֶׁבַּשָּׁמַיִם עָלָיו. — *R' Shimon ben Elazar says: He deviates and causes his Father in Heaven to turn from him.*

R' Shimon ben Elazar explains homiletically that the term *shaatnez* indicates the gravity of violating the laws of *shaatnez*. Taking the letters נז as a contraction of נלוז, a root meaning to *bend* or *turn* (see *Proverbs* 4:21), R' Shimon ben Elazar remarks that the one who wears *shaatnez* is a deviate, and at the same time he distances Hashem from him (*Rav; Rosh; Rash*). The sin of wearing *shaatnez* is especially acute in view of the fact that it has no obvious benefits and is thus not the type of thing which people crave (see *Tosafos HaRosh* to *Horayos* 11a, s.v. רבי יהודה). The sinner who wears *shaatnez* is not succumbing to an overpowering desire to enjoy *shaatnez*; he is simply rebelling against Hashem. He is thus not worthy of Hashem's mercy (*Rambam Comm.; Tos. Yom Tov*).

Rabbeinu Tam (*Tosafos* to *Niddah* 61b; *Rosh*) views R' Shimon ben Elazar's statement as support for the definition of נז as twining, a process involving bending and turning. [However, the warp of a loom is constantly bent during the process of weaving, and hence weaving too is suggestive of bending and deviating (*R' Shlomo Sirilio* quoted by *Meleches Shlomo*).]

9.

As explained in the previous mishnah, most commentators assume that unless the production of a mixture of linen and wool includes all the three processes of *shua*, *tavui*, and *noz*, it is not Biblically forbidden as *shaatnez*. Nevertheless, even such fabrics were Rabbinically forbidden, as taught in the following mishnah. [According to *Rambam* these are also Biblically forbidden, and the mishnah here illustrates the different types of Biblically forbidden mixes.]

לְבָדִים אֲסוּרִים מִפְּנֵי שֶׁהֵם שׁוּעִים. — *Felts are forbidden because they are carded.*

Although only fabrics which have undergone the three processes of *shua*, *tavui*, and *noz* are considered *shaatnez* under Biblical law, by Rabbinic enactment even a fabric produced by only one of these processes is forbidden to wear. Accordingly, felts made from a mixture of wool and linen which were carded together are Rabbinically forbidden to wear as *shua* even though there is no spinning or weaving involved (*Rav; Rosh; Rash*).

We have rendered *shua* as carding in keeping with *Rav's* definition in the previous mishnah. As noted by *Rav* there, however, the actual meaning of *shua* is smooth (see *Targum Onkelos* to *Genesis* 27:11, *Leviticus* 14:42). Carding of fibers prior to spinning is a form of smoothing and comes under *shua*, but the process of pressing fibers together to form felt is also a form of smoothing. Thus, even if a tangle of flax and wool was felted together without first being

R' Shimon ben Elazar says: He deviates and causes his Father in Heaven to turn from him.

9. Felts are forbidden because they are carded. A border of wool on linen is forbidden because it surrounds the weave. R' Yose says: Belts of purple wool are forbidden because he bastes them before tying.

YAD AVRAHAM

carded, the resulting felt would still be *shua* [and according to *Rambam*, Biblically forbidden]. See also *Rambam Comm*. Kafich ed.

פִּיו שֶׁל צֶמֶר בְּשֶׁל פִּשְׁתָּן אָסוּר מִפְּנֵי שֶׁהֵם חוֹזְרִין כָּאֱרִיג. — *A border of wool on linen is forbidden because it surrounds the weave.*

[Most editions read פִּיף rather than פִּיו, and there is also variation with regard to כָּאֱרִיג, some texts having בָּאֱרִיג (with a ב) and others having לָאֱרִיג (with a ל).]

On completing a garment, it was the practice of weavers to add a border of three or four thick threads as reinforcement (*Rav; Rash*). These were not woven with the garment but were inserted into the weave near the edge (*Rosh*). The mishnah states that if the garment is linen, it is forbidden to insert border threads of wool, even though the wool is not actually woven together with the linen. This is because the border threads run along the perimeter of the garment and prevent it from coming apart. As such they uphold the weave, and are viewed as part of it. Accordingly, the garment was viewed as a weave of linen and wool which is forbidden Rabbinically as *noz* (see *Ri ben Malki Tzedek*). Alternatively, the border threads were viewed as part of the weave not because they reinforced it, but because the insertion of these threads resembles weaving (*Rav; Rosh; Rash*).

The phrase of the mishnah מִפְּנֵי שֶׁהֵם חוֹזְרִין כָּאֱרִיג is understood, according to the above, as explaining the category under which this case is prohibited — i.e. weaving (which comes under *noz*). The thrust of the mishnah is that the insertion

of the border threads resembles weaving and the garment is forbidden as a mixed weave. A different approach to this statement is found in the commentary to *Toras Kohanim* (*Lev.* 19:19) attributed to *Rash* and in *Maharach Ohr Zarua* §54 in the name of R' Moshe ben R' Chasdai. This approach defines פִּיף as fibers, and explains אֱרִיג as the web on a loom. The mishnah teaches that it is forbidden to keep wool fibers in the vicinity of a loom supporting a web of linen. This is because the fibers inevitably become entangled in the web and the resulting twisting of these fibers as the web is woven resembles spinning. Thus, the garment is forbidden Rabbinically as containing *tavui*, a forbidden spin of linen and wool. [It might be in order to note here that according to one opinion recorded in *Aruch*, s.v. שעטנז, twining of linen and wool threads to produce two-ply mixed thread comes under *tavui*, not *noz* (cf. *Rabbeinu Tam* quoted in previous mishnah, s.v. שנאמר).]

רַבִּי יוֹסֵי אוֹמֵר: מְשִׁיחוֹת שֶׁל אַרְגָּמָן אֲסוּרוֹת מִפְּנֵי שֶׁהוּא מוֹלֵל עַד שֶׁלֹּא קוֹשֵׁר. — *R' Yose says: Belts of purple wool are forbidden because he bastes them before tying.*

This refers to a rope-like belt of purple wool which it is forbidden to tie around a linen robe (*Rav; Rosh; Rash*). Although tying a woolen belt around a linen robe should not be forbidden, since no connection is established between the wool and the linen, the mishnah forbids this *because he bastes them before tying.* That is, it was the style to loosely sew the belt to the robe to keep it in place. Although this is not a permanent con-

לֹא יִקְשׁוֹר סֶרֶט שֶׁל צֶמֶר בְּשֶׁל פִּשְׁתָּן לַחֲגֹר בּוֹ אֶת מָתְנָיו, אַף עַל פִּי שֶׁהָרְצוּעָה בָּאֶמְצַע.

יד אברהם

nection, it is sufficient to render the combination shaatnez.[1]

It is not made clear by the commentators whether the prohibition in the present case is Rabbinic or Biblical. Certainly, the thrust of the mishnah seems to be that the basting of the belt to the robe constitutes a forbidden attachment of linen to wool. There is no indication, however, that this case illustrates a combination of linen and wool which has undergone only one of the three critical processes of shua, tavui or noz. Thus, there is no sound basis for assuming that the rope-belt has not undergone combing and spinning. If we posit for the sake of argument, that the belt has indeed been combed and spun, then an analysis of this case according to the opinions outlined in the commentary to mishnah 8 yields the following results.

According to Rashi, the term shaatnez indicates linen and wool which were combed together, spun together, and woven. Clearly, the woolen belt here was not combed or spun together with the linen of the robe. Nevertheless, this does not definitely mean that the prohibition in question is at most Rabbinic. In an attempt to defend Rashi's position against serious difficulties raised by Tosafos (to Niddah 61b et al.) and others, it has been suggested that according to Rashi there are two types of Biblical kilayim. The first type, derived from the Biblical term shaatnez (Lev. 19:19, Deut. 22:11), involves a mixture or blend of linen and wool, and is the result of combing together a mixture of linen and wool, spinning the mixture, and then weaving the resultant thread. The second type derives from the term יַחְדָּו, together, in the phrase wool and linen together (Deut. 22:11; see Yevamos 5b). This refers to wool and linen garments which are independently produced but later connected one to another by sewing or tying, for example (see Maharach Ohr Zarua §54; R' Eliyahu Mizrachi to Rashi, Leviticus 19:19; and Chiddushei HaGrach [stencil] §74). In the present

case, if attachment of the woolen belt to the linen robe by basting is viewed as bringing linen and wool together, wearing this combination while the belt is basted into place should be Biblically forbidden.

According to the view of Rabbeinu Tam, attachment of independently produced linen to independently produced wool creates Biblically prohibited kilayim. This is provided that the linen and wool have each been combed, spun, and twined. In the present case there is no evidence that the belt and robe have not been thus prepared, and hence their connection should be Biblically prohibited. However, attachment by basting, which is not as permanent as regular stitching, or tying, might not count as a connection under Biblical law, and hence the belt-robe combination here might only be regarded as connected and forbidden under Rabbinic law.

It will be recalled that the view of Rash, favored by Rav to mishnah 8, understands the term shaatnez as alluding to a fabric woven from linen and wool threads, which have independently been combed and spun. Obviously, the belt here has not been woven with the robe. However, Rash agrees that sewing linen to wool also creates Biblically forbidden shaatnez (see Tos. Yom Tov to mishnah 8 and see mishnah 10 below). Thus, again, if the basting here satisfies the Biblical criteria for connection of fabrics, the robe-belt combination would be Biblically forbidden.

Clearly, even if the prohibition here is merely Rabbinic, the nature of the basis of the prohibition differs from that of the preceding cases. There, the Rabbis prohibited even mixed materials which were produced by only some of the critical shaatnez processes. Here, the issue is not the production of the materials, but the nature of their connection. If the connection counts as together, the combination will be forbidden to wear under Biblical law. If it does not, it was nevertheless forbidden as such by the Rabbis.[2]

1. For examples of the root מלל meaning loosely sewed or basted, see Moed Katan 26a-b (Rash; Rosh).

2. Tif. Yis. (Hilchesa Gevirasa) suggests that the mishnah forbids wearing these belts even without basting them to the robe. Evidently he assumes that basting linen to wool qualifies

9
9

It is forbidden to tie a strip of wool to a strip of linen to gird his waist, even though the [leather] strap is in the middle.

Rambam Comm. defines מוֹלֵל as rolling between the fingers (see e.g. *Beitzah* 13b) and explains the case here differently. The belts of purple wool mentioned here were made by taking a bunch of strips of purple wool and tying the bunch with a linen thread. This alone does not constitute *shaatnez*, since the linen is not tied *to* the wool but is wrapped around the wool and tied to itself (see *Rosh, Hil. Kilei Begadim* §19; see also *Chiddushei R' Akiva Eiger* to *Taz, Yoreh Deah* 300:6; *Aruch HaShulchan, Yoreh Deah* 300:18). However, it was also the practice to roll part of the linen string together with the strips of wool before tying it. This rolling together prior to tying was regarded by R' Yose as spinning (*tavui*), so that the belt created by tying the linen thread around the bunch of woolen strips contained a forbidden spin of linen and wool. Thus, *because he rolls* the linen thread together with the woolen strips *before he ties* the linen thread around the strips, R' Yose maintains that these *belts of purple wool are forbidden* to wear.

According to *Rambam*, the case of felts, the first case of the mishnah, illustrates a Biblically forbidden combination of linen and wool via *shua* alone; the case of פִּיף illustrates a Biblically forbidden combination via *noz* alone; and the present case illustrates wool and linen combined via *tavui* (cf. *Beur HaGra, Yoreh Deah* 300:1). Each of these is Biblically forbidden, since according to *Rambam*, attachment of linen to wool by *any* of the processes of *shua, tavui,* or *noz* constitutes *shaatnez* (see *Rambam Comm.* Kafich ed. fn. 27). [*Rambam Comm.* writes, however, that the halachah does not follow R' Yose's opinion, presumably because this rolling is not in fact treated like spinning.]

לֹא יִקְשׁוֹר סֶרֶט שֶׁל צֶמֶר בְּשֶׁל פִּשְׁתָּן לַחֲגֹר בּוֹ אֶת מָתְנָיו, אַף עַל פִּי שֶׁהָרְצוּעָה בָּאֶמְצַע. — *It is forbidden to tie a strip of wool to a strip of linen to gird his waist, even though the [leather] strap is in the middle.*

If a leather strap has woolen strips connected to one of its ends and linen strips connected to the other, it is forbidden for use as a belt. This is because the belt is closed by tying the woolen strips to the linen ones and this constitutes *kilayim* (*Rav; Rosh; Rash*; see *Teshuvas HaRashba* 1:288 [quoted by *Meleches Shlomo* to mishnah 10, s.v. השק]). It would, however, be permitted to tie an additional strap of leather to the loose end of wool, for example, so that closing the belt would now involve tying leather to linen. Although the belt contains both linen and wool, since these are not in contact with each other, their mutual connection to the leather strap in the middle does not render them connected to each other. Thus, a prohibited *kilayim* connection of linen to wool is only when the linen and wool are directly connected to each other.

Rambam Comm., however, maintains that even when the linen and wool are connected indirectly (i.e. they are both attached to a third material, in this case, leather), the combination constitutes forbidden *kilayim* (see also *Rambam, Hil. Kilayim* 10:9, and cf. *Rash* to mishnah 9:1 above). Thus, it is forbidden to wear this belt even if the linen strips are not tied to the woolen ones (e.g. another strip of leather is tied to the woolen end, as above). The same opinion is expressed by *Ritva* (*Beitzah* 15a; also quoted by *Shitah Mekubetzes* loc. cit.).

under Biblical law as *together*. The mishnah thus teaches that it was Rabbinically forbidden to tie such woolen belts around linen robes lest the wearer come to baste them together and then wear them (see also *Tur, Yoreh Deah* 300).

[י] **אוֹתוֹת** הַגַּרְדִּין וְאוֹתוֹת הַכּוֹבְסִים אֲסוּרוֹת
מִשּׁוּם כִּלְאַיִם. הַתּוֹכֵף תְּכִיפָה
אַחַת, אֵינָהּ חִבּוּר, וְאֵין בָּהּ מִשּׁוּם כִּלְאַיִם, וְהַשּׁוֹמְטָהּ
בְּשַׁבָּת פָּטוּר. עָשָׂה שְׁנֵי רָאשֶׁיהָ לְצַד אֶחָד, חִבּוּר,
וְיֵשׁ בָּהּ מִשּׁוּם כִּלְאַיִם, וְהַשּׁוֹמְטָהּ בְּשַׁבָּת חַיָּב.

10.

The following mishnah discusses how many stitches are needed for two cloths which have been sewn together to be considered connected under Biblical law. This question has bearing not only for *kilayim* law (in the case of linen sewn to wool), but also for Sabbath law, as well as for the laws of *tumah* (ritual impurity) and *taharah* (ritual purity).

אוֹתוֹת הַגַּרְדִּין וְאוֹתוֹת הַכּוֹבְסִים אֲסוּרוֹת מִשּׁוּם כִּלְאַיִם. — *Labels of weavers and labels of launderers are forbidden as kilayim.*

In order to prevent confusion of one person's garments with those of another, it was common for weavers and cleaners to sew the owner's initials onto garments brought to them for repairs or laundering. If the garment was woolen, and the thread used to sew the initials was linen, or vice versa, the garment becomes forbidden to wear as *kilayim* (*Rav; Rosh; Rash*). Even though the lettering is not an integral part of the garment, and even though the owner does not care for it, the garment is forbidden for wearing as long as the *shaatnez* is not removed (*Rambam, Hil. Kilayim* 10:23; *Meleches Shlomo*).

הַתּוֹכֵף תְּכִיפָה אַחַת, אֵינָהּ חִבּוּר, וְאֵין בָּהּ מִשּׁוּם כִּלְאַיִם, — *[If] someone thrusts [the needle] a single thrust, this is not a connection, it does not count as kilayim,*

[A stitch in sewing refers to an in-and-out movement of a threaded needle. When executing a stitch, the needle penetrates the cloth twice. An in movement or an out movement alone is accomplished by a *single thrust* of the needle. In a single thrust of the needle, the cloth is penetrated a single time by the needle. The translation assumes that the term תְּכִיפָה is synonymous with תְּחִיבָה,

inserting or pushing (see *Rav*).]

If two cloths are connected by a *single thrust* [i.e. the result of a single penetration of the cloths by a threaded needle], they are *not* considered joined with respect to the laws of *tumah* and *taharah*. If one of the cloths contracts *tumah*, the status of the other is unaffected, and likewise, if both cloths happen to be *tamei*, then the sprinkling of the waters of the red heifer (part of the process of *taharah*) on one of the cloths does not make the other one *tahor*.

Similarly, if a linen garment is connected to a woolen one by a *single thrust*, the two are not considered joined under the laws of *kilayim* (*Rav; Rosh; Rash*).

From *Rambam* (*Hil. Kilayim* 10:24) it seems that the assertion here that a *single thrust* does not constitute a connection is valid only if no knots were tied. However, if the person brings the two ends of the thread together and ties them, this would be considered a connection and the resultant combination of a linen with a woolen garment would be forbidden to wear as *kilayim*. [However, *Rambam Comm.* appears to maintain that a *single thrust* is never considered a connection, not even if the ends are tied together (*Beur HaGra, Yoreh Deah* 300:5).]

Additionally, it is possible that the mishnah's ruling refers only to a case in which some neutral thread (e.g. cotton) was being used to connect a linen garment to a woolen

10. **L**abels of weavers and labels of launderers are forbidden as *kilayim*. [If] someone thrusts [the needle] a single thrust, this is not a connection, it does not count as *kilayim*, and someone who undoes it on the Sabbath is exempt. [If] its two ends are brought to the same side, this is a connection, it counts as *kilayim*, and someone who undoes it on the Sabbath is liable.

YAD AVRAHAM

one. In such a case, a *single thrust* does not create *kilayim*. However, if a person sews a woolen garment with linen thread, or vice versa, then a *single thrust* will create *kilayim*, at least in the case in which the ends of the thread are tied (*Tos. R' Akiva* to mishnah 8 from *Perishah, Yoreh Deah* 300:10; *Taz* loc. cit. §5).

We have followed the standard commentators in assuming that the case under discussion involves connecting a linen garment to a woolen one by sewing. According to this explanation, the first case of the mishnah in which letters are embroidered to a woolen garment using linen thread is an entirely separate case. There the thread is one of the components of the *kilayim* whereas here the thread serves to connect two garments such that the garments constitute *kilayim*. It is possible, however, that the mishnah is in fact continuing to discuss the case of thread as a component of *kilayim*. After stating that linen thread embroidered into a woolen garment creates *kilayim*, the mishnah adds that this is only if the thread will stay in place. But a single thrust of linen thread inserted into a woolen garment will not constitute *kilayim* (see *Meiri* to *Yevamos* 5b [ed. Dickman] p. 39, s.v. ומכל מקום). According to this explanation it is not at all clear that connecting a woolen garment to a linen one by sewing will constitute *kilayim*, since this issue is not addressed by the mishnah. Indeed, some *Geonim* understood that two garments, one of linen and the other of wool, which are sewn together are forbidden Rabbinically on the grounds that sewing presses the garments together and this resembles *shua* (*Rav Sherira* in responsum preserved in *Sefer HaEshkol, Hil. Shaatnez* [ed. Albeck] p. 43; see also *Otzar HaGeonim, Beitzah* 14b, Responsa Sec. 28; *Teshuvos HaRif*, Responsum 316; *Orchos Chaim*, vol. 2, p. 221; and see *Rambam Comm.* end of mishnah 9 above).

וְהַשּׁוֹמְטָה בְּשַׁבָּת פָּטוּר. — *and someone who undoes it on the Sabbath is exempt.*

To undo stitching in order to resew is forbidden on the Sabbath as the prohibited labor called tearing (see *Shabbos* 7:2). However, if a person undoes a *single thrust* he is not liable. Since the *single thrust* does not count as a connection, separation of the unconnected garments is not tearing (*Rav; Rosh; Rash*).

It is somewhat curious that the mishnah speaks about *undoing* single thrusts on the Sabbath, rather than sewing them. Just as undoing sewing is forbidden on the Sabbath, so also sewing is forbidden. Thus, consistent with the case of *kilayim* which deals with sewing single thrusts, the mishnah could have illustrated the applications to the laws of the Sabbath in terms of sewing single thrusts as well (*Tos. Chadashim*; see *Tos. Anshei Shem* and see below, end of s.v. עשה).

עָשָׂה שְׁנֵי רָאשֶׁיהָ לְצַד אֶחָד, חִבּוּר, וְיֵשׁ בָּהּ מִשּׁוּם כִּלְאַיִם, וְהַשּׁוֹמְטָה בְּשַׁבָּת חַיָּב. — *[If] its two ends are brought to the same side, this is a connection, it counts as kilayim, and someone who undoes it on the Sabbath is liable.*

If a full stitch was used to connect the linen to the woolen garment, this is a connection. [A full stitch refers to an in-and-out motion of the threaded needle. This involves two penetrations of the cloths, one in and one out, and results in both ends of the thread on the same side of the cloth.] *Rav*, following *Rosh, Rash,* and *Ri ben Malki Tzedek*, adds that a full stitch is a connection only if the two ends of the thread are tied together, since otherwise even a full stitch does not hold. [However, from *Rambam* (*Comm.* and

רַבִּי יְהוּדָה אוֹמֵר: עַד שֶׁיְשַׁלֵּשׁ. הַשַּׂק וְהַקֻּפָּה מִצְטָרְפִין לְכִלְאָיִם.

יד אברהם

Hil. Kilayim 10:24) it seems that a full stitch counts as a connection for the laws of kilayim even if it is not tied. For Sabbath law, however, Rambam (Hil. Shabbos 10:9) maintains that a stitch is a connection only if it is tied (see Radbaz to Hil. Kilayim 10:24).]

Rosh, who maintains that a full stitch is only a connection if it is tied, questions why a single thrust does not count as a connection if the ends are tied. The question is left unresolved.

The fact that a full stitch is considered a connection has consequences in several areas of law, as illustrated by the mishnah. In the context of the laws of tumah and taharah, if one garment is connected to another by a full stitch, then if one of the garments contracts tumah, or is sprinkled as part of the process of taharah, the adjoining garment is likewise affected. For kilayim, if a linen garment is sewn to a woolen one with a full stitch, the result is forbidden to wear. For Sabbath law, a full stitch counts as a connection which if undone renders the perpetrator liable for illegally disconnecting the garments.

As noted, Rambam regards a full stitch as a connection for kilayim even if it is not tied (Rambam, Hil. Kilayim 10:24). For Sabbath law, however, if such a stitch is sewn on the Sabbath, it is not considered lasting and is not a violation of the prohibition on sewing on the Sabbath unless it is tied (Rambam, Hil. Shabbos 10:9 from Shabbos 74b). It has already been noted that the prohibition on undoing stitches during the Sabbath falls under the prohibition to tear during the Sabbath, a prohibition which is not limited only to things connected via sewing. Since an untied stitch counts as a connection for kilayim, removal of an untied stitch which

connects linen to wool might count as tearing even with respect to Sabbath law. Sewing of kilayim on the Sabbath, however, would not constitute a violation of the prohibition on sewing on the Sabbath unless the stitch was tied. That the garments are considered connected for kilayim does not mean that they have been sewn together, and for the Sabbath prohibition on sewing, what matters is whether sewing has taken place. For the prohibition on tearing however, what matters is whether or not the items being separated were connected. Since the garments are considered connected for kilayim, their separation constitutes a violation of the Sabbath prohibition on tearing. It follows from this analysis that the mishnah's example of undoing rather than sewing is not accidental. Sewing a full stitch (even to connect linen to wool) on the Sabbath, without tying it, does not engender liability for sewing; undoing an untied full stitch which connects linen to wool on the Sabbath does engender liability for tearing, [since for kilayim that stitch counts as a connection] (see Chavos Yair §143).

רַבִּי יְהוּדָה אוֹמֵר: עַד שֶׁיְשַׁלֵּשׁ. — R' Yehudah says: Until he trebles.

Rabbi Yehudah maintains that a full stitch, even if tied, does not constitute a connection, whereas a stitch-and-a-half, even if not tied, does count as a connection. A stitch-and-a-half refers to three thrusts or penetrations of the threaded needle: one in, one out, and another one in (Rav; Rosh; Rash). According to Rabbi Yehudah, two garments joined by less than a stitch-and-a-half are considered separate for tumah and taharah, they do not constitute kilayim, and someone who undoes the connection on the Sabbath is not liable (Rambam Comm.). Yerushalmi explains that in

R' Yehudah says: Until he trebles. The sack and the wicker box combine for *kilayim*.

Rabbi Yehudah's opinion, only a stitch-and-a-half is sufficiently enduring to count as a connection (cf. *Ri ben Malki Tzedek* to mishnah 1:9 above, and see *Ridbaz* to *Yerushalmi* 9:6, s.v. א ר"ד (סימון).

It is not clear why R' Yehudah distinguishes between a stitch which is tied and a stitch-and-a-half which is untied. One would have thought that a single tied stitch is no less enduring than an untied stitch-and-a-half. The question is left unresolved by *Rosh*.

הַשַּׂק וְהַקֻּפָּה מִצְטָרְפִין לְכִלְאַיִם. — *The sack and the wicker box combine for kilayim.* [A *sack* was woven from hair of animals such as goats, camels, horses and cows (*Rambam, Hil. Keilim* 1:12). A קוּפָּה was a type of wicker container (*Tif. Yis.;* see mishnah *Keilim* 16:3). Normally these were used independently, and if for some reason they were connected, it was not likely to be on a long-term basis (see *Yerushalmi*).]

The mishnah teaches that if a piece of woolen cloth which is attached to a sack is connected by a full stitch to a piece of linen which is attached to a box, the resulting combination of linen and wool is *kilayim*. Since the sack and the box are separate entities, it might have been thought that the stitch joining the linen to the wool should not be considered a connection. The mishnah therefore states that *the sack and the box combine* and the connection between the linen on one and the wool on the other constitutes *kilayim* (*Rav; Rosh; Rash*). Accordingly,

it would be forbidden for example to cover oneself with the sack or with the box (*Tur, Yoreh Deah* 300; *Shach* and *Taz* to *Yoreh Deah* 300:7; see also *Shulchan Aruch, Yoreh Deah* 301:3 that if a garment has *kilayim* at one end, it is forbidden to cover oneself even with the other end which does not contain *kilayim*).

According to the preceding explanation, the case under discussion is one in which a sack is connected to a wicker box. A much different explanation is adopted by *Rambam* (*Comm.* and *Hil. Kilayim* 10:3) and *Ri ben Malki Tzedek* who explain that the case in question involves linen and wool contained inside a sack or a wicker box. *Sifrei* (*Deut.* 22:11) infers from the term יַחְדָּו, *together* (ibid.), that any union of linen and wool constitutes *kilayim*, including linen and wool kept inside the same closed container. Accordingly, the mishnah teaches that if linen and wool are kept inside the same sack, or inside the same wicker box, the sack or box unites them, and it becomes forbidden to carry the sack on one's back (see above, mishnah 5). The mishnah would thus translate: *The sack "or" the wicker box unite* linen and wool contained inside them *to produce kilayim*. [*Rambam* seems to have read מְצָרְפִין, a transitive verb referring to the capacity of the box to unite its contents, rather than מִצְטָרְפִין, a passive form referring to the combination of the sack to the box (see *Rambam Comm.* Kafich ed.).]

סליק מסכת כלאים